Veg

Britain

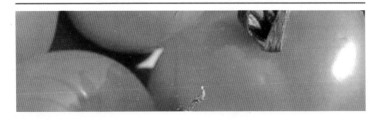

2006

Always find the best place to eat, sleep and shop veggie

Edited by Alex Bourke
with Sophie & Stephen Fenwick-Paul, Katrina Holland,
Claire Insley, Sarah Richards and Suzanne Wright

Design by Mickaël Charbonnel, assisted by Alexandra Boylan

 Vegetarian Guides

Contents Vegetarian Britain 2006

ENGLAND

REPUBLIC OF IRELAND

WALES

East

London

West

South

145 East
148 Bedfordshire
150 Buckinghamshire
153 Cambridgeshire
158 Essex
166 Hertfordshire
171 Leicestershire
178 Norfolk
182 Northants
184 Suffolk

187 London

241 South
244 Berkshire
249 Cornwall
263 Devon
284 Dorset
290 East Sussex
310 Hampshire
315 Kent
320 Middlesex
326 Somerset
345 West Sussex
347 Isle of Wight
351 Wiltshire
356 Channel Islands

361 West
364 Bristol
371 Gloucestershire
374 Herefordshire
382 Oxfordshire
387 Shropshire
393 Staffordshire
397 Warwickshire
401 West Midlands
408 Worcestershire

447 WALES
466 Cardiff

Contents
Vegetarian Britain 2006

For regular updates, visit
www.vegetarianguides.co.uk/updates

100% Natural and Tasty Meat-free Meal

- Vegetarian and Vegan Products
- No Cholesterol
- No Preservatives
- Non-GMO

Certified

Simply **VEGGIEMASTER**™ Everyday

Vegetarian Britain 2006 (3rd edition)

edited by Alex Bourke, with Sophie and Stephen Fenwick-Paul,
Katrina Holland, Claire Insley, Sarah Richards and Suzanne Wright

ISBN 1-902259-06-8

Published November 2005, by Vegetarian Guides Ltd,
PO Box 2284, London W1A 5UH, England
www.vegetarianguides.com   info@vegetarianguides.com
Fax (+44) (0) 870-121 4721

Cover design by Mickaël Charbonnel, contact mick@humanbeans.net
Cover photo Juliet Coombe, Lonely Planet library
Layout and maps by Mickaël Charbonnel assisted by Alex Boylan
Vegetarian Guides logo design: Marion Gillet
Inside photos: Mike Bourke, Tony Bishop Weston and various. Wherever
possible copyright has been established. Please inform us of any errors.
Contributors: Tony & Yvonne Bishop Weston, Ankaret Harmer, Sam Calvert,
Vanessa Clarke, Dr Cynthia Combe, John Curtis, Peter Despard, Sophie and
Stephen Fenwick-Paul, Paul Gaynor, Alexandra Geen, Dr Michael Grill, Carol
Hart, Brian Jacobs, Laurence and Christine Klein, Philippa Lennox, everyone at
London Vegans, Nana Luke, Laurence Main, Caroline Malkinson, Kari Manovitch,
Harry Mather, Scott Nelson, Joy Olver, Marc Palmer, Karin Ridgers, Beverly Riley,
George Rodger, Julie Rosenfield, Bani Sethi, Peter Simpson, Patrick Smith,
Natalie Tharraléos, Frank Thunder, Patricia Tricker, Lisa Wilkinson, Ronny
Worsey and everyone else ... THANK YOU!!

UK and worldwide bookshop distribution: Portfolio Books
Unit 5, Perivale Industrial Park, Horsenden Lane South, Greenford,
Middlesex UB6 7RL, England. sales@portfoliobooks.com
Tel: (+44) 020-8997 9000, Fax: (+44) 020-8997 9097

UK health food shop distribution by KHS Books For Health
31 Middle Bourne Lane, Lower Bourne, Farnham, Surrey GU10 3NH
Tel: 01252 716660 Fax: 01252-821295 booksforhealth@tiscali.co.uk

Distributed in USA and Canada by Casemate, 2114 Darby Road,
Havertown, PA 19083. casemate@casematepublishing.com
Tel 610-853 9131, Fax 610-853 9146

Printed and bound in Wales by Cambrian Printers

8

New in this Edition

This third edition of Vegetarian Britain has 25% more entries, over 1,250 places to eat, sleep and shop. For those of you who've been patiently waiting, we apologise for the delay. We had no idea just how many new places you'd tell us about!

This guide uses colour for the first time. Green borders on pages highlight veggie Hot Spots such as Brighton, Bristol, Edinburgh and Cumbria. We've changed the layout to fit 30% more into the same space. The book is now arranged by regions to facilitate touring but retains the county side tabs for ease of reference. The number of indexes has increased to eight so that you can search on accommodation, restaurants, location, 100% vegan (or super-vegan-friendly), retreat centres, and now also child-friendly and dog-friendly. We've also included more information in the listings about smoking, alcohol, whether they take credit cards, and availability of vegan desserts.

Our Top 10 Destinations highlight parts of Britain with an especially high concentration of vegetarian delights. The Top 10 restaurants is our personal selection of innovative places that are making an outstanding contribution to taking vegetarian food mainstream.

What to do late at night when the vegetarian restaurant is closed? We've included omnivorous restaurants with big veggie menus where we recognised that many vegetarians eat there, either through choice, or in a group of friends who don't want to go where we do. Top of the list of handy places for when your mates veto a veggie venue are of course Indian restaurants, some of which have more dishes for us than most vegetarian eateries. Lebanese, Italian, south-east Asian, Greek and Mexican restaurants aren't far behind, and we've found the best ones all over the country. Pizza Express has been a veggie standby for years, with vegan pizza bases that can be without cheese. A couple of Pizza Express branches will sometimes even make pizzas with vegan cheese, or let you bring it in, a trend some of our readers are working to encourage. Bella Pasta and Bella Italia are also ahead of other chains in their provision of vegetarian and vegan food.

The Small Print:

Restaurants are continually changing their owners and opening hours and sometimes close for holidays. Every effort has been made to ensure the accuracy of information in this book, however it is impossible to account for every detail and mistakes can occur. It's worthwhile calling before making a special journey to be on the safe side. Sometimes vegetarian guest houses do not continue to be so when they change hands. If you discover changes or a new veggie friendly place, please email us at: updates@vegetarianguides.co.uk
For regular updates, visit: www.vegetarianguides.co.uk/updates

Top 10 Destinations

Romantic dinners, birthday and anniversary celebrations don't have to be limited to your county. Why not whisk your loved one, or just yourself, off to the veggie hotspots of Britain and Ireland? Each has its own character and there are enough here to keep you coming back every month for years.

1 Brighton, East Sussex (South) p290

Veggie capital of the south with a dozen great vegetarian eateries between the central station and the sea, Brighton is the ideal day out as a side trip from London. The area around the Laines is packed with lovely little shops, veggie cafes and even a veggie pub. There are clubs galore and even a naturist beach by the marina. Don't miss Vegetarian Shoes in Gardner Street (closed Sunday). We've given you several places to stay, but make sure you book ahead.

2 Cornwall (South) p249

At the far south-west corner of England, Cornwall has sandy beaches, surfing, sailing, coastal walks, the fabulous Eden project and Heligan Gardens, arty St Ives, and lots of gorgeous guest houses. The top place to relax for a week in summer, or come for a quiet recharge weekend out of season.

3 Cumbria (North) p42

One of Britain's top walking destinations, the Lake District National Park covers the county of Cumbria in the north-west of England. Stunning scenery, stone houses, cafes galore, boat trips on Lake Windermere, and a huge concentration of veggie guest houses.

4 Devon (South) p263

Next door to Cornwall, yet totally different, Devon is much more hilly, with wild and windswept moors, cute coastal towns, and many lovely veggie retreats.

5 Edinburgh (Scotland) p417

Veggie capital of Scotland and the north, packed with history, a castle, parks and squares, tremendous bars and nightlife and a dozen yummy veggie restaurants.

6   Glastonbury, Somerset (South)   p327

The town (not the huge festival nearby in the last weekend of June)
with the magical Tor, veggie guest houses and cafes, and a New Age
spirit, make this the best little place in Britain for a spiritual makeover.
(Totnes in Devon and Hebden Bridge in Yorkshire are alternative too.)

7   Dublin (Ireland)   p478

The friendliest city in Europe, a cheap flight away by Ryanair.
Fantastic pubs and nightlife, plenty to see and buy, and several
veggie places to dine. This young, fashionable, trendy capital is very
popular for weekends away, hen and stag nights, for example at Bono
and the Edge's nightclub the Grafton on the river Liffey, close to the
Temple Bar area where young folks go to party and dance away Friday
and Saturday night. Everything is within walking distance including
some very nice shops.

8   London's West End   p217

With one hundred vegetarian restaurants, a dozen of them vegan,
London veggies are the envy of the world. When not on a veggie cafe
crawl around the West End, there is fantastic fashion shopping in the
mile long Oxford Street, the cutest boutiques in Covent Garden,
outstanding theatre and nightlife around Soho, and heaps of attractions from the ancient relics of the British Museum to the London Eye
ferris wheel. Plus veggie guest houses, a luxury hotel with superb
cuisine for rock and movie star readers, and central backpacker
hostels and campsites (yes in London!) for budget travellers.

9   Scottish Highlands   p427

To truly get away from it all, you can't beat a highland guest house.
Like the couples who leave the city to start a new life running these
wonderful places, you too can wake up to birdsong with not a car in
sight. Walk amongst the glens, sit by a loch, enjoy the beautiful
wilderness, soak up the history of a ruined castle or whisky distillery,
and stuff yourself silly on yummy Scottish veggie grub.

10 Wales   p447

Britain's other great unspoiled natural escape, north and west Wales
offer walking, mountains, peace and relaxation. And stacks of
vegetarian guest houses.

A Top 15 would also include these vibrant cities with excellent veggie
dining: Birmingham, Bristol, Glasgow Manchester and York. Other
great cities are Bath, Leicester, Nottingham and Sheffield.

Our Top 10 Veggie Restaurants in Britain

1 De Muths – Bath, Somerset   P335

Top tourist venue has a top class veggie restaurant and vegan dessert heaven.

2 Manna – Primrose Hill, London   P205

Classy gourmet international dining in Primrose Hill.   Ideal for a romantic dinner.

3 Terre a Terre – Brighton, East Sussex   P302

The gourmet restaurant in a town full of veggie cafes. If you don't reserve, you won't get in.

4 Two Two Two – Hammersmith, West London   P235

Outstanding new licensed gourmet vegan international restaurant near Olympia, with charming staff and a superb dessert menu.

5 Cafe Maitreya – Bristol   P368

The capital of the West of England has a top vegetarian restaurant near the M32.

6 Black Bo's – Edinburgh, Scotland   P422

Cordon Vert with an amazingly eclectic menu for a romantic evening.

7 Hitchcocks – Hull, East Yorkshire   P126

All you can eat buffet restaurant run by a couple who've travelled all over the world collecting recipes. The first to book choose which country the menu of the night will be from.

8 Riverside Vegetaria – Kingston, Surrey   P342

Superb restaurant with gorgeous views over the Thames.

9 Bob Trollop's Pub – Newcastle-upon-Tyne   P106

A comprehensive vegetarian food menu in a proper British pub. They even have a magic vegan button on the till.

10 Wild Ginger – Harrogate, Yorkshire   P117

Cosy and homely vegetarian restaurant that is particularly good for vegans.

The Good Island Guide

Veggie eateries may be few in these places, but if you're well supplied, nothing beats a good island break.

Isle of Wight

Enjoy a slower pace of life just below Southampton off the south coast of England. Perfect for sailing or just watching. There's even a vegan guest house.

Isle of Man

Get away to where no one will ever find you on this big island in the Irish Sea. Open an offshore bank account and relax in complete tranquility. (except during the annual TT motorcycle races)

Jersey

Of the two main Channel Islands, close to the coast of France, Jersey is the fun island for a self-catering holiday with sunbathing, surfing, swimming, country walking and a couple of great places to eat out. It's no wonder bronzed Aussie lifeguards come over in droves during their winter to work the beaches. For an altogether quieter time head for Guernsey.

Scottish Islands

To truly get away from it all, watching seabirds, seals and beautiful sunsets on a windswept, deserted beach, head for Orkney, Shetland or the outer Hebrides.

"One of the simplest and most powerful ways to rekindle passion is to get out of the house on a romantic getaway.... Try to get away at least one night a month."

John Gray, Mars and Venus In The Bedroom

Special Interest Holidays

Vegetarian Britain gives you places to sleep and eat. But what about the time in between meals? How about a holiday or weekend where you are pampered or provided with fun activities to enjoy in the company of other veggies?

Retreat Centres

Throughout the accommodation listings, you'll occasionally see the words Retreat Centre, indicating that this is a place offering a lot more than bed and breakfast. Burn out is a constant risk of modern life. Come and rejuvenate at guest houses run by holistic health practitioners. Be pampered with massage, Reiki, yoga and other revitalisers. Two particularly well recommended retreat centres are Heartspring in Wales and Shekinashram in Glastonbury, Somerset. You'll find more in the Retreat Centres index.

Yoga centres are usually run by vegetarians and the food is almost always veggie. Find them in the yoga magazines in WH Smith or larger health food stores.

Annual Vegan Festivals in Britain

Heart of England, check www.veganfestivals.org.uk for 2006 venue.
East Midlands, Sat 10th Dec 2005, 11am to 5pm, at the Council House, Market Square, Nottingham. See page 97.
London September at Kensington Town Hall, Hornton St W8, www.londonveganfestival.org.uk
Bristol end October, see www.yaoh.co.uk (p362)
London Christmas Without Cruelty on the closest Sunday to 1st December at Kensington Town Hall. www.animalaid.org.uk
One World Summer Festival www.macrobios.com

Veggie Holidays Abroad

The International Vegetarian Union (www.ivu.org) and European Vegetarian Union (www.european-vegetarian.org) organise week long World and European Vegetarian Congresses, based around a hotel with talks, cookery demos and excursions, every couple of years. You can come to learn all about activism, or just hang out and socialise with veggie voyagers from all over the world. The next World Vegetarian Congresses are in Goa Oct 2006, and Dresden 2008.

Vegi Ventures offer guided vegetarian holidays for small groups from Peru to Turkey. (See page 36, www.vegiventures.com) For keen and leisure cyclists, Bicycle Beano tour around the UK.

If you fancy a city break in Paris, Amsterdam or Barcelona, make a romantic investment in our Vegetarian Europe guide. It contains capitals and tourist hotspots from Seville to St Petersburg. (See the end pages of this guide.)

Music and Arts festivals

The Edinburgh Festival throughout August is heaven for theatre and music fans. Make sure you book accommodation well ahead. There are plenty of other festivals all over Britain throughout the year, which you can find listed in music magazines and via tourist offices.

For a bargain weekend away, pack a tent for festivals such as Glastonbury, on the solstice weekend at the end of June, where there veggie cafes in the Green Fields area. At other events such as Reading Festival, WOMAD and the Big Green Gathering, you'll also find specialist veggie caterers like Leon Lewis (see Essex). For all these events, buy tickets in advance or you probably won't get in!

Veggie pages

Free Help and Advice for Veggies

If you want to go veggie or vegan, or know someone who might be interested, the organisations below have stacks of literature to help and can answer questions. If you want to help spread the word and get active for animal rights and health, or you just need more recipes, they would love to hear from you. They all have brilliant websites. Always enclose a stamped addressed envelope or a donation, or better still join (by covenanted standing order is best) and help them make the world a better place for veggies, meat reducers and, of course, animals.

The Vegetarian Society

www.vegsoc.org
See advert page 15.

Vegetarian and Vegan Foundation

www.vegetarian.org.uk
See advert page 21.

The Vegan Society

www.vegansociety.com
See advert page 29.

Viva! (Vegetarians International Voice for Animals)

www.viva.org.uk
See advert page 13.

Animal Aid

www.animalaid.org.uk
See advert page 31.

ARCNews

www.arcnews.org.uk
PO Box 339, Wolverhampton WV10 7BZ
Tel: 0845-458 0146

Network of 500 local animal groups and campaigners. For news, subscribe to 12 monthly issues of ARCNews for £10.

People for the Ethical Treatment of Animals (PETA)

www.peta.org.uk
See advert page 24.

Realfood

PO Box 339, Wolverhampton WV10 7BZ
Tel: 0845-458 0146
www.realfood.org.uk

Campaigning vegan group making it easy to follow a vegan diet.

Vegan Buddies

www.veganbuddies.org.uk

If you want to go vegan but find it hard sign up and get a local buddy to help you make the transition. New and aspiring vegans can advertise for help, while isolated vegans can find out more easily who is in their area. They also need people to give advice, and to advertise the fact that they exist. You can also post specific questions and requests for advice.

Veggies

www.veggies.org.uk
Tel: 0845-458 9595

Publishes the Animal Contacts Directory, available on line, which lists every veggie and vegan business and animal group in the country and many overseas.

Booze

Festival Wines, page 22.
Vintage Roots, page 16.

Charities

Vegfam, page 28.

Cleaning Products

Ecover (page 13) manufacture all kinds of cleaning products that have not been tested on animals and have no animal ingredients. You can find them in many wholefood stores and take the bottles back to be refilled..

Cosmetics

BUAV (page 36) have a Little Guide to Cruelty Free, as do PETA (page 24). One of the most innovative vegan companies is Yaoh, page 10.

Dating

Contact Centre, page 16.

Dog and Cat Food

Many veggies aren't thrilled about having to feed companion animals. A number of companies make veggie dog food, including Happidog (see page 8), and Vegecat and Vegekit for cats is available from the Vegan Society (page 29). Realfood's cats love Redwoods fake tuna and salmon (in health food shops) and Fry's mince from Beanies (page 19 and 312).

Holidays

Vegi Ventures, page 28, and see the feature on holidays, page 18.

Meat and cheese substitutes

VeggieMaster page 5.
Fry's page 19.
Redwood page 22.

Nutrition and Recipes

Yvonne and Tony Bishop Weston's Vegan cookbook, page 29.

Nutritionist and caterer Liz Cook has produced a gorgeous colour illustrated vegetarian (in fact vegan) nutritional chart with which foods to eat for vitamins, minerals, carbohydrates, protein, fibre and essential fatty acids. 18cm high by 88cm wide, with wipe clean finish, it's on kitchen walls and cupboards in thousands of veggie homes. Price £3.95.

So,What do you eat? is Liz's beautiful full colour hand drawn A4 cookbook full

21

of nutritional advice and easy recipes. The covers are tough, clear plastic and the pages are wipe clean, designed for years of kitchen use by children of all ages, teenagers and anyone starting a vegetarian or vegan diet. Price £12.95 with a free copy of the wallchart.

Wall chart and book available direct from Liz on 01273-388864 or email lizcook@onetel.com

Shoes

Beyond Skin, page 7.
Ethical Wares, page 30.
Total Liberation, page 13, and shop in Axminster, page 278.
Vegetarian Shoes, page 26, or visit their shop in Brighton, page 305.

Travel

Vegetarian Guides sells guides to London, Britain, Europe, Spain, Italy, USA/Canada, New York etc. The website has links to restaurant listings all over the world. See end pages and inside front cover for more details.
www.vegetarianguides.co.uk

Food for Life

by Yvonne Bishop-Weston, BSc Dip ION

Probably the single most persuasive argument you could have to encourage others to join you in making a difference is yourself. Just being a happy, healthy looking vegetarian or vegan speaks for itself.

There are huge benefits in living meat free not only for your long term health but also for the viability and health of our planet.

In 2004 Britain's largest ever health and diet survey of over 37,000 people, by the Institute for Optimum Nutrition (ION), revealed only 6% were in 'optimal health'. 44% were in poor health, with frequent low energy (80%), constipation (81%), high stress (75%), PMS (women 64%), abdominal bloating (64%), frequent colds (50%), headaches or migraine (46%) and depression (46%). The good news is that it found that the healthiest people ate 8 or more servings of fruit and vegetables a day.

Here are my Top 10 Tips for being a super-healthy veggie:

1 Start the day with a BANG! You've been asleep all night busy repairing the damage of a modern lifestyle – give your body a break! Feed it! A mug of caffeine and a bit of toast with sugar-laden marmalade, or worse still a pop-tart, just won't do it long term. Try a bowl of porridge with strawberries or blueberries and some nuts and seeds sprinkled on top. If you are a toast-a-holic aim for wholemeal or rye breads spread with nut or pumpkin seed butter instead of jam.

2 Put a rainbow in your life! Oranges are not the only fruit. Eat a wide variety of colourful fruit and vegetables. Many are appealing bright colours for a reason – to attract you to them and their myriad of phytonutrients, vitamins and minerals. Research on benefits of foods such as blueberries, broccoli, carrots and mangoes claims benefits ranging from warding off Alzheimer's to protecting against cancer. Buy organic or wash them with water and vinegar. Your dinner plate should be at least half full with a mixture of colourful vegetables (not including potatoes) with a bias towards green leafy veg. Drizzle flax or hemp oil on them to get your quota of essential fats.

3 Just Say "No" to Drugs You may think coffee and sugary foods and drinks are giving you the energy to drag yourself out of bed in the morning, but in actual fact they are what make you feel like you need them so much. Try decaff coffee or tea or better still experiment with polyphenol and anti oxidant rich teas such as Rooibosch (redbush) instead.

What Do You Mean, You "ONLY" Eat Fish?

Go Vegetarian!

4 Have a drink! A glass of red wine has been shown in some studies to benefit you with its anti-oxidants and relaxing effects. Much more than that and the toxic effects of the alcohol on your liver and brain will start to outweigh any benefits. Give your body a chance to flush itself out. Drink 1fi litres (6 mugs) of water a day – between meals and especially in hot weather.

5 Get Fat not Fatter Bizarrely you can lose weight by eating fat. You need the right sort, the kind your brain rather than your bottom is made of. Even among the good fats balance can be a problem. Many people struggle to get enough vital omega 3 fats which can be found in their most useful form in high lignan flax oil, hemp oil and also in walnuts. Drizzle flax oil on your vegetables, cereal, soup or salad. You can also sneak it in your smoothies.

6 Step Outside! Grab yourself some sunshine to boost vitamin D. Take a tip from the birds – hitch hike towards the equator in winter. Yes too much is bad for your skin but not enough could be even worse. Nothing is ever that simple – there is a new study that suggests that sunshine slows melanoma growth – remember everything in moderation.

7 Get up and Go! There's nothing quite like a bit of exercise to promote health – so get your heart beating a little faster for at least 15 minutes a day. Also follow the example of your neighbour's cat – do a bit of stretching and yawning – yoga is even better, Tai Chi anyone? Remember all those exercises you used to do at school, crouching, leg raises? Walk, cycle, swim, dance and wherever possible don't take the lift or escalator.

8 Atkins Smatchkins Remember protein? OK so Dr Atkins was on a bridge too far but he had a point. A white bread base with a sugary red sauce and a bit of animal fat on top (pizza) or a bowl of white flour and water (pasta) with a sugar laden tomato sauce on top, or corn flour and water (tortilla) with vegetables and sugary chilli sauce (Fajitas) is not real food – it tastes great, but unless you throw a whole load of beans, nuts and tofu on there you are barely one step away from eating nothing but sugar. If you live in a basement and you had to run up 3 flights of stairs to answer the door to the pizza boy then maybe your body could use a few instant calories – if not – you're stuffed. Aim for about 20% or at least a quarter of your dinner plate to be mixed protein-rich foods such as lentils and mushrooms, beans, nuts and seeds, quinoa, buckwheat, tofu, hemp or meat-free alternatives without hydrogenated–fat.

9 Carb Crawling Yes carbohydrates are delicious, but in their refined (white) form, unless you are down the gym every night – forget it. One nutritionist is recommending a maximum safe limit of 5 French fries a day – you get the picture? Pick unrefined complex carbohydrates, with a bit of how nature intended them to be, complete with fibre.

Try to ensure no more than a quarter of your dinner plate is starchy, complex carbohydrate such as brown rice, wild rice, wholemeal pasta, millet or potatoes. Try buckwheat pasta, other protein rich pseudo-grains such as quinoa and amaranth, and fresh bean sprouts. Have some protein with your snacks such as hummus with your oatcakes or nuts with organic chocolate. Avoid eating carbs separately unless you have just been working out in the gym for 40 minutes. For French bread think sugar stick. Try not to have too many carbs at night.

10 Vive la difference! One of the failings of modern western medicine is that it tries to treat everyone as equal when we are all so different. Many factors affect how healthy you are and one of the keys to the success of alternative and complementary therapies is they look at the whole body and underlying causes, not just symptoms.

If you are struggling with life, don't be afraid to take a multi-vitamin and mineral supplement. Pick a good brand as they are more reliable, better quality and in the long run cheaper than getting extra vitamins secondhand from fortified foods. It's not a cop out if you are a vegetarian – many meat eaters could benefit from extra selenium, calcium, zinc, magnesium, iron and even vitamin B12. The Soil Association will explain how the soil (from which food is made!) has been depleted of key minerals.

The role of B12 as a health biomarker is taking on Eureka proportions with its importance in protecting against heart

www.festivalwines.co.uk

ORGANIC & BIODYNAMIC WINES

Festival Wines Ltd
PO Box 5088
Brighton & Hove
BN52 9BZ
t/f: 01273 325307
e: ben@festivalwines.co.uk

disease by lowering homocysteine levels. We don't live in a natural world – please recognise that and at the very least take a sublingual vitamin B12 under your tongue on a regular basis until someone proves its bio-availability in algae in addition to cow-pooh and Marmite!

If you have any health problems then seek out a member of The British Association of Nutrition Therapists (BANT).

Yvonne Bishop-Weston is a BANT registered nutrition therapist and Foresight practitioner. She has held key roles at Holland & Barrett, Cranks and is currently a Senior Consultant at the Food Doctor. She also runs her own nutrition and catering consultancy

www.foodsforlife.org.uk

in partnership with her husband Tony and together they have written the new cookbook Vegan, published by Hamlyn, £12.99, ISBN 0600609154.

29

30

Animal Aid
Campaigning for all animals

Animal Aid is Britain's leading animal rights group, campaigning against vivisection, factory farming and all other animal abuse. We also promote vegetarianism and cruelty-free living, and have an active educational wing offering free school speakers, campaign literature and videos for teachers.

We urgently need more members if we are to continue with and expand our vital work. Please use the form on this page or send your details on a piece of paper with a cheque made payble to Animal Aid. For more information or to join by credit card see our website or call the number below.

We need you to help us to help animals.

Please Join Animal Aid Today

Your details (please use block capitals)

Surname: .... First name:... Title: ....

Address: ....

.... Post code: ....

What it costs (please tick appropriate boxes)

Annual membership: ❏ £14 waged ❏ £9 Unwaged ❏ £6 Youth (16 or under) ❏ £240 Life

I enclose a donation of £ .... I enclose a cheque for a total of £ ....

Please return this form to:

Animal Aid, The Old Chapel, Bradford St, Tonbridge, Kent TN9 1AW
Tel: (01732) 364546
email: info@animalaid.org.uk
web: www.animalaid.org.uk

NORTH

Northern England Counties

Northumberland

Tyne & Wear

Durham

Cumbria

Yorkshire

York

Isle of Man
(not to scale)

Lancashire

Liverpool   Manchester

Lincolnshire

Cheshire   Derbyshire

Nottinghamshire

Northern England

Cheshire

The Greenhouse

Vegetarian restaurant and shop

41/43 Oxford Rd
Altrincham, Cheshire WA14 2ED
Tel: 0161–929 4141 restaurant
Tel: 0161–929 4141 shop
Restaurant open: Mon–Sat 08.30–17.30

Vegetarian restaurant near the head-quarters of the Vegetarian Society. Always have vegan options available such as homemade spicy African soup, £5.50. Ten different salads, homemade cakes. No smoking throughout. Visa, MC.
Adjoining health food shop has a vast selection of allergy–free food and herbal teas. Chiller cabinet.

Bella Italia

Omnivorous Italian restaurant

29 Eastgate Street, Chester CH1 1LG
Tel: 01244–325 420
Open: Mon–Thu 10:30–22:30,
Fri–Sat 10–23:00, Sunday 11–22:00

Lots of veggie options and they have a list of all the dishes suitable for vegans if you ask. The pizza bases are vegan, so is the bruschetta starter and there are a couple of vegan pasta dishes.

Pizza Express

Omnivorous pizza restaurant

4 Market Place, Macclesfield
Cheshire SK10 1EX
Tel: 01625 425 175
Open: 11.30–23.00

Vegan pizza bases and can leave off the cheese for vegans.

Holland & Barrett

Health food shop

7 Paddock Row, Grosvenor Precinct
Chester, Cheshire CH1 1ED
Tel: 01244–348 153
Open Mon–Sat 09.00–17.30
Sun 11.00–17.30

25 Victoria Street
Crewe, Cheshire CW2 2JE
Tel: 01270–253 022
Open Mon–Sat 09.00–17.30

Mill Street Mall
Macclesfield, Cheshire SK11 8AJ
Tel: 01625–424 256
Open Mon–Sat 09.00–17.30

39 High Street
Nantwich, Cheshire CW5 5DB
Tel: 01270–610 041
Open Mon–Sat 09.00–17.30

Cleveland

The Waiting Room

Vegetarian daytime cafe/coffee shop and evening restaurant.

Muesli, porridge, fruit bowl all £2.45. Roast tomato & coriander soup £3.95, Indian savouries £4.50, risotto £4.50–6.95, pasta £4.95–5.95, salads £4.50–6.50. Sandwiches farmhouse, baguette, flat bread, chappati and pitta. Cakes £2.45 and puddings from the evening menu.

Evening starters £3.95–£4.50 include roast aubergine; mushroom, garlic and cashew nut paté; warm avocado salad with raspberry vinaigrette; hummous and hot bread. One main course £8.50 or two half courses £11.90, include carrot and cashew nut loaf with spiced plum sauce, Thai green curry, mushroom and leek stroganoff, hot three bean chilli with veg and sesame potatoes or rice. Salad bowl £2.50.

Numerous desserts £4.50 include summer fruit pudding.Tea and herbal tea, £1.45; coffee, from £1.85. House wine £2.50 glass, £9.90 bottle.

Vegetarian restaurant

9 Station Road
Eaglescliffe
Stockton on Tees
Cleveland
(between Eaglescliffe Station and Yarm Road)

Tel: 01642–780 465

www.
the-waiting-room.co.uk

Open: Mon–Sat 10.00–16.30
(lunches available between 11.30–14.30)
& 18.30–22.00.
Sunday 12.00–14.30 (for lunches) & from 19.00 to close.

Light entertainment most Sunday evenings

Credit cards accepted

Holland & Barrett

Health food shop

184 Middleton Grange Shopping Centre
Hartlepool TS24 7RG
Tel: 01429–860 810

Holland & Barrett

Health food shop

16 Castle Way, Stockton TS18 1BG
Tel: 01642–671 127

The Lake District **Cumbria**

DUMFRIES
& GALLOWAY

NORTHUMBERLAND

SOLWAY FIRTH

SOLWAY
COAST

Longtown

A74

A685

Brampton

Carlisle

Wigton

A595

M6

A686

Alston

Maryport

A590

A596

DURHAM

River
Derwent

Cockermouth

A66

Penrith

A66

A591

Appleby-in-
Westmorland

Brough

Workington

A66

Keswick

Ullswater

A6

M6

A685

Kirkby
Stephen

Whitehaven

A591

A592

ST BEES
HEAD

Egremont

Grasmere

Rydal

A683

Wast
Water

Ambleside

A595

Ravenglass

Hawkshead

Windermere

River Lune

Coniston

Near
Sawrey

Kendal

Sedbergh

A683

Broughton
in Furness

A593

Windermere

Witherslack

A590

A591

Millom

Ulverston

Kirkby
Lonsdale

NORTH

Barrow-in-Furness

Grange-
over-Sands

YORKSHIRE

MORCAMBE BAY

LANCASHIRE

Cumbria

43

The Lake District, in the heart of Cumbria, is the largest of England's National Parks and offers some of the best walking in Britain. It is an extremely beautiful area with high fells, rocky crags, lush green dales, huge peaceful lakes and busy villages. As a vegetarian, it is an excellent place to take a holiday, as there are veggie friendly guesthouses and restaurants in many of its villages. The main bases for the Lakes are Keswick in the North and Windermere and Bowness in the South.

Windermere and Bowness is the largest tourist centre and is full of bed & breakfasts, restaurants and attractions such as The World of Beatrix Potter. It gets inundated by tourists and can feel like a seaside resort, so don't come if you're after peace and quiet. One of its good qualities though is the veg-friendly Kirkwood Guesthouse. If the weather's not so great for walking, visit the Lake District Centre at Brockhole, by Lake Windermere, which has an adventure playground, interactive exhibitions, beautiful gardens, games' lawn and a gift shop.

Keswick, next to Derwent Water is particularly popular with walkers. It's still a busy town, but it feels more relaxed than Windermere. A pleasant four mile circular walk from the town centre to the Castlerigg Stone Circle, believed to be around 3000 years old, offers excellent views. Have lunch at the vibrant wholefood veggie café, Lakeland Peddlar, or take a tasty snack away with you. Take a boat trip or row a hired boat around the lake for a refreshing change from walking.

Ambleside, Just north of Windermere and Bowness, is a pretty town and a popular centre for walkers and climbers. It's a good base to explore the Southern Lake District, but although slightly less hectic than Windermere and Bowness, it is still regularly inundated. Beechmount Guesthouse caters well for veggies.

Grasmere is an essential place to visit if you're into the poetry of Wordsworth. It is the home of Dove Cottage, where he wrote many of his poems, and the Wordsworth

Museum. It is a very pretty village but is often overrun with tourists, so it is best to visit out of season.

Coniston Water and the town are both beautiful. There are some lovely walks in the area, particularly up the Old Man of Coniston. If it's a clear day, the view from the top is breathtaking.

Cockermouth. Be sure to dine at least one evening at the Quince and Medlar in Cockermouth, one of the best veggie restaurants in Britain. If you're not staying in Cockermouth, it's worth the drive. Cockermouth is just outside the Lake District, which makes it quieter than many of the places.

Kendal, on the eastern outskirts of the Lakes, is a busy market town with several interesting museums and galleries. Its selling point for veggies and vegans has to be Fox Hall vegan bed and breakfast serving imaginative breakfasts and delicious three course dinners, or Lakeland Natural vegetarian guesthouse.

If you'd prefer to be out of the main hub of the Lake District, consider Grange-over-Sands on the southern edge of the park or Alston, close to The Pennines.

The Lake District offers many opportunities for learning about the area. It is possible to do navigated walks and bike rides and learn to map read.

If you're tired of walking or it's just not your thing, most of the lakes have boat trips around them, which can be a relaxing way to still see some gorgeous scenery. There are also some great cycling routes around the Lake District, particularly the Cumbria Cycle Way which takes five to seven days. There are many books available on cycling in Cumbria.

A word of warning: try to avoid the Lake District on summer weekends as it is the second most visited area in Britain behind London. It's quite hard to enjoy nature when you have a crowd of strangers around you!

Hall Croft

Large detached four storey and lovingly restored Victorian villa in the classic English village of Dufton offering quality accommodation: one double with private bathroom £23–26 per person per night, one double ensuite £23–26, one twin ensuite £23–26. Tea and coffee making facilities in rooms as are TV, VCR and hairdryer.

Breakfast is substantial and includes a wide range of cereals, vegan muesli, fresh fruit, homemade wholemeal and speciality breads with homemade marmalade and jam. Orange or grapefruit juice and Fair Trade tea and coffee are also offered. Cooked breakfast is available on request with advance notice such as croissants, veggie/vegan sausages, baked beans, pancakes, homemade muffins, and grapefruit cocktail.

Special diets can be catered for and vegan margarine, soya yoghurt, soya milk and other gluten free foods are all available. The vegetarian owners Ray and Frei pride themselves on their personal service and nothing (almost!) is too much trouble. Also for vegetarians nearby is Little Salkeld Watermill vegetarian organic wholefood tea room and also The Village Bakery organic cafe.

The Eden Valley is a little known part of Cumbria, ideal for a peaceful break – walking, cycling touring or just chilling out. It is ideally placed for touring the Lakes (30 minute drive away), Northumberland, Scotland, the Yorkshire Dales. Carlisle is an interesting city and there are many fascinating small market towns within easy reach. A beautiful, tranquil area in which to relax. Also right on The Pennine Way.

Vegan/vegetarian bed and breakfast

Hall Croft
Dufton
Appleby-in-Westmorland
Cumbria CA16 6DB

Tel: 01768–352 902

Email: r.walker@lease holdpartnerships.co.uk

Train station: Appleby 3 miles

Collection available from train station

Open: all year, except Christmas

Directions: A66 to Appleby – Dufton is signposted. The village is 3 miles out of Appleby. Hall Croft is situated at the lower end of the village green.

Parking: available

Children of all ages welcome

Pets by arrangement

Owners more than willing to advise on routes, or occasionally, to lead runs or cycle rides

Packed lunches available on request £5

Homemade cake and tea/coffee offered each afternoon

No smoking throughout

AA 4 Diamonds

Lakeland Living

Big family house with a large organic vegetable garden and lots of pets. Two double ensuite rooms at £20 per person, one in country cottage style, the other modern and minimalistic.

Start the day with a selection of fresh and dried fruit and nuts and cereals, followed by cooked potato and seaweed cakes. Also toast or bread, homemade marmalade, jams, and an own recipe spread of tahini and mullberry extract, all organic. Soya milk, vegan margarine, yoghurt and muesli are all available.

The owner Anita is vegan and used to run her own restaurant. There is a fabulous evening menu for £10. Choose from lentil and veg soup, garlic and herb mushrooms, nutty strudel or homemade haggis. Or a traditional Corfu dish of tomatoes, baked aubergine, red onions, haricots and olives. All served with veggies from the garden.

Dessert can be homemade vegan chocolate ice-cream or fruit crumble. Homemade fruit juice is also available all day.

There are several cats in the house, and rabbits and guinea pigs in garden. There are no resident children, but frequent visits from baby grandchildren.

A few minutes walk from Quince & Medlar vegetarian restaurant and the Granary health food store.

On the edge of the National Park, with mountains and lakes within walking distance. Watersports, walking, swimming and a seaside 6 miles away. Museums such as Wordsworth House and 2 mins away, the Toy and Doll Museum. Brewery with visitor centre close by. The town centre has a theatre and cinema.

Cockermouth

Vegetarian and Vegan B&B

15 Challoner Street
Cockermouth
Cumbria CA13 9QS

Tel: 01900-824 045

Email: anita@yuvaorganic-foods.wanadoo.co.uk

Train station: Maryport, 6 miles, then bus or taxi or collection

Open: all year

Directions: Challoner Street is in the centre of town, almost opposite Barclays Bank.

Parking: the street is very narrow and one-way (away from main street), therefore there is only space for one car. However, parking is available in a nearby area.

Children of all ages welcome

High chairs and facilities for babies

Dogs welcome if they don't chase cats!

No smoking throughout

Tea and coffee making facilities, washbasin and hairdryer in rooms.

10% discount for Vegan Society, Viva! and people with this book

Beech Tree Guest House

Beech Tree Guest House is set in its own grounds, at the foot of the Old Man of Coniston, 150 yards from the centre of the village. There are six double rooms, three with ensuites and two twin rooms, one with an ensuite. Rooms with ensuites are £26–£27 per person per night and those without are £20–£23 per person per night.

Begin the day with fruit juice, cereals and grapefruit followed by vegetarian sausage-burgers or vegetarian sausages, mushrooms, beans, tomatoes and toast. Vegan margarine, soya milk and vegan muesli are available. Special diets catered for. Let them know your requirements when you book. No evening meal is offered, but there is a wide range of restaurants and pubs in Coniston and the surrounding villages.

There are walks right from the house to local waterfalls, the lower valleys or to Coniston Old Man and the high fells. Some of the most beautiful scenery in the Lake District is nearby, as well as many famous houses and attractions.

Coniston is an ideal stopover on the Cumbria Way. It is an excellent centre for many activities. There is much to do for people of all interests and abilities, such as walks ranging from gentle strolls to difficult climbs, sailing and canoeing, and of course just sightseeing and relaxing. Coniston makes a good base to explore the Langdale Valleys, Wastwater and the Southern Fells.

Guests are welcome to enjoy the small but interesting garden. Drying facilities are available. Tea and coffee making facilites in rooms. Guest lounge with television.

Vegetarian Guest House

Yewdale Road
Coniston
Cumbria LA21 8DX
England

Tel: 01539–441 717

Train Station: Windermere, 12 miles, then bus

Open: all year

Directions: phone for details and map

Parking: ample private parking

Children over 10 only

No pets

No smoking throughout

Glenthorne Country House

Victorian country house set in one of the most peaceful locations in Grasmere. It's as large as a hotel but not as formal. There is accommodation to suit everyone including self catering apartments and three simple bunk style rooms for walkers and cyclists.

There are 25 rooms in all: 4 standard singles £28 per person per night, 1 single ensuite £35; 6 double ensuites £49; 2 standard twins £42 and 12 ensuite twins £49.

Cereal and a full cooked veggie breakfast are offered. There's not so much for vegans although they do have soya milk.

A three course dinner is available for £16.50 and the restaurant is open to non residents too. There is always one veggie option available for example, melon cocktail, followed by nut roast with provençale sauce and for dessert, fresh fruit salad, cheese cake or chocolate torte. If you are vegan or have any other dietary requirements, let them know in advance.

Glenthorne is surrounded by fells and beautiful scenery. Take strolls around Grasmere village and lake, or set out for the day with a packed lunch provided by the guest house for a more challenging walk.

Alternatively, have a lazy day relaxing in the lounges or gardens with a book.

There is a conference room which seats up to 45 people. Tea and coffee making facilities are available in the rooms.

Omnivorous Guest House & Restaurant

Easedale Road
Grasmere
Cumbria LA22 9QH
England

Tel and Fax:
01539-435 389

www.glenthorne.org

Email: info@glenthorne.org

Train Station: Windermere, 10 miles, then bus or taxi

Open:
February–November

Directions: from junction 36 on the M6 take the A591 to Grasmere. Turn left into the village, then go past the Red Lion Hotel and Heaton Cooper Studio. Turn left onto Easedale Road. Glenthorne is at the top of the hill on the left.

Parking: available

Conference room

Clothes drying and bike storage facilities

Discounts available on long stays and with large group bookings

No smoking throughout

Children welcome

Cots and high chairs provided

49

Lancrigg

Lancrigg is set in 30 acres of idyllic gardens overlooking the serenity of Easedale. You will appreciate the total absence of traffic noise and the sound of nearby waterfalls and birds. There is excellent walking right from the doorstep.

There are 13 rooms, with singles, doubles, twins and families, all with ensuite bathrooms. Most have special features such as gorgeous views and whirlpool spa baths. Prices range from £50–£99 per person per night and include a four course dinner. Cheaper rates for stays of three nights or more. Deduct £20 if you don't want dinner.

In the morning help yourself to fruit juices, fruit salads and natural cereals. This is followed by a continental or full cooked breakfast of basil tomatoes, vegetarian burgers, baked beans, mushrooms and toast. Vegan margarine, soya milk, soya yoghurt, vegan muesli, veggie sausages and vegan croissants are all available.

Dinner could be roasted aubergine and tomato torte with a romesco sauce, followed by carrot and fennel soup. Your main might be provençal mushroom, leek and pinekernel stuffed pepper, with a tomato and olive sauce and new potaotes, roasted in lemon and fresh herbs, served with salad. For dessert, chocolate and walnut cake. Finish off with fresh ground coffee and chocolates. Organic wine available. Special diets catered for. Food is organic where possible and free from artificial additives.

Champagne and luxury chocolates may be ordered to be in your room on arrival. Tea & coffee making and TV in rooms.

Vegetarian
country house hotel

Easedale
Grasmere
Cumbria LA22 9QN
England

Tel: 015394 35317

Fax: 015394 35058

www.lancrigg.co.uk

Email: info@lancrigg.co.uk

Train Station:
Windermere 8 miles
then taxi

Open: all year

Directions: From the M6, take the A591 to Grasmere. In the centre of the village, turn left up Easedale Road. The entrance is 1/2 mile on the right.

Parking: available

Children and pets welcome. They have cots and high chairs.

Smoking in rooms only

Breakfast can be served in rooms if requested

10% discount to members of the Vegetarian Society, Vegan Society, Viva! and people presenting this book.

Fox Hall Vegan B&B

Vegan Bed & Breakfast

Seventeenth century converted barn in the rural village of Sedgwick, four miles south of Kendal, with two rooms sleeping up to five people ensuite. Children aged five to sixteen stay for £10 and those under five are free.

Breakfast is entirely vegan and is a selection of cereals or porridge with soya milk, soya yoghurt and fresh fruit followed by a choice from several dishes including creamed mushrooms on toast; tofu, onion, mushrooms and dill on toast; home made lemon and sultana pancakes or the Big One- two nut rissoles or bean burgers with scrambled tofu, mushrooms, onions and plum tomatoes. Organic and GMO free foods are used where possible.

There is an extensive evening meal menu from which you could choose leek and potato soup, wholemeal pancakes layered with fennel, spinach and tomato and for dessert, chocolate and orange gateau. A child's meal is £3.50. Packed lunches are available for £3. They can cater for all types of special diet including gluten or sugar free and raw.

From Sedgwick, there are good local walks along the disused Lancaster to Kendal Canal towpath, the banks of the River Kent and into Leven Park. Levens Hall and Sizergh Castle are within walking distance. The town is ideally situated for exploring the lakes and mountains of Cumbria and the North West coast. It's only twenty drive minutes to Windermere.

Tea and coffee making and colour TVs in the rooms.

Sedgwick
Kendal
Cumbria LA8 0JP
England

Tel and Fax:
015395 61241

www.fox.hall@
btinternet.co.uk

Email: www.fox.hall.
btinternet.com

Train Station: Oxenholme, 3 miles, then bus or taxi.

Open: all year

Directions: From junction 36 on M6, follow A590 to Barrow-in-Furness. Drop down to roundabout for A590/A591. Follow Sedgwick one mile. Go under canal bridge. Fox Hall is the first house on the left.

Parking: three spaces

Travel cot and high chair.

No smoking throughout.

No pets

They no longer have a self-catering cottage.

FOX HALL VEGAN B&B

Sedgwick, Kendal, Cumbria, LA8 0JP

Come and stay with a vegan family who care about your holiday in our 17th century converted barn 4 miles south of Kendal, South Lakes. Extensive menu - all vegan. Comfortable, well-equipped cottage and happy family home. Children very welcome, travel cot and high chair available. Sorry, no smoking or pets. Good local walks. Ideal base for exploring the English Lake District.

Tel/Fax: Sylvia or Chris on 015395 61241
E-mail: Fox.Hall@btinternet.com or
Visit our Website: www.fox.hall.btinternet.co.uk
for more info and pictures.

Anworth House

Relax in this small friendly Victorian guest house quietly situated within walking distance of the town centre and run by vegetarian staff. Quality accommodation with one twin ensuite £23–£28 per person per night, three double ensuites and one fourposter ensuite £23–£28. Single person supplement £5.

All meals are served in the attractive dining room. Start the day with cereal or vegan muesli with soya milk or soya yoghurt followed by a full vegetarian or vegan cooked breakfast of scrambled tofu and sausage. Vegan margarine is also available.

Vegetarian evening meal £10 is available for residents only by request and could start with hot and sour soup or hummous, followed by moussaka and red peppers, then a dessert of strawberry and coconut terrine or peach and apricot puffs.

A small market town Keswick is surrounded by beautiful mountains and lakes in the heart of the Lake District National Park with Scafell Pike, the biggest Lake Windermere and the Solway coastline and Walney Island. A walker's paradise, Keswick is on the 'Cumbria Way', the 'Allerdale Ramble' long distance footpath, and the C2C cycle way.

As well as sailing and canoeing on Lake Derwentwater there are always plenty of things to do from theatre, cinemas, and museums, to shops, two parks, and a leisure pool. Other places to visit include Puzzling Place, Historical Mire House, and in Cockermouth the birthplace of Wordsworth.

Nearby is the Lakeland Pedlar restaurant and Sundance health food shop.

Vegetarian
Bed and Breakfast

27 Eskin Street
Keswick
Cumbria CA12 4DQ

Tel: 01768–772 923

www.anworthhouse.co.uk

Train station: Penrith, 16 miles, then bus or taxi.

Open: all year

Directions: Turn off M6 at junction 40 onto A66 Penrith. Anworth House is found off Penrith Road in Keswick, fourth left after Derwent petrol station into Greta Street leading to Eskin Street.

Parking: available

Adults only

Visa, Mastercard, JCB

All rooms have tea and coffee making facilities with washbasin, television and hairdryer

No pets

No smoking throughout

ETC 3 diamonds

Edwardene Hotel

Omnivorous hotel with a veggie proprietor, in an 1885 traditional grey slate, three storey building. There are eleven rooms, all with ensuite bathrooms; two singles at £28–£33 per night, and six doubles, two twins and one family all at £29–£37.50 per person.

For breakfast you could have Morning Glory – oats and fruit steeped in maple syrup and soya milk, or a full cooked veggie breakfast. For vegans muesli, margarine, soya milk and sausages are all available.

Dinner is £16.95. The main course could be Fruity Bean Casserole with savoury rice, served with naan bread. They are open to non-residents for dinner too. Visit the veggie cafe The Lakeland Pedlar in town for lunch.

The hotel is in a quiet position, and is only two minutes walk from the town centre and all attractions. Keswick has shops, restaurants, numerous pubs, a theatre, a cinema, as well as galleries and museums.

Keswick is set amidst spectacular scenery and is paradise for walkers. The town is overlooked by Skiddaw, the fourth highest mountain in England. It is an excellent base from which to explore the Central and Northern Lake District.

Co-proprietor Margaret is a qualified chiropodist and Reiki therapist, and is happy to attend to your needs.

There is a guest lounge with a fireplace, television, video player and hi-fi. It has no bar although is licensed to sell alcohol. All rooms have a direct dial telephone, alarm clock and radio, television, hairdryer and tea and coffee making facilities. Some rooms contain videos, bars and other luxury upgrades.

Omnivorous
Hotel

26 Southey Street
Keswick
Cumbria CA12 4EB
England

Tel: 01768-773 586

Fax: 01768-773 824

www.edwardenehotel.com

Email: info@edwardene
hotel.com

Train Station: Penrith,
16 miles, then bus or taxi

Open: all year

Directions: From the M6 junction 40, follow the A66 west towards Keswick. Turn left on the A591 and follow signs to town centre. Just before pedestrian traffic lights turn left, then sharp left again into Southey Street. They are 150 yards on the right.

Parking: 2 spaces

Children of any age welcome

Cot and high chair available

Pets in special circumstances

Credit cards accepted

No smoking throughout

32 Skiddaw Street

Veggie B&B set in the popular Lake District town of Keswick. There are one double and one family room at £20–£25 per person per night.

A full cooked vegetarian breakfast is available on request, and vegan by arrangement.

Dinner is not offered, but veggie food is easily available in Keswick. For lunch, try Keswicks only fully vegetarian cafe, the Lakeland Pedlar.

Keswick is an excellent centre for exploring the fells, walking and climbing. There are many museums, galleries and country houses to visit nearby. See entertainment at Keswick's Theatre by the Lake, open throughout the year. It hosts a wide range of visiting drama, music, dance, talks, comedy and film.

The Keswick Museum and Art Gallery reveal Keswick's past, from an industrial mining centre to home of the Lakeland Poets.

If you need a day off walking, but still want to take in fresh air and magnificant scenery, take a boat trip around Derwentwater. You can spend all day hopping on and off at any of the seven landings.

Tea and coffee making facilities are available and there is a television in the family room.

Vegetarian
Bed and Breakfast

32 Skiddaw Street
Keswick
Cumbria CA12 4BY
England

Tel: 01768–772 752

Train Station: Penrith, then get a bus

Open: all year, except Christmas and New Year

Directions: A66 from Penrith, left hand slip road to Keswick. Right at Chestnut Hill, past BP petrol station, under bridge, past fire station, then second left into Blencathra Street. Follow to right, then turn left into Skiddaw Street.

Parking: on street

A lock-up garage is available for bicycles and canoes

Children aged five and over welcome

No smoking throughout

Honister House

Centrally located 18th century home in the lovely market town of Keswick. There are three rooms all with ensuite bathrooms: double, twin and family accommodation from £27 per person per night.

A breakfast of fruit juice, fresh fruit and cereal or porridge is offered followed by hash browns, veggie sausages, mushrooms, tomatoes, baked beans, toast and preserves. Soya milk, and vegan margarine are available as is home-baked organic vegan bread.

Dinner is not offered but there are plenty of restaurants, pubs and a veggie cafe for example, the Lakeland Pedlar. After dinner you could take in a movie at the cinema or go to the 'Theatre by the Lake'.

Keswick is surrounded by beautiful mountains and lake Derwentwater. There is unlimited walking for all abilities, as well as cycle routes.

If you want to take it easy, go for a cruise on Derwentwater and take in the magnificent views from a different angle.

There are many places of historical and cultural interest within easy reach such as the 4,000 year old Castlerigg Stone Circle and William Wordsworth's home.

Packed lunches on request. They have bicycle storage, boot storage and a drying area. Facilities for making Fairtrade tea and fresh coffee are available in the rooms with vegan and handmade vegetarian biscuits.

Keswick

Omnivorous
Guest House

1 Borrowdale Road
Keswick
Cumbria CA12 5DD
England

Tel: 01768-773 181
Fax: 08701-202 948

www.honisterhouse.co.uk

Email:
philandsueh@aol.com

Train station:
Penrith, 20 miles, then bus or taxi

Open: all year

Directions:
From the town centre and tourist information follow the right hand fork, Lake Road. After one minute walk they are on the left hand side.

Parking: available

Discounts to Viva! members

Children welcome.
Cot and high chair available.
Baby sitting by arrangement.

Baby sitting available

Drying area and bicycle storage

Credit cards accepted

No smoking throughout

RAC Four Diamond Rating
RAC Sparkling Diamond & Warm Welcome Awards

Pickle Farm

Eighteenth century farmhouse in a secluded location with panoramic views over the surrounding countryside. There are three rooms: two double ensuites with balconies and one twin ensuite for £28–£34 per person per night. On arrival you will be offered complimentary homemade veggie or vegan afternoon teas.

Breakfast is whatever you would like, for example fresh and dried fruits, homemade muesli and granola, followed by a variety of cooked foods and homemade breads and preserves. For vegans homemade sausages, muesli, margarine, soya milk and soya yoghurt are all available. There are many restaurants in and around Kirkby Lonsdale where veggie food can be found.

Pickle is located in the Lune Valley between the Yorkshire Dales and the Lake District. Walk from the door to the climbing spot of Hutton Roof Crags and to the Rakes, a spectacular limestone pavement. A few minutes drive away is the nature reserve and bird sanctuary at Leighton Moss. Kirkby Lonsdale is walking distance where you could visit Devil's Bridge, Ruskin's View and the many interesting shops. Ingleton is a short drive away for waterfalls and caves, or for serious walking go to the Three Peaks of Whernside, Ingleborough and Pen y Ghent. You could also visit the market towns of Dent, Settle and Skipton. In the other direction is the Lake District, famous for its scenery and fell walking.

There is also a spacious one-bed two-person cottage attached to the Farm with fabulous views. One week from £195 in low season to £325 during high season.

At night relax in the sitting room in front of the wood-burning stove. Tea and coffee making facilities in the rooms.

Vegetarian / Vegan Bed and Breakfast

Pickle Farm
Hutton Roof
Kirkby Lonsdale
Cumbria CA6 2PH
England

Tel: 01524-272 104

www.picklefarm.co.uk

Email:
stay@picklefarm.co.uk

Train station: Carnforth, 10 miles

Open: all year

Directions: From Kirkby Lonsdale Tourist Information Centre, take New Road out of town to mini roundabout. Turn left and pass Booths Supermarket. Turn right at roundabout onto A65 towards Kendal, then take the first left, signposted Hutton Roof 3 miles. At the T junction turn right. After another mile turn right into Hutton Roof. Proceed through village to the church on the left. Pickle gateway is on the right 200 yards past the church.

Parking: plenty available

Exclusively for adults

No smoking throughout

Michelin BIB award

Five Diamonds Gold Award with Visit Britain

See pictures (facing page)

For updates to this guidebook

visit

www.vegetarianguides.co.uk/updates

For links to sites covering other
countries

www.vegetarianguides.co.uk/links

Kirkwood Guest House

Omnivorous guest house that's been trading for twenty years.

There are seven rooms: four double ensuites (all with four poster beds), two twin ensuites and a family room (one double and two singles). From £25 per person per night for a standard room, and from £27 per person for the four posters.

Breakfast could be fruit, juice and cereal or muesli followed by beans, tomatoes, mushrooms, hash browns and veggie sausages. They sometimes have pancakes. Soya milk, vegan muesli and soya yoghurt are available, but it is best to let them know in advance if you are vegan.

Windermere is a very popular base to explore the Lake District and at times can feel like a seaside resort. If you are wanting a lively stay in the Lakes, this is the town to come to. There are lots of restaurants and bars, many offering veggie food.

There are cruises around Lake Windermere or you could hire your own rowing boat. For rainy days, there are museums including the Steamboat Museum and the World of Beatrix Potter.

Orrest Head is a one and a half mile climb from the train station and offers great Lakeland views. Another good viewpoint is Brant Fell. Beatrix Potter's cottage at Hill Top and the village of Hawkshead are walking distance away.

There is a guest lounge. Rooms have tea and coffee making facilities, radio, hairdryer and TV.

Windermere

Omnivorous
Guest House

Princes Road
Windermere
Cumbria CA23 2DD
England

Tel: 01539-443 907

www.kirkwood51.co.uk

Email:
info@kirkwood51.co.uk

Train Station: Windermere, 1/2 mile, then walk or get a taxi.
Collection possible by arrangement.

Open: all year

Directions: Please phone or see map on website for directions

Parking: available

No smoking throughout

Children welcome

Animals welcome

Credit cards accepted

Discounts for longer stays

Quince and Medlar

Gourmet vegetarian food, three times winner of 'vegetarian restaurant of the year' and four times runner up. Situated in a listed Georgian building with a wood panelled candlelit dining room featuring work by local artists. Very swish, recommended for a special occasion.

Starters £3.95–£6.95 such as soup, roast aubergine and sundried tomato paté, and baked French onion tart.

Main courses £12.75 include parsnip, fennel and basmati rice discs with white truffle oil and Madeira sauce; lentil and apricot strudel in filo pastry on a bed of wilted spinach leaves with tomato and red wine sauce; spiced Moroccan vegetable cone with creamed coconut, lemongrass and tumeric, with a ring of wild rice and chutney.

Home-made garlic bread £1.35.

Desserts £4.75 include chocolate orange pie, lemon tart, and coffee and Tia Maria parfait. Vegan ice cream is available.

The menu changes every 6–8 weeks. Vegan options are available but not marked on the menu. About half the ingredients used are organic.

House wine £11.15 a bottle, £2.95 glass, other wines up to £30.

They appreciate advance notice of special diets.

The owners take great pride in their restaurant and have even won 'loo of the year' award!

Vegetarian
Restaurant

13 Castlegate
Cockermouth
Cumbria CA13 9EU

Tel: 01900–823 579

www.quinceandmedlar.co.
uk

Open:
Tue–Sat from 19.00

Booking advisable

Licensed

Children over 5 years welcome

No smoking throughout

Visa, MC

Ambleside

Nab Cottage

Omnivorous guest house

Rydal, Ambleside, Cumbria CA22 9SD
Tel: 01539–435 311. Open: all year
www.rydalwater.com, tim@nabcottage.com

One single, two twin/doubles £24 per person, four twin/double ensuites £26 per person. Vegans and special diets catered for with advance notice. Children of all ages welcome at a discounted price. Pets by arrangement. Smoking in the sitting room only

Granny Smiths

Wholefood shop

Market Place, Ambleside, Cumbria LA22 9BU
Tel: 015394–33145

Organic fruit & veg, soya milk, Tofutti vegan cream cheese.

Caldbeck

The Watermill Restaurant

Vegetarian restaurant

Priest's Mill, Caldbeck, Wigton,
Cumbria CA7 8DR. Tel: 01697–478 267
Open: Mon 11–16.00, Tue–Sun 10–17.00,
closed from start Jan until mid Feb
www.watermillrestaurant.co.uk

Light refreshments to full meals. Some tables overlook the river or you can sit outside on the grassy terrace over-looking the village cricket pitch. Starters from £2.95, mains £6. Always something vegan and gluten-free. No smoking throughout. Cash and cheque only. Evening parties and outside catering by arrangement. Disabled access. Free parking. Summer 2005this restaurant was due to change hands and the new owners may introduce meat dishes.

Cockermouth

The Granary

Health food shop

15 Main Street
Cockermouth, Cumbria CA13 9LE
Tel: 01900–822 633
Open: Mon–Sat 9.30– 17.30

Pride themselves on their individual service. Fully veggie shop with chiller and freezer cabinets. Stocks toiletries and offers clothes washing.

Grasmere

How Beck

Vegetarian bed and breakfast

Grasmere, Cumbria, CA22 9RH
Tel: 01539–435 732
Email: trevor.eastes@btinternet.com
Open: all year, except Christmas and New Year

Two double ensuite rooms £27–£30 per person per night. No children or pets. No smoking throughout. Visa, MC.

The Rowan Tree

Vegetarian cafe

Church Bridge, Grasmere, Cumbria CA22 9SN
Tel: 01539–435 528
www.therowantreegrasmere.co.uk
Open: Spring–Autumn Mon–Sun 10–17.00,
18–21.00; Jan–Feb just weekends daytime.
Closed Xmas and New Year holidays

Located beside the river Rothay, this vegetarian café becomes a restaurant at night. Choose from starters such as hummous £3.50, mushroom, hazelnut and red wine paté £4.50, spring rolls £4.50 and mains including fruit and vegetable curry £7.75. No smoking throughout. Visa, MC.

Waterside Wholefoods

Kendal

Vegetarian cafe,
restaurant and shop

Kent View
Waterside
Kendal
Cumbria LA9 4DZ

Tel: 01539 729743 shop
01539 733252 office

Toni@glenrae.
freeserve.co.uk

Train: Oxenholme

Open: Mon– Sat 9.00–
16.30

Licensed with food

Vegan and vegetarian
wholefood 50% organic

No smoking

All credit cards accepted

High chairs for children

This vegetarian café and shop, which has been going for over 25 years, offers cosmopolitan food and strives to be as organic as possible.

The daily changing menu includes pizzas with toppings such as spinach and pine kernal, mushroom or pineapple. Pates such as hummous or fennel and orange.

Main meals include pasta and vegetable bake, mushroom and bean stroganoff, Turkish pilaff, spiced vegetable and chickpea tagine, cauliflower and cashew nut curry, from £3.20 per portion.

Salads include bulgar wheat with mint, cucumber and tomato; cauliflower, cashew nut and date; pasta with mixed peppers, French dressing & herbs.

Cakes and slices such as chocolate fudge, luscious lemon with lemon curd topping, coffee & walnut, fig & ginger, orange & poppy seed, carrot cake.

Usual selection of coffees £1.10 filter to £1.60 for lattes. Fairtrade available also.

Organic wine is available.

Special diets are catered for, such as wheat and gluten free, diabetic, raw and of course vegan. They always have vegan margarine, soya milk, cappucino and milkshakes/ smoothies.

They cater for children and also do outside catering

Kendal

The Tapestry Tearooms

Vegetarian cafe

Stramongate, Kendal, Cumbria LA9 4BH
01539-722 975
Open: Mon–Fri 10.00–16.30
www.quaker-tapestry.co.uk

This delightful cafe is part of The Quaker Tapestry Exhibition Centre. They do a good range of usual cafe foods much of which is vegan. All vegetarian. Also has space for 1-3 people to stay.

Kan Foods

Wholefood shop

9 New Shambles, Kendal, Cumbria CA9 4TS
01539 721190
Open: Mon–Sat 9.00–17.00

Veggie shop, selling grains, pulses etc. Organic cosmetics and natural skin care products. No ready-made foods.

Keswick

Lakeland Pedlar

See full page listing page 66.

Mayson's Wholesome Food Restaurant

Omnivorous restaurant

33 Lake Road, Keswick, Cumbria CA12 5DQ
01768-774 104
www.maysonsrestaurant.btinternet.co.uk
Open: 7 days, summer 10–20.45,
winter 10.30–16.00

Omnivorous restaurant with about 30% of meals veggie. All salads vegetarian. Always have a vegan dish such as vegan biryani curry £6.25. Desserts around

£1.95, vegan flapjacks 95p.
House wine £2.10 glass, half carafe £5.15, litre carafe £10.25. Lots of bottled and draft beers. Pot of tea 85p, coffee £1.10. No soya milk.
No smoking from 12 noon. Cash or cheque only. Small portions for children. High chairs available.
They own a take-away called Mayson's directly opposite which does veggie and vegan sandwiches, around £2.65.

Sundance Wholefoods

Wholefood shop

33 Main Street, Keswick CA12 5BL
017687-74712
Open: Daily 09.00–17.00

Veggie and vegan shop offering take-away food. Chiller cabinet with cakes and samosas.

Milnthorpe

Living Well

Wholefood shop

26 The Square, Milnthorpe, Cumbria CA7 7QJ
Tel: 01539-563 870
Open: Mon–Fri 9.00–17.00, Sat til 13.00

Veggie shop with fridge and freezer.

Penrith

Little Salkeld Watermill

Vegetarian organic tea room

Little Salkeld, Cumbria LA10 1NN
6 miles NE of Penrith
01768-881 523
Open: Feb–Christmas every day 10.30–17.00
www.organicmill.co.uk

Organic vegetarian cafe using flour from the next door traditional 18th century

65

The Lakeland Pedlar

Keswick

Vegetarian cafe & bicycle centre

Hendersons Yard
Bell Close Car Park,
Keswick
Cumbria CA12 5JD

Tel: 017687–74492
Fax: 017687 75752
www.lakelandpedlar.co.uk
lakeland.pedlar@btclick.com

Open: Mon–Sun 9.00–17.00

Licensed for cider, beer and wine. Organic and vegan

Allergies catered for

No smoking

Visa, MC, Maestro

10% discount to Viva!, Vegetarian and Vegan Society members

Children's menu

Private parties caterred for

Situated in central Keswick, this veggie cafe, popular with cyclists and walkers, has great views of the fells. Decorated in warm deep reds and yellows with the walls festooned wirh cycling prints and memorabilia, the cafe makes a memorable and relaxing place to pass the time. Most dishes are or can be made vegan.

Start the day with a full "Pedlars"veggie breakfast including beans, grilled tomatoes, mushrooms, hash browns and toast for £5.85. Or try the Bacon Ciabatta Buttie £3.75, made with vegan rashers. Breakfast served until 11.30am.

Lunchtime specials include spinach, carrot and cashew nut filo pie, baked butternut squash and leek crepes or roast Mediterranean vegetables and sundried tomato tart.

Homemade soups with organic bread are £3.05.

Main courses, £5.95, include veggie chilli with pitta bread and side salad; 3 bean burritos with jalapenos. The soup, salad and bread combo is £5.15.

Children's menu, £2–£3.40, such as the "Pirate" soup with wholemeal bread or veggie burgers.

Lots of desserts and dairy–free organic ice cream £1.85.

Fair trade coffee and tea, £1.30–£1.60 and herbal teas £1.25. Cold drinks, £1.25–£1.60 including ginger beer, juices and Purdey's.

At certain times of the year the Pedlar is open for an evening menu with vegan wines, beers and ciders.

Outside seating is available where you may smoke.

water-powered mill, which is open to visitors for £3.50 adult, £1.50 child. Veggie cafe has little for vegans. Soups, biscuits and fruit pies, all made from their own flour. Bring your own alcohol. No smoking throughout. High chairs and children's portions. MC, Visa.

Nature's Health Store

Wholefood shop

1 King Street, Penrith, Cumbria CA11 7AR
01768 899262.
Open: Mon–Sat 9.00–17.00 (16.30 Wed)

Good range of cruelty-free cosmetics and special dietary products. Can also offer advice.

The Village Bakery

Omnivorous organic cafe

Melmerby, 9 miles NE of Penrith on A686
Tel: 01768–881 515
www.village-bakery.com
Open: Mon–Sat 8.30–17.00, Sun 9.30–17.00
Special evening meals on certain Saturdays

Snacks and light meals using ingredients from the wood-fired bakery and smallholding. Wheat, gluten and dairy free catered for. Shop sells organic bread, cakes (apricot and date flapjacks are vegan), groceries, baking books and equipment. Exhibitions, demonstrations, talks and events, books and pamphlets on organic gardening and agriculture. Baking courses.

Ulverston

World Peace Cafe

Vegetarian cafe and meditation centre

5 Cavendish Street, Ulverston LA12 7AD
Tel: 01229–587793
Open: Tue–Sat 10–16.30, Wed –15.00,
Fri Stop the Week evening from 19.30

Soup £2.80. Lunch £5 such as veg biryani with tarka dal, falafel. Open sandwich £4 with salad. Coffees, teas, smoothies in summer with soya milk, gluten free and vegan cakes £1–1.50. Garden area. Sofas in front window. No smoking. No alcohol. Children welcome, high chairs. No credit cards. Meditation room upstairs for recentering yourself. (You don't have to be a Buddhist) Tuesday and Thursday meditation 12.30–13.00 £3 which entitles you to soup afterwards for £1.50. Classes Thursday 19.30–21.00/21.30 £4 followed by refreshments. Stop the Week Friday night 19.30 meditation class and three course dinner £9.50.

Appleseeds

Health food shop

59 Market Street, Ulverston CA12 7LP
Tel: 01229–583 394
Open: Mon–Sat 9.00–17.00 (Wed 15.30)

Veggie shop offering a variety of organic veggies and alcohol, gluten-free products, healthy drinks such as smoothies, soya foods, ready meals, pre-bagged and organic fruits, nuts and grains. Chiller cabinet. Books on health, complementary therapies, music tapes.

Holland & Barrett

Health food shop

206–208 Dalton Road, Barrow-in-Furness
Tel: 01229–835795

2 Globe Lane, The Lanes, Carlisle
Tel: 01228–530827

54 Stricklandgate, Kendal
Tel: 01539–733828

53 Pow Street, Workington
Tel: 01900–62214

Derbyshire

Jennifer and David's Guest House

New bed and breakfast between Matlock and Bakewell, ideal for exploring the Peak District National Park. One double room with sole use of adjacent private bathroom, £22.50 per person. No single supplement.

Breakfast (can be in room) is a choice of: fruit juice, cereals, fresh fruit salad and soya yoghurt followed by any or all of the following: vegan sausage, beans, tomatoes, mushrooms, home made rosti, organic toast, preserves mainly from fruit grown in garden (damsons, raspberries, strawberries, white/red/blackcurrants, rhubarb and marmalade). They have vegan muesli and margarine and soya milk.

They do not provide an evening meal but you can bring in take-aways from the Shalimar Indian restaurant within 100 yards. Caudwells Mill (listed below) is excellent.

The lovely garden has views across the valley. Footpath by river opposite the house. David is an outdoor pursuits instructor and can provide activities at a reasonable cost.

Ideal location for walking, cycling or sight seeing and there is a good local bus route to explore the area. Chatsworth House and Haddon Hall are nearby. Mining Museum and Heights Of Abraham theme park in Matlock Bath. Show caves in Castleton and Buxton. There are numerous local villages, which have well dressing festivals throughout the summer – an ancient tradition not to be missed! The nearby Peak Rail steam railway station has a café and small play area. There are regular special trains such as real ale/curry night, Roaring 40's weekend. Formal dining car for Sunday lunch etc.

Matlock

Vegetarian and vegan bed & breakfast

3 Unity Villas,
Dale Road North,
Darley Dale, Matlock,
Derbyshire DE4 2HX

Tel: 01629-732 445

www.dm-adventure.co.uk

Email:
dm-adventure@
supanet.com

Train Station: Matlock 5 miles. Bus from Derby / Matlock / Bakewell / Manchester.
There are several local taxi firms and we can collect from Matlock or Bakewell

Open: all year

Directions: The house is situated on the A6 between Matlock and Bakewell. From Matlock proceed in the direction of Bakewell for approximately 4 miles. Toll Bar Racing is on the left and we are opposite on the right.

Parking: behind the bouse

TV lounge

Children welcome

No smoking throughout

No credit cards

Tea/coffee making and hairdryer in room.

Stonecroft

Second generation family run guest house situated in the historic hamlet of Edale. There are two rooms, one double with private facilities from £30 per person per night and one double ensuite from £35 per person.

Start your day with fruit juice and cereal or muesli followed by a continental or cooked breakfast. Continental breakfast could be home made bread rolls, preserves, tahini, soya yoghurt and fruit. If you opt for the cooked, you'll have veg sausages, baked beans, mushrooms, tomatoes and fried bread. If these choices don't take your fancy, there's more, like mushrooms on toast with garam masala and baked soya bean crunchy balls, scrambled tofu on toast with tomatoes, kitchiri or stuffed pancakes. Your host is a qualified chef and a vegan on a gluten and wheat-free diet. She caters well for vegans and those on special diets. For your evening meal, most hotels, pubs and cafes in the area cater for veggies.

Stonecroft is situated at the start of the Pennine Way, in the heart of Derbyshire's Peak District National Park. It is a haven for those seeking peace, beauty and the countryside. There are many attractions within easy reach. It is six miles from Castleton with its show caves and Norman Castle, and twelve miles from Buxton. Chatsworth House and Haddon Hall are only a short drive away.

Rooms have tea and coffee making facilities, clock radio, hair dryer and dressing gowns. Iron and drying facilities available.

English Tourist Board four diamonds gold award.

Omnivorous guest house

Edale
Hope Valley
Derbyshire S33 7ZA
England

Tel and Fax:
01433–670 262

www.stonecroftguesthouse.co.uk

Email:
stonecroftedale@aol.com

Train Station: Edale, 1/4 mile then collection by arrangement.

Open: all year, except Christmas

Directions: Edale is five miles from the village of Hope. Stonecroft is the third house on the left after the church.

TV lounge

Parking: available

No children or dogs

No smoking throughout (house and grounds)

7.5% discount for stays of three nights or over (excluding bank holidays)

Riber Hall

Omnivorous hotel

Riber, Matlock, Derbyshire, DE4 5JU
Tel: 01629-582 795
Fax: 01629-580 475
www.riber-hall.co.uk info@riber-hall.co.uk
Open: All Year not Xmas Day

Historic country manor on the edge of the Peak District National Park. Many different ensuite rooms £52.50-£91 per person double or £78-£112 single. Vegetarian lunch £24 two courses or £27 for three served 12.00-13.30. Dinner £32 or £37 served 19.00-21.30. Rooms have tea and coffee making facilities, TV with satellite channels, hair dryers. Dogs welcome. Children over 10 welcome. RAC and AA 3 stars.

Bakewell

Caudwell's Mill Craft Centre
Rowsley, nr Bakewell DE4 2EB
Tel: 01629-733 185
Open: summer 10-17.30, winter 10-16.30

Snacks and starters from £3.45 and mains at £5.95 such as Homity pie. Home made cakes including vegan £1.15-2.35. Unlicensed. Children welcome, high chairs. No smoking. No credit cards.

The Cottage Tea Room

Vegetarian tea rooms

3 Fennel Street,
Ashford-in-the-Water, Bakewell DE45 1QF
Tel: 01629-812 488
Open: every day except Tue and Fri, 14.30-17.00 in summer, earlier in winter

Vegetarian traditional tea rooms on the old Roman road. Accent on home cooking with traditional English cakes, hand kneaded breads and scones. 6 variations of afternoon tea or just a pot and a slice of cake for £3-£5.25. Big selection of teas and herbals. Can cater for gluten free and diabetic with advance warning.

Unspoilt conservation area, in exquisite Peak District village. The cottage is 2 miles north of Bakewell and 8 miles south of Buxton Spa, just above the ford by the sheepwash bridge.

Buxton

The Wild Carrot

Vegetarian wholefood organic shop

5 Bridge Street, Buxton SK17 6BS
Tel: 01298-22843
www.wildcarrot.freeserve.co.uk

Predominantly vegan with a take-away selection of Indian, Italian and Mexican snacks, 45p to £1.66. Organic VegBox scheme for collection or delivery. Vegan ice cream and other sweet items. 10% discount to Vegetarian and Vegan Society members.

Chesterfield

The Natural Choice Health Food & Cafe

Vegetarian cafe and shop

5 Long Shambles, Chesterfield S40 1PX
Tel: 01246-558 550
Open: Mon-Sat 9.00-17.00 closed Sunday.

Cooked breakfast £2.95 including drink. Afternoon tea £1.65 with scone, cookie or toasted teacake (can be vegan). Soup £2.95. Salads, mains £2.95-£5.50 include vegan pasties, pies, casserole, savoury roasts. Sandwiches and jacket potatoes. Many cakes and desserts suitable for diabetics, gluten free and vegans. Menu changes daily. Children welcome, no high chairs. No smoking. Visa, MC.

Holland & Barrett

Health food shop

59 Low Pavement, Chesterfield S40 1PD
Tel: 01246–232 536

Pizza Express

Omnivorous pizza restaurant

25 Irongate, Derby DE1 3GL
Tel: 01332–349 718
Open: every day 11.30–midnight

Sound Bites

Vegan wholefood shop

Unit 23, Guildhall Market, Derby
Tel: 01332–291 369.
Open: Mon–Sat 9–17.00
www.soundbitesderby.org.uk

Mainly Fairtrade and organic food, bread, fruit & veg, lunchtime munchies such as pasties and sausage rolls, body care and household products. Phone before coming as they plan to move to a larger shop or check website, which includes their brilliant Nibbler newsletter which you can sign up to by email.

Holland & Barrett

Health food shop

Unit 18, Crown Walk, Eagle Centre, Derby
Tel: 01332–360 664

The Globe

Vegan kitchen within a pub

144 High Street West,Glossop, SK30 HJJ
Tel: 01457–852 417
foodattheglobe@hotmail.com
www.globemusic.org
Open for food: Mon, Wed–Sat 17.00–late; Sun 13.00; closed Tue.

Vegan kitchen within the pub owned by vegans. Menu changes regularly. Beer garden won first prize in 'Glossop in Bloom' in 2003. £1–£1.50 snacks such as samosas, parsnip chips, hummous and pitta bread. Mains such as spinach and chickpea curry,cauliflower, hot–pot with bread, Mexican bean chilli with sundried tomatoes and rice £2–£2.50. To finish it off they do Swedish Glace, in three flavours. The Globe is a live music venue with global bands playing upstairs. Musicians downstairs perform on Mon, Thu and Sun.

The Walnut Club

Omnivorous organic restaurant & bar

Unit 6, The Square, Main Road, Hathersage, Derbyshire, S32
1BB. (Peak District.)
Open: every day 12–23.00
Tel: 01433–651155

100% organic. Veggie and vegan friendly, meals £12–25. Live music at week–ends. Child friendly. Door–to–door taxi service. No rush policy, the table you book is yours for the evening.

The Cafe in Scarthin Books

Vegetarian cafe in a bookshop

Scarthin Books, The Promenade,
Scarthin, Cromford, Derbyshire, DE4 3QF
Tel: 01629–823 272
clare@scarthinbooks.com
Open: Mon–Sat 9.30–18.00, Sun 12–18.00

Vegetarian cafe within a bookshop. Soup with organic wholewheat rolls £3.20 is usually vegan. Savoury items £1.50–£3.20. Cakes £1–£1.95, of which only the flapjack is vegan. Organic Fairtrade coffee, wide selection of teas and cold drinks.

County Durham

Barnard Castle

33 Newgate B&B

Omnivorous Bed and Breakfast

33 Newgate, Barnard Castle,
Co. Durham, DL12 8NJ
Tel: 01833-690208
Open: all year
Email: peter.whittaker@tinyworld.co.uk
Train Station: Darlington, 20 miles

One family room with private facilities £22–£27 person per night. Vegetarian or vegan evening meal £12.50 available with advance notice. Children welcome. No pets. No smoking throughout.

Darlington

Pizza Express

Omnivorous pizza restaurant

1 Skinnergate, Darlington DL3 7NB
Tel: 01325-488 771
Open: every day midday–midnight

Outside courtyard garden in summer. Children welcome, baby changing facilities. Disabled access.

Health Warehouse

Health food shop

15 Post House Wynd, Darlington DL3 7LU
Tel: 01325 468570
Open: Mon–Sat 9–17.30 (17.00 Wed & Sat)

Health food shop with lots of take–away food like pasties and flapjacks, very handy as Darlington does not have a veggie café, though you can get veggie food in many places. They have a bakery on–site. Working towards organic status.

Holland & Barrett

Health food shop

5 Queen Street, Darlington DL3 6SH
Tel: 01325–365 656

Durham

Pizza Express

Omnivorous pizza restaurant

64 Saddler Street, Durham DH1 3PG
Tel: 0191–383 2661
Open: every day 11.30–24.00

Off the market square. Children welcome, baby changing facilities. Sometimes live music.

The Alms Houses

Omnivorous cafe

Palace Green, Durham DH1 3RL
Tel: 0191–386 1054
Open: every day
summer 09–20.00, winter 09–17.00

Right outside the cathedral and castle. Always have a veggie meal, gluten free meals and cake on the board.

Holland & Barrett

Health food shop

13 Milburngate, Durham DH1 4SL
Tel: 01913–842 374

Lancashire

Crazi Carrots

Vegetarian, vegan or raw bed & breakfast in a quiet semi-detached house in Bolton near a country park, 15 minutes from Manchester. One simple twin room with wooden floor and en suite shower room, £25 per person. No single supplement.

Breakfast is fresh fruit salad, yoghurts, nuts and seeds, cereals, cooked if required. There is vegan muesli and margarine, soya milk, veggie sausages. There is a small garden frequented by frogs, birds and butterflies where you can have breakfast on the patio.

It is a bright, calm, private space with no nasty chemicals. Food is organic where possible. You can use the diner, sitting room and kitchen. There is a reverse osmosis water filter and juicer and a library.

Evening meal not generally available. Ten minute walk to shops and pubs – the local does veggie but not vegan meals. The nearest veggie places to eat out are in Manchester such as Eigth Day, the Greenhouse and Earth Cafe.

The owner teaches yoga and massage by arrangement and there are therapists nearby including a Life Coach, sports massage, reflexology, aromatherapy.

Bring walking books (for outside, the house is shoe free) for the many nearby walks including to Entwistle Reservoir by a real ale pub The Strawberry Duck which serves good food. Rivington Pike hill walk is in Horwich with views across to the sea. There is an old fashioned coffee shop in a chapel.

5 minutes from Moses Gate Country Park, with a lake with ducks and geese and a path suitable for prams or wheelchairs. 30 minutes from areas of outstanding beauty: Jumbles, Entwistle, Wayoh, Rivington Pike.

Veggie/Vegan or raw bed & breakfast

123 Aintree Road
Little Lever
Bolton
Lancashire BL3 1ES

Tel: 01204-704600
07050 262819

www.wellbeingwork
shopsworldwide.com

Email:
alwynne@wellbeingwork
shopsworldwide.com

Train Station: Bolton, 2 miles, then taxi/bus or owner can collect you

Open: all year

Directions: 15 minutes from Manchester on the A666, exit Farnworth/Kearsley

Parking available

Children welcome

Well behaved pets welcome

No smoking throughout

No credit cards

Disabled access: downstairs bathroom and sofa-bed available

10% discount to members of the Vegetarian Society, Vegan Society, Viva!, PETA, Animal Aid and people presenting this book.

Vegan owner

Hairdryer available

Cameo Hotel

Omnivorous hotel

30 Hornby Road, Blackpool
Lancashire FY1 4QG
Tel/Fax: 01253 626144
Open: all year
www.cameo-hotel.co.uk
janetandphil@cameo-hotel.co.uk

Vegetarian owned hotel, though not actually vegetarian but they'd love to be if they can get enough of us. 12 rooms. One night £18 per person (£23 with evening meal), 2 nights £35, 3 £52 (£66 with evening meals). 5+ nights under £16 per night. Prices increase during the illuminations. Close to the Tower, seafront, piers, Winter Gardens and town centre. Smoking allowed in rooms. MC, Visa, debit cards.

Wildlife Hotel

Vegan hotel

39 Woodfield Road
Blackpool, Lancashire FY1 6AX
Tel: 01253 346143

The only vegan hotel in Blackpool, 12 rooms all ensuite, £20 per person. Animal rights folk especially welcome. Evening meal usually available £6. They have vegan wine. No smoking throughout. No credit cards. Dogs by arrangement. Children welcome, cot. TV in rooms and in the lounge. Close to pleasure beach and those wonderful trams, between central and south piers. 10% discount for Vegetarian and Vegan Society, Animal Aid, PETA and Viva members. There is a JD Wetherspoon pub nearby with veggie food and Thai and Indian restaurants in town.

Surya Snack Bar

Indian vegetarian snack bar

98 Derby Street, Bolton, Lancashire BL3 6HG
Tel: 01204-380 679
Open: Mon–Fri 12-14.00, 18-22.00
Sat–Sun 12-22.30

Very vegan friendly Indian vegetarian restaurant with dishes from throughout the sub continent. Starters, £1.50-£4, with samosas and kachoris, and mains from £2-£6.99 with stir fried aubergines, dosas and spinach mung daal. Plan to introduce menu with vegan items clearly indicated. Desserts, £2, including they tell us, vegan gulab jamun. 35cl half bottle of wine £2.80. Outside catering. Separate smoking section. Visa, MC. 20% discount to members of the Vegetarian or Vegan Society. Children welcome, no high chairs.

Patagonia Cafe

Omnivorous café

116 Bradshawgate, Bolton,
Lancashire BL2 1AY
Tel: 01204-528 533
Open: Mon–Thu 8.00-17.00,
Fri–Sat 08-22.30, Sun closed.

Omnivorous café that considers itself a cross over for families and groups that include veggies. Half the menu is vegetarian, some vegan. Soup, sandwiches £4, hummous, potatoes, bean. No smoking. MC, Visa.

Bolton

Sokrates

Omnivorous Greek restaurant

80–84 Winter Hey Lane, Horwich
Bolton, Lancashire BL6 7NZ
Tel: 01204–692100
Open: every day 18–22.30 last orders

Lots of vegetarian dishes. Starters £5–6, mains £9.50–11 such as vine leaves, moussaka, oven baked butterbeans. Vegetarian banquet £17.90 minimum two people, with a bit of 25 different dishes. House wine £10.50, glass £2.55. No smoking room. Children welcome, high chairs. Visa, MC, Amex, Diners. Reservations advised weekends.

Burnley

Red Triangle Cafe

Vegetarian restaurant

160 St James Street, Burnley, Lancs BB11 1NR
Tel: 01282–832 319
Open: Tue–Sat 10.30–19.00,
Fri & Sat night 19.00–22.30
(you must book, only open for bookings in evenings).
closed Sun & Mon

Vegetarian café and restaurant that also has occasional music nights. Mains £3.50 during the day and £5.95 in evenings such as Moroccan couscous with pumpkin seeds. Desserts £1.50 day, £1.95, such as fruit filled oat pancake with soya custard. House wine £5.95 for a bottle, £1.50 glass. Children welcome in the day, high chair. No smoking policy. No credit cards.

Colne

Vegetarian Restaurant (Jim's Caff)

Vegetarian restaurant

19–21 New Market Street, Colne
Lancashire BB8 9BJ
Tel: 01282–868 828
Open: Thu–Sun 19–23.00 or later

Licensed vegetarian restaurant with world food influences. Specials change weekly, such as Polynesian sweet and sour with pineapple, deep–fried tofu, green beans, Chinese leaves, peppers, beansprouts, gomasio, brown rice, crispy noodles, nori £7.45. Always something vegan but can offer more variety with advance notice. Smoking permitted but hardly anyone does and the ceilings are high. House wine carafe 75cl £7.65. Organic wine by the bottle £8.95–13.50. Children welcome, no high chair. No credit cards, cash machine outside. Occasional live acoustic music.

Lancaster

The Whale Tail

Vegetarian cafe

78a Penny Street, Lancaster LA1 1XN
Tel: 01524–845 133
www.10000things.org.uk/whale_tail_cafe.htm
Open: Mon–Fri 9.00–16.00,
Sat 9.30–17.00, Sun 10.30–15.00

Vegetarian café above Single Step Wholefoods. Always has vegan options available. Breakfast every day. Soups at £2.20 and mains for £2.95–£5.15. Vegan chocolate cake £1.95. House wine £8 for a bottle, £2 glass. No smoking inside but have a patio garden. No credit cards.

Bella Italia

Omnivorous Italian restaurant

26/28 Church Street, Lancaster
Tel: 01524-36340
Open: Mon–Sat 11–23.00, Sun –22.00

Near the city centre and university.

Gregson Centre

Omnivorous cafe in arts centre

33 Moorgate, Lancaster
Tel: 01524-849959
Open: Mon–Fri 12–21.00, Sat–Sun 11–21.00
www.gregson.co.uk

Cafe and bar in a community arts centre, 500 metres up the hill from the Dukes Playhouse. Good community feel and lots of events. Can make all its vegetarian dishes vegan, £4–6 for a main such as jacket potato £3.50, baguettes, ciabattas all 3.50, salads £4.75. Veggie sausage, champ (mash with onion) and peas £5.75. Desserts £2.95 but maybe not vegan. House wine £2.20 glass, £9.50 bottle. Children's menu with veggie sausages, pasta, high chairs. MC, Visa.

The Sultan of Lancaster

Indian omnivorous restaurant

The Old Church, Brock Street, Lancaster LA1 1UR (opposite Whale Tail)
Tel 01524-61188
Open: every day 17–23.00

Amazing atmospheric place in an old chapel. Veggie dishes cooked separately, dinner for £13–15. Children welcome, high chairs. Smoking allowed at present. No alcohol. MC, Visa.
(All the Indian restaurants in Lancaster are vegan aware and friendly.)
Downstairs is the daytime Mediterranean and Middle Eastern Sultan Food Court & Art Gallery with meals, snacks and coffees. Open Mon–Thu 10–17.00, Fri–Sat 10–22.00, Sun 11–16.00. Tel. 01524-849494.

Single Step

Vegetarian Co-op

78a Penny Street,, Lancaster LA1 1XN
Tel: 01524-63021
Open: Mon–Sat 9.30–17.30

Organic veggies. Loose food in hoppers. Vegan cheese, milk, yoghurt, ice-cream. Organic vegan wines and beers. Vegan cosmetics, eco-friendly household products. Fresh bread daily. Gluten free foods. Cash or cheque only.

For a veggie map of Lancaster:
http://tofubandits.org.uk/guide2.html

City Deli

Omnivorous cafe

8b Winckley Street, Preston PR1 2AA
Tel: 01772-204777
Open: Mon–Sat 9–17.00, Sun 11–17.00

90% vegetarian and some of it vegan, including Mexican wraps. Average meal £4.95 such as chimichanga tortilla wrap with spicy potato, salad and couscous. Three desserts but none vegan. Glass wine £2.75. Children welcome, no high chairs. No smoking. MC, Visa.

Waterslack Tearoom

Omnivorous tea room

Waterslack Garden Centre
Silverdale, Lancashire LA5 OUU
Tel: 01524-701 862
Open: Mon–Sat 9–15.00, Sun 9–16.00

Tea room based in garden centre. Vegetarian breakfast. Salads and soups from £2.80. Main salad an 79 d specials £5.75–7.50, normally something veggie but not necessarily vegan, but they will make something such as a salad with avocado and walnuts. Farm shop adjacent has some gluten and dairy-free food that they can bring in.

Tameside

Tameside Vaidic (Health) Foods

Health food shop

61 Penny Meadow, Ashton-under-Lyne
Tameside, Lancs OL6 6HE
Tel: 0161–330 9853
Open: Mon–Fri 9.30–17.00,
Tue closed, Sat 9.30–16.30
Special evenings 18.00–21.00

Todmordon

Bear Cafe

Vegetarian café and wholefood shop

29 Rochdale Road, Todmorden
Lancashire OL14 7LA
Tel: 01706–813 737
Shop: Mon–Thu 9.30–17.30, Fri–Sat 9.30–20.00. Cafe: Mon–Sat 10–16.30 & Fri–Sat 19–21.00 tapas

Vegetarian café and fair trade gift shop above a wholefood shop. Café serves light meals and snacks with sandwiches from £2.50, Mexican, Greek and Italian ciabattas, various wraps, plated salads, jacket potatoes and mini flans. Plenty for vegans with almost everything having a vegan alternative – such as a Ploughman's lunch with vegan cheese. In their desserts they are famous for their vegan hot chocolate cake £2, which can be served with non dairy cream or ice cream £2.50. Friday and Saturday nights they stay open as a tapas and antepasta bar, average £12.50 per head. BYO or buy from their choice of organic and vegetarian wines and beers from the shop below (no corkdate). Can cater for private functions. No smoking. MC, Visa.

Holland & Barrett

Health food shop

3 Cobden Court, Blackburn
Tel: 01254–693 010

33 Corporation Street, Blackpool
Tel: 01253–299 393

26 Newport Street, Bolton
Tel: 01204–385 954

33 The Mall, Burnley
Tel: 01282–459 833

26 Penny Street, Lancaster
Tel: 01524–848 633

24 Euston Road, Morecombe
Tel: 01524–401383

Lower Mall, 37 The Spindles Shopping Centre, Oldham
Tel: 0161–622 0180

Unit 1, 13 Friargate Walk,
St Georges Centre, Preston
Tel: 01772–259 357

Unit 51 Market Way, Rochdale Exchange
Rochdale
Tel: 01706–353 445

97/99 Princess Street, Stockport
Tel: 0161–480 2314

Lincolnshire

Maud's Tearoom

Omnivorous cafe

Maud Foster Windmill, Willoughby Road,
Boston, Lincs PE21 9EG. Tel: 01205–352 188
Open: Wed 10.00–17.00, Sat 11.00–17.00,
Sun 12–17.00. Jul & Aug Thu–Fri 11–17.00

Previously vegetarian cafe serving
2 or 3 vegetarian and vegan (on
request) meals around £5, such as
soups and vegetable fajitas. Large
variety of cakes, some vegan. Unlicensed. Non smoking. MC, Visa.
Children welcome, one high chair.
10% discount to members of the
Vegetarian Society. You can go into
the mill which is a separate
business, £2.50 adults, £2 senior,
£1.50 children, family (2+2) £6.50.

Pimento Tearooms

Vegetarian tearoom

27 Steep Hill, Lincoln LN2 1LU
Tel: 01522–524 851
Open: every day 10–17.00 (10.30– Sun)

Vegetarian and vegan cafe and tearoom
on the steep hill between the high street
and the cathedral, near the cathedral
end. Main meal £5.50 such as veg and
bean casserole with speciality breads;
spring veg curry; salads. Home made
cakes £1.75, at least one vegan. No
smoking. Children welcome, one high
chair. Unlicensed, bring your own by
prior arrangement. MC, Visa.

Pasquale at Beradis

Omnivorous Italian restaurant

292–3 High Street, Lincoln.
Tel: 01522–529 360
Open: Tue–Sat 11.30–14.30, , 17.30–22.30,
closed Sun–Mon

Big menu, mains from £5.95,
including vegan and gluten free.
Children welcome, high chair. No
smoking. No credit cards.

Thailand Number One

Omnivorous Thai restaurant

80–81 Bailgate, Lincoln. Tel: 01522–537000
Open: Mon–Sat 12–14.30 (not Sun),
every day 18–23.00

Extensive vegetarian section on
their menu. Two set menus £16.95
or £18.95, and 10 a la carte dishes.
Special lunch of starter and main
course with rice £6.95. Desserts
include vegan Thai coconut
pancake roll or banana fritters £3.
House wine £2.10 glass, £9.95
bottle. No smoking. Children
welcome, high chair. MC, Visa.

Greens

Wholefood shop

175 High Street, Lincoln. Tel: 01522–524874
Open: Mon–Sat 9–17.30, Sun 11–15.00

There is another health food shop
in Gordon Rd near the cathedral
and Pimento.

Holland & Barrett

Health Food shop

47 Market Place, Boston PE21 6NF
Tel: 01205 359712

61 Friargate, Freshney Place Shopping Centre,
Grimsby DN31 1ED. Tel: 01472–344 115

319 High Street Lincoln LN5 7DW
Tel: 01522–567 615

37 High Street, Scunthorpe DN15 6SB
Tel: 01724–278 157

37 Lumley Road Skegness PE25 3LL
Tel: 01754–764 412

Manchester is a large, hectic city, famous for its nightclub culture. There is a strong gay scene, and a massive population of students, so the city has had a cosmopolitan feel for a long time and really comes alive at night.

The shopping centre has all the chain and department stores and some great little independent stores.

Vegetarians are well catered for in Manchester. There are some good restaurants and a few excellent cafes and health food shops, including an entirely vegan supermarket.

Manchester

Earth Café

Vegetarian cafe

Central vegetarian café near the Arndale shopping complex, housed in the same building as the Manchester Buddhist centre, and run by Buddhists. 95% of the food is organic, prepared on the premises and is suitable for vegans.

16-20 Turner Street
Northern Quarter
Manchester M41 1DZ

Tel: 0161-834 1996

Soups and sandwiches £2–£2.60, with fillings such as olive tapenades, Italian style tofu or Brazil nut and tofu.

www.earthcafe.co.uk
fabulousfood@
earthcafe.co.uk

There are at least 2 mains £2.50–£5.80 such as Indonesian stew, sweet vegetable curry, polenta bake, shepherd's pie, and perrico (scrambled tofu and mixed veg). 3–4 side dishes and 7 salads: hummous, coleslaw, green beans, beansprouts, rice-noodle, lettuce, carrot salad.

Open: Tue–Sat 10–17.00, closed Sun–Mon

Can cater for special diets, ie. wheat and nut-free

High chairs

No smoking

Cakes from £1.50, including chocolate and coffee and walnut. Organic juice bar with juices from £1.70 and soya smoothies from £2.75.

No credit cards

Eighth Day Café

Vegetarian cafe and wholefood shop

Vegetarian café and health food shop run by a workers co-op, with an international wholefood menu. Over 75% vegan and much is wheat-free. Seats over 100.

111 Oxford Road
Manchester M1 7DU

Breakfast, served until 11.30, from £1.40 for beans on toast and £4.95 for a full veggie house or vegan option.

Tel: 0161-273 1850 cafe
       0161-273 4878 shop

www.eighth-day.co.uk
mail@eighth-day.co.uk

Soups £2. Salads £2.55 small bowl, £3.70 large. Baked potatoes with fillings from £2.50; casseroles £3.30. Specials from £4.50 such as homemade falafel, tofu and mushroom burgers. Desserts are also usually vegan such as chocolate cake £1.75 and crumbles, sponges and hot puddings £2. Special diets catered for and they always soya milk and vegan margarine. All food is available for take-away.

Cafe: Mon–Sat 9.30–19.30
Shop: Mon–Sat 09.30–17.30
(Thu till 19.00). Closed Sun

No smoking throughout

Visa, MC

5% discount to Vegetarian Society members and 10% for students

The Basement

Bookshop with vegan cafe

24 Lever Street (off Piccadilly Gardens), Manchester M1
Tel: 0161-237 1832
Open: Wed-Sat 12-18.00

New vegan collective not-for-profit cafe run by volunteers. (and they always need more!) Mostly organic, light stuff such as soup £1.50, great mixed salads with rice or couscous £2 for a bowl. Specials include curry, butterbean stew £2-2.50 a bowl. Home made cakes £1. Freshly squeezed juices £1.80. You can use the internet and they've got a library of activist type books, novels, campaigning stuff, video library. Gallery space with exhibitions. No smoking. Children welcome, Wednesday is vegan Mums's day, one high chair, settees and low tables. No credit cards. No alcohol but they're hoping to change that at the end of 2005 with new licensing laws. Available for grassroots meetings evenings. Health food shop planned to open here summer 2005.

Bean Counter

Vegetarian cafe and restaurant

535 Wilbraham Road, Chorlton, Manchester M21 0UE. Tel: 0161-882 0700
Open: Mon-Fri 10-18.00,
Sat 10-21.00, Sun 11-17.00

All day full British (with haggis) veggie cooked breakfasts £5.95. Pies, soups, panini, sausage sandwiches, veggieburgers £4.25 with salsa and salad,; specials £6-7 vary such as curry, nut roasts, mushroom Wellington. Cakes including vegan chocolate £1.85. Unlicensed, BYO. No smoking. Children welcome, high chairs. MC, Visa, Amex.

Diamond Dogs

Vegetarian cafe

52 Beeech Road, Chorlton, Manchester M21 9EG
Tel: 0161-882 0101
Open: Mon-Fri 10-17.30 (last order 16.30), Sat-Sun 9-18.30 (last order 17.30)

Everything organic and fair trade, lots of vegan options. Do really good breakfasts £2.95-5.95 for the works. Paninis, toasted sandwiches. Main courses £5.95-7.95 such as vegan pizza with pesto roast veg, olives, capers and pinenuts; sweet potato gumbo. Desserts include vegan cheesecake £3.95. Not licensed. No smoking except outside tables. Good disabled access. Children welcome, high chairs. No credit cards.

Fuel Café Bar

Vegetarian café

448 Wilmslow Road, Withington Greater Manchester M20 3BW
Tel: 0161-448 9702
Open: Mon-Sat 9.00-24.00, Sun 10-23.30
www.fuelcafebar.co.uk

Full breakfast £4.50. Cafe meals £2.20-£5.90 include paninis, bruschettas, salads and burritos. Desserts £1-80-2.80, some flapjacks are vegan. House wine £2.30 glass, £8 bottle. Children welcome during the day, high chair. Smoking permitted. Visa, MC. 2 internet terminals, WiFi.
Nearby at 486 is Withington Wholefoods, tel 0161-445 6696.

The Greenhouse

Vegetarian & vegan restaurant

331 Great Western Street
Rusholme, Greater Manchester M14 4AN
Tel: 0161–224 0730
UK Freephone booking: 0800 092 2733 or
through website www.dineveggie.com
greenhouse@dineveggie.com
Lunch: Tue–Sat 12.00–18.30, Sun 12–15.00
(last booking 14.00, later for 6+ people)
Dinner: Mon–Fri 18.30–23.00 (last order
21.30), half hour later Sat, half hr earlier Sun
Closed afternoon and 21.30 if no bookings.
Closed 24.7.05–5.9.05, Xmas–17 Jan, see
website for more details.

The original vegetarian restaurant
in Manchester since 1983 with an
astounding 200 a la carte dishes,
half of them vegan, all listed on the
website. Starters £1.95–£4.455.
Mains £5.45–£9.85 such as vegan
Sunday roast. A stunning 30
desserts £2.45–3.95, of which just
under half are vegan. 10% discount
for Vegetarian or Vegan Society
members (except Sat after 17.00,
Xmas, New Year and Valentine's).
Non smoking. Visa, MC.

Greens Restaurant

International vegetarian restaurant

43 Lapwing Lane, West Didsbury
Greater Manchester M20 2NT
Tel: 0161–434 4259
Open: Mon–Sun 17.30–22.30,
Tue–Fri 12–14.00, Sun 12.30–15.30

Modern international and ethnic
vegetarian restaurant. Starters
from £3.25. Mains £10.25 such as
aubergine and potato mussamam
curry with peanuts served with
Thai sticky rice. Always vegan
options, but can be limited especially vegan desserts which are not
always on the menu so worth
asking about. Bring your own

booze, no corkage charge. No
smoking throughout. Visa, MC

Herbivore

Vegetarian cafe

The Burlington Rooms, in centre of
Manchester University campus,
Burlington Street, Manchester M15 6HQ
Tel: 0161–275 2408
Open term time: Mon–Fri 09–19.00,
Sat–Sun 11–17.00.
During exams they match the library's
longer opening hours, sometimes as late as
23.00+ at weekends. No wheelchair access.

Main course with salad £3.50, e.g.
stuffed aubergine. Soup and bread
£2. Always a vegan option. Carrot
cake, flapjacks. Not licensed.
Children welcome, no high chairs.
No smoking. No credit cards. Don't
come between 12 and 2pm during
term time unless you want to join a
queue of 100 people!

Misty's Vegetarian Café

Vegetarian & vegan café

Unit 3, Longsight Shopping Centre
531 Stockport Road, Longsight
Greater Manchester M12 4JH
Tel: 0161–256 3355
phil@mistys-cafe.fsnet.co.uk
Open: Mon–Sat 9–17.00, Sun closed

Vegetarian café with food from
around the world and predominantly vegan menu. Mains such as
chickpea curry with rice £3. They
specialise in vegan desserts, with
typically 9 including strawberry
cheesecake and apricot and
pistachio cake, £1.50. Always have
soya milk. Children welcome, 2
high chairs. Smoking permitted.
No credit cards.

v2go

Vegetarian cafe and take-away

At The Orient, in the Trafford Centre
Manchester M17 8EB
Tel: 0161–747 2700. www.v2go.co.uk
Open:Mon–Fri 07.30–22.00,Sun 7.30–19.00

Arndale Centre, Market St,
central Manchester
Tel 0161–839 8878
Open: Mon–Sat 08.00–20.00, Sun 9–17.00

Vegetarian food on the move. Traditional veggie burger or spicy Mexican beanburger £3. Falafel £4. Hummous and salad pitta £3.75. Mixed salads £3.25. Crunchy potato wedges £1.50. Fries £1.30. Sandwiches £1.95–£2.35. Two types of muffin £1.50 and different flavoured flapjacks £1.
Mineral water £1.00. Freshly squeezed juices from £1.50. Fizzy drinks 90p–£1.40.

Marble Brewery

Vegan real ale brewery

4 pubs including The Bar at 553 Wilbraham Road, Chorlton, M21 0UE
Tel: 0161–861 7565
Open: pub hours

The Bar does a range of vegan dishes, including Sunday roast, baked aubergine, and falafel platter.

Nawaab

Indian buffet restaurant

1008 Stockport Rd, Levenshulme, Manchester
Tel: 0161–224 6969
Open: every day 17.30–23.00

Huge restaurant, all-you-can-eat £10. 50% vegetarian. Licensed.

Punjab Sweet House

Indian omnivorous

177 Wilmslow Road
Rusholme, Greater Manchester M14
Tel: 0161–225 2960
Open: Open every day 12–24.00 (Mon from 17.00), Fri–Sat till 01.00

Indian omnivorous restaurant with about half the menu vegetarian. Many South Indian dishes, main dishes under £5. 10% student discount. They try to keep one side non-smoking. Visa, MC. Licensed.

Tampopo

S.E. Asian omnivorous restaurant

16 Albert Square, City Centre, Manchester M2 5PF
Tel: 0161–819 1966
Open: Mon–Sat 12–23.00, Sun 12–22.00

Noodle, Eastern and fusion dishes with a strong Thai and Vietnamese slant. Veggie items clearly marked. Some vegan dishes and menu items can be adapted. Vegan desserts. Licensed. No smoking. Children welcome, high chairs.

Wagamama

Omnivorous Japanese Restaurant

1 The Printworks, Corporation Street, Manchester, M4 4DG
Tel: 0161 839 5916
www.wagamama.com
Open: Mon–Sat 12.00–23.00
Sun 12.30–22.00

This chain is GMO-free and offers something for vegans. Watch out for egg in one of the rice dishes. 5 vegan side dishes from raw salad to edamame £2.65–£4.50. Mains from £4.95 a soup, 3 noodle dishes, 2 rice dishes are mostly vegan. Various raw, fresh juices £2.65, Japanese beer £2.90–£4.20, wine £3.10 a glass to £13.50 for a bottle. Sake and plum wine also available.

Unicorn Grocery

Vegan supermarket

89 Albany Road, Chorlton, Manchester M21 0BN. **www.unicorn–grocery.co.uk**
Open: Tue–Sat 9.30–18.00 (Wed–Thu – 19.00), Sun 11–17.00, Mon closed

Co-operatively run all vegan supermarket round the corner from Bean Counter in Chorlton on Barlow Moor Road, south Manchester, with a stunning range of wholesome and organic foods, beer and wine. Specialists in vegan, gluten and sugar free.

Holland & Barrett

Health food shop

Unit 34, Lower Mall, Trafford Park
Manchester M17 2BL
Tel: 0161–747 2699

87 Deansgate, Manchester, M3 2BW
Tel: 0161–834 5923

Unit 122 Market Way, Upper Mall, Arndale Ct, Manchester
Tel: 0161–834 5975

607 Wilbraham Road, Chorlton Cum Hardy, Greater Manchester MX1 1AN
Tel: 0161–881 1539

Merseyside **Liverpool**

Liverpool

Liverpool attracts a lot of tourists due to the worldwide success of the band the Beatles who put it firmly on the map in the 1960's. Today's fans can visit a museum, a shop and can even see the houses where the "fab four" grew up.

Liverpool boasts some splendid Victorian architecture including many unspoiled city centre pubs. Most of its docks are still in operation but Albert Dock has now been turned into a tourist attraction with lots of little shops and cafes and the impressive Tate modern art gallery. There are lots of museums to visit, including ones with certain historical themes, such as the Maritime Museum and the Museum of Liverpool Life.

Liverpool is a very compact city and it is easy to walk around the city centre. If you want all the usual high street shops, leave Central Station and walk straight up Church Street. The Beatles attractions and the Tourist Information Centre are also situated off this and the Docks are at the far end.

The most interesting area for vegetarians is Bold Street, which runs to the left of the station in the opposite direction. The small streets running parallel to and branching off Bold Street are full of pubs, clubs and cafes and are very lively in the evenings.

Liverpool is well served by railways and motorways and is a good base for exploring North Wales and the North West.

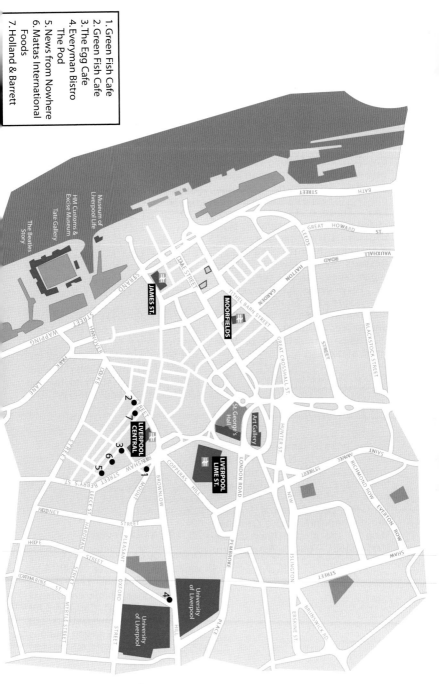

1. Green Fish Cafe
2. Green Fish Cafe
3. The Egg Cafe
4. Everyman Bistro
   The Pod
5. News from Nowhere
6. Mattas International
   Foods
7. Holland & Barrett

Liverpool

Green Fish Café

Vegetarian café

11 Upper Newington, Off Renshaw Street
Liverpool,Merseyside L1
Tel: 0151–707 8592
www.greenfishcafe.co.uk
Train Liverpool Central
Open: Mon–Sat 11–17.00

Cheap, modern-looking vegetarian café with at least two vegan meals per day. Smaller and more up-market in appearance than The Egg. Starters £1.70 upwards include soup and salads. Main courses £3.75 include curry, mousakka, burritos and pasta. Desserts £1.20 upwards but no vegan cakes. Tea and coffee 90p–£1. They always have soya milk and spread. Smoking area. Children welcome, no high chairs. Unlicensed. No credit cards.
Directions: turn left out of Lime Street station.

The Door, 65–67 Hanover Street
Liverpool,Merseyside L1 3BY
Tel: 0151–702 0705
www.greenfishcafe.co.uk
Open: Mon–Fri 10–17.00, closed weekend.

Second branch, same menu as the other one. No smoking throughout. Children welcome, no high chairs. Unlicensed. No credit cards.
Turn left out of Central Station, and it's opposite Black's Camping Shop on the ground floor of the Merseyside Youth Association building.

The Egg Café

Vegetarian café

Top Floor, Newington Buildings,Newington
Liverpool, Merseyside L1 4ED
Tel: 0151 707 2755
Train: between Liverpool Central and Lime Street (main railway station)
Open: Mon–Sat 10–22.30, Sun 10–16.00

Vegetarian café with plenty of menu vegan. Mains £4.75 such as spaghetti bolognaise, potato and pea Madras with rice and/or salad, spinach dal.. Always have vegan desserts £1.85–2.10 – cakes and crumbles, e.g. banana cake, chocolate crunch £1. Very smal smoking section, will be phased out. Children welcome, high chairs. No credit cards.Top floor, no lift.
Walk up Bold Street and turn right at the big Oxfam shop onto Newington (it is not signposted) and about half way along look out for a tall scruffy building on your right. Climb the stairs to the top (2nd) floor and you're there.

Everyman Bistro

Omnivorous bistro

5–9 Hope Street, Liverpool,
Merseyside L1 9BH
Tel/Fax: 0151–708 9545
www.everyman.co.uk
Open: Mon–Wed 12.00–24.00,
Thu & Fri 12.00–02.00,
Sat 11.00–02.00 Sun closed

Omnivorous bistro with 45% menu vegetarian. Mains at £5.95–6.50 include aubergine and potato curry, spicy vegetable enchilladas and vegetable daal. Can cater for vegans and other special diets, but get there early as vegan options can run out. Gluten-free desserts and mains are available. Licensed. House wine is £2.75 for a glass, £9.95 for a bottle. Separate non smoking section. Children welcome, high chairs. Visa, MC.

The Pod

Omnivorous bar-restaurant

137-139 Allerton Road, Liverpool,
Merseyside L18 2DD
Tel: 0151 724 2255
Open: Mon–Sat 12–15.00 lunch,
brunch menu, daily 18.00–21.30 tapas
menu

Omnivorous bar-restaurant with a lot of vegetarian food. Lunch main meal £6 such as garlic focaccia with aubergine, salad, tomato and olive penne, spicy vegetable chilli served with couscous or homemade chips. They can make anything vegan and charge less. Soup £3.
For a tapas evening meal you'll need about three dishes at £3 each, such as potato agnioli, vegetable tempura.
Smoking allowed in the whole restaurant as it's quite small. Visa, MC, Diners, Amex. Children over 14 welcome with parents, younger ones before 8pm when the drinking gets going. Reservations advised for evenings as they get quite busy though you can just turn up.

News From Nowhere

Bookshop

Bold Street (almost right at the top)
Liverpool, Merseyside L1
Train: Liverpool Central
Open: Mon–Sat 9–5.30

Radical bookshop run by a women's workers' co-op. Stocks a wide range of human and animal

rights, gay and lesbian, environmental and personal development books, postcards and magazines. Good selection of vegetarian and vegan cookbooks. Very knowledgeable and helpful staff. Huge noticeboard by the door packed with events and contacts in Liverpool.

Mattas International Foods

International food shop

Bold Street, Liverpool
Train : Liverpool Central
Open: Mon–Sat 9–18.00,
Sun 10–16.00

Cheap international food shop, selling some meat but also very well stocked with vegan products. Cheapest soya milk, tofu and take away vegan pasties and samosas in town. Delivery of vegan Turkish Delight every Thursday, ask at the counter! Walk up Bold street and it's on the left, near the top.

Holland & Barrett

Health food shop

17 Whitechapel, Liverpool,
Merseyside L1 6DS
Tel: 0151–236 8911

3a Bold Stret, Liverpool, Merseyside L1 4DG
Tel: 0151–708 9343

6 Borough Pavement
Birkenhead,Merseyside L41 2XX
Tel: 0151–647 7327

28 Marina Walk, Ellesmere Port
South Wirral, Merseyside L65 0BS
Tel: 0151–355 9228

Unit 12 Station Arcade, Chapel Street
Southport, Merseyside PR8 1BH
Tel: 01704–530 734

Northumberland

The Byre

19th century stone-built farm byre which has been converted into a modern unique house offering vegetarian bed and breakfast and self catering. There are two rooms: one twin ensuite and one double with private bathroom, £25–£28 per person per night. Self catering is £40 per room (1 or 2 people).

Breakfast could be fresh fruit salad and cereal, muesli, dried fruit or porridge followed by veggie sausages, rashers, baked beans, tomatoes and mushrooms. Vegans are well catered for.

A two course dinner by arrangement is £12 and could be Chinese stir fry, Thai sweet potato curry, chickpea and spinach curry, followed by bread and butter pudding, or Tracey's sticky toffee pudding with toffee sauce. Meals are served with juice, tea or filter coffee, and you can bring your own wine. As much local fresh produce as possible is used and they cater for special diets.

Harbottle is a small village in the Northumberland National Park. The park offers glimpses of ancient landscapes and wilderness found nowhere else in England.

The ancient ruins of Harbottle castle overlook the Reivers Way along the Coquet Valley. Harbottle is at the foothills of the Cheviots making it a perfect base for walking, cycling and birdwatching and it is just fifteen minutes from the village of Rothbury. Northumberland has a magnificent coastline with wide sandy beaches, quaint villages and dramatic castles.

Tea and coffee making facilities, television and video in the sitting room.

Vegetarian
Bed and Breakfast

Harbottle
near Rothbury
Northumberland
NE65 7DG
England

Tel: 01669-650 476

www.the-byre.co.uk
rosemary@the-byre.co.uk

Train station:
Morpeth, then taxi or bus or they can collect.

Open: Apr–Oct Thurs–Sun

Directions: A1 north past Newcastle, A697 to Coldstream, B6344 to Rothbury, go west for 4 1/2 miles, turn right at signpost marked Sharperton /Harbottle/Alwinton

Parking: available off road

Children welcome by arrangement

No smoking throughout

Disabled access, category three

West Woodburn

Bay Horse Inn

Omnivorous bed & breakfast

West Woodburn, Near Hexham
Northumberland NE48 2RX
Tel: 01434–270 218

---

5 ensuite rooms £25 per person: 2 double, 2 twin, 1 family with a four-poster and 2 singles. Children £15, under-5 free. Vegetarian or vegan breakfast. Dogs welcome.

Hexham

Hexham Tans

Vegetarian cafe

11 St Mary's Chare, Hexham,
Northumberland NE46 1NQ
Tel: 01434–656 284
Open: Tue–Sat 08.30–1600, closed Sun–Mon

Cheap, friendly veggie cafe. All specials £4 such as veg curry, chili. Pizzas made to order, can be cheeseless. Sandwiches. Cakes £1.30 and scones £1 are all vegan. 25cl bottle of wine £2.40. Very child friendly, high chairs. No smoking. No credit cards.

Morpeth

The Chantry Tea Room

Omnivorous restaurant

9 Chantry Place
Morpeth, Northumberland NE61 1PJ
Tel: 01670–514 414
Open: Mon–Sat 9.00–16.30

Several vegetarian choices on menu, jacket potatoes, sandwiches, various pies and hot dishes, from £2.85. Can cater for vegans with advance notice. Non smoking. No credit cards.

West Woodburn

Bay Horse Inn

Omnivorous pub–restaurant

West Woodburn, Near Hexham
Northumberland NE48 2RX
Tel: 01434–270 218
Open: Mon–Sun 11–23.00

Under new ownership since our last edition but still catering well for vegetarians and vegans, with everything clearly marked on the menu. Soup £2.50. At least 3 vegan mains from £4.95 such as veg tikka masala, tomato and basil penne, stuffed peppers, mushroom stroganof. No smoking. Children can eat in dining room, but not in pub after 6pm. Visa, MC.

Holland & Barrett

Health food shop

23 Station Road, Ashington, Northumberland NE63 9UZ
Tel: 01670–853883

31–33 Fore Street, Hexham, Northumberland NE46 1LU
Tel: 001434–609067

97

Notinghamshire Nottingham

Anson's Place

Veggie B&B in a large Victorian house situated in Gedling Village, three and a half miles north east of Nottingham city. There are two rooms, one double and one twin costing £40 per room per night. If you are alone, the room will cost you £30. One of the rooms overlooks the garden and can be made into a family room.

Breakfast comprises fruit juice, a selection of cereals or muesli with fresh fruit salad or grapefruit, followed by baked beans, tomatoes and mushrooms on toast with tea or coffee. Soya milk, vegan margarine and vegan muesli available. Food is organic when possible. It's best to give notice if you are vegan.

No evening meal is offered, but the Windsor Castle pub only 5-10 minutes away offers good vegetarian and vegan options, and there are a few veggie restaurants in the city.

Sherwood Forest (a Special Site of Scientific Interest) is thirty minutes drive away.

The Peak District is forty minutes away and historic Newark is twenty five minutes away.

Visit Nottingham Castle, The River Trent, Greens Windmill and The Lace Market. There are also many museums, shops, nightclubs and theatres in town, as well as a National Ice Arena, water sports and Tennis Centre.

Tea and coffee making facilities and televisions in the rooms. Guests are welcome to use the garden.

Gedling

Vegetarian
Bed and Breakfast

21 Waverley Avenue
Gedling
Nottinghamshire
England NG4 3HH

Tel: 01159-618 090

Email: ansonsplace21@ hotmail.com

Train Station: Midland Nottingham, 3 1/2 miles, then bus or taxi

Open: all year

Directions: 3 1/2 miles north east of Nottingham off the A612 Nottingham to Southwell Road

Parking: available

High chairs for the little ones

No pets

No smoking throughout

10% discount for stays of three nights or more

Croft Hotel
Omnivorous hotel

6–8 North Road, West Bridgford,
Nottinghamshire, NG2 7NH
Tel: 0115 9812744
Open: all year except Xmas
Train Station: Nottingham, 1 mile

Fourteen rooms £20–£25 per person per night. Children and pets welcome. No smoking.

Screaming Carrot
Vegan bakery and wholefood shop

42 Foxhall Road
Forest Fields, Nottingham NG7 6LJ
Tel: 0115–910 3013
Open: Mon–Fri 07–18.00, Sat 10–16.00, Sun closed

Entirely vegan bakery stocking a range of health foods and snacks. Take-away pasties, wraps and cakes range from 50p to £2. Under new (still vegan) management, so the range might change.

Squeek
Gourmet vegetarian restaurant

23–25 Heathcote Street
Hockley, Nottingham NG1 3AG
Tel: 0115–955 5560
Open: Mon–Sat 18.00–22.00

Vegetarian gourmet restaurant where everything on the menu can be made vegan. Starters £4.95, mains £10.95. Any two courses £13.95, three for £15.95. Desserts £4.95 including vegan ice cream. House wine £10.50 bottle, £3.50 glass. No smoking. Children welcome, no high chairs. Visa, MC.

Sumac Centre
Vegan cafe & campaigns centre

245 Gladstone Street, Forest Fields,
Nottingham NG7 6HX
Tel: 0845–458 9595
www.veggies.org.uk/sumac
sumac@veggies.org.uk
Open: Cafe Fri–Sun 10–15.00.
Bar Thu–Sat 18.30–23.00, Sun 12–17.00.
Phone for further openings.

Campaigning resource centre for animals, humans and the environment. Pure vegan café with meals, snacks, cakes and fresh local produce. Soup £1.50. Fried breakfast with sosages, potato cake, beans, toast, tomatoes and mushrooms £2.60. Main meal £2.75–3.75. Banana split with Swedish Glace vegan ice-cream £1.80. Cakes 60p–£1. Vegan social club/bar selling a range of local vegan real ales and continental lagers.

They can host gatherings, meetings (centre occasionally closes for this, so check if travelling any distance). Thu–Sun internet access, library. Home of Veggies Catering Campaign, volunteers always needed.

The Vegetarian Pot
Indian vegetarian restaurant

375 Alfreton Road, Radford
Nottingham NG7 5LT
Tel: 0115–970 3333
www.vegetarianpot.com
Open: Mon–Sat 11–14.00, 17–21.00, closed Sun

Friendly vegetarian North Indian restaurant and takeaway with a predominantly vegan menu. Non-vegan items are clearly indicated with a star. Main meals from £5 such as channa (chickpeas), aloo bhangan (potatoes and aubergine) and saag (spinach and mustard leaves flavoured with freshly ground ginger and garlic). Set meals include choice of 2 thalis which comprise vegetable dishes, daal, pilau rice and chapattis or pooris. Desserts happily include vegan friendly yellow rice (rice cooked with sugar and raisins), £1. Non smoking. No credit cards. Offer outside catering.

Nottingham – omnivorous

Broadway Café

Omnivorous cafe in cinema

Broad Street, Nottingham
Tel: 0115–952 1551
Open: Mon–Fri 9–23.00,
Sat 11–23.00, Sun 12–22.30

Omnivorous café within the Broadway cinema, serving drinks, snacks and meals. Vegetarian and vegan dishes typically around £6, always a vegan option. Often have veggie and vegan staff.

Lincolnshire Poacher

Real ale pub with food

161–163 Mansfield Road, Nottingham
Tel: 0115–941 1584
Open: Mon–Sat 11.00–23.00, Sun 11–22.30

This real ale pub usually has 5 veggie dishes, and they are happy to cater for vegans.

Muchachas

Omnivorous Mexican restaurant

140 Alfreton Road, Nottingham
Tel: 0115–979 2191
Open: Mon–Sat 12.00–14.30, 18.00–23.00;
Sun closed.

Co-operative run Mexican restaurant, training people with learning difficulties. 8–9 veggie dishes,

served with rice or potatoes – many can easily be made vegan.

The Old Angel

Omnivorous pub

7 Stoney Street, Hockley,
Nottingham NG1 1LG
Tel: 0115–950 2303
www.oldangel.ukpub.net
Open normal pub hours,
serve food Mon–Sat 11–19.00,
Sun 12–16.00.

Busy pub with regular music events and a large selection of vegetarian and vegan meals, including veggie breakfast.

Q in the corner (at Ziggis)

Omnivorous cafe

3 Victoria Street, Nottingham
Tel: 0115–950 6956
Open: Mon–Sat 10–17.00, closed Sun

Omnivorous café at rear of boutique, with good selection of homemade vegetarian and vegan dishes.

Royal Thai

Omnivorous Thai restaurant

189 Mansfield Road, Nottingham
Tel: 0115–948 3001
Open: Mon–Sat 12–14.30, 18–23.00
closed Sun

Omnivorous Thai restaurant. 12 main courses on vegetarian menu, 7 suitable for vegans, from £2–£6; set meals £14.

Their sister restaurant Siam Tsini is open the same hours plus Sunday eve 18–22.30 at 16–20a Carlton Street, Nottingham NG1 1NN. Tel 0115–958 2222. Smoking allowed. Licensed. MC, Visa.

Alley Café

Friendly vegetarian and vegan café bar in the centre of Nottingham opposite the main library, located in a courtyard near the market square.

Vegetarian and vegan organic cafe

1A Cannon Court
Long Row
Nottingham
NG1 6JE

Starters, £2–£2.95, include organic potato wedges with dips; soups, and crunchy Oriental tofu orbs.

Tel: 0115–955 1013

www.alleycafe.co.uk
alleycafe@hotmail.com

Large selection of sandwiches, with a choice of 5 different breads (foccacia, Italian, baguette, granary and rye) all of which are £3.10 and come with names, Ethel is a vegan cream cheese, avocado and pine nuts sandwich; Mildred – smoked tofu, vegan pesto with artichoke hearts; and Winston – roasted vegetables and hummus.

Open: Mon–Sat 11.00–23.00

Fully licensed and all wines are organic and vegetarian or vegan

Smoking permitted

Specials are cooked by famous vegan chef Ronny. They're vegan 99% of the time, and change every other day. A typical example would be stuffed peppers with mushroom and smoked tofu mousse, served with grilled tomato salad and cous cous. You can have a pizza with practically any toppings, including tofutti mozzerella, and a choice of 2 burgers at £4.25 – a tempeh burger and a hemp burger.

Visa, MC

Desserts, £1.50–£2 are all vegan and hugely popular. The cheesecake can range from raspberry and mango to blueberry and cranberry. There's also choc hemp slice, mocha cake with coffee toffee sauce and blueberry brownies.

They try to cater for special diets and there are wheat–free options.

There is a DJ Thu–Fri evenings with a mellow funk sound.

They try to have environmentally sound initiatives using eco products and recycling waste wherever possible.

V1 Vegetarian Fast Food

Vegetarian fast food, where you'll usually get your food in just 2 or 3 minutes and no more than 6.

Oven-baked veggieburgers are a speciality, choose from spicy, nut, beany, VLT, ranch with fries and a drink £4.20–£4.50, or burger only £2.50. Or have the organic version with organic mushroom burger, organic tortilla chips and organic drink for £5.20, burger only £3.20. Vegan cheese add 25p, double burger £1.20. Jungle box for kids with sausages or jungle burger with fries and drink £2.50.

Extras £1.05–£1.90 fries, hash browns, onion rings, sausages & dip, spicy wedges & dip, garlic mushrooms, beany chips.

Chilli or ratatouille with rice or chips £3.50.

Breakfast served until 11am, sausage, rasher and beans in a bun with hash browns and drink £2.95. Hot sausage sandwich £1.75. Toasted teacake 85p. Toast and jam 75p.

Dozens of freshly made sandwiches and wraps on white or granary bread from £1.90.

Soft drinks 90p–£1.30, fresh orange juice £1.30, hot drinks including cappuccino 75p–£1. Also fruit smoothies, mineral water, soya and organic drinks.

Special offers include soup and sandwich £2.90, large meals for students for the price of a regular. Doughnut or tea cake and hot drink 3–6pm £1.30.

Special diets are catered for, and vegan and gluten free options are always available.

Vegetarian and vegan burgers and cafe

7 Hounds Gate
Nottingham
NG1 7AA

Tel: 0115-941 5121

Open:Mon–Sat 08.00–18.00, Sun 12–16.00

Full menu and details of external catering on their superb website:
www.v-1.co.uk
mail@v-1.co.uk

Kids parties available upon request

No eggs used on premises

10% discount for members of The Vegetarian and Vegan Society, Viva!

STOP PRESS:
As we go to press, sadly V1 has closed down. They are hoping to find a buyer and there is a good chance it will re-open.
See www.v-1.co.uk for the latest.
If you are interested in investing or managing the restaurant contact Tamsin 07966 178211 or email webenquiry@v-1.co.uk

Wagamama

Omnivorous Japanese Restaurant

The Cornerhouse, Burton Street,
Nottingham, NG1 4DB
Tel: 0115 924 1797
Fax: 0115 924 1797
www.wagamama.com
Open: Mon–Sat 12.00–23.00,
Sun 12.30–22.00

See Manchester entry for menu

Natural Food Company

Wholefood shop

37a Mansfield Road, Nottingham
Tel: 0115 955 9914
Open: Mon–Fri 9.15–18.00, Sat 9.30–17.30

Vegan–friendly, all–vegetarian wholefood shop. Cakes and savouries. Natural remedies.

Roots Natural Foods

Wholefood & Organic shop

526 Mansfield Road, Sherwood
Nottingham NG5 2FR
Tel: 0115 960 9014
Open: Mon–Fri 9–18.00 (Wed 18.45),
Sat 9–16.30

100% veggie. Natural foods, organic fruit and veg, take–away foods, free range eggs, cleaning and health products, supplements, Veggies burgers and sosages.

Holland & Barrett

Health food shop

95c Victoria Centre, Nottingham NG1 3QE
Tel: 0115–958 0753

14 Broadwalk, Broadmarsh Centre
Nottingham NG1 7LE
Tel: 0115–979 9409
Both above branches open Mon–Sat 9–17.30,
Wed late until 19.00, Sun 10.30–16.30

Unit 2, Co-op Development, High Rd,
Beeston NG9 2JP
Tel: 0115 922 4302

63–65 High Street, Long Eaton,
Nottingham NG10 1HZ
Tel: 0115–9725561

617 Mansfield Road, Sherwood,
Nottingham NG5 2PW
Tel: 0115 962 4527

17 Bridge Street, Worksop, Notts S80 1DP
Tel: 01909 476185

Durham Ox

Omnivorous inn

Newark Road, Wellow NG22 0EA
Tel: 01623 861026
Open: Mon–Sun 11.30–21.30

17th century coaching inn with vegetarian menu lunch and evening, £5.20 for main of which there are eleven such as Thai mushroom noodles. Non smoking dining areas. Visa, MC. Children welcome, high chairs.

Tyne and Wear

Bob Trollop's Pub

100% Vegetarian PUB with a terrific British veggie food menu and good value.

All day breakfast with sausages, burger, tomato, mushrooms, baked beans and hash browns. Mixed grill similar plus garlic mushrooms, onion rings, jacket wedges.

Starters like garlic bread, samosas, garlic mushrooms with tomato and garlic dip, hummus with toast, pakoras, taco triangles. Dips and dippers with salad garnish like deep fried coated veg with peanut satay sauce, deep fried jacket wedges with garlic mayonnaise, vegetable nuggets with tomato and garlic dip.

Main courses: for £5.95 Chinese stir fry, vegetable tikka masala, vegetable bake, penne pasta bake, homemade chilli, mushroom risotto, bean burrito, and creamy mushroom penne, veg and nut roast, giant Yorkshire pud with sausages.

Paninis £4.95 such as Mediterranean roast veg, sundried tomato.

Hot butties made with wholemeal hoagie, baguette, or tortilla wrap, containing veggie sausages, spicy beanburger, quarter or halfpounder. Spice it up with chilli, beans, salsa, crispy onion rings, or mushrooms. Extra veg and spuds available. Sandwiches can also be made with the same range of breads. .

Lots of desserts like blackcurrant and apple crumble, chocolate fudge cake, treacle sponge. They do coffee and teas.

Vegetarian pub

32–40 Sandhill
Quayside
Newcastle
Tyne & Wear NE1 3JF
Tel: 0191–261 1037

www.wessextaverns.co.uk

Pub open:
Mon–Sat 11–23.00,
Sun 10–22.30

Full menu:
Mon–Sat 11–19.00
Sun 10–19.00

Children until 7pm

Happy hours 4–7pm with cut price wine, draught beers, lager and cider.

There's a list behind the bar of which dishes are vegan and a magic vegan button on the till to inform the chefs not to put butter in your sandwich etc.

Wine £8.50 bottle, glass from £1.75

Smoking allowed, no non smoking area

Visa, MC, Switch and they do cashback if you spend over £5

Directions: right by Tyne Bridge and opposite the Guildhall

Supernatural Cafe

Vegetarian organic cafe

100% organic vegetarian cafe in the big health and wholefood store Almonds & Raisins in the city centre.

Anytime snacks: organic breakfast cereals £2.50 (soya or rice milk on request), bagel with preserve or sugar free fruit spread £1.50 or with vegan alternative to cream cheese and fruit £1.99, wholemeal toast with spread £1.50.

Lunches change every day based upon seasonal variations and best available produce. For example, soup with roll £2.99, vegan quiche £4 with salad, jacket potatoes £3-4 with beans or hummous or Balti. Pizza and pastie. Burgers £1.70 take-away, £2.80 eat in.

Lots of people come here for a take-away lunch and it can all be gone by 2pm. Sandwiches in a big long roll, such as tofu with olive pate, fake meats, all with salad and beansprouts, £2.10 take-away, £2.89 eat in.

Carrot cake 75p. Vegan chocolate cake £1.19-2.10, strawberry or black cherry or blueberry crumble 85p, fruit cake £1.20. Florentine 65p. Chocolate fudge brownie 65p. Vegan ice-cream £2.25, with soft fruit £2.60.

Over 100 types of herb, green and black teas, £1.50 per pot for one person, £3 for two people. Pot of Fair Trade coffee £1.95 for one, £3.50 for two. Mugs of Bamby, dandelion coffee, Barleycup, Wake Up £1.50, hot chocolate £1.99 (can be with soya or rice milk).

15/17 Upper Princess Square,
Newcastle-upon-Tyne
NE1 2AB
(in Almonds & Raisins wholefood shop in the heart of the city centre)

Tel: 0191-261 5959

Metro station: Monument

Open:
Mon-Sat 08.30-16.30 (mains till 14.00), closed Sun

No smoking

10% discount for students and senior citizens

Not licensed

Gluten and wheat-free, raw, macrobiotic, vegan and diabetic catered for.

MC, Visa, Amex

The Sky Apple

Vegetarian cafe, in the style of a coffee bar, cloudscape walls and crystal chandeliers.

Soup of the day £3. Home made veggie burgers. Sandwiches with salad £4.50–5.00. Mains £5–6.40 include tortillas, burritos, chilli non carne, tacos, moussaka, vege-burger, mixed salad. Baked potatoes £4–5.50, toppings include refried beans, hummous, roast Mediterranean veg. Felafel salad £4.40. Proper chips £1.80. Olives £1.70.

Evening menu has 5 starters such as Chinese dim sum £4.50 with spring rolls and dumplings. 5 mains £7.50–£8 such as Asian sweetcorn and veg pancakes with Thai coconut and lime sauce; yam and pepper stew. Desserts £4.50 include vegan banana tarte tatin.

Bring your own alcohol £1 per person. Candles on the tables in the evening.

Vegetarian cafe

182 Heaton Road, Heaton, Newcastle–upon–Tyne
NE6 5HP
Tel: 0191 209 2571

Metro: Chillingham Rd or Byker

www.skyapplecafe.co.uk

Open: Tue–Sat 10–17.00
Thu–Sat evening menu 18.00–22.00 (last orders)

No smoking

No credit cards

BYO alcohol

Children welcome, high chairs

Outside catering

Heartbreak Soup

Omnivorous restaurant

77 Quayside, Newcastle NE1 2BJ
Tel: 0191-222 1701
Open: Tue–Sat 18–22.00ish (last orders),
subject to change
ww.heartbreaksoup.com

Lively international place. The Tex–Mex chef has moved on but the new Asian and North African chefs offer rotating veggie dishes, with always at least one vegan starter £5.45 such as beetroot, radish and rocket salad with falafel, hummous and flatbread. Soup £3.75. Mains £10.25 such as tofu and squash lasagne. Desserts £4.95 and they always have some Swedish Glace in the fridge. House wine £9.95 bottle, glass £2.50. Children welcome, no high chair but you can bring in a car seat. Smoking. Visa, MC.

Almonds & Raisins

Health food shop & cafe

17/19 Upper Princess Square,
Newcastle-upon-Tyne NE1 2AB
Tel: 0191-261 5959
Open: Mon–Sat 8.30–17.00, Sun closed
All the usual health food vitamins and an organic and wholefood supermarket with bodycare and household products too, Ecover, Veggiewash.

The Last Days of Raj

Indian omnivorous restaurant

168 Kells Lane, Low Fell, Gateshead
Tel: 0191 4826494
Open: Mon–Sat 12.00–14.30,

Mon–Sun 18.00–24.00.
Closed Sun lunch.

Indian restaurant with some vegetarian dishes and more that can be adapted. Lunch £6.50 for 4 courses. House wine £10.50 bottle, £1.90. Children welcome, high chair. MC, Visa.

Out of This World

Organic supermarket and deli

Gosforth Shopping Centre, High Street
Gosforth NE3 1JZ
Open: Mon–Sat 9–18.00, closed SUn
Tel: 0191-213 0421

Big ethical organic supermarket, with lots of veggie food and a take-away delicatessen with pasties (many vegan), sandwiches (not Saturday), bhajias, cakes (some vegan), olives to enjoy in the nearby park.

Holland & Barrett

Health food shop

5 Cameron Walk, Metro Centre, Gateshead
Tel: 0191-460 2546

Unit 12, Hill Street Centre
Middlesborough TS1 1SU
Tel: 01642-220 179

11 Bigg Market, Newcastle NE1 1UN
Tel: 0191-232 7540

21 Blandford Street, Sunderland
Tel: 0191-565 6249

27 Albany Mall, Washington NE38 7SA
Tel: 0191-417 8451

287–289 Whitley Road, Whitley Bay NE26 2FN
Tel: 0191-251 6107

Yorkshire

North Yorkshire   Rugged Moors to windswept beaches on the coast are enough to take your breath away. Stay at Falcon Guest House in the former whaling port of Whitby, or North Cliff in picturesque Robin's Hood Bay, a seaside resort that was once a stamping ground for smugglers. Further south in Scarborough, Ranworth vegetarian guest house is set in a handsome stone villa – be sure to bring a big appetite as breakfast comes with fresh soya smoothies and vegan muffins in addition to a full cooked feast plus vegan yoghurt and muesli.

Tourists flock to York for its wonderfully preserved Roman walls and rambling streets, covered on both sides by handsome Tudor-style buildings. Come in early July and you'll have a chance to see the York Early Music Festival, that is if you can fight off the crowds. Stay in Cornmill Lodge vegetarian guest house and rest assured that Blake Head vegetarian world cafe and El Piano tapas bar are just two of the many places to get great veggie eats in the city. Vanilla Black is the newest place in town, quite upmarket and open late.

The spa town of Harrogate is well worth a trip. After a luxurious dip in the Turkish Baths, have lunch or dinner at Wild Ginger, who even serve vegan cream cheese. If you are on the go, pop into the Green House for vegan/veggie snacks, ice cream and take-aways that are usually organic.

East Yorkshire   If you are ever in Hull, stay at Acorn Guest House. An absolute must is the famous Hitchcocks, one of the most unique vegetarian restaurants in the UK. Be first to book for the evening and you could choose the cuisine for the evening from Thai, Cajun, Indian, Chinese, Afro-Caribbean, Russian, Nepalese, etc.

West Yorkshire Bronté country, Haworth, nuzzles the northwest corner of the county. Nearby, lush green hills spill over into the magnificent valleys and quaint villages of The Dales. The Dales are a wonderful place to spend the night and Archway Cottage does it in style. This early Victorian villa in beautiful Ilkley offers B&B from just £20 per person.

In Hebden Bridge, enjoy the breath-taking scenery of the Pennines. Stay in Myrtle Grove if you have time to spare and explore the town which offers live music, theatrical performances, heaps of cafes and an Alternative Energy Centre. If you plan a June visit, don't miss the Arts Festival. The Organic House, a veggie wholefood shop, has great lunches in their cafe.

Two industrial towns Bradford and Leeds, major centres of the late-medieval wool trade and the 19th-century Industrial Revolution, have evolved into two separate worlds. You're less likely to visit Bradford, but if passing through do enjoy its world renowned National Museum of Film & Television. Or make the short trip to nearby Saltaire to soak up the fascinating history of the industrial revolution, or visit the David Hockney exhibition at the 1853 gallery. Try South Square vegetarian cafe on Thornton Road for daily lunch specials. Leeds has evolved into one of the trendiest, hippest cities in England and has a little more to offer in the way of food: Hansa's is famous for its traditional Gujarati vegetarian cuisine; Roots and Fruits offers veggie breakfasts and lunches.

South Yorkshire. Sheffield has lots of great places for veggies to eat, including several new ones, such as the two branches of Kumquat Mae, Blue Moon Cafe, Green Edge Cafe and Airy Fairy coffee shop. It's on the doorstep of The Peak District National Park which offers an abundance of walking and climbing.

North Yorkshire

Falcon Guest House

Vegetarian bed and breakfast set in a quiet part of Whitby, a town with an 'old world' feeling. Falcon Guest House has two rooms, interchangeable as singles at £20–£30 per night, double or twin at £18 per person per night, or a family at £50 per night for three people, or £60 per night for four people. Reductions are often available for children.

You won't go hungry at this bed and beakfast where breakfast is more than ample! Choose from vegan organic muesli, organic cornflakes or Weetabix along with bananas, dates and nuts. Then follow up with a cooked brekkie of veggie sausages, organic baked beans, fried mushrooms and tomatoes and organic wholegrain bread and toast with organic marmalade. Tea and herbal teas, Fair Trade coffee, vegan margarine and soya milk are available.

No evening meals are provided, but nearby the wholefood restaurant Sanders Yard provides daytime and evening meals for both veggies and vegans.

Whitby is betwixt a two mile beach and unspoilt North Yorkshire Moors National Park. The latter contains 'Heartbeat' country and the North York Moors Steam Railway. The town boasts its own authenticity and quaintness, and its Abbey, Captian Cooke Museum, Dracula Museum, Sutcliffe Photo Gallery and annual August Folk Festival, offer an enjoyable stay.

There are tea making facilities in the rooms. TV in the lounge.

Vegetarian Bed & Breakfast

29 Falcon Terrace
Whitby
North Yorkshire
YO21 1EH
England

Tel: 01947–603 507

Train Station:
Whitby, 7 minutes walk

Directions:
From train station, go along Windsor Terrace, skirting opposite side of train station from dockend side. Windsor Terrace soon winds up a short hill (North Road). Falcon Terrace is topmost street off North Road on the right.

Parking: available on the street

Children welcome

No animals please

No smoking throughout

Bransdale

Lidmoor Farm

Vegetarian guest house

Lidmoor Farm, Bransdale, York, North Yorkshire YO62 7JL (40 miles north of York)
Tel: 01751–432214
e-mail juleswatson62@yahoo.co.uk
www.lidmoor.co.ukL

An isolated sheep farm in the heart of the North Yorkshire Moors, surrounded by heather moorland, ancient oak-wooded valleys and your very own lake to swim in.
Two double rooms, one with an extra bed £22.50 per person with continental breakfast, children 12 and under half price, babies free. Cooked vegetarian breakfast for an added £3.50. Vegans catered for. No dogs. No credit cards. Ideal base for walkers. Pubs and restaurants with veggie menus 15 minutes drive. Relaxation massage available

Scarborough

Ranworth

Vegetarian Guest House

Church Road, Ravenscar, Scarborough, North Yorkshire YO13 0LZ
Tel: 01723–870366
Train: Scarborough 10 miles, then bus or taxi
Open: All year

Victorian local stone villa with two doubles £20 per person, one double en suite £22, and twin with a play room attached £20. Children under 14 £12. No charge for under 2. £5 single supplement. Packed lunche £5. Evening meal £10 (£7 children). Organic and fair trade where possible. TV lounge with video and board games, conservatory, and wild garden visited by deer and badgers with a summer house and seating areas. Children welcome. Cots and high chairs available. Pets welcome. No smoking throughout. Cash or cheque only.

Hutton–le–Hole

Burnley House

Omnivorous bed and breakfast

Hutton–le–Hole, North Yorkshire YO62 6UA
Tel: 01751–417 548. Fax: 01751–417 760
www.burnleyhouse.co.uk
Email: info@burnleyhouse.co.uk

There are three double ensuites and two twin ensuites at £65–70 double occupancy, or £45 for single occupancy.
Breakfast could be muesli or cereal with fresh fruit followed by tomatoes, mushrooms, baked beans Soya milk and vegan muesli are available. Local, organic and home made ingredients are used when possible.
Rooms have TV's and tea and coffee making facilites. One has a four poster bed. Ground floor rooms so some disabled access. Children are welcome, cots and high chairs available. No smoking throughout.
Previously called "Moorlands".

115

Horton-in-Ribblesdale

The Women's Holiday Centre

Vegetarian holiday centre

The Old Vicarage, Horton-in-Ribblesdale,
Settle, N Yorks BD24 0HD
Tel: 01729-860 207
www.hortonwhc.org.uk
Train: Horton-in-Ribblesdalde 10 mins, Settle
to Carlisle line

Only veggie and vegan food at this centre for women and girls, and boy children up to 10 (up to 16 for 4 weeks per year) in the Three Peaks part of the Yorkshire Dales. Very inexpensive sliding scale, from £7 inc. Two dorms and two double rooms. Open fires. Large garden. Winter themed weekends.

Robin Hood's Bay, nr Whitby

North Cliff

Omnivorous bed & breakfast

Mount Pleasant North, Robin Hood's Bay
near Whitby, North Yorkshire YO22 4RE
Tel: 01947-880481. www.north-cliff.co.uk
Email: northcliff@bayfair.co.uk
Train: Whitby, 6 miles, then bus

Beautiful Victorian villa still retaining many original features. Two double rooms and one twin, £27.50 per person per night, all ensuite bathrooms. Full cooked English veggie breakfast. Vegan no problem. Evening meal or packed lunch may be available and there is a health food shop in Whitby. The rear rooms have views over the bay.

Grassington

The Retreat Tea Rooms

Vegetarian cafe and tea-room

14-16 Main Street, Grassington,
N Yorks BD23 5AA. Tel: 01756-751887
www.theretreatcafeingrassington.co.uk
Open: Fri-Wed 10-18.00, summer also Thu

Very chilled new vegetarian cafe in old market town a few steps from the cobbled square with wall to wall grade 2 listed buildings. The whole of July is a music festival from folk to rock to classical.
Starters like soup £3.50 Always 5 or 6 vegan choices on the menu. Most expensive meal £6.50 for a proper salad and meal of the day. Light meal of salad and chips. Always at least 3 vegan cakes £1.50-2.50. Pot of all sorts of teas £1, latte and cappuccino (can be soya) £1.30. House wine £1.75 glass. £2 bottle of Grolsch or Bud or Yorkshire bitter. No smoking. Children welcome, high chair. Dogs welcome. No credit cards.

Harrogate

The Green House

Wholefood shop

5 Station Parade, Harrogate HG1 1UF
Tel: 01423-502 580
Open: Mon-Sat 9-17.45

The only wholefood shop in Harrogate that is 100% vegetarian. Mainly organic. Located at the front of Wild Ginger award-winning vegan restaurant. Chiller and freezer cabinet is great for vegan cheeses, tofu, six flavours of Swedish Glace. Also vegan wines, beers, cider and perry. MC, Visa.

Wild Ginger

Cosy and homely vegetarian and vegan award winning wholefood restaurant where everything on the menu is either vegan or has a vegan alternative, and much of it is organic.

Breakfast until 12 noon, £5.95, vegetarian rashers and sausages, mushrooms, beans, tomato and toast.

Homemade soup with roll £3.25. Small salads £3.25, £4.95 for a Greek salad. Daytime menu includes several burgers £5.95 and hot and cold sandwiches around £3, including dairy-free cream cheese and tomato and basil, and spicy red bean and salad. Jacket potatoes from £4.95 with filling and salad.

Evening menu mains £5.95-£7.50 such as vegetarian roast haggis served with potato wedges, swede and carrot, seasonal vegetables and Wild Ginger gravy; French bread pizza with special topping of homemade fresh herbs and tomato sauce with spring onions and peppers; and a sausage special.

Large choice of tempting desserts start from £1 for a scoop of speciality dairy-free ice cream (vanilla, strawberry, chocolate and raspberry), ice cream sodas from £2 and hot chocolate cake with a rich chocolate sauce and ice cream, £4.95.

Can cater for special diets – gluten-free, wheat-free, raw, diabetic and will try to cater for anyone.

Fully licensed with all organic alcohol. House wine £8.50 for a bottle, £2.60 a large glass. Lots of fruit wines.

They also hold special gourmet evenings. See website for details and mailing list.

Vegetarian cafe bistro

5 Station Parade
(behind the GreenHouse)
Harrogate
North Yorkshire HG1 1UF

Tel: 01423-566 122

www.wild-ginger.co.uk

Train: Harrogate

Open:
Mon–Thu 10.00-15.00 (last orders),
Fri & Sat 11.00-19.00 (last orders)

No smoking throughout

All major cards

5% discount for Vegan Society members

2004 Observer Award for Best Sheik Cheap Eats in Yorkshire and Humberside

Wild Oats / Healthy Life

Vegetarian cafe and wholefood shop

190 High St, Skipton BD23 1JZ
Tel 01756-790619
Cafe: Mon-Sat 9.30-16.30, closed Sun
Shop: Mon-Sat 9-17.30

Wild Oats cafe is upstairs from the
Healthy Life wholefood shop. Soup
£2.95 with wholemeal bread. Main
courses such as stuffed pancakes with
two salads £5.50. Cakes £2.20-2.50,
some vegan. Freshly squeezed orange
juice, (soya) cappuccino. MC, Visa. No
smoking. Children welcome, high
chairs. Unlicensed.
Shop has take-away sandwiches, soup
& salad from the cafe.

The Old Oak Tree

English omnivorous restaurant in pub

South Kilvington, Thirsk, N Yorks YO7 2NL
Tel: 01845-523 276
Pub 11-15.00 & 18.30-23.00. Closed Mon
Food: Tue-Sun 12-14.00
& 18.30-21.00 (last orders),

English omnivorous restaurant
with a vegetarian menu that
changes, some vegan but best to
ring first. Licensed. Smoking area.
Visa, MC, Amex. Children's menu,
one high chair.

Stone House Inn and Tea Room

Omnivorous pub

Thruscross, near Harrogate, HG3 4AH
Tel: 01943-880325. Meals Tue-Sat 12-
14.00, 18-21.00; Sun 12-15.00
stonehouseinn@hotmail.co.uk

Always several vegetarian meals
and vegan nut roast. The pub itself
features stone flagging, beams and
open fires. Totally non-smoking.
Close to Thruscross Reservoir for
walking and bird watching.
Contact them for details of walks.

Magpie Cafe

Omnivorous restaurant

14 Pier Road
Whitby, North Yorkshire YO21 3PU
Tel: 01947-602 058
www.magpicafe.co.uk. info@magpie.co.uk
Open: Mon-Sun 11.30-21.00

Omnivorous restaurant which has
several hot and cold vegetarian
dishes such as leak and pasta
bake, and shepherds pie. Happy to
adapt for vegans. Vegetarian
specials change weekly. Mains at
£6.95 which include a dried fruit
and nut salad. Will try to cater for
other special diets, some gluten-
free items menu. No smoking
throughout. Visa, MC.

First Season

Wholefood shop

1 St. Anne's Lane
Whitby, North Yorkshire YO21 3PF
Tel: 01947 601 608
Open: Mon-Sat 9-17.00

Vegetarian wholefood shop with
supplements, a few pasties and
vegan ice-cream.

Holland & Barrett

Health food shop

1a James Street, Harrogate, N Yorks HG1 1QF
Tel: 01423-503 469

30 Market Place, Thirsk , N Yorks YO7 1LB.
Tel: 01845-526868

York

Cornmill Lodge

Vegetarian Guest House

Small family run vegetarian guest house within fifteen minutes walk of York Minster. There are five rooms: two double ensuites, one twin ensuite, one single (with private facilities) and one family all priced at £20–£35 per person per night.

120 Haxby Road
York
North Yorkshire YO31 8JP

Breakfast is organic wherever possible and is comprised of fruit juice, fruit salad and organic or gluten-free cereal. You are then spoilt for choice with a selection of mushrooms with buckwheat pancakes, banana with sunflower seeds on toast, almond and sesame seed tofu, vegetarian or vegan sausages or burgers. Any of these can be accompanied by mushrooms, tomatoes, baked beans, and wholemeal toast with preserves. Organic tea and coffee, fruit and herb teas, soya and rice milk, vegan margarine, vegan muesli and soy yoghurt available.

Tel and Fax:
01904–620 566

www.cornmillyork.co.uk
cornmillyork@aol.com

Train Station: York, 2 kms then get bus no.1 towards Wiggington. Get off at Havby Road School. Walk back towards city centre.

Dinner is not offered but the veggie tapas bar El Piano is nearby.

Open: all year

Born in Yorkshire the owner, Jen, knows a lot about the county and is always willing to advise guests about the many attractions of the city and surrounding area.

Directions: From outer ring road, A1237, follow signs to York District Hospital. Take a sharp left turn at traffic lights after hospital. Cornmill Lodge is on the right, just before the pedestrian crossing.

For those who enjoy walking, Cornmill Lodge is only half an hour's drive to the Yorkshire Moors, Dales and the coastline. Or you could spend a day in the medieval city of York with its excellent shopping and restuarants.

Parking: off street

Children of all age welcome; those under fourteen half price
Cots and high chairs available

Leave your soap at home as toiletries are free from animal ingredients and are not tested on animals.

No smoking throughout

10% discount to members of the Vegetarian Society, Vegan Society, Viva!, PETA, and people presenting this book

Tea and coffee making facilities in the rooms.

Visa, MC

The Blake Head

Vegetarian world food café at the back of a bookshop which caters for vegans and has wheat-free options. It was recently described as 'Vegetarian Heaven' by a local newspaper.

Breakfasts, snacks and main meals are all available and there is even a children's menu.

Typical breakfasts, £2.95-5.95 include beans on toast; potato and parsnip rosti with sauteed mushrooms; or hot apricot muesli.

Lunches, £3.50-£5.95 include soup with bread; jacket potatoes with mixed salad; or spicy bean burger with ciabatta roll and salad.

Main courses include mushroom timbale with cranberry and onion gravy; sun dried tomato and olive puff parcels with a white wine sauce; and arame ginger filo parcels with toasted sesame seeds.

Children can tuck into burgers, salads, beans on toast or jacket potatoes, £2-4.

There is a good range of cakes and biscuits, 95p-£2.40. Their chocolate fudge slice; banana, apricot and nut loaf; and orange and syrup biscuits are all vegan.

A wide range of drinks is available, including teas and herbal teas, £1.25; coffees from £1.20; hot chocolate; barleycup, £1.50, soft drinks; juices and mineral water, from £1.25. Wine, £2.95 per glass, £10.95 per bottle. A variety of beer is also available.

Organic and fresh local produce is used where possible and all food is prepared on the premises.

Vegetarian world cafe

104 Micklegate
York
North Yorkshire YO1 1JX

Tel: 01904-623 767

www.blakeheadcafe.co.uk

Train station: York

Open:
Mon-Sat 9.30-17.00,
Sun 10.00-17.00

Children very welcome

High chairs available

No smoking except in the outside courtyard

5% discount for Viva! members

El Piano

Vegetarian tapas bar in the heart of York. Other than nightclubs, it is the latest opening premises in the city. Organic where possible, the cuisine is Hispanic and internationally influenced and presented in individual tapas dishes.

Homemade soup £3.25, with bread and/or Spanish crisps and/or buckwheat cakes. Meals come in three sizes: £2.25, £3.95 and £6. Choose from 70 savouries, which can be gluten-free or vegan, or both.

Desserts £2.25, £3.95 and £6, with vegan choices – flapjacks, chocolate brownies, chocolate pie, crema Catalana, carrot cake; all can be served with non-dairy toppings.

Customers can use their musical instruments. Special diets catered for – gluten-free, wheat-free, raw, macrobiotic, vegan, diabetic, candida and sugar free.

Vegetarian tapas bar

15/17 Grape Lane, York
North Yorkshire YO1 7HU
Tel: 01904-610 676
www.elpiano.co.uk

Open:
Mon-Sat 10.00-24.00
Sun 12-17.00 low season,
12-19.30 high season

Fully licensed

Wheelchair and pushchair access

3 function rooms upstairs

Smoking throughout

MC, Visa

Live music on Fridays and Saturdays.

Vanilla Black

York's newest and most formal vegetarian restaurant (with candles at night), in the centre, with dark oak floors, minimalist white walls, 1930's dark oak furniture.

7 lunch main courses such as refried borlotti beans in tomato and smoked paprika sauce with olive oil toasted bread £5.50; baked beetroot, spiced cucumber and cherry tomato salads with leaves £5.65.

Evening starters £4.85. Mains include tomato and caramelised shallot tart £11.25; aubergine and mint dumplings in lemon and bean chowder £10.95. All served with a choice of new potatoes and roasted veg or dressed local leaves.

4 desserts which change daily, always one vegan such as oven roasted plums.

Vegetarian restaurant

26 Swinegate,
York YO1 8AZ

Tel: 01904-676 750

Open:
Wed-Sat 12-14.00, and
Tue-Sat 18-21.15 (last food order). Closed Sun-Mon.

Vegetarian wines (some vegan or organic) glass £2.65, bottle £10.80. Vegan local beers.

MC, Visa

Dairy Guest House

Omnivorous Guest House

3 Scarcroft Road York, YO23 1ND
Ten minutes walk from train station
Tel: 01904 639 367
www.dairyguesthouse.co.uk
Open: all year

Doubles and twins £60–£70 per room. Family rooms and king size beds available. See website for full details. Disabled access. No pets. Vegetarian and vegan breakfasts. No smoking throughout. MC, Visa.

The Spurriergate Centre

Omnivorous restaurant &
Fair Trade shop

St. Michael's Church, Spurriergate, York
Tel: 01904 629 393
www.thespurriergatecentre.com
Open: Mon–Fri 10–4.30, Sat 9.30–5

12th century church offers a place to meet, shop and eat. Two shops with cards, books, fair trade coffees, teas, and third world crafts. Child friendly.

Jumbo

Omnivorous Chinese restaurant

2–4 Hudson Street, York YO1 6LP.
Tel:01904-623656.
Open every day 12–23.00.

Omnivorous Chinese all-you-want buffet with lots for veggies and vegans including mounds of fresh fruit. Rice contains egg or ham but they always have plain boiled rice though you may have to ask for it. Prices vary according to time: 12–16.45 £4.99; 16.45–18.45 £6.99 (but till 23.00 on Sun); 18.45–23.00 £8.99, £9.99 on Sat.

Tower Street Pantry

Omnivorous sandwich bar

14 Tower Street, York YO1 9SA
Tel: 01904-647963
Open: Mon–Sat 08.15–17.00, Sun 10–17.00

Take-away or eat-in sandwich bar right opposite Clifford's Tower, the only bit of castle left above ground. Each sandwich, £1.60–2.40, made to order so you can pick your ingredients. Lots of salad boxes with 12 ingredients £2.10. Hummous, roast veg, cakes, flapjacks and fahiras (a big pasty).

Holland & Barrett

Health food shop

28–30 Coney Street, York
Tel: 01904–627 257

123

East Yorkshire

Acorn Guest House

Omnivorous guest house with vegetarian owners. There are nine rooms, all ensuite but with showers only, two singles at £28, two doubles, three twin rooms at £20 per person per night and two family rooms at £50–£60 for the room. One of the twin rooms is a loft with doors and a balcony overlooking the garden.

A selection of cereals and a cooked breakfast is offered. Soya milk and vegan margarine are available on request, and veggie sausages and veggie bacon are provided.

There are many museums, cinemas, sports arenas and an ice rink. Shop until you drop at the Princess Quay centre on the river which is built almost entirely of glass. Check out the markets on Sunday.

There is plenty of night life including lots of old worldly pubs, restaurants and clubs.

The town is pedestrianised and flat so is very easy for wheelchair users to get around.

Acorn Guest House has disabled access. There are three ground floor rooms and one has access to a wheel-in shower room.

Televisions and tea and coffee making facilities are in the rooms.

Hull

Omnivorous Guest House

719 Beverley High Road
Hull
East Yorkshire HU6 7JN
England

Tel: 01482–853 248
Fax: 01482–853 148

Train station:
Hull, 2 1/4 miles

Open: all year

Directions:
2 1/4 miles north of Hull city centre on the A1079 Beverley to York Road.

Parking: ten spaces

Children welcome

Animals welcome

No smoking throughout

Disabled access

Hitchcock's

Vegetarian Restaurant

Superb vegetarian all-you-can-eat buffet restaurant that attracts lots of meat eaters and is worth stopping in Hull for. One price £15 (£12 concessions) for three courses and coffee, with one sitting starting from 8.15pm.

1-2 Bishop Lane
Hull
East Yorkshire HU1 1PA
(on corner of Bishop Lane
and High Street)

Being in a quiet area of the Old Town, they only open when enough people book, usually 15-20 are sufficient, either as a single group or several separate bookings.

Tel: 01482-320 233

Open:
Tue-Sat 20.00-24.00, Sun-Mon closed

The menu is chosen by the first person to book and is based around a particular country, such as Italian, Chinese, Mexican, Thai, Cajun, Indian, Afro-Caribbean, Russian. But they could do Nepalese, Patagonian, Israeli, Tibetan, German and even English. Or a mixture.

Children welcome, prices to suit as they like haggling.

Licensed

Outside catering

Almost all food is vegan, for example the Cajun menu starts with salsa red bean, dips with crudites and toasted bread. The awesome main course buffet includes okra gumbo, red beans and rice, banana bread, Jamaican curry, fried plantain bananas and sweet potatoes, lemon spinach, sweetcorn, hot salsa, salads, chillies.

Cash and cheque only

£2 discount for members of the Vegetarian or Vegan Society

Several desserts such as pecan pie, crumble and (vegan) ice cream.

House wines from £1.30 glass, £7 bottle. Beer £2 pint. Spirits from £1. Or bring your own wine and pay £1 per bottle corkage.

Caters for coeliacs, nut-free and other diets on request.

This is one of the best vegetarian restaurants ever, anywhere.

Bean There

Organic vegetarian restaurant, mainly Mediterranean cuisine. 95% of ingredients are organic. They have a chocolate shop upstairs which sells vegan, no added sugar chocolate and gelatine–free Turkish delight.

Evening starters £3.75, including brushetta (vegan option), chick pea and garlic pate, winter vegetable soup. Mains £6.95 include African sweet potato stew, pepper, parmesan and nut filo bake (vegan), vegetable moussaka. Dessert £3.95. They have vegan cream, ice–cream and custard, but if you really can't decide on a pudding, try their selection of 3 for £7.50.

Lunchtime meals are similar with starters ranging from £2.60–£4, mains £3.75–£4.60 and desserts/cakes £1.30–£2.25.

Bridlington

Vegetarian cafe

10 Wellington Road
Bridlington,
East Yorkshire YO15 2BL
(near the war memorial)

Tel: 01262–679 800
www.beentherecafe.co.uk

Open: Tue–Sat 11–15.00;
Sat 18–20.30 last orders

No credit cards

No smoking

BYO for £1

Hull .

The Zoo Cafe

Vegetarian cafe

80B Newland Avenue, Hull HU5 3AB
Tel: 01482–494 352
Open: Mon–Sat 10.00–18.00 closed Sunday

Soup, salads, burritos, casseroles and veggieburgers. Four daily options for vegans, usually two gluten free. Desserts such as chocolate brownies and banana cake. Soya milk available. Smoking. Large open doors and courtyard. Cheques over £10.

Thai House Restaurant

Omnivorous Thai restaurant

51 Princes Avenue, Hull HU5 3QY
Tel: 01482–473 473
Open: every day 17.30–23.30, Fri–Sat –24.00

Almost every dish has veggie option £6.95–8.75. 2 courses and drink £13–16. Wine £8.95 bottle,

£2.25 glass. Children welcome, high chair. 2/3 no smoking. MC, Visa.

Holland & Barrett

Health food shop

Unit 1, 47/49 Kings St, Bridlington

21 Whitefriargate, Hull.

New Ellerby

Ellerby B&B

Vegan bed & breakfast

The Croft, Main Road, New Ellerby,
East Yorks HU11 5AP. Tel: 01964–562676
www.ellerbycroft.co.uk

New 100% vegan B&B 10 miles east of Hull. Doubles and twin £27.50 per person (under–7 free, 7–10 £10, 11–16 £17). Evening meal £17 (£0, £5, £10). Packed lunch £5 (£3). Reflexology, Reiki, massage. BYO or real ale pub nearby.

South Yorkshire

The Fieldgate Centre

Vegan bed & breakfast and camping

Mill Field Road, Fishlake,
nr Doncaster DN7 5GH (five minutes away
from junction 6 of the M18, see website map)
Train: Thorne two miles then they pick up in
electric car.
Tel: 01302–846 293
www.fieldgatecentre.org

Beautiful, peaceful, rural location, 7
miles north–east of the centre of
Doncaster. One twin and one double,
both ensuite, £27.50 per person with
vegan organic breakfast. £2.50 single
person supplement.
Camping £5.50 per tent or caravan for
any number of people. £1.50 electric
hookup.
Vegan organic cafe on site, see below.

Holland & Barrett

Health food shop

19 Cheapside, Barnsley S70 1RQ
Tel: 01226 770069

The Fieldgate Centre

Vegan organic cafe

Mill Field Road, Fishlake, near Doncaster
Open: Tue–Sun 9.30–18.00, Fri–Sat till 22.00
Tel: 01302–846 293
www.fieldgatecentre.org

£3.75 main course such as nut cutlets
with salad picked that morning, bean
salad and bread. Home made soup
£2.95. Deluxe organic chocolate cake
£1.95.
Tuesday is vegan organic pizza night,
eat in or take away.
Independent cinema Fri–Sat evening.
Conference room at back used for businesses, tai chi and pilates evenings.
(Motor) bikers club every second
Sunday of the month 15–18.00, to
promote good fuel in your biker not just
yer bike, with films, prizes.

Eating Whole

Vegetarian restaurant

25 Copley Road, Doncaster DN1 2PE
Open: Mon–Sat 09.00–16.00,
also Thu–Sat 19.30–22.30. Closed Sun.
Tel: 01302–738 730
eating.whole@doncaster.co.uk

Soups from £2.10. Mains such as spicy
lentil rissole with chilli sauce £4. Always
a vegan dessert, fruit salad or treacle
tart, £2.30. Organic wines and beers.
Xmas and New Year dinners. Smoking
section. No credit cards. Vegetarian and
Vegan Society members 10% discount.

Holland & Barrett

Health food shop

Unit 23 Frenchgate, Doncaster DN1 1ST
Tel: 01302 360082

Airy Fairy

Vegetarian coffee shop

239 London Road, Sheffield,
South Yorkshire S2 4NF
Tel: 0114–249 2090
www.airyfairy.org. anwen@airyfairy.org
Open: Mon–Tues 11–18.00 (Summer closes
15.30, Wed–Fri 11–18.00, Sat 11–17.00

Vegetarian Fair Trade gift and coffee
shop. Coffee from 80p, lots of fruit and
herb teas, vegan hot chocolate and
cappucino. All food is homemade and
mostly organic. Cakes 60p–£1.20, such
as fruit cakes, Bakewell tart and vegan
blueberry crumble. Handmade and local
crafts with pagan influences, and Fair
Trade items from around the world.
Cruelty free bodycare products.   129

Blue Moon Cafe

Vegetarian cafe

2 St James's Street, Sheffield S1 2EW
Tel: 0114–276 3443
Open: Mon–Sat 8.00–20.00

Big vegetarian self service restaurant by the Anglican cathedral. Soup £2.75, mains £5.25 with salads, scones 85p and desserts from £1.60 for a range of vegan cakes. Organic wines and beers. No smoking throughout. Visa, MC.

Exodus New Age Store and De Light cafe

Vegan/vegetarian cafe

85 Laughton Road, Dinnington, Sheffield S25 2PN. Tel: 01909–518 333
Email: exodus03@btconnect.com
Open: Tues–Sat 08.00–23.00,
Sun 10.00–22.00, Mon 08.00–19.00

Veggie restaurant and deluxe coffee bar. Eat in and take away. Evening entertainment includes poetry readings, live music and story telling. No smoking. MC, Visa. Licensed.

Green Edge Cafe

Vegetarian cafe

4 Nether Edge Rd, Sheffield S7 1RU
Bus 22 from centre of town, also 75, 76, 97
Tel: 0114–258 8550
Open: Tue–Sat 9.30–16.30, closed Sun–Mon

Brand new vegetarian cafe opposite Zed Wholefoods in a leafy stone suburb of Sheffield near parks. Hummous with salads, olive paste, soup, starter or main salads such as roast veg and couscous, £2.50–4.00. Sweet tarts £2.75 such as vegan lime and polenta. Cakes 80p–£1.50, none vegan at present. Organic drinks. Children's portions, 2 high chairs. BYO, no corkage. No smoking. No credit cards. Art on walls.

Heeley City Farm Cafe

Vegetarian cafe

Richards Rd, Heeley, Sheffield S2 3DT
Tel: 0114–258 0244
Open: every day 10–16.00

Vegan–friendly veggie cafe in a city farm with horses, cows, pigs, sheep – all rescued and not to be eaten. Great breakfasts with fake bacon. Cooked lunch £2.50 such as jacket potato, veggieburger, toasties, hummous and salad with pitta. Specials Tue and Thursday £3.25 such as pies, stuffed tortilla or pepper. Children welcome, high chair. Wheelchair friendly. No smoking. No credit cards.

Kumquat Mae Vegetarian Restaurant

Vegetarian restaurant

353 Abbeydale Road, Heeley, Sheffield S7 1FS
Tel: 0114–250 1076
Open: Wed–Sat 18.00–22.30.
Closed Sun–Tue. Will open for parties of 12+.

Starters £4.95 such as griddled marinated aubergine rolls with basil and smoked tofu stuffing. Main £11.75 such as roast red pepper filled with refried beans, lime chili and coriander with (vegan) melted cheese, rice, salad. Desserts £4.50 such as nectarine and elderflower crumble. Bring your own alcohol, no corkage charge. MC, Visa. No smoking area. Children welcome, high chair. Reservations recommended Friday and Saturday.

Kumquat Mae @ Out to Munch

Vegetarian cafe

at Sheffield Antiques Centre, 178–188 Broad-field Rd, Heeley, Sheffield S8 0XL
Tel: 0114–258 4994
Open: every day 11–16.00

New vegetarian cafe in Sheffield Antiques Centre, near the established restaurant. £2.50 snacks, £3.50 light meals such as aubergines with Mediter-ranean veg and almond stuffing; tortilla with almonds and potatoes. Cakes £1.50 big slice. Unlicensed. Juices. Children welcome (they could nip round to their restaurant to get a high chair). No credit cards.

Momtaz

Omnivorous Indian/Bangladeshi restaurant

115A Chesterfield Road, Sheffield S8 0RN
Tel: 0114–258 8822
Open: every day 18–24.00, –01.00 Fri–Sat

New restaurant with lots for veggies £4.80–6.50 such as Balti. House wine £8.50 bottle, £2.20 glass. Children welcome, high chair. Smoking. MC, Visa.

Nirmal

North Indian omnivorous restaurant

189–193 Glossop Road, Sheffield S10 2GW
Tel: 0114–272 4054
Open: every day 18.00–24.00

Vegetarian owned with lots of veggie dishes £4.95, a good meal for £7–8. House wine £8.95 bottle, £4.50 very large glass. Children welcome, high chairs. One side smoking. MC, Visa, Amex, Diners.

Beanies Wholefoods

Wholefood shop

205–207 Crookes Valley Road, Sheffield
Tel: 0114–2681662. Open: Mon–Fri 9–20.00, Sat 9–18.00, Sun 10.00–17.00

Organic fruit & veg and box scheme.

In a Nutshell

Wholefood shop

31 Chesterfield Road, Heeley, Sheffield S10 0RL
Tel: 0114–250 8555
Open: Mon–Sat 9.30–17.30, –18.30 Wed

Sells sandwiches, cakes and pastries.

New Roots Wholefood

Wholefood shop

Glossop Road, Sheffield. Tel: 0114–272 1971

Spital Hill, Sheffield. Mon–Fri 11.00–15.00

Veggie deli counter with soup, pastries, pizzas, cakes. The second location has meditation and healing courses.

Zed Wholefoods

Wholefood shop

3A Nether Edge Rd, Sheffield S7 1RU
Tel: 0114–255 2153
Open: Mon–Sat 9–19.00, Sun 10–17.00

Sandwiches, pasties to take–away. Organic veg box scheme.

Holland & Barrett

Health Food Shop

10 Barkers Pool, Sheffield S1 1HB
Tel: 0114–275 5438

47 Crystal Peaks, Mossborough
Sheffield S19 6PQ. Tel: 0114–251 0369

West Yorkshire

Archway Cottage

Two early Victorian cottages linked together make this large family home and B&B. Situated in the heart of Ilkley, it enjoys outstanding moorland views.

There are four rooms; one double ensuite at £22.50 per person per night, one twin at £20, one family room at £40–52 per night and a family ensuite at £52–60.

For breakfast choose from a selection of fruit juices and cereals with fresh fruit salad followed by tomatoes, mushrooms or beans on toast. With prior notice they can provide vegan sausages, soya milk and soya yoghurt. Tea, coffee, fruit and herbal teas are all available.

Dinner is not offered but Ilkley has a variety of restaurants most with veggie options.

Ilkley also has a nightclub and three bars with late night licences. There is a wide variety of shops and a museum. It is also an ideal walking base with the famous Ilkley Moor and Cow and Calf Rocks. The Dales Way walk starts here and goes all the way to Windermere.

The nearby towns of Otley and Grassington and village of Malham are lovely and well worth a look.

Packed lunches are available. Tea and coffee making facilities, washbasins and televisions are in the rooms.

Yorkshire Dales

Omnivorous B&B

24 Skipton Road
Ilkley, West Yorkshire
LS29 9EP England

Tel: 01943–603 399

Email:
thegreens@archcottage.fsnet.co.uk

Train Station:
Ilkley, 1/4 mile

Open: all year, except Christmas

Directions: Situated on the A65, two minutes from the town centre.

Parking: 2 spaces

Children welcome

High chair available

No smoking throughout

Cash and cheque only

Myrtle Grove

Veggie B&B set in the busy thriving town of Hebden Bridge. There is one spacious double ensuite room with views over the garden, the town and across the valley to Heptonstall. It costs £25–£35 per person per night in a double room. Up to two children can be accommodated at an extra charge. Single occupancy £30-35 Sun-Thu, £45 Fri-Sat, £50 bank holidays.

Begin your day with home grown organic fruit with soya yoghurt and cereal followed by a full cooked breakfast. Soya milk, vegan margarine and vegan muesli are available. The veggie proprietor uses organic produce where possible, bakes her own bread and makes preserves. She is happy to cater for special dietary requirements if given notice.

Walk from the B&B down to the canal and town centre to do some shopping, or eat dinner at one of the many restaurants providing veggie food. The town of Hebden Bridge promotes the arts and has theatrical performances, poetry readings, story telling and live music. There is an arts festival every June. There are alternative therapy and healing clinics as well as an Alternative Energy Centre, canal boats, a marina and a cinema providing a varied selection of films.

For walkers, Hardcastle Crags are nearby and there are footpaths beginning at the house. You could take easy and relaxing strolls along the canal or do more challenging walks into the hills and onto the moors.

The room has tea and coffee making facilites, a television and radio.

Vegetarian Bed and Breakfast

Old Lees Road
Hebden Bridge
West Yorkshire HX7 8HL
England

Tel: 01422 846 078

www.myrtlegrove.
btinternet.co.uk

Email: myrtlegrove@
btinternet.com

Train Station: Hebden Bridge, 1km, then bus or taxi or collection is possible.

Open: all year

Directions:
At Hebden Bridge (A646) take A6033 to Howorth after the first set of traffic lights. Myrtle Grove is 200 metres on the right. (A B&B sign hangs from the railings).

Parking: available on the street

Dogs welcome by arrangement

No smoking throughout

South Square Vegetarian Cafe

Vegetarian cafe

South Square, Thornton Road, Thornton
Bradford, West Yorkshire BD13 3LD
Tel: 01274 834 928
Open: Tue–Sat 11.30–15.00, Sun 12–15.00.
Mon closed.
Last orders 30 mins. before closing.

Vegetarian cafe. Mix of fast food, Indian, Mediterranean and Mexican dishes, with a wholefood approach. Fixed and today's menu. Most food cooked on premises. Always have vegan options.

Prashad Vegetarian Chaat House

Vegetarian restaurant

86 Horton Grange Road, Bradford BD7 2DW
Tel: 01274-575 893. www.prashad.co.uk
Open: Tue–Fri 11–15.00, 18–21.30;
Sat–Sun 11–22.30

The food is mainly very spicy and salty in keeping with the authentic Indian dishes but they may offer mild versions in the future as they find out what new customers want. They also do corporate catering. Family business run by Mrs Patel and her son Bobby.
sales@prashadcatering.com
www.prashadcatering.com

1 in 12 Club

Vegetarian cafe

Top floor, 21–23 Albion St, Bradford BD1 2LY
Tel: 01274-734 160. www.1in12.com
Open: Thur–Sat 12–15.00, some evenings

An amazing example of workers' taking charge, the entire building was bought, renovated and is run by a local anarchist collective. The midle floor is a social centre and on the ground are a recording studio and practice rooms. The top floor cafe has standard cafe fare from veggieburgers and sosrolls, pasties and salad to exquisite dishes and you won't pay more than £3, except on benefit nights when 3 or more courses comes to £5–6. Also flapjacks, organic fair trade coffee, teas, soft drinks. No alcohol. No smoking. No credit cards. Children welcome, 4 high chairs.

Fair Trade Cafe

Vegetarian cafe

Basement of the Anglican Chaplaincy, 2 Ash
Grove, Bradford, W Yorks BD7 1BN
Open: Mon–Fri 12–15.00 during term

Small soup with roll £1.50. Daily special £3.50 such as curry, chili. Gluten free and vegan desserts like chocolate brownies, cheesecake £1–2. No credit cards. No smoking. Children welcome, high chair. Run mainly by voluneters. Use the entrance on Great Horton Road, opposite the Chesham Building of Bradford University. Look for the mural on the garage door. Regular themed daytime and evening events – tickets in cafe.

Courtyard by Marriott

Omnivorous restaurant

The Pastures, Tong Lane
Bradford, West Yorkshire BD4 0RP
Tel: 0113 285 4646
www.courtyard.com

3–star hotel and restaurant 5 miles from both Bradford and Leeds city centres. Some vegetarian food in the restaurant such as pasta, and they say the can cater for vegans if you call ahead.   Three course a la carte dinner £20, main meal £10–15. The hotel is £95 single occupancy Mon–Thur, falling at weekends to £76 double, £53 single, but watch out for weddings.

Halifax

World Peace Cafe & Meditation Centre

Vegetarian Buddhist meditation centre

5 North Bridge, Halifax HX1 1XH
Tel: 01422 353 311
www.worldpeacecafehalifax.com
Open: Tues–Sat 9.30am–4.30pm,
Closed Sun & Mon

100% organic, 100% vegetarian, many vegan options including falafels. On selected Friday evenings at 19.30, a 3 course meal with coffee and meditation costs £8.50. Take away is available.

Pharo's

Vegan gourmet cafe

5/6 Causeway Foot, Ogden, Halifax,
West Yorkshire, HX2 8XX (4 miles north of
Halifax on A629, corner of Ogden Lane and
Keighly Rd). Tel: 01422–248 049
Menus at www.halifaxvegan.co.uk
Email: veganferrit@yahoo.co.uk
Open: from June 2005, initially Fri eve,
Sat–Sun all day, plus bookings other times.

New cafe in a walkers' paradise. Seasonal fresh organic locally grown produce. Main courses include Oriental, curry, chilli, Mediterranean and Western dishes. Evening starters £3.30, mains £7.30, dessert £3.40. Saturday buffet lunch 11.30–3.30pm £9.90 with all–you–can–eat jacket potato, salads, fruit juice and smoothie, speciality breads, dips, teas and coffee. Sunday 4 course roast lunch 12–3pm £12.50 with choice of two soups, three starters, 2 vegan roasts or pie plus side veg and gravy, 3

desserts. Vegan alcoholic and alcohol-free drinks. Freshly prepared juices, slushies and smoothies, Fair trade teas and coffees. Take–aways later in 2005. Sugar–free, gluten–free no problem. No smoking. Bikers/cyclists welcome. MC, Visa. Older children welcome, discount for 8–12. Stop press: Closed as we go to press until further notice, check website for updates.

Hebden Bridge

Canalside Community Cafe

Vegan cafe

9 Hebble End, Hebden Bridge HX7 6HJ
(on the canalside next to Alternative Technology Centre, parallel with Market Street).
Tel: 07870–727373
Email: kurlykathb@yahoo.co.uk
Open: Tue–Thu 10.00–18.00 (it's another
cafe at other times, not veggie) Kath Baker

Food from 70p to £4 such as toasties sandwiches, stuffed pittas, jacket potatoes, vegan fry–up, soup, salad bar, specials like satay, moussaka, lasagne, curry £4. Home baked cakes. Kids menu, 3 high chairs, toys. Garden seating outside too. Huge range of teas. BYO, no corkage. Cash or cheque only. Smoking outside only. Community info shop too.

Laughing Gravy

Vegetarian restaurant

The Birchcliffe Centre, Birchcliffe Road,
Hebden Bridge West Yorkshire HX7 8DG
Tel: 01422 844425
www.laughinggravy.co.uk
Open: Fri–Sat from 19.30

Vegetarian restaurant which you'll need to book for. They do a mezze menu, like a buffet that comes to your table, for £17.95, with loads

Organic House

100 % organic vegetarian food influenced by Chinese, Mediterranean, Thai, Turkish etc.

Organic vegetarian cafe

Starters £2–£2.75 include vegan savoury pate with toast and relish, soup with homemade bread, salads £3.95–£4.75. Mains £3.95–£4.95 such as flatbread pizza (vegan if you want) and salad; potato and lentil cakes, coconut and coriander broth and peas; Brazil nut and mushroom pie with potato salad.

2 Market St, Hebden Bridge, West Yorkshire, HX7 6AA
Tel: 01422 843429

oh@organic–house.co.uk
www.organic–house.co.uk

Open: Tue–Wed 9–18.00,
Thu–Fri 9–19.00,
Sat 9–18.00, Sun 9–17.00
Planning to open Fri–Sat eve

Desserts £1.80–£2.50 such as vegan Fair trade cakes.

Children's portions, high chairs

House wine £5.49. Beer £2.10. Coffee£1.10. BYO with £2 corkage fee.

No smoking

MC, Visa

There is an exhibition space for local artists. Also bodywork such as shiatsu, reflexology, acupuncture and massage. Shop, see next page.

Special diets are catered for and they are allergy–aware.

for vegans. They change the menu every week based on what's in season. Ashley and James the chefs have worked in many kinds of restaurants so the cuisine is taken from all over the world. Licensed for alcohol. Just outside Hebden Bridge, a four minute walk from the train station. No smoking. Visa, MC. Child friendly, six high chairs. Will open for parties of 10+ other nights. During the day it's a residential centre running courses and they do the catering, and they do outside events too.

Closed Mon, some bank holidays.

Big shop plus cafe (seeabove), all veggie organic, good for vegans. Do your shopping then relax. The shop has lots of hard to find allergy suitable and special diet stuff, fruit and veg, alcohol, books. Dietary advice can be given. Proprietor is vegan. MC, Visa.

Organic House

Organic vegetarian shop

2 Market Street, Hebden Bridge HX7 6AA
Tel: 01422–843 429
Open: Tue–Wed & Sat 9–18.00.
Thu–Fri 9–19.00, Sun 9–17.00.

The Blue Rooms

Vegetarian restaurant

9 Byram Arcade, Huddersfield HD1 1ND
Tel: 01484 512 373
Open: Mon–Fri 10.00–17.00, Sat 9.00–17.00

Vegetarian restaurant. Mains, £4.50–£5, and there are always vegan friendly dishes. No smoking throughout. No credit cards.

Roots and Fruits

Friendly vegetarian restaurant. All day breakfast, which can be made vegan, £4.95. Starters from £3.25 include nachos, samosas and New York potatoes (wedges). Sandwiches £3.95 such as wild mushroom pate or hummous. Jacket potatoes £3.95 with various fillings.

Mains £4.75–£6 such as burgers and chilli burritos. There is a specials board, from £6.95, which varies and typically includes pasta, salad or curry.

Desserts, £3.50.

Many dishes can be made vegan and they always have soya milk.

Private parties for up to 30 people.

Vegetarian restaurant

10–11 Grant Arcade
Leeds
West Yorkshire LS1 6PG
Tel: 0113–242 8313

Open: Mon–Fri 11.00–18.50
(last orders),
Sat 10.00–19.00

Licensed

Separate smoking section

Wheelchair access

Visa, MC

5% discount (food only) to
Vegetarian Society members

Hansa's

Gujarati vegetarian restaurant

72–74 North Street, Leeds, West Yorkshire
Tel: 0113–2444 408
www.hansasrestaurant.com (menu)
Open: Mon–Thu 17.00–22.30 (last order),
Fri –Sat 17.00–23.00, Sun 12–14.00 buffet

Starters £3.25–3.75, platter of mixed bhajiyas for two £6.95. Mung bean dhosa £3.95–5.25, idli with daal £4.50. Mains from £3.50 such as whole Kenyan aubergine stuffed with spicy masala £6.25, curries and daals. Thali and dessert £7.95 or 9.25. Banquet for six £11.50 or 12.95 with dessert and coffee. Vegans desserts such as sweet vermicelli cooked in vegetable ghee with sultanas, almonds and cardamon, £3.25. All you can eat Sunday buffet £7.95, children 6–12 £3.75.
Organic, vegetarian and vegan wine from £2.95 glass, £11.50. bottle. Beer £2.50 bottle. Coffee £1.50. No soya milk available. High chairs for children. MC, Visa. 10% service charge. 10% discount for Animal Aid, PETA, Vegetarian or Vegan Society, Viva! Gift vouchers available. Cookery demos.

The Common Place

Vegan co-operative cafe

23 Wharf Street, Leeds LS2 7EQ
Tel: 0845–345 7334, 0113–246 8640
www.thecommonplace.org.uk
Open: Wed 12–15.00, Thu–Fri 12–20.00
Sat 12–19.00

Leeds' autonomous, collectively run, radical social centre in an old textile mill has a vegan cafe run by volunteers, 50–seat cinema, bookshop, internet, meeting rooms, art space and a music venue. Around £2 for a meal such as curry with rice and salad. Several really tasty cakes 50p.

Beano Wholefoods

Vegetarian shop and deli

36 New Briggate, Leeds LS1 6NU
Tel: 0113-243 5737
Open: Mon–Sat 9–17.00 (Tue from 9.30,
Thu–Fri till 17.30), closed Sun
www.beanowholefoods.co.uk

Regular wholefood shop plus organic fruit and veg, non-dairy ice-cream and yoghurts, plus a take-out counter that is 90% vegan. Sandwiches £1.80-2.50. Pasties, pizzas, cakes. MC, Visa. They are looking for bigger premises.

Anand Sweets

Vegetarian Indian take-away in shop

109 Harehills Road, Leeds LS8 5HS
Tel: 01130248 1234
Open: Tue–Sun 10–20.00, closed Mon

Mainly sweets including vegan ladhu. Samosas, pakoras, allu tikki, cold curry and rice.

Strawberry Fields Cafe-Bar

Omnivorous cafe-bar

159 Woodhouse Lane
Leeds, West Yorkshire LS2 3ED
Open: Lunch Mon–Fri 12–14.10,
Bar snacks only Mon–Sat 19.00 to late,
closed Sun
Tel: 0113 243 1515. www.strawbs.com

Small and friendly omnivorous cafe-bar. They make everything themselves. Proprietor is vegetarian and caters well for veggies and vegans with Mediterranean and Mexican dishes. Starters £1.85-£3.99 include vegan garlic bread or hummous. Veggieburger £2. Main dishes £5.50-7.50 such as pizzas (can be without cheese), wild mushroom enchilada. Wine £8.50 bottle, £2 glass. Situated between the universities, day clientele tend to be professionals / academics and students. Lively in the evening. Long cocktails from £2.75 and double spirits for £1.50.

Org

Omnivorous organic food shop, deli/ juice bar & holistic treatment centre

79 Great George Street, Leeds LS1 3BR
(opposite LGI Hospital nearr Millenium Sq)
Tel: 0113–234 7000
www.org-organics.org.uk
Open: Mon–Fri 9.30–17.30, Sat 10–17.00.
Sometimes Sun 11–15.00 summer, call first.
Deli Mon–Fri 19–16.00, Sat 10–15.00

Sandwiches, salads, veggieburgers, soup, curries in winter. Meal in £4.49, take-away 99p–£3.29. Meal, coffee and cake £4.99. Platter £5–8 per head. Juices, smoothies, shakes £2.35-4.19. Organic food shop with fruit and veg, home deliveries, Artesan breads, wines and spirits. They do the full range of Dr Hauschka cosmetics. Sandwiches, salads, veggieburgers, soup, curries in winter. Meal in £4.49, take-away £3.49. No smoking. MC, Visa.

The Hungry Caterpillar

Wholefood shop and take-away

8 The Crescent, Hyde Park Corner,
Leeds LS6 2NW.
Tel: 07968–302 382
Mon–Fri 10–18.00, Sat 10–17.00
Closed Sun

Vegetarian take-away Mediterranean lunch £2.50 includes butter beans, dolmades, olives, sundried tomatoes, hummous. Organic drinks. Wholemeal and non-wheat breads. Organic fruit & veg boxes to order.

139

The Beehive

Fair Trade shop and mini-cafe

67 Potternewton Lane
Chapel Allerton
Leeds, West Yorkshire LS7 3LW
Tel: 0113-262 2975
Open: Tue-Fri 10.30-16.30, Sat 10-17.00

Small Fair Trade shop near the Roundhay Park, with crafts, gifts, some organic and wholefoods. Food is clearly labelled dairy free, gluten free and nut free. Chilled drinks. Locally sourced household cleaning products that are eco-friendly.
Mini-café with one table and four chairs. Herbal teas 60p cup, pot for two 90p. Freshly ground coffee 80p cup.

Corner Cafe

Omnivorous Indian cafe

104 Burley Road, Leeds, LS3.
Tel: 0113-2346677
Open: Tue-Sat 18-23.00

Nearly half of menu is vegan. Non-smoking. No credit cards.

Spiral

Vegan catering service

Leeds, West Yorkshire. Tel: 0113-248 4044

Catering service, cooking workshops, short courses, for animal, gluten or sugar free diets.

Cheerful Chilli

Vegetarian restaurant

Yorkgate Farm, East Chevin Road
Otley, West Yorkshire LS21 3DD
Tel: 01943 466 567
Open: Tue, Wed, Fri, Sat 18.30-late, last orders 21.30

Vegetarian evening restaurant that gets heavily booked. Call to reserve and they'll call you back. Bring your own alcohol. £12-13 for three courses, plenty for vegans or allergies. During the daytime it's called the Ramblers Cafe with non-vegetarian food.
Location: on the right-hand side of East Chevin Road, which comes south out of Otley and eventually, after changing its name to Otley Old Road, joins the A658 airport road a mile or so N.E. of the airport.

Dandelion and Burdock

V egan cafe

16 Town Hall Street, Sowerby Bridge,
West Yorkshire HX6 2EA (near Halifax)
Tel: 01422-316000
Open: Wed -Thu: 18.00 - 22.00 (last serving), Fri-Sat 18.00 - later close, Sat-Sun 11-15.00

Fully licensed. Nouvelle cuisine type.

Holland & Barrett

Health food shop

Unit 1, 58 Kirkgate, Bradford BD1 1QT
Tel: 01274 723289

4 Crown Street, Halifax HX1 1TT
Tel: 01422 365794

64 Towngate, Keighley, West Yorks
BD21 3QE. Tel: 01535 663 338

11 Crossgates Centre, Arndale, Leeds LS15
Tel: 0113 264 8326

21 Bond Street Mall, Bond Street Centre,
Leeds LS1 5ER. Tel: 0113 2467011

37 The Merrion Centre, Leeds LS2 8NG
Tel: 0113 234 2828

Saints Walk, The Riding Centre, Wakefield,
West Yorkshire WF1 1US. Tel: 01924 367195

The Isle of Man is so different, with a history that stretches right back to the Vikings. The island is also very scenic, with beautiful coastal walks. Being in the Gulf Stream the weather is mild. There is lots of sea wildlife such as seals and basking sharks.

Fly there from Manchester, Liverpool or London, or get the ferry or Seacat from Liverpool, Heysham (Lancashire), Belfast or Dublin.

There's one vegetarian restaurant on the island, which is only open during the day. In the evenings and on Sundays you'll find plenty of pizza places, Italian and Indian restaurants.

Isle of Man

Fernleigh Hotel

Omnivorous hotel

Marine Parade, Peel, Isle of Man IM5 1PB
Tel: 01624 842435. Fax: 01624 842435
Open: all year except around Christmas
ferneleigh@manx.net. www.isleofman.com

On the sunny West side of the island, 13 miles from Douglas. Happy to do vegetarian or vegan breakfast if you let them know in advance. 4 en suite rooms £25 per person. 8 standard rooms £20. No supplement for single occupancy. They make their own Glamorgan and chick pea vegetarian sausages, vegan lentil and carrotburgers, oat cakes, a different breakfast every day. Soya milk and soya cream available and they will get soya margarine if you ask beforehand.

Castletown Health Store

Health food shop

21 Malew Street, Castletown IM9 1AD
Tel: 01624–825812. www.health-store.co.uk
Open: Mon–Sat 9–17.30, closed Sun

Green's

Vegetarian restaurant

Steam Railway Station, Douglas IM1 4AA
Tel: 01624–629 129
Open: Mon–Sat 9–17, food served 12–14.30
E-mail: nigelkermode@excite.com

At the railway station in Douglas. Substantial bowl of vegan soup £2.95. Main £6.95 such as Red Dragon pie, homity pie, pasta bake, wholemeal pizza, moussaka. Baked potatoes with fillings and 5 to 7 salads. Desserts like fruit crumble or sticky toffee pudding (not vegan). House wine £7.95 bottle, glass £1.50. Smoking section. Children welcome, 3 high chairs and a baby table. Parking outside. No cards.

Millennium Saagar

Omnivorous Indian restaurant

1 Sherwood Terrace, Broadway, Douglas, Isle of Man, IM2 4EN Tel: 01624 679871

Plenty for vegetarians.

Julian Graves Health Store

Health food shop

62 Duke Street, Douglas, Isle of Man
Tel: 01624–616 933
Open: Mon–Sat 9–17.00, closed Sun

Savoury pre-packed foods, dried fruits and nuts, snacks, flapjacks, and they have multi-vitamins.

Holland & Barrett

Health food shop

Unit 2, 26–30 Strand Street, Douglas
Tel: 01624–676 527

Isle of Man Health Food Store

Health food shop

90 Bucks Road, Douglas, Isle of Man IM1 3AG
Tel: 01624–675 647
Open: Thu 10.30–13.00, Sat 9–17.30,
Mon–Tue, Wed & Fri 9–13.15, 14.15–17.30

Multi-vitamins, health food supplies. Good for veggies.

Good Health

Health food shop

Shop F, Museum Bldngs, Church Rd, Port Erin

Small shop with flapjacks, drinks etc

EAST

Eastern England Counties

Bedfordshire

Buckinghamshire

Cambridgeshire

Essex

Hertfordshire

Leicestershire

Norfolk

Northamptonshire

Suffolk

Leicestershire

Kings Lynn

Norfolk

Cambridgeshire

Northamptonshire

Cambridge

Suffolk

Bedfordshire

Buckinghamshire

Colchester

Essex

Hertfordshire

East England

Bedfordshire

Bedford

Pizza Express

Omnivorous pizza restaurant

22 St Peters St, Bedford MK40 2PN
Tel: 01234 271124
Open: Mon 11.30–23.00,
Tues–Sat 11.30–24.00, Sun 11.30–23.30

Close to the John Bunyan Statue. This branch has said they're not taking part in the Pizza Express scheme to offer vegan pizzas – let us know if they change their minds!

Green Cuisine

Vegetarian & Vegan catering

10 Ribble Way, Bedford MK41 7TY
Tel: 01234–305 080
tanna.tanna@ntlworld.com

Any function from dinner parties and house parties to wedding receptions for up to 150 people.

Holland & Barrett

Health food shop

10 Horne Lane, Harpur Centre, Bedford
Tel: 01234–352 866

Dunstable

Golden Dragon

Omnivorous Chinese restaurant

1 Tring Road, Dunstable LU6 2PX
Tel: 01582–661 485
Open: Mon–Sun 12.00–14.00, 18.00–23.00

Extensive separate vegetarian and vegan menu. Several mock meat dishes, starters £2.70–£6.50; mains £3.20–£6 and desserts from £2.50. House wine £9.50 bottle, £2.50 glass. Separate smoking section. Children welcome, high chairs. Visa, MC.

Leighton Buzzard

Nature's Harvest

Vegetarian wholefood shop

19 North Street, Leighton Buzzard LU7 1EF
Tel: 01525–371 378

Organic and vegan chilled and frozen foods, vegan ice-cream. Skin-care products. Cookbooks. Therapy room with homeopathy, massage, reflexology, allergy testing, nutritional advice.

Luton

Poco Loco

Omnivorous cafe

at the Hat Factory, 65–67 Bute St, Luton
Tel: 01582–401603. www.pocoloco.co.uk
Open: Mon–Sat 07.00–20.30, closed Sun

Avocado, houmous and falafel wraps from £3.50 and a couple of other vegan dishes. Soya milk available.

Pizza Express

Omnivorous pizza restaurant

The Lodge, 3 Church Street, Luton
Tel: 01582–456 229
Open: Mon–Sat 11.30–23.00; Sun –22.30

In a converted Masonic temple.

First Health

Health food shop

87–88 The Market Hall, Arndale Centre, Luton
Tel: 01582–451170

Family business, very friendly.

Holland & Barrett

Health food shop

158 Arndale Centre, Luton
Tel: 01582–482 574

149

Buckinghamshire

Amersham

GNC

Health food shop

100 Sycamore Road, Amersham HP6 5EN
Tel: 01494-727273

Aylesbury

Carlos

Omnivorous Portuguese restaurant

11 Temple Street, off Friar's Square Shopping
Complex, Aylesbury. Tel: 01296-421 228
Open: every day, closed Sunday night

---

14 items on a separate veggies and
vegan menu such as nut roast, chilli
beans, and vegan-fried vegetables in
champagne sauce.

Eat As Much As You Like

Omni Chinese buffet restaurant

35-37 New Street, Aylesbury, HP20 2NL
Tel: 01296-422 191
Open: Mon-Sat 12-14.30, 18-23.15,
Sun 12-20.15

Up-market buffet restaurant.
Lunchtime around £5-6, evening £9-
10. 30% suitable for veggies. Round the
back of Sainsbury's.

Health Right

Health food shop

48c Friar's Square Shopping Centre
Aylesbury. Tel: 01296-397 022 / 435 542
Open: Mon-Sat 9-17.30

Veggie and vegan takeaways such as
pies and pasties. They sell soya
yoghurts, cheeses and margarines,
Swedish glace, Tofutti and carob ices.

Also recommended by local veggies: On
the outside of Friars Square Shopping
building is the Noodle Bar with Chinese
vegetarian and vegan options, a popular
venue for young and mobile people.
Just Baguettes at 10 Bourbon Street,
(Tel: 01296 399555) bake on the
premises and make to order. There is a
large whiteboard with the vegetarian
menu and includes humus for vegans.
Long queue at lunch-times.
At 71 High Street is Bon Appetit French
fast food take away and restaurant (Tel:
01296 489877) with veggie options.
Finally, look out for the mobile outdoor
catering unit near WHSmiths in the High
Street, specialising in jacket potatoes.

Bletchley

Veggie World

Vegan Chinese restaurant

150-152 Queensway, Bletchley MK2 2RS
Tel: 01908-632 288.
www.veggie-world.com
Open: Tue-Sat 11.30-14.30,
Tue-Sun 17-22.00

Chinese vegetarian restaurant, with 90
vegan dishes in the evening and low
priced lunches. Lots of meat substitutes
like fake chicken and pork, plus tofu,
stir-fried veg etc. Big menu. Starters and
soups around £2. Chef's recommenda-
tion main course £3.60. Main courses
£3.80. Rice from £1.70. Cheaper at
lunchtime, about £3-4 to eat there. No
alcohol, although bring your own wine.
Non smoking throughout. Frozen and
dried meat substitutes may be
purchased for home cooking.

Holland & Barrett

Health food shop

Unit 16, The Concourse, the Brunel Centre,
Bletchley. Tel: 01908-642 437

151

Buckingham

Back to Nature

Health food shop

14 The Cornwalls Centre, off the High Street
Buckingham. Tel: 01280-812 694
Open: Mon-Sat 9.15-17.30 (17.00 Sat)

Soya alternatives to rice, cheese, margarine etc.

Chesham

Health Right

Health food shop

27 High Street, Chesham, Bucks
Tel: 01494-771 267
Open: Mon-Sat 9-17.30

Take-away pies and pasties. They sell soya yoghurt, cheeses and margarines, Swedish glace, Tofutti and carob ices.

Gerrards Cross

GNC

Health food shop

2D Station Road, Gerrards Cross
Tel: 01753-889040

Milton Keynes

The Eating Point

90% Vegetarian wholefood restaurant

Christ Church, Stantonbury Campus,
Stantonbury (Saxon St side),
Tel: 01908-315 627
Open: Mon-Fri lunchtimes (School term only)

Lots of beans, pasta, rice, vegetables and very cheap as they have a staff of volunteers. Off the V7 road that runs north-south through the centre, in north Milton Keynes. Snack menu too.

Also recommended in MK: Absolutely Souper cafe in Midsummer Place

shopping building. Half the menu is vegetarian with vegan options, a salad buffet, soups, chowders and goulashes, baguettes/sandwiches, jacket potatoes, fresh fruit smoothies. Only open daytime.

Brunches sandwich bar in the main centre shopping building, though the margarine in the roasted vegetable sandwich is not vegan. Eat in or take away. Open daytime. Good Indian restaurants are La Hind at Elder House, 502 Elder Gate, Station Square (Tel 01908 675948) and Jaipur at 599 Grafton Gate East (Tel 01908 669796). Chiquito Mexican restaurant & bar at 199 Midsummer Boulevard (Tel 01908-670456)

Alternatives

Vegetarian health food shop and complementary health centre

Burchard Crescent, Shenley Church End
Milton Keynes. Tel: 01908-526 524
Open: Mon-Fri 10-18.00, Sat 10-17.00

Chiller cabinet with dairy-free food.

Holland & Barrett

Health food shop

Unit 17, the Food Centre, near Sainsburys
Milton Keynes. Tel: 01908-690 721

Milton Keynes Vegetarians & Vegans

Vegetarian Society

Peter Simpson
psimpson@vegcac-mkveg.fslife.co.uk
Tel: 01908-503 919, 07967 589663

Monthly meals at Veggie World restaurant on Wednesdays. Stalls at local events.

Peter is the General Secretary of the Vegetarian Cycling & Athletic Club and represents the athletics side. See www.vegcac.co.uk

Cambridge is full of students in the winter, and tourists in the summer, who enjoy punting down the river, or chilling in one of the city's many open spaces. The city has a lot of elegance, character and history, a great shopping centre and some excellent health food shops.

There is only one good vegetarian place, the Rainbow, which is particularly good and recommended by local vegans. A number of other places cater well for us, and these are usually packed as demand is high.

Cambridgeshire

Dykelands Guest House

Detached guest house on the south side of the city offering modern, spacious, well laid out accommodation. There are nine rooms; one single ensuite at £35 per night, one double and one twin at £42 per room per night, two double ensuites and one twin ensuite at £52 per room per night and three family rooms at £60–£75 per room per night.

For breakfast choose from a selection of cereals with juice, toast and preserves. A cooked veggie breakfast is available and vegan options can be arranged by request for example, mushrooms on toast. Soya milk and soya spread are also provided.

There is no shortage of trendy cafes and restaurants in this university town, most offering veggie food. For a cheaper alternative you could take a picnic and enjoy it by the river. Make sure you try punting down the river, but try not to fall in!

Cambridge has lots of tourist attractions including National Trust sites Anglesey Abbey, Houghton Mill, Wicken Fen and Wimpole Hall as well as English Heritage sites Audley End, Bury St Edmunds Abbey and Denny Abbey. There's also the American Military Cemetry, Ely Cathedral, the Iron Age Fort on Gog Magog Hills, Mountfitchet Castle, Norman Village and an RSPB Nature Reserve all nearby.

Omnivorous
Guest House

157 Mowbray Road
Cambridge
Cambridgeshire CB1 7SP
England

Tel: 01223–244 300

Fax: 01223–566 746

www.dykelands.com

Email:
dykelands@fsbdial.co.uk

Train Station: Cambridge 1 mile, then taxi or bus.

Open: all year

Directions: From A10/M11 junction 11 A1309. At seventh set of traffic lights turn right into Long Road. At next roundabout first exit is Mowbray Road.

Parking: available

Children welcome

Dogs welcome (in ground floor rooms only)

Credit cards accepted (no surcharge)

No smoking throughout

Three Diamond Award (English Tourist Board)

Rooms have tea and coffee making facilites, televisions and radios.

Joan's B&B

Vegan bed and breakfast

74 Sturton Street, Cambridge CB1 2QA
Train Station: Cambridge, 10 minutes walk
Tel: 01223-311 828
Fax: 01223-300 318
Open: by arrangement

Two rooms, one double and one single £23 per person per night. Evening meal by arrangement, two courses, £8. No children or pets. No smoking throughout.

Stockyard Farm B&B

Omnivorous bed and breakfast, vegetarian owner

Wisbech Road, Welney, Wisbech PE14 9RQ
Tel: 01354-610 433
Fax: 01354-6104 22
Train Station: Littleport, 7 miles
Open: all year, except Christmas

Two rooms, one double and one twin £18-£20 per person per night. Double let as single from £25 per night. Children over ten years welcome, pets welcome. No smoking throughout. Three miles from wildlife and wetlands centre. Between Ely and Wisbech on A1101, at north end of village.

The Jolly Abbot

Omnivorous pub with a vegetarian kitchen

Abbotsley, nr St. Neots, Cambrdge PE19 6UL
Tel: 01767-677 765
jolly.abbot@virgin.net

This pub has both omnivorous and vegetarian kitchens. They cater for other special diets also.

Rainbow Bistro

Vegetarian restaurant

9A Kings Parade, Cambridge CB2 1SJ
Tel: 01223-321551
www.rainbowcafe.co.uk
Open: Tues-Sat 10–22.00 (last orders 21.30).

The Rainbow is totally vegetarian, using freshly made food without additives, colourings or flavourings. Vegan, gluten or nut free is clearly indicated. Soupe du jour £2.95. Menu changes at regular intervals, with mains priced at £7.25. Children's choices £3.25 such as risotto, pasta and small versions of the mains. All cakes are home made, and half are vegan, £3.75. All ice cream is vegan Swedish glace. All wine, beer and cider is vegan organic. Wine £12.95 bottle, £3.25 glass. Non smoking. Visa, MC.

Cafe Naz Curry Centre

Omnivorous Indian restaurant

45–47 Castle St, Cambridge
Tel: 01223-363 666

Indian with some south Indian food like dosas (but beware of yoghurt in coconut chutney). Curries and sambar are excellent.

Cambridge Blue

Omnivorous restaurant

85 Gwydir Street, Cambridge CB1 2LG
Tel: 01223-361 382
Open: Mon-Sat 12.00–14.30, 18.00–21.30

Vegetarian dishes change daily and there is at least one hot dish, £4.75. Can cater for vegans on request with advance notice. Visa, MC.

Cambridge – restaurants

Charlie Chan's

Omnivorous Chinese restaurant

14 Regent Street, Cambridge CB2 1DB
Tel: 01223–359 336
www.visualaid.co.uk
/charliechan/htm/menus.htm
info@charliechan.co.uk
Open: every day 12–17.00, 18–23.00

They offer a vegetarian set dinner, which includes soup and at least four different vegan dishes, and costs £32 per couple. Vegan desserts are also available. In the centre of town opposite Parker's Piece.

The Gardenia

Omnivorous Greek restaurant

2 Rose Crescent, Cambridge CB2 3LL
Tel: 01223–356 354
Open: every day 11.00–03.00

Omnivorous Greek take-away and restaurant with lots of cheap vegetarian and vegan food. Most options £3–3.50.

Mai Thai @ Hobbs Pavilion

Thai Omnivorous restaurant

Parkers Piece, Cambridge CB1 1JH
Tel: 01223–367 480
Open: every day 12.00–15.00, 18–23.00

Now a Thai restaurant under new ownership and with 15 vegetarian dishes £4.95–9.95. Set meal for at least two people £17 or £23 which could include mixed platter, bean curd, mushroom, green curry, mixed veg stir-fry, steamed rice, sweet and sour, salad. House wine £9.80 for a bottle, £2.20 for a glass. No smoking. Visa, MC, Amex. Reduction for students.

Cambridge shops

Al Amin

Oriental grocery shop

Mill Road, Cambridge

Wide selection of Asian foods including fresh tofu, spring roll skins, red bean dumplings, mock duck and lots more.

Arjuna Wholefoods

Vegetarian co-operative shop

12 Mill Road, Cambridge
Tel: 01223–364 845

Good range of things for lunch.

Daily Bread Co-op

Vegetarian wholefood shop

Unit 3, Kilmaine Close, King's Hedges
Cambridge CB4 2PH
Tel: 01223–423 177
Open: Tue–Fri 9–17.30, Sat 9–16.00

GNC

Health food shop

Unit 6, Lion Yard Centre, Cambridge CB2 3ET
Tel: 01223–315603

Nasreen Dar

Indian food shop

20 Histon Road, Cambridge
Tel: 01223–568 013
Open: Mon–Sat 8–20.00 Sun 8–17.00

Excellent shop selling nearly everything including lots of bags of pulses and fresh vegetable samosas, potato patties, battered aubergines and a fantastic range of frozen curries etc.

Organic Health

Organic health food shop

87 Church Road, Hauxton CB2 5HS
Tel: 01223-870 101
www.organichealth.biz
Open:Tues-Sat 9-17.00, Thu til 18.30

Offers dairy-free, wheat-free, gluten-free, yeast-free foods that are fair trade and/or biodynamic.

Holland & Barrett

Health food shop

4 Bradwells Court, Cambridge CB1 1NH
Tel: 01223-368914

Unit 7 Shopping Mall, Grafton Centre, Cambridge CB1 1PS
Tel: 01223-314544

1 Coronation Parade, High Street, Ely, Cambs CB7 4LB
Tel: 01353-662330

Unit G, Saint Benedicts, Huntingdon, Cambs PE18 6PN
Tel: 01480-417203

33 Long Causeway, Peterborough PE1 1YJ
Tel: 01733-311268

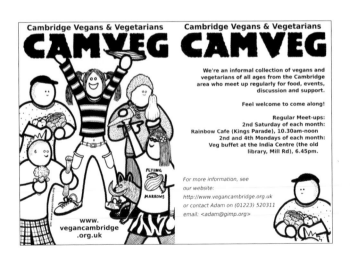

The UK's answer to New Jersey, Essex is next to London and near to "Veggie Capital of Europe" Brighton. If we can survive famous Essex girl/man jokes we can survive anything!

Lively clubs, reasonably priced theatres, new cinemas, country walks, seaside towns, good shops, shopping malls, some decent eateries and like minded people – what more could you want?

by Karin Ridgers. Viva! Essex

For the latest on what's on in Essex see www.thisisessex.co.uk

Essex

Billericay

Nature's Table

Health food shop

Unit 8, The Walk, 128 High Street, Billericay
Tel: 01277–655 444
Open: Mon–Sat 9–17.00

Brentwood

Pizza Express

Omnivorous pizza restaurant

5 High Street, Brentwood CM14 4RG
Tel: 01277–233 569
Open: Mon–Sun 12.00–23.00

Pizza chain that can make vegan pizzas. You ask them to leave off the cheese and they can manage to do this. They also do salads. Vegetarian options include margharita, giardinera, mushroom and Veneziana.

Chelmsford

Cosmopolitan

Omnivorous restaurant & patisserie

8–10 Broomsfield Road
Chelmsford CM1 1SN
Tel: 01245–493 929
www.cosmopolitan.quickonthenet.com
Open: Mon–Sat 18.30–22.00

Separate big vegetarian menu including vegan items. Starters £4–6.25 such as avocado and mango salad, grilled mushrooms. Mains £6.90–10.25 include bean polenta; Ragu di ceci, a rich sauce of chickpeas with tomato on pasta; Vegetali Delizia, sauté of potato, pepper and onion baked in Italian style. Organic produce used whenever possible. Licensed.

Pizza Express

Omnivorous pizza restaurant

219 Moulsham Street
Chelmsford CM2 0LR
Tel: 01245–491 466
Open: Mon–Sun 11.30–24.00

See Brentwood branch for details.

Centre of Natural Health

Health food shop

20 New London Road, Chelmsford CM2 0SW
Tel: 01245–350 881
Open: Mon–Sat 9.30–17.30

They sell fresh veggies, cereals, tinned beans, alternative milks, soya desserts, bottled juices and water, freshly made veggie meals and vegan chocolate.

Clacton–on–Sea

All Natural

Health food shop

27 Pier Avenue, Clacton–on–Sea
Tel: 01255–435 629
Open: Mon–Sat 8.45–17.00

Avalon Natural Health & Therapy Centre

Health food shop

6 St. John's Road, Great Clacton,
Clacton–on–Sea CO15 4BP
Tel: 01255–436 059
Open: Mon–Fri 9–17.00

Large range of dried herbs and supplements. Small range of teas and toothpaste. Homeopathic and Bach remedies.

Colchester

Chef Canton

Chinese restaurant & take-away

2A Crouch Street, Colchester
Tel: 01206-572 703
Open: every day 12-14.00, 17.30-23.00,
Fri-Sat till 23.30

Set vegetarian meal £12 each, minimum two people. Wine £2.70 glass, £9.50 bottle. Beer £2.80. Children welcome. Smoking. MC, Visa.

China Chef

Chinese restaurant & take-away

73 Crouch Street, Colchester
Tel: 01206-546 953
Open: every day 12-1.45 from 17.30 10.45,
11.15 Fri-Sat

Special set vegetarian dinner for two people £20.40 take-away, eat in £25. House wine £10.50 bottle, £2.80 glass. Children welcome. Flexible on smoking. MC, Visa.

Garden Café

Omnivorous cafe

74 High Street, Colchester CO1 1UE
Tel: 01206-500 169
Open: Mon-Sat 10.00-16.30, meals 12.00-15.00. Open Bank holidays except Xmas.

Café at the back of the Minories art gallery boasts a fair selection of vegan lunches and cakes. Two soups daily £4, vegan home made bread, and at least one of the main meals is vegan. Recommended by vegans and they are looking into introducing more vegan items such as soya milk smoothies in summer, vegan sandwiches and oat milk. Soya cappuccinos available.

The Lemon Tree

Omnivorous brasserie

48 St John's Street, Colchester
Tel: 01206-767 337
Open: lunchtime and evenings 12-21.30
Mon-Sat, closed Sun

Brasserie in centre of town, built into the old Roman city wall. Set lunch £8.95, dinner £10.95, such as soup followed by pasta or baked butternut squash and mushroom risotto, and they can always rustle up something vegan. House wine £11.95 bottle, £3.15 glass. Children's menu. No smoking inside. Terrace in good weather. MC, Visa, Amex.

Pizza Express

Omnivorous pizza restaurant

1 St Runwald's Street, Colchester
Tel: 01206-760 680
Open: Mon-Sun 11.30-24.00

See Brentwood branch for details.

Natural Foods

Health food shop

27 Sir Issacs Walk, Colchester CO1 1JJ
Tel: 01206-542 844
Open: Mon-Sat 9.30-17.30

Natural Bodycare & Giftshop

Health food shop

55 High Street Wivenhoe, Colchester CO7 9AZ
Tel: 01206-822 478
Open: Mon-Fri 9.30-17.30

Stocks mostly vitamins and minerals (including vegan varieties) and also snacks and drinks to take away. They also sell toiletries that haven't been tested on animals.

Devon Centre Tea Room

Vegetarian tea rooms

Arts & Crafts Centre, High Street
Dedham CO7 6AD
Open: every day 10.00–17.00, except 24–26
Dec. Closed Mondays Jan–March
Tel: 01206–322 677

Vegetarian tea rooms. Serve light lunches, £2.60–£6, but nothing vegan we've been told by a local. Tea 95p for a pot. Non smoking. No credit cards.

The Healthfood Centre

Health food shop

130 High Street, Epping
Tel: 01992–570 100
Open: Mon, Tue, Thu–Sat 9.30–17.30

The Shadhona

Omnivorous Indian restaurant

200 Main Road, Hawkwell, Hockley SS5 4EH
Tel: 01702–207 188
Open: every day 12.30–14.30, 18–23.00 inc. bank holidays

Around 6 veggie main dishes and 14 side dishes are vegetarian or vegan. House wine £10.95 bottle, glass £2.75.

Sunrise Health Foods

Health food shop

31 Spa Road, Hockley SS5 4AZ
Tel: 01702–207 017
Open: Mon–Sat 9–18.00

Large stock of chilled and frozen food for veggies and vegans and dairy–free cheese and yoghurt.

Suruchi

Vegetarian South Indian restaurant

506 High Road, Ilford IG1 1UE
Tel: 020–8598 2020
Open: every day except Tuesday 12–15.00 and 18–24.00, last order 23.00

Specialists in south Indian and Chinese vegetarian dishes in an Indian style. Many vegan items marked with 'V'. Value for money, good–sized portions, recommended by many vegans! Starters £3.50–4.00 and mains £5.00. New owner from May 2005 but it's likely to stay the same with possibly longer opening hours.

Pizza Express

Omnivorous pizza restaurant

410–412 Cranbook Road, Gants Hill, Ilford
Tel: 020–8554 3030
Open: Mon–Sun 12.00–23.00

See Brentwood branch for details.

Café Pulse

Vegetarian cafe

80 Leigh Road, Leigh-on-Sea SS9 1BZ
Tel: 01702–719 222
Open: Mon–Sat 9.00–16.00

Vegetarian world cuisine. They use locally grown produce with many organic ingredients and 95% of the food is made on the premises. Salads £3.50, starters from £3.20 such as soup of the day, vegan paté, hummous, served with warm pitta or rice cakes. Main meals (11am–4pm) £4.25–4.85 such as chilli bean wrap with couscous; lentil and red pepper flan with garlic mash plus carrot, peanut and banana salad. Can cater for special diets.

161

The Vitamin Service

Health food shop

8 Madeira Avenue, Leigh-on-Sea SS9 3EB
Tel: 01702-470 923/0800-652 7855
www.vitserve.com
Open: Mon-Fri 9-16.00

Postal service for food supplies.
Discounts on most products and free
delivery.

Pizza Express

Omnivorous pizza restaurant

281-283 High Road, Loughton IG10 1AH
Tel: 020-8508 3303
Open: Mon-Sun 11.00-23.30

See Brentwood branch for details.

GNC

Health food shop

16N Laurie Walk, Liberty Shopping Centre
Romford RM1 3RT
Tel: 01708-747 192
Open: Mon-Sat 9-18.00, Sun 11-16.00

Stocks vegetarian capsules, supplements, and snack bars.

Pizza Express

Omnivorous pizza restaurant

9-11 London Road, Southend-on-Sea
Tel: 01702-435 585
Open: Mon-Sun 11.30-23.30

See Brentwood branch for details.

Singapore Sling

Oriental restaurant

12 Clifton Parade, Southend-on-Sea
Tel: 01702-431 313
www.locallife.co.uk/singaporesling
Open: Tue-Sun 12-15.00, 18.00-late

Food from China, Japan, Thailand,
Singapore and Malaysia. Several vege-
tarian items on the menu and can cater
for vegans with green curry, Japanese
udon noodles and Thai crispy tofu.
Smoking permitted. Visa, MC.
They have another restaurant called
Fujiyama at 126 Hamlet Court Road,
Tel: 01702 331666.

Pizza Express

Omnivorous pizza restaurant

131-3 St Mary's Lane, Upminster RM14 2SH
Tel: 01708-224 111
Open: Mon-Sun 12.00-23.00

See Brentwood branch for details.

Health Lines

Health food shop

32 Corbets Tey Road, Upminster
Tel: 01708-220 495
Open: Mon-Sat 10-17.30, Wed -13.00

Abbey Health Foods

Health food shop

3 Sun Street, Waltham Abbey
Tel: 01992-650 014
Open: Mon-Wed, Fri-Sat 9-13.00, 14-17.00.
Closed Thu.

Owner is a qualified nutritional therapist
and happy to advise. Most products are
vegetarian. Chiller cabinet with oils,
drinks, superfoods etc.

Kia

Omnivorous global restaurant

264 London Road, Westcliff-on-Sea
Tel: 01702–342 424
Open: Wed–Sat 18–22.00 or later,
Fri–Sat –23.00, Sun 12.30–22.00,
closed Mon–Tue

Some vegetarian and vegan options, particularly on the tapas menu. Starters such as melon, pear and hazelnut salad with elderflower dressing £4. Main courses include baked aubergine stuffed with onions, tomatoes, peppers and garlic served with tabouleh £9.50. House wine £10.50 bottle, 2.95 glass. Children welcome, no high chair. No smoking areas. MC, Visa.

T. M. Health Shop

Health food shop

348 London Road, Westcliff-on-Sea
Tel: 01702–335 327
Open: Mon–Sat 9–17.00

VegSX

Vegan activism

www.veganessex.org
www.veggievision.co.uk
http://essex.veganfestival.org
veganessex@hotmail.com

World Vegan Day events, socials, school speakers training, demos, stalls, fun runs, helping the local animal sanctuary, making new friends, catering.

VegSX!

Several years ago I woke up!

I found vegetarianism! A revelation! I had to share this new found obvious answer to the world's problems and to start this, form a veggie group in Essex. Despite being in the local press, my novice attempts at Viva! Essex were dashed. Well kind of. I carried on campaigning on my own.

However now in Essex we have a strong group known as VegSX, Vegan Essex, Viva! Essex and Essex Animal Rights, and we are mainly vegan. We are networking with other veggie groups throughout Essex, such as Southend Veggies, Southend Animal Aid and St Francis Foundation. So veganism and vegetarianism are growing in our affluent county.

For more info please email veganessex@hotmail.com
www.veganessex.org
http://essex.veganfestival.org
veganessex@hotmail.com

Mail Order & Catering

Leon's Vegetarian Catering

Gourmet vegetarian catering

132b London Road, Brentwood CM14 4NS
Tel: 01277-218 661
leonsveg@aol.com. www.leonlewis.co.uk

Mouthwatering vegetarian and vegan catering, buffets, cookery demonstrations, any event nationwide. Amazing fungus forays in the woods in autumn and late spring followed by cooking the booty and quaffing from Leon's extensive wine cellar.

Minerva

Mail order chocolate

7A Eld Lane, Colchester CO1 1LS
Tel: 01206-560 338
www.MinervaChocolates.com
Amanda@MinervaChocolates.com
Business hours: Mon–Sat 10.00–17.30

Alll vegetarian with wonderful vegan selection and Easter eggs.

Spiralseed

Vegan books and permaculture

www.spiralseed.co.uk

Vegan, ethical initiative based in Essex. Earthright books, posters and T-shirts, forest gardening, permaculture design, consultancy and teaching. Books for young green vegans.

Platypus Creek

Omnivorous catering

44 Lower Holt Street, Earls Cone, Colchester
Tel: 01787-222 281

The Australian chef has been on a veggie/vegan cookery course.

164

Holland & Barrett

Holland & Barrett

Health food shop

49 East Street, Barking. Tel: 0208 591 8017

42 Eastgate Centre, Eastgate, Basildon
Tel: 01268-282 084.
Open: Mon–Sat 9–17.30

4–5 Exchange Way, Chelmsford
Tel: 01245-258 748
Open: Mon–Sat 9–17.30

11 Station Rd, Clacton–on–Sea
Tel: 01255 435551

8 Pelhams Lane, Colchester.
Tel: 01206-546 009
Open: Mon–Sat 9–17.30

5 Priory Walk, Colchester. Tel: 01206–369129

6 Grays Town Centre, Grays
Tel: 01375 387357

11 Broad Walk, Harlow. Tel: 01279 425543
Open: Mon–Sat 9–17.30

52 Cranbrook Rd, Ilford. Tel: 020–8553 2808

Unit 250, Lakeside Shop Ctr., Grays
Tel: 01708–869226

212 High Rd, Loughton. Tel: 0208–5321163

55 High Street, Rayleigh
Tel: 01268 779249

Unit 16, Laurie Walk, Romford
Tel: 01708–747 192

25 King St, Saffron Walden.
Tel: 01799 516736

185–7 High St, Southend Tel: 01702–338356

Veggie Vision

new internet TV station
cookery, celebs, info

TV presenter and businesswoman Karin Ridgers spent 18 months liaising with TV stations to get a healthy compassionate TV programme off the ground. Having been told she was "too ahead of her time", Karin decided to launch her own internet TV station and VeggieVision.com was born.

Poet Benjamin Zephaniah, No.B.E, and actor Jerome Flynn (Soldier Soldier) have already appeared in exclusive interviews about their lives and being vegetarian. "At the moment we have a small selection of mini programmes that people can click and watch – with many more coming soon. With more and more people going over to broadband, VeggieVision is quick, informative, fun and educational, with the benefit of worldwide 24/7," says Karin.

Vegans and veggies all over the UK and the world can send in a mini film about why they are veggie, what they cook, or film their local veggie restaurant which in return can donate some meals as competition prizes.

"It's really to promote the positive side of being veggie & vegan, and vegan products. It's a bit like my veg events – a positive party atmosphere – entertaining but educational at the same time."

VeggieVision.com has already received an amazing response with thousands of viewers from as far away as Australia, USA, Italy, Germany, Holland and Israel. In a few years we will all be watching programmes on demand, especially on the internet, and VeggieVision is proud to be "ahead of its time".

The VeggieVision team are all professional cameramen, editors and presenters, from private production companies and Sky TV, who share Karin's passion to promote non-animal eating.

www.veggievision.co.uk
www.mad-promotions.com
www.karinridgers.tv

Hertfordshire

The Violin B & B

Grovehill

A pure vegetarian, homestyle B&B based in Hemel Hempstead. Run by Sarah and David who offer vegetarian accommodation for £25 per person per night, £30 for single occupancy. Prices include continental breakfast. Discounted rate if staying 7+ nights.

They will cook a 3 course evening meal if booked in advance for £10 per person. Food is organic where possible.

Toiletries contain no animal products and are cruelty-free.

Broadband wireless internet available.

10 miles from Luton Airport and 22 miles from Heathrow. They can collect or deliver you to either airport. £15 for Luton, £25 for Heathrow, any time of day/night.

Vegetarian bed and breakfast

24 The Dee
Grovehill
Hemel Hempstead
Herts HP2 6EN

Tel: 01442-388 977

www.theviolinbnb.co.uk
contact@theviolinbnb.co.uk

Trainstation: Hemel Hempstead, 3 miles

Open: all year

Directions: From M1/M25 Leave the M25 at Junction 21 for the M1 North. Leave the M1 at Junction 8 for Hemel Hempstead (A4147). As you come off the Motorway, go over the first roundabout. At second roundabout, turn right into Maylands Avenue (this is an industrial area, lots of offices etc). Stay on Maylands Avenue all the way to the end, where you get to another roundabout, turn left, up the slope for about 300 meters, where there is another roundabout – turn right (this is called Redbourn Rd). Follow road past 'Sky Ford' and you get to a roundabout (nearly there!) Go straight over, into the Grovehill estate, go over two mini-roundabouts, you will pass a school on the left-hand side, and take the first left into The Dee. We are just up on the right hand side, No.24.

King William IV

Omnivorous pub with Olde Worlde restaurant and quiet alcoves around the pub for a business lunch or something more romantic. Big vegetarian menu that you can view on their website.

Starters such as soup £4.25, roast Mediterranean veg £5.95, roast parsnip salad £5.95.

10 main dishes, a couple of them vegan, £9.95–10.65, such as mushrooms in ale, risotto, enchiladas, ravioli, nut curry, shepherd's pie, 3–bean casserole.

Desserts such as fresh strawberries £5.95, apple crumble £5.45.

Lunchtime there's the same menu plus panini from £5.45, jacket potatoes from £4.95, wraps from £4.95.

Reserve evenings, and lunchtime if you want a good table.

Heydon

Omnivorous country pub and restaurant

Chishill Road
Heydon
Cambridgeshire SG8

(technically in Cambridgeshire, for practical purposes it's Royston, Hertfordshire)

Directions: on the main road through Heydon, 17 miles from Cambridge off A505

Tel: 01763-838 773
Fax: 01763-837 179

www.kingwilliv.freeuk.com
kingwilliv@freeuk.com

Open: pub hours
Lunch:
12-14.30, Sat 12-15.00
Dinner:
Mon-Fri 18.30-21.30/22.00
Sat from 18.00
Sun from 19.00

Car park

Well behaved children welcome, but not small ones Sat, or Fri if busy. No high chairs.

Some smoking areas, restaurant is no smoking

10 tables outside

MC, Visa

Bella Italia

Omnivorous Italian restaurant

21 – 23 Chequer Street, St Albans
Tel: 01727–844 264
Open: Mon–Thu 11–22.00,
Fri–Sat 12–23.00, Sun 12–22.00

Lots of veggie options and they have a
list of all the dishes suitable for vegans
if you ask. The pizza bases are vegan,
so is the bruschetta starter and there are
a couple of vegan pasta dishes.

Pizza Express

Omnivorous pizza chain

11/13 Verulam Road, St Albans AR3 4DA
Tel: 01727–853 020
www.pizzaexpress.co.uk
Open: every day 12–23.30

They can make vegan pizzas if you ask
them to leave off the cheese. They also
do salads. Vegetarian options include
margharita, giardinera, mushroom and
Veneziana.

The Pasta Bowl

Omnivorous Italian restaurant

5a High Street, St Albans
Tel: 01727–812 683
Open: Mon–Thu 12–15.00, 18.00–23.00;
Fri –23.30; Sat 12–23.30; Sun 17.00–22.00

Lots of veggie options. Pizza bases and
garlic bread are vegan, and where
possible will adapt dishes to make them
vegan.

Bar Meze

Omnivorous Mediterranean tapas bar

8 Adelaide Street, St Albans
Open: Tue–Sat 11.30–14.00, Sun 11–14.00,
closed Mon lunchtime. Every day 18–22.00
Tel: 01727–847 799

Plenty for veggies. Children welcome,
high chairs. House wine £11.50 bottle,
glass £3. Partly smoking. MC, Visa.

Wagamama

Omnivorous Japanese restaurant

Unit 6, Christopher Place, St Albans AL3 5DQ
Tel: 01727–865 122
www.wagamama.com
Open: Mon–Sat 12.00–23.00 Sun –22.00

See Manchester entry for menu.

Zizzi

Omnivorous Italian restaurant

20 High Street, St Albans
Tel: 01727–850 200
Open: Mon–Sat 12–23.30, Sun –23.00

Owned by ASK chain. Pizza bases are
vegan and can be made without cheese.
House wine £11.95 bottle. Children
welcome, high chairs. Smoking and no
smoking. MC, Visa.

Down to Earth

Vegetarian cafe

7 Amwell End, Ware SG12 9HP
Tel: 01920–463358
Open: Mon–Sat 9–17.00, closed Sun

In a tudor building. Large variety of
mains £3.95, many vegan or gluten
free, such as moussaka, mushroom
pasta bake, pizza (can be vegan with
Cheezley), cottage pie, risotto, chili,
roasted veg, ratatouille, curry. Soup
£2.50. Large sandwich list, toasties,
jacket spuds. Wide variety of cakes 75p,
some vegan or gluten free. Fruit salad in
summer, sometimes a crumble. No
smoking. Children welcome but beware
steep stairs, two high chairs. No cards.
Unlicensed but BYO, offie opposite.

EAST

Hertfordshire

Watford

Edwins @ 143 The Parade

Omnivorous Italian restaurant

143 The Parade, High Street, Watford
Tel: 01923–211 283
Open: Mon–Fri 12–15.00, 18–23.00,
Sat 12–23.00, Sun 12–17.00

Lots of veggie options. Pizza bases and garlic bread are vegan. They are very accommodating and where possible will adapt dishes to make them vegan.

ASK Restaurant

Omnivorous pizza & pasta restaurant

Market Street, Watford
Tel: 01923–213 111
Open: Mon–Sat 12–23.30, Sun 12–22.30

They've told us the pizza bases are vegan, can be without cheese. House wine £11.95 bottle, £3.25–4.20 glass. Smoking at the back. Children welcome, high chairs. MC, Visa.

Pizza Express

Omnivorous pizza restaurant

137 High Street, Watford
Tel: 01923–213 991
Open: Mon–Sun 11.30–24.00

In a 1614 building next to the Harlequin Centre in the centre of town. Vegan no problem.

Cafe Mezza Lebanese Restaurant

Omnivorous Lebanese restaurant

144 Lower High Street, Watford
Tel: 01923–211 500
Open: Sun–Thu 12–22.00, Fri–Sat 12–22.30

Lots of veggie and vegan meze dishes, including falafel, hummous, baba ganoush, kibbe potatoes. Two hot pitta-style take-away sandwiches: Al Bustan £2.80 with char-grilled vegetables and baba ganoush, and falafel. Licensed. Children welcome, high chairs. MC, Visa.

Ambala Foods

Indian sweet shop

96 Queens Avenue, Watford WD18 7NS
Tel: 01923–817 560
Open: every day 11–23.00

Plenty of sweets and savouries for vegetarians, only samosas for vegans.

Holland & Barrett

Health food shop

115 High St, Barnet EN5 5Uz
Tel: 0208–449 5654

12a South St, Bishops Stortford CM23 3AT
Tel: 01279–651 637

Unit 187c The Marlowes Centre,
Hemel Hempstead HP1 1BB
Tel: 01442–211 356

25/27 Birchley Green, Hertford SG14 1BN
Tel: 01992–504 751

99 Hermitage Road, Hitchin SG5 1DG
Tel: 01462–451 643

6 Angel Pavement, Royston SG8 9AS
Tel: 01763–249 468

61 St Peters St, St Albans AL1 3EA
Tel: 01727–845 333

Unit 44 Queensway, Stevenage SG1 1EE
Tel: 0438–727 749

105 High Street, Watford WD17 2DQ
Tel: 01923–221 602

54 Howards Gate,
Welwyn Garden City AL8 6BP
Tel: 01707–376 285

Leicester is a great place for vegetarians to live and visit, as it has a huge range of veggie eateries, possibly due to the large populations of Hindus, Jains and students who live here.

Leicester city centre has a lot of character, with more small shops than chain stores, and lots of lovely old buildings, though it certainly isn't quaint. It is a small city, yet has good facilities, including a huge library, friendly pubs and possibly the largest outdoor market in Britain, where you can buy very cheap fruit and veg, textiles and clothes. There are several large parks on the edges of the city centre, and you can walk by the canal which runs from North to South through the middle of the city.

There is a strong green movement in Leicester, and cycling paths are better than average, though air pollution can be a big problem in hot weather. The city also seems to have a strong spiritual feel.

Leicestershire

Mirch Masala

Family oriented Indian vegetarian restaurant with Mexican, Italian and South Indian menus and several pizzas.

Vegetarian Indian restaurant

South Indian starters from £2.50–£3.50, such as kachoris – spiced crushed lentil balls covered in deep fried pastry, and pani puri – crispy puri filled with potatoes and chickpeas served with tamarind chutney and coriander mix.

Unit 19/20 Belgrave
Commercial Centre
Belgrave Road
Leicester
Leicestershire LE4 5AV

Tel: 0116–261 0888

Main dishes include favourites like masala dosa, £4.25–5.75; idli sambhar – flat rice and lentil flour cakes served with coconut chutney and sambhar (lentil soup); and mixed vegetable curry.

Open:
Mon–Sun from 11am–22.30

Small children's menu
High chairs

6 Italian menu mains with Mirch Masala special spaghetti £4.50.

Non smoking inside but small outside seating area where it is permitted.

Large Mexican menu with various starters including nachos £3.25, and burritos, tacos, enchiladas, £4.50–£5.75 as mains.

Visa, MC

They also have wraps for £3.95 with fillings ranging from herb and garlic to Mexican rice or chilli.

The snack menu includes jacket potatoes from £1.20, corn on the cob £1.20, vegetable burgers £1.80, with chips £2.50, chips £1.10, and toasted sandwiches £2.25. Pizzas eat in £10.95–£16.95, for take-away buy one get one free, .

Not licensed. Fresh juice bar with smoothies.

Ambica Sweetmart

Vegetarian Indian restaurant

147 Belgrave Road, Leicester, LE4 6AS
Tel: 0116-266 2451
Open: Wed-Sun 12-20.00 except Tue

Eat well for a fiver with food from all over India. Indian desserts all contain dairy. House wine £1.25 glass, £1.25. Children welcome, high chairs. Smoking section. MC, Visa.

Bobby's

Vegetarian Indian restaurant

154 Belgrave Road, Leicester, LE4 5AT
Tel: 0116-266 0106
Open: every day 11-22.00 (Sat from 10am)

Indian vegetarian restaurant with some vegan curries, chapattis and snacks.

Chaat House

Vegetarian Indian restaurant

108 Belgrave Road, Leicester
Tel: 0116-2660 513
Open: Wed-Mon 12.00-20.30, close Tue

Indian vegetarian restaurant. There is no such thing as bad Indian food in Leicester which has curry houses everywhere. However there is such a thing as outstanding Indian food which you'll find here being munched by the local vegetarian Buddhists, Hindus, Sikhs and vegan Jains. Mains from £8. Non smoking. Visa, MC.

Good Earth Restaurant

Vegetarian restaurant

19 Free Lane, Leicester
Tel: 0116-262 6260
good.earth-restaurant@virgin.net
Open: Mon-Fri 10-15.00, Sat 10-16.00

Vegetarian buffet style restaurant which always has something vegan. Salads £2.75-3.60. Mains £3.60-4.75 such as beany casserole with roasted veg. Desserts and puddings 75p-£2 include vegan date or apricot slice. Glass of wine £2, beer £2. Children welcome, high chair. Separate smoking section. No credit cards.

Indigo

Vegetarian Indo-Chinese restaurant

Indigo at the Fosseway, 432 Melton Road
Leicester, LE4 7SN
Tel: 0116-261 1000
Open: Mon-Sat 12-14.30, 18.00-22.30;
Sat 12-22.30m Sun 12-21.00

Popular Indo-Chinese vegetarian restaurant with a fairly extensive menu of South Indian and Indo-Chinese dishes £3-6.50. Weekday lunch buffet £5.50. House wine £8.50 bottle, £1.95 glass. Children welcome, high chairs. No smoking. MC, Visa.

Jalsa

Indian Gujarati vegetarian restaurant

87 Belgrave Rd, Leicester, LE4 6AS
Tel: 0116–266 6186
Open: Mon, Wed–Fri 18–22.00, closed Tue,
Sat–Sun 14–23.00

Gujarati and some East African dishes.
Starters £1.50–4.75 such as mixed
samosa, Tandoori Moghul sizzler
(cassava and yam). Main dishes £4–7.95
such as kari bhindi or baingan barta
(grilled aubergines with parathas and
onion salad). Desserts (none vegan yet
but they're looking into vegan ice-
cream). House wine £1.95 glass,
£10.50 bottle. No smoking. Children
welcome, 2 high chairs. MC, Visa.

Pizza Pride

Vegetarian fast food take–away

21 Melton Road, Leicester
Tel: 0116–2669 522
Open: Tue–Thu 11–15.00, 16.15–21.00, Fri
11–15.00, 16.15–22.00, Sat 12–15.00,
16.15–22.00, Sun 16.00–22.00

Vegetarian pizza take–away and
delivery which also does burgers, chips
and jacket potatoes, from £1. Pizza
bases are vegan and they can make
them without cheese. Pizzas start at
£3.49 for an 8 inch pizza, £1.50 when
they run special offers. No credit cards.

Sardaar

Vegetarian Indian restaurant

30 Narborough Road, Leicester, LE4 5AT
Tel: 0116–299 3300
Open: every day except Christmas 10–22.00

North Indian Punjabi near MFI on the
south–west side of town. Great value

dishes £2.30–3.50, 70% vegan.
Samosas 30p. Desserts including non-
dairy. Take–away too. Children
welcome, high chairs. Toilets not
disabled accessible but they are about
to fix that. No smoking.

Sayonara Thali

Vegetarian Indian restaurant

49 Belgrave Road, Leicester
Tel: 0116–266 5888
Open: All week 12.00–21.30, Sat till 22.00

North and South Indian dishes and
thalis and take–away. Choice of 50
starters from £2.25, all the usual mains
from £7 and always vegan options.
Separate smoking section. Children
weolcome, high chairs. Visa, MC.

Sharmilee Restaurant

Vegetarian Indian restaurant

71–73 Belgrave Road, Leicester LE4 6AS
Tel: 0116–2610 503
Open: Tue–Fri 12–14.30, 18.00–21.00,
Sat 12–21.30, Sun 12–21.00

North, South and Gujarati, average £10
for a meal. Vegan desserts are on the
way. House wine £8.95 bottle, £2.50
glass. Children welcome, high chairs.
Smoking not encouraged. MC, Visa.

Sonal's Bhajiya House

Vegetarian Gujarati Indian restaurant

122 Narborough Road, Leicester LE3 0BT
Tel: 0116–2470 441
Open: Mon & Wed–Fri 16.00–21.30; closed
Tue; Sat 07.30–21.30 Sun 10–21.30

Full meal for £5.95 or £7.95. House
wine from £4.95 bottle, £1.25 glass.
Children welcome, no high chairs. Cash
or cheque only. Smoking and non-
smoking.

Oriental Chinese

Omnivorous Chinese restaurant

70 High Street, Leicester
Tel: 0116-2532 448
Open: every day 11.30–16.00, 17.00–23.30

Lots of vegetarian dishes such as stir-fried veg, crispy veg with chili and garlic, monk's veg and bean curd, around £5. £4.20 buffet, evening £6.99, weekend evening £7.99. House wine £10 a bottle, £2.45 glass. Children welcome, 2 high chairs. Smoking and non-smoking sections. MC, Visa.

Currant Affairs

Vegetarian wholefood shop

9A Loseby Lane,, Leicester, LE1 5DR
Tel 0116-251 0887

Friendly knowledgeable staff. Excellent vegan take-away food, including 4 or 5 filled rolls, pies, pasties, vegan and vegetarian pizza, and they also do soup in winter. Vegan "cheese", organic cheese and milk, Redwoods sausages, bacon, etc. Also sell toiletries, and vitamins and supplements. Small selection of freshly baked breads normally available on the counter. 10% discount for Vegetarian or Vegan Society members.

Leicester Wholefood Co-operative

Organic co-operative

Unit 3, Freehold Street , off Dysart Way , Leicester, LE1 2LX
Tel: 0116-251 2525

Warehouse-style organic and wholefood shop. All vegan items are labelled as such on the shelves. Soya milk and yogurt, and deli items such as hummous, olives, etc.

GNC

Health food shop

18 Silver Street, Leicester LE1 5ET
Tel: 0116-262 4859

Wide range of veg-friendly items (though supplements may not be vegetarian). All takeaway food vegetarian, approximately 50% vegan. Chilled cabinet with samosas, pasties and sweet items. Taifun tofu sausages, Sojasun soya yoghurt, Vegemince, as well as frozen ready meals and desserts. 10% discount on production of Vegetarian or Vegan Society membership card.

Holland & Barrett

Health food shop

48 Castle Street, Hinckley, Leics LE10 1DB
Tel: 01455-251258

5-6 Humberston Mall, Haymarket Centre
Leicester LE1 3YB
Tel: 0116-251 6270

33 The Horsefair Street, Leicester LE1 3BP
Tel: 0116-262 1547

11 Manor Walk, Market Harborough
Leicestershire LE16 9BX
Tel: 01858-431 250

VEGAN
PASSPORT

2nd edition July 2005

now with even more languages

edited by George Rodger of the Vegan Society

We've all been in a foreign restaurant and explained to the waiter in basic English what we want, only for the cook to serve up soup with a bone at the bottom or salad with tuna. Not any more! This passport sized book contains a page for each of 56 languages covering over 93% of the world's population, saying what vegans do and don't eat in great detail.

Let the waiter show it to the cook and you'll be sure of a totally animal free feast even if no one speaks a word of your language. Includes Afrikaans, Albanian, Arabic, Basque, Bengali, Bulgarian, Catalan, Chinese, Croatian, Czech, Danish, Dutch, English, Esperanto, Finnish, French, Goan, Greek, Hebrew, Hindi, Hungarian, Indonesian, Italian, Japanese, Kannada, Korean, Malagasay, Malay, Maltese, Marathi, Mongolian, Nepali, Norwegian, Persian, Polish, Portuguese, Romanian, Russian, Serbian, Shona, Sinhalese, Slovak, Somali, Spanish, Swahili, Swedish, Tagalog, Tamil, Thai, Turkish, Ukrainian, Urdu, Vietnamese, Yoruba. Plus a page of pictures of what we do and don't eat if all else fails.

£3.99 + postage from Vegetarian Guides
Order at www.vegetarianguides.co.uk

For restaurants all over the world, visit /links

VEGETARIAN LONDON

edited by Alex Bourke

100 vegetarian restaurants across the capital
Detailed reviews with sample dishes and vegan offerings
50 ethnic restaurants with big veggie menus
150 wholefood and health food shops
12 indexes: including cheap eats, posh, vegan, kids
Lots of maps

"More important than the A–Z." The Vegetarian Society

ISBN 1-902259-05-X (2005), 1-902259-08-4 (2006)
280 pages, pocket size, £6.95

Buy in London at Waterstones, Foyles, Books Etc, Borders,
Planet Organic, Fresh & Wild, Bumblebee, Red Veg

Mail order worldwide at www.vegetarianguides.co.uk

UK and worldwide bookhops order from Portfolio, Gardners
UK health food stores order from KHS
US/Canada bookstores from Casemate

Norfolk

Greenbanks Hotel

Hotel and restaurant with vegetarian proprietors in the heart of the Norfolk countryside. There are nine luxury ensuite rooms consisting of doubles and twins for £35–60 per person per room per night and family rooms for £100 per room per night.

Begin your day with cereal and juice followed by a cooked breakfast of herbed potato pancakes, beans, spiced tomatoes, home made veggie sausages and muffins or nut scones. Soya milk, soya yoghurt and vegan margarine are available. Veggie and vegan specialities are available on request.

A three course dinner is offered in their licensed Alexanders restaurant for £23. It could be miniature vegetable spring rolls followed by ginger roasted root vegetables with stuffed peppers and for dessert, apple cake and coconut custard. 50% of the produce is organic. Open to non-residents. Special diets catered for.

Greenbanks is set in eight acres of meadows and has a bog garden, wild flower walk and lakes. They also have a heated indoor hydrotherapy pool.

The coast and beaches are nearby as well as Peddars Way walk and Thetford Forest where you can walk or cycle.

Not far away is the thriving city of Norwich with its huge churches, interesting castle and museums. It has the best night life in the region behind Cambridge.

Tea and coffee making facilities and televisions are in the rooms.

Wendling

Omnivorous hotel & restaurant

Swaffham Road
Wendling
Norfolk NR19 2AB
England

Tel: 01362–687 742

Fax: 01362–687 760

www.greenbankshotel.co.uk

Email: jenny@greenbankshotel.co.uk

Train station: Norwich, 20 miles, then bus

Open: all year

Directions: Midway between Swaffham and East Dereham on A47, turn off at sign saying Wendling/Longham

Parking: 20 spaces

Children are welcome and they have facilities such as high chairs

Pets by arrangement

Disabled access: 5 ground floor rooms and full access to showers

Credit cards accepted

No smoking throughout

Please state that you are veggie on arrival or when booking

Castle Acre

Old Red Lion

Wholefood vegetarian bed and breakfast/hostel

Bailey Street, Castle Acre, PE32 2AG
Tel: 01760–755 557
Train Station: Downham Market, 12 miles
Bus route: National Express from Victoria to Swaffam daily
www.oldredlion.here2stay.org.uk

Two doubles (one ensuite), two twins, one dorm room and one family room £15–£25 per person per night. Evening meal by arrangement. Can use the kitchen to cook your own meals if desired.
Dogs and children by arrangement. No smoking throughout.

Diss

Les Amandines

Vegetarian restaurant

Norfolk House Yard, St Nicholas Street, Diss IP22 4LB
Tel: 01379–640 449
Open: Tue–Sat 10–16.00

Vegetarian and vegan café–restaurant established 17 years ago, in the centre of the town, a stone's throw from the old church and market place. They serve breakfasts, teas, cakes and lunches.

Natural Food Store

Vegetarian health food shop

Tel: 01379–651 832
Open: Mon–Fri 9–17.30, Sat 9–17.00

Adjacent to Les Amandines. They sell organic bread, scones, pasties, cakes, savouries, deli stuff like wrapped vine leaves, and vegan cheeses. The chiller has homemade hummous, pate, etc.

Norwich

The Tree House

Vegetarian restaurant & take–away

14–16 Dove Street, Norwich NR2 4DE
Tel: 01603–763 258
Open: Mon–Wed 10–17.00, Thu–Sat 10–21.00

Vegetarian wholefood café–restaurant with mostly organic and vegan food. Starters from £2.70 such as lentil and miso soup and mains start at £5.50 and change daily. Normally all desserts are vegan, including tofu cheesecake £2.40, and they always have vegan ice cream. Non smoking. No credit cards. 10% student discount.

Butlers

Vegetarian take–away

98 Vauxhall Street, Norwich NR2 2SD
Tel: 01603–665 066
Open: Mon–Fri 07–17.00, Sat 07–15.00

Take–away only (no seats) from £1.50 per portion such as pasta or lentil and aubergine bake. Salads and veg by the kilo, around £3 for 500g. Slab cakes £3, some vegan or gluten free. Bottled and canned drinks.

Holland & Barrett

Health food shop

9/10 Victoria Arcade, Great Yarmouth
Tel: 01493–855 316

15 Norfolk Street, Kings Lynn
Tel: 01553–765 969

19/21 White Lion Street, Norwich
Tel: 01603–762 955

The Greenhouse

Organic and Fair Trade
vegetarian restaurant

The Greenhouse is both a café and an environmental centre which offers cheap food and a relaxed atmosphere, so mobile phones should be turned off at the door!

42–46 Bethel St
Norwich
Norfolk NR2 1NR

Soup of the day with bread, £3, salad bowls £3 and Ploughmans salad with the option of vegan cheese £5.25.

Tel: 01603-631 007

www.greenhousetrust.co.uk

A selection of other sandwiches is also available: mushroom pate, mixed salad, peanut butter, etc.

Open:
Tues–Sat 10.00–17.00,
closed Sun and Mon

They also have jacket potatoes with a range of fillings, plus hummous and pitta platters.

Licensed

There is a range of cakes, including vegan and gluten–free options.

High chairs

No smoking

Hot and cold cordials 90p. Organic teas, mug 90p, large pot £2.50. Organic, fair-trade coffees from 90p–£2.60. Soya milk and soya cappuccinos.

MC, Visa

Wines, beer and cider are available with meals. Wine around £2 a glass or £6–10 for a bottle.

A strong emphasis is placed on ethics, so fair-traded and organic ingredients are used where possible.

EAST

Norfolk

Northamptonshire

Balti King

Omnivorous Indian restaurant

73 Earl Street, Uppermounts, Northampton
Tel: 01604-637 747
Open: every day 11.30–14.00, 17–23.00

25 vegetarian dishes £3–5 such as mixed veg Balti £2.95. You can bring your own alcohol from the off license opposite. Located in the city centre. Half smoking. Children welcome, no high chairs. MC, Visa.

The Old Bank

Omnivorous pub

Opposite the Guildhall, Northampton centre
Tel: 01604-239 534
Food: Sun 12–20.00, Mon–Sat 11–20.00

Spacious pub with a good view of the Guildhall, one of the town's most interesting buildings, and a courtyard garden for the summer. A number of vegetarian dishes are served such as spicy beanburger (vegan) £3.45, nachos, jacket potatoes.

The Penny Whistle

Omnivorous pub

31–33 Abington Square, Northampton
NN1 4AE
Tel: 01604-824 471
Open: Mon–Thu 12–23.00,
Fri– Sat 12–24.00, Sun 12–22.30

Student-filled pub serving food in the daytimes, 12.00–20.00, with six vegetarian options such as smokey bean-burgers, salads, veggie sausage and mash, average £4.50. Popular, filling and cheap.

Daily Bread Co-op

Vegetarian wholefood shop

The Old Laundry, Bedford Road,
Northampton NN4 7AD
(on the town side of the Bedford Road round-about near the Council office)
Tel: 01604-621 531
www.dailybread.co.uk
northampton@dailybread.co.uk
Open: Mon–Fri 8.30–17.30, Sat –17.00

Wholefood co-operative with non-food fairly traded products too, and the best place in Northampton for vegetarian/vegan food. They sell vegan ice cream. There is another branch in Cambridge.

Pooja

Vegetarian Indian restaurant

33 Alma Street, Wellingborough NN8 4DH
Tel: 01933-278 800
Open: Tue–Sun 18–23.00

Punjabi, Gujarati and South Indian food for £3.50–4.75 per dish. £10–12 for a meal. House wine £9.50 bottle, £2.50 glass. Children welcome, high chair. No smoking. MC, Visa.

Holland & Barrett

Health food shop

8 Mercer Row, Northampton NN1 2QL
Tel: 01604-639 603

43 Queens Square, Corby NN17 1PD
Tel: 01536-408 914

34 High Street, Kettering NN16 8SU
Tel: 01536-417 209

33 Long Causeway, Peterborough PE1 1YJ
Tel: 01733-311 268

Suffolk

Western House

Vegetarian bed and breakfast

High Street, Cavendish CO10 8AR
Tel: 01787–280 550
Train station: Sudbury, 7 miles
Open: all year

One single, one double and two twins at £17–£18 per person. Vegans catered for with prior notice. Children aged 2 onwards welcome. No pets. No smoking throughout. There is a small wholefood shop on the premises, open Mon–Sat 9–13.00.

Kwan Thai

Omnivorous Thai restaurant

14 St. Nicholas Street, Ipswich
Tel: 01473–253 106
Open: every day 12–14.00,
18–23.00 (Sat till 23.30)

Thai restaurant with several vegetarian dishes. Set menu from £16.25 per person includes sweet and sour panang, stir fried mushrooms and sweetcorn, phad thai and steamed rice. A la carte veggie dishes £3.15–£5.50 including phad puk nam mun hoy – fried mixed vegetables in soya sauce; and gairng keow wahn – bean curd, mushrooms and bamboo shoots cooked with coconut milk and fresh Thai herbs. There is a smoking section. Children welcome, high chair. House wine £2.95 glass, £10.95 bottle. MC, Visa, Amex. Take–away 10% off.

The Linden Tree

Omnivorous English restaurant

7 Out Norgate, Bury St. Edmunds
Tel: 01284–754 600
Open: Mon–Thu 12–14.00, 18–21.30;
Fri –Sat 12–21.30 all day,
Sun 12–15.00, 17.30–21.30

There are at least 5 vegetarian mains daily and 1 veggie special £7.99. They always have something vegan or can fix it for you. House wine is £10.99 per bottle, £3.25 for a glass. Separate smoking section. Visa, MC. Fri–Sat afternoon 14.30–18.00 light menu. Children welcome, high chairs.

Holland & Barrett

Health food shop

6 Brentgrovel Street, Bury St. Edmonds
Tel: 01284–706 677

91 Hamilton Road, Felixstowe
Tel: 01394–671 796

7 The Butter Market, Ipswich
Tel: 01473–219 153

27 Westgate Street, Ipswich
Tel: 01473–233 477

17 The Britton Centre, Lowestoft
Tel: 01502–500 832

Unit 7, The Rookery Centre, Newmarket
Tel: 01638 561511

8/10 Market Place, Stowmarket
Tel: 01449–676 046

LONDON

London Accommodation

Central London Restaurants

Outer London Restaurants

This chapter includes a selection of key places from our 280 page book Vegetarian London (see page 201)

We start with veggie-friendly accommodation (page 190) from camping to five star hotel. This is all you need before coming to London.

Next we list places to dine and shop in the main tourist centres around the centre of London:
Camden and Primrose Hill, The City, Covent Garden, Noho (north of Oxford Street: Bloomsbury, Euston, Marylebone, Tottenham Court Road) and finally Soho (the West End).

Soho – the central area to the south of Oxford Street – is where visitors normally spend the majority of time. Here there are a hundred cinemas and theatres, shops galore, cafes and sightseeing. Our munchie map of Soho enables you to locate the closest place in seconds. Some of the most popular and good value veggie eateries include the all-you-can-eat buffets for £6 at Tai in Greek Street, and £5.95 at Govinda's off Soho Square. Don't miss the fab falafel bar Maoz at 43 Old Compton Street, where you can fill up for only £3, and Red Veg at the north end of Dean Street now also does several kinds of falafels. For an international veggie restaurant in the evening try Mildreds (party atmosphere, good wine list). Mantra is a great new Indian restaurant and VitaOrganic has opened a branch nearby..

We also supply a map for Covent Garden, a hot spot for tourists and vegetarian locals alike. The area around Neal's Yard, Long Acre and Neal Street is jam-packed with unique and amazing shops and all sorts of designer gear. Indulge in international delicacies at World Food Cafe, or enjoy a light meal at Neal's Yard Salad Bar. If you're after a fast lunch, pop around the corner to the basement cafe, Food for Thought.

Finally we list a selection of terrific restaurants outside the centre in the Rest of London (page 221), including East, North, South and West London.

If you've come to Wembley for a conference, concert or match, check out the many places to eat in the Middlesex chapter (page 324).

For comprehensive reviews of 100 vegetarian restaurants and 150 wholefood stores throughout London, pick up a copy of our pocket-size Vegetarian London guide (page 201) at London bookshops such as Waterstones, Books Etc, Borders (soya cappuccino in the cafe), Foyles (cafe with soya cappuccino and vegan cake), food stores such as Planet Organic, Fresh & Wild; or order at any UK, US or Canadian bookshop; or buy online at: www.vegetarianguides.co.uk

Accommodation

Mount View

Smart Victorian house with garden in a quieter area of North London, combining tranquility and the gentle pace of village life but within easy reach of central London. A quiet haven after a busy day sightseeing. Rooms decorated using natural materials.

Double en suite with sofa in bay window and antique furniture £35 per person. Double £25 per person. Twin with shower £27.50. Single £40–45. 10% discount for 7+ nights.

Vegetarian breakfast available. Vegan and other diets on request.

No evening meal, but Haelan Centre health food store is nearby and Jai Krishna vegetarian restaurant. There are plenty more vegetarian restaurant on the Victoria and Piccadilly underground lines which go right through central London.

15 minutes walking from Finsbury Park tube and rail station, luggage can be collected when you arrive.

Near Highgate cemetery, Hampstead Heath with Kenwood House, Alexandra Palace.

All rooms with tv, hairdryer, washbasin, tea and coffee making facilities. Washing machine and dryer and internet access available on request. Payphone.

AA 5 diamonds.

Finsbury Park

Vegetarian friendly Guest house

31 Mount View Road
London N4 4SS

Tel: 020 8340 9222
Fax: 020 8342 8494

Tube: Finsbury Park
15 minutes walk.
They will collect you and your luggage on arrival.

Open: All year round

www.
mountviewguesthouse
.com

Email:
MountViewBB@aol.com

Unrestricted parking in street.

No smoking throughout.

No pets.

Children welcome but no high chair.

Dutch and French spoken.

MC, Visa

Dora Rothner

Vegetarian bed and breakfast in a friendly home twenty minutes by tube from central London.

There are three rooms: one single and two doubles (not twins) costing £20 per person per night. No single person supplement. Shared bathroom.

A light breakfast is served and includes fresh grapefruit, muesli, a selection of cereals, and toast with various jams. Soya milk, vegan margarine and vegan muesli are available.

Dinner is not offered but Rani Indian Vegetarian restaurant is just a few minutes away.

The bed and breakfast is close to shops, bus routes and the tube station. It is set in a well kept garden overlooking the park.

All rooms have televisions.

Finchley

Vegetarian
Bed and breakfast

23 The Ridgeway
Finchley
London N3 2PG
England

Tel: 020-8346 0246

Tube Station: Finchley Central (Northern Line), then an eight minute walk

Open: all year including Christmas

Directions: Close to Finchley Central tube (Northern line), the North Circular Road and the M1

Parking: available

Only children over 12

No pets

No smoking throughout

Stephanie Rothner B&B

Friendly B&B with a well kept garden on a quiet residential road. The single room is £18 per person per night, whilst sole occupancy of the double room is £22 or for two sharing £36 per night.

A light breakfast is served comprising of fresh grapefruit, fruit juice, cereals and toast with various preserves. Other types of fruit can be provided on request. Soya milk and vegan margarine are always available.

Whilst dinner is not offered there are plenty of shops and restaurants serving veggie food nearby. Rani Indian Vegetarian Restaurant is not far away in Finchley, N3.

Friary Park is only 10 minutes away from the house. At the end of Grove Road there are bus routes to central London and the tube station (Woodside Park – Northern Line) is only a fifteen minute walk away. Journey time on the tube to the centre is about thirty minutes.

One friendly resident cat.

Short stay guests welcome.

Televisions in the rooms.

Vegetarian
Bed and Breakfast

44 Grove Road
North Finchley
London N12 9DY
England

Tel: 020–8446 1604

Mobile: 07956 406446

Tube Station: Woodside Park (Northern Line), then a 15 minute walk, or Finchley bus terminal.

Open: all year

Directions: Close to the M1 and off the A406 North Circular Road. Follow signs to Finchley.

Parking: available nearby

No children

No pets

No smoking throughout

LONDON Accommodation

193

Hampstead Village Guest House

Veggie friendly hotel

Veggie friendly 1872 Victorian guest house in a peaceful setting close to the heath and tube. In the heart of lively Hampstead Village, a fun area with art cinema, restaurants with veggie food, coffee shops and pubs.

2 Kemplay Road
Hampstead
London NW3 1SY

The large, very comfortable rooms are full of character with sitting area, writing desk, remote control TV, hairdryer, iron, fridge (brilliant for veggies), kettle, telephone, books and even a hot–waterbottle to cuddle.

Tel: 020–7435 8679

Fax: 020–7794 0254

Tube: Hampstead

Parking can be arranged

En suite double £90, en suite single £70. Double £75, singles £50 and £60. Large studio with kitchen and shower £95 for 1, £125 for 2, £145 for 3, £160 for 4, £170 for 5. Parking £10 per day.

5 rooms from
£50–70 single,
£77 upwards for double

No smoking anywhere

Optional breakfast £7 from 8.00 a.m., 9.00 at weekends until late, can be in the garden in summer and you can invite guests.

See page 205 for nearby restaurants

Booking requires credit card, pay on arrival in cash, sterling (travellers) cheques or credit card (5% surcharge).

No meals except breakfast, but there are veggie restaurants and a wholefood store in the area and veggie dishes in other nearby restaurants.

www.HampsteadGuesthouse.com
info@HampsteadGuesthouse.com

HAMPSTEAD VILLAGE GUESTHOUSE
2 Kemplay Road, Hampstead
London NW3 1SY

www.hampsteadguesthouse.com
tel: +44 (0)20 7435 8679   **Fax:** +44 (0)20 7794 0254
e-mail: info@hampsteadguesthouse.com

- Peaceful setting, close to Hampstead Heath, yet in the heart of lively Hampstead Village.

- Close to underground and bus. Centre of London in 10 minutes.

- Large rooms full of character, plus modern amenities: TV, kettle and direct-dial telephone.

- Breakfast in the garden, weather permitting.

- Accomodation from £50.

- No smoking.

"If you're looking for something a little different, make a beeline for Annemarie van der Meer's Hampstead home."

Chosen as one of the "Hotels of the Year". The Which? Hotel Guide 2000.

Liz Heavenstone's

Cosy top floor apartment in a Regency terrace in Primrose Hill village, on the edge of Regent's Park. Two double/twin rooms, £55–65 per room per night, one with own bathroom, one with shower, which become a self contained apartment with living room when both rooms are taken. There's also a futon for an extra bed in one room.

Good for self-catering as the kitchen-breakfast room has fridge, dishwasher, cooker, and microwave-cum-oven.

Add £5 for self-service vegetarian organic breakfast, which can easily be veganized, and they'll happily cater for special diets if you tell them in advance. There are always tea, coffee and herbal drinks, and the breakfast room has a bowl of fruit.

They have plenty of info on London for guests. Good location, close to the centre but not in the centre. Nearby are Triyoga Centre (www.triyoga.co.uk), which has drop-in classes and the Little Earth veggie cafe, Primrose Hill, Regents Park, Manna vegetarian restaurant, Cafe Seventy Nine and Sesame wholefood store. Camden is a short walk away. Two minutes walk to Chalk Farm underground.

Prior telephone booking is essential, do not just turn up.

Self catering bed and breakfast / apartment

Liz Heavenstone's Guest House,
192 Regents Park Road,
Hampstead,
London NW1 8XP

Tel: 020–7722 7139

Fax: 020–7586 3004

lizheavenstone@
onetel.com

Tube: Chalk Farm

Open: all year

Children welcome.

No pets.

Discreet smokers tolerated.

Temple Lodge

Temple Lodge is a quiet oasis in the middle of London. There are four single rooms at £30 per night or £195 per week, and three twin rooms at £50 per room per night or £330 per week, plus two double rooms from £50 per night.

A hearty continental breakfast is served. Soya milk and vegan margarine are available on request.

You won't have to walk far for lunch or dinner as The Gate vegetarian restaurant is on the same premises. (closed Sunday) There is also a vegetarian Indian restaurant Sagar at 157 King Street and the new vegan restaurant 222 at 222 North End Road which does a great lunchtime buffet.

Visitors are invited to join in with activities of the Christian Community and will have the opportunity of joining the Temple Lodge Club for a nominal fee. The house offers many facilities for the use of guests, such as a kitchen, a quiet and secluded garden and a large library.

The house is thought to be built on the foundations of a seventeenth century building. The artist Sir Frank Brangwyn lived there during the early part of the twentieth century, and both house and grounds have been restored to their former glory.

All major tourist attractions are reached easily by public transport. Pleasant walks along the River Thames are easily accessible. Historical houses, Kew Gardens, the Waterfowl sanctuary of the Wetlands Centre and three theatres are all within walking distance. Close to Olympia and Earls Court Exhibition Centres.

Washbasins are in the rooms, and hairdryers are available on request.

Vegetarian bed and breakfast

51 Queen Caroline Street
Hammersmith
London W6 9QL
England

Tel: 020–8748 8388

Fax: 020–8563 2758

Email:
m.beaumont@rdplus.net

Tube Station: Hammersmith, 5 minutes

Open: all year

Directions: By car, directly from the west along A4/M4 and from westerly directions along A3 and A40. The North/South Circular Roads give access from other directions.

Parking: metered parking available on the street

No smoking throughout

MC, Visa

Children welcome, please enquire.

LONDON Accommodation

Knightsbridge

The Lanesborough

Luxury hotel & veg-friendly restaurant

Hyde Park Corner,
Knightsbridge, London SW1X 7TA
Tel: 020-7259 5599. Fax: 020-7259 5606
For reservations in USA call toll free 1-800
999 1828, fax: 1-800 937 8278
Tube: Hyde Park Corner
Open: All Year Round
www.lanesborough.com

Luxury hotel popular with veggie rock and movie stars and C.E.O.'s. Singles £285, doubles £395 up to the royal suite at £5000. That's per night, plus VAT. If a veggie/vegan breakfast is required you have to give prior notice at the time of booking. Services include 24 hour butler, fitness studio, spa studio, business centre, complimentary internet access in your room with on-demand film.

The in-house restaurant The Conservatory features gourmet vegetarian dinners, prepared by top chef Paul Gayler or one of his brigade of 40 chefs. Lunch is £24 for 2 courses or £27.50 for three, dinner prices depend on the day of the week but usually range from £32-£44 per head. The vegetarian a la carte menu often has vegan options but not always so phone ahead. There is live music every night and dancing on Friday and Saturday nights.

It's a few minutes taxi or bus ride to the veggie delights of Soho.

Streatham

Barrow House

Vegetarian bed & breakfast

45 Barrow Road, Streatham Common
London SW16 5PE
Tel: 020-8677 1925. Fax: 020-8677 1925
Open: all year round
Train: Streatham Common British Rail

Close to the A23 London to Brighton road.
barrowhaus@hotmail.com

Vegetarian and vegan bed and breakfast in south London, in a Victorian family house in a quiet location, 15 minutes by rail from Victoria Station and close to the A23. Three double/twin rooms, £60 double or £40 single. Non smoking. No pets. No credit cards. Two vegetarian restaurants and a wholefood store nearby.

Hemel Hempstead

The Violin B&B

Vegetarian bed and breakfast

24 The Dee, Grovehill, Hemel Hempstead
Hertfordshire HP2 6EN
Tel: 020-01442-388977
Train: Hemel Hempstead 3 miles
Open: all year round
contact@theviolinbnb.co.uk
www.theviolinbnb.co.uk

Vegetarian, homestyle B&B on the M1 side of Hemel Hempstead. 20 miles NW of London, conveniently close to the motorway and an ideal base if you're coming for a concert or theatre. There is a rail link with Euston station and a very economical Green line Bus 758 service almost every hour into central London for £7 return.

£25 per person per night, £30 for single occupancy, including continental breakfast. Discounted rate for 7+ nights.

A 3 course evening meal may be available if booked in advance for £10. Food is organic where possible.

Toiletries contain no animal products and are cruelty-free.

Broadband wireless internet available.

By train: three miles from Hemel Hempstead Station, which is on the main line from Birmingham to London Euston.

By air: 10 miles from Luton Airport and

22 miles from Heathrow. They can collect or deliver you to either airport. £15 for Luton, £25 for Heathrow, any time of day/night.
See also Hertfordshire

HOSTELS

Generator Hostel

The king of hostels, fab location

Compton Place, behind 37 Tavistock Place,
Bloomsbury, London WC1H 9SD
Tel: 020-7388 7666. Fax: 020-7388 7644
Tube: Russell Square, Kings Cross, Euston
Open: All year, 24 hours
info@the-generator.co.uk
www.the-generator.co.uk

International 837 bed hostel in Blooms-bury. The cheapest dorms you have to wait for, so you'll probably pay £17 for a 4-bed room. Nearby are Vegetarian Paradise restaurant and Alara Whole-foods (where vegans can buy breakfast). Age 18-35, but older young-at-hearts welcome. Busy bar. Bring earplugs and a padlock for your locker. Towels provided.

Other Hostels

Rock bottom accommodation

www.piccadillyhotel.net
www.astorhostels.com
www.st-christophers.co.uk
www.wakeuplondon.co.uk
www.yhalondon.org.uk
www.ukhostels.com
www.totalhostels.com

Our favourite guidebooks for budget places are Lonely Planet, Rough Guides or Let's Go London, England, Britain or Europe. Off season you can often just turn up, but at weekends and in summer you absolutely must reserve ahead for your first night.
If you've just got off a coach or airport train at Victoria station, there are some accommodation agencies that can sort out your first night's stay for a small commission.

CAMPING

Crystal Palace Campsite

Camping in South-East London

Crystal Palace Parade,, London SE19
Tel: 020-8778 7155
Train: Crystal Palace BR
Open: All year round

This is a caravan park so electricity is available but no shop or cooking facili-ties. They do have laundry and washing facilities though. Rates vary according to the time of year. Backpackers £5 per tent winter, £7 summer, car £8/£10. Then £3.80 per adult winter, £5 summer.

Lee Valley Park

Camping in North-East London

Pickets Lock Centre, London N9
Tel: 020-020-8803 6900
www.leevalleypark.com
Tube: Tottenham Hale, Edmonton BR
Open: All Year except Xmas Day,
Boxing Day & New Year

Huge well equipped camping site set in 6 acres with sports centre and leisure complex with 12 screen cinema, swimming pool, golf course, kids' play area, 3 pubs and pizza restaurant. Acts as bus terminal for those going into town. There is a minimum charge for everyone £6.10 for adult or £2.60 for children 5-16, for individuals this goes up to £9.00 (i.e. one person and tent). Electricity is £2.50 per night. Charge for dogs and awnings £1.50. Another site is nearby at Sewardstone Road, Chingford, E4 7RA Tel 020-8529 5689, closed in winter.

Moving to London

If you're moving to London for at least six months, then an apartment (flat) with friends can be cheaper than a hostel and much quieter. And much nicer too if you share a kitchen with veggies. Finding an apartment is a full time job for a few days but it can be done if you're persistent.

A single or double room in a houseshare will be £70–120 per week, a studio flat £100 per week and up. You'll need a month's deposit, a month's rent up front, and the contract will normally be a six months assured shorthold tenancy. Staying in a hostel for the first weeks is a lot less hassle while you find a job and you can get some mates there, or go to vegetarian and vegan events to find new friends. (page 230)

A word of warning: London is expensive. The majority of people work hard so they can afford to enjoy it to the full, but live in a small space, probably just one or maybe two rooms. People who turn up wanting to move in with them without paying rent create awkwardness and embarrassment all round. So before coming, make sure you have plenty of money to tide you over for a few weeks while you find a job.

LOOT

London's free ads newspaper

www.loot.com

If you want to rent a whole apartment, this is the place. Buy an early bird token on line to see all the latest ads, of just browse to get a feel for prices. You can place a free ad yourself and let the landlords come to you. Search on "veg" to find veggie houseshares. A printed version of LOOT can be bought in newsagents.

VegCom

Veggie accommodation adverts

www.vegcom.org.uk or
www.veganlondon.org.uk
and click on VegCom

Vegans and veggies in the London area looking for flatmates.

Vegan Village

UK vegan accommodation adverts

www.veganvillage.co.uk

National classified adverts including sublets and flatshares.

Camden was once the working class district on the north-east edge of Regent's Park. These days it attracts an eclectic mix, who flock in the thousands to London's most popular market (actually six markets) off the High Street and around the Lock, which give you the best choice of hip new and secondhand clothes in town. There are some veggie and veggie-friendly food stalls and take-aways (including falafel and a juice bar) and the psychedelic Dream Temple Café has vegan snacks and meals at weekends. The arty bit around the Lock is more expensive but has an interesting range of stalls. You can buy all your presents here in one go.

Camden features some of the best bars, clubs and pubs in London which are the basis of a lively music scene. For a fast and good value bite beforehand try the Healthier Eating Café or Tai Buffet. Gourmet dining can be had at Manna. Café Seventy-Nine is a more laid-back experience before or after a walk on Primrose Hill with its terrific views over London, or try the new ultra-healthy Little Earth Cafe opposite Manna or Green Note restaurant (often with live music) near Fresh & Wild.

Camden & Primrose Hill

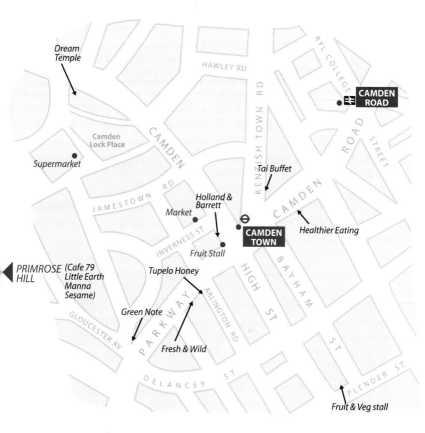

Dream Temple

HAWLEY RD

RYL COLLEGE

CAMDEN ROAD

Camden Lock Place

CAMDEN RD

KENTISH TOWN RD

ROAD

STREET

Supermarket

Tai Buffet

JAMESTOWN RD

Holland & Barrett

Market

CAMDEN

INVERNESS ST

CAMDEN TOWN

Healthier Eating

Fruit Stall

PRIMROSE HILL

(Cafe 79 Little Earth Manna Sesame)

Tupelo Honey

HIGH ST

BAYHAM

Green Note

GLOUCESTER AV

PARKWAY

ARLINGTON RD

ST

Fresh & Wild

DELANCEY ST

PLENDER ST

Fruit & Veg stall

Camden Town

Dream Temple Cafe

Almost vegan cafe

Above the Dream Temple record shop,
21–22 Stables Market NW1 8AH
Tel: 020–7267 8528
Open: Everyday 10.30–18.30, Fri–Sun 21–late
Tube: Camden Town

This cafe is the last one on the left going north up Camden High Street at the back of Camden Stables Market.
Herbal, Arabic, Moroccan teas, chai, organic coffee, (soya) latte or cappuccino, £1.30–2.00, or £3.00 for a pot. Smoothies £3, organic hemp milk and organic vegan lassi £2. Also kombucha, guava drink, coconut water.
Vegan brownies, flapjacks and cakes £2. At weekends there are vegan meals.

Green Note

Vegetarian restaurant–cafe–bar

106 Parkway, NW1 7AN
Tel: 020–7485 9899
Open: Tue–Fri 18–23.00, Sat–Sun 12–23.00
Tube: Camden Town. www.greennote.co.uk

Mostly vegan or vegan option. Tapas £3.95–4.95. Lunch sandwiches, wraps and burgers £6.95. Evening mains £7.95–9.45 such as Green Thai curry, butternut squash tagine, pasta. 6 desserts £4.95. Sat–Sun brunch. Licensed. See website for live music.

Tai Buffet

Vegan Chinese buffet

6 Kentish Town Road NW1
Tel: 020–7284 4004
Open: Every day all day
Tube: Camden Town

Lots of fake meat and Chinese favorites. Open every day for lunch and dinner. All you can eat £5, £6 after 6pm and Sunday or take–away for £3–4.

The Healthier Eating Cafe

Omnivorous cafe

24 Camden Road NW1 9DP
Tel: 020–7267 2649
Open: Mon–Fri 6.30–19.30, Sat 8.–20.00, Sun 11–20.00
Tube: Camden Town

Beautiful modern design, with bright yellow frontage and a very light interior. Local artists' pictures hang on the walls. Take–away salads and sandwiches £2.50–3.00 such as roast pepper with hummous and roquette with black olives.

Tupelo Honey

Omnivorous cafe

27 Parkway NW1 7PN (corner of Arlington St)
Tel: 020–7284 2989
Open: Tue–Sat 9.30–23.30, Sun 12–20.00, Mon 9.30–18.00
Tube: Camden Town

Popular and chilled out place with several rooms on three floors, a small outside area and a roof garden.

Fresh and Wild

Organic supermarket

49 Parkway NW1 7PN
Tel: 020–7428 7575
Open: Mon–Fri 8–21.00, Sat 9.30–21.00, Sun 10.30–20.00
Tube: Camden Town

Huge organic supermarket with a small café. The store sells everything from tea to toothpaste and has a big take–away food and juice bar. Prepared food is sold by weight, £1–1.50 per 100g, with lots of salads, baked tofu and savouries (not all vegetarian). Natural remedies, bodycare, books. Great choice of organic fruit and vegetables.

Cafe Seventy Nine

Vegetarian cafe and take-away

79 Regents Park Road NW1 8UY
Tel: 020-7586 8012
Tube: Chalk Farm
Open: Mon-Sat, 8.30-18.00, Sun09-18.00

All day full English cooked breakfast special £6.45; organic soup of the day with organic Neal's Yard roll £4.45; Hummous and warm wholemal pitta £3.65; and main courses such as pasta with pesto, pine nuts, cherry tomatoes and green salad £6.25 or bagel burger and deep fried new potatoes £5.75.
Milkshakes £2.95, can be made with soya milk. (Soya) cappuccino £1.65-1.95.

Little Earth Cafe

Vegetarian organic cafe and juice bar

i(n Triyoga Centre) 6 Erskine Road NW3
Tel: 020-7483 3344
www.triyoga.co.uk
Tube: Chalk Farm
Open: Mon-Fri 9-15.00 17-20.00, Sat 10-18.00, Sun11-15.00

Organic vegan hot food menu includes hummous sandwich £3.50 with biodynamic spelt-rye bread, braised red pepper and watercress; Johnny sandwich £4 with beetroot pate, watercress, avocado, balsamic, red onion, cucumber, alfalfa and olive oil; soup £3; quinoa of the day £5.50.
Raw food menu features organic pink sushi £4; rainbow salad £4.50; and almond burgers £5.50 with pinenut "cheese", avocado, sprouts and cucumber relish.
Raw desserts menu £3.50 has chocolate banofie, carrot cake, blue fig tart with lavender-walnut cream, blueberry cake with lemon cashew cream.
Special juices for pregnancy and mummy. Organic baby food £1.50. No mobile phones. Non smoking.

Manna

Vegetarian restaurant

4 Erskine Road, Hampstead NW3 3AJ
Tel: 020 7722 8028
www.manna-veg.com
Tube: Chalk Farm
Open: Mon-Sat18.30-23.00, Sun12.30-15.00 18.30-12.30

Very classy international gourmet vegetarian restaurant. Mains £10.95-12.50, half vegan, such as Tapas Olé with smoky tofu albondigas al jerez, Catalan minted broad beans, grilled sour dough panboli, spinach and carrot croquetas, garbanzo salad and orange, avocado and olive salad; or Summer Tomato, Coconut & Ginger Curry with baby carrots, sweetcorn, mangetout and yellow courgette served with cashew rice and a sweet cucumber salsa topped with crispy noodles.
Desserts £3.95 to £6.75, plenty vegan, like petits fours, a plate of truffles, chocolates and biscuits. Organic fruit crumble and pecan chocolate cake.
Service not included. Discretionary 12.5% added to parties of 6 or more.

Sesame Health Foods

Wholefood shop and take-away

128 Regents Park Road NW1
Tel: 020-7586 3779
Open: Mon-Fri 9-18.00, Sat 10-18.00, Sun 12-17.00
Tube: Chalk Farm

Take-away items include soups, salads, rice and vegetables, snacks, pasta, stir-fries and cakes. They have all you need for a summer picnic on nearby Primrose Hill. Natural remedies and body care.

The City is the 'Wall Street' of London, and also has St Paul's Cathedral and the Tower of London. In this square mile you are likely to see young and not so young professional men and women heading for the gym or a healthy lunch, as fitness clubs and multicultural food continue to expand and thrive in London.

From noon till 2pm there's a feeding frenzy in take-away specialists such as Futures!, Fresh & Wild and Pure, or treat yourself to a sit-down lunch at The Greenery or The Place Below.

For an altogether more relaxing experience on the quieter City fringes, Rye Wholefoods has a peaceful café within their shop, whilst Antimony Balance has added a juice bar in theirs.

Although St Paul's is free on Sundays during church services and the district is pleasantly uncongested, be forewarned that all the vegetarian restaurants are closed.

The City

Carnevale

Vegetarian Mediterranean restaurant and take-away

135 Whitecross Street EC1Y 8JL
Tel: 020-7250 3452
www.carnevalerestaurant.co.uk
Tube: Old Streeet, Barbican, Moorgate
Open: Mon-Fri 10-22.30, Sat 17.30-22.30

Near the Barbican Centre and Museum of London with a glass roofed backyard. Starters include vegan soup of the day £3.75; warm salad with chestnut mushrooms, tomatoes and spinach £5.50; roasted aubergines tossed in Romesco sauce £5.50; and watercress, fennel, and kalamata olive salad £5.

Main courses £11.50 such as potato and shallot panisse with fennel, red pepper and flageolet beans; butternut squash Thai curry with spiced tofu balls. Five puddings £4.95 with vegan options including baked stuffed quince with cardamon cream. Visa, MC.

CTB

Vegetarian Oriental buffet

88 Leather Lane EC1
Tel: 020-7242-6128
Open: Mon-Sat 12.00-22.00, Sun closed
Tube: Farringdon. Bus 55, 243

All you can eat for £5.00 (all day) or you can have a take-away box for £3 or £4. Typical dishes include sweet and sour veg balls, lemon grass pot, spring rolls, crispy aubergine and black bean with mixed veg, spiced aubergine, several tasty veg curries with tofu and all kinds of fake meats. Licensed.

Futures!

Vegetarian take-away

8 Botolph Alley Eastcheap EC3R 8DR
Tel: 020-7623 4529
Open: Mon-Sat breakfast 7.30-10.00, lunch

11.30-15.00
Tube: Monument

Tucked away in a pedestrianised alley in the heart the City, this little shop offers several hot dishes £4 including bakes, pasta dishes and stir fries.

They also have four salads such as mixed bean; cabbage, apple and raisin with grain mustard dressing. £1.30 single portion, £3 combos.

Desserts £1.80 include apricot Bakewell tart. Smoothies sold here as well as tea, coffee and juices. Cash only.

Pure

Vegetarian take-away

In one of the entrances of Moorgate tube at the corner of Moor Place and Moorfields, opposite Dixons electrical store.
Tel: 020-7588 7800
Tube: Moorgate
Open: Mon-Fri 6.00-22.00, Sat 7.30-18.00, Sun 7.30-15.00

Fill up take-away boxes with hummous, avocado, grilled veg, moussaka, lentils and rice for £4.35. Or choose from 10 sides including country veg with pasta, beans and lentils, vine leaves and Moroccan salad with dates.

Breakfast options include porridge £1.85-2.50, tropical fruit and nut muesli and fresh fruit salads.

The Greenery

Vegetarian cafe and take-away

5 Cowcross St EC1M 6DR
Tel: 020-7490 4870
Open: Mon-Fri 7.00-17.00
Tube: Farringdon

Muesli, croissants, fruit scones, soups, baps and salads in addition to mains like Homity pie, pasta, curries, veggie satay: £1.30-£3.75 take-away, £4.25 eat in, £5.50 with salsa platter.

The Place Below

Vegetarian restaurant and take–away

St Mary–le–Bow Church Crypt
Cheapside EC2V 6AU
Tel: 020–7329 0789
Tube: St Paul's
www.theplacebelow.co.uk
Open: Mon–Fri 07.30–15.30

The chefs at this excellent little hideaway make their own granola, muesli £1.80, organic porridge £1.50, muffins £1.30, croissants £1.50 and freshly squeezed orange juice £1.95 .
Lunch could be soup £3.10 eat in, take–away £2.70, salads £7.50 eat in, £6.20 take–away, or a hot dish £7.00 in, £5.70 out, such as ratatouille with Asian flavours, spiced chickpeas and coconut rice. £2 discount on dish of the day 11.30–12.00.

Wheatley's

Vegetarian cafe

33–34 Myddleton Street EC1R 1UA
Tel: 020–7278–6662
Open: Mon–Fri 8.00–16.00
Tube: Angel, then 38 or 341 bus

Not far from Saddlers Wells, this cafe has a garden with a canopy for summer showers and heaters in winter.
Soup £2.30; custom–made sandwiches £2.95; hot tortillas, savoury crepes and falafels £3.95. Vegan cakes £2.20.

Antimony Balance

Wholefood shop and juice bar

47 Farringdon Road EC1M
Tel: 0870–3600 345
Tube: Farringdon
Open: Mon–Fri 8–19.00, Sat 10–16.00

Bodycare includes Dr Hauschka, Neal's Yard, Barefoot Botanicals, Birds Bees,

Weleda, Spizia Organics.
They also carry aromatherapy goodies, candles, incense, lavender wheat bag hot/cold compresses and a big range of vegetarian health and diet books.
For the munchies, they stock veggie sandwiches, pies and pastries, delicious flapjacks and organic juices £2.50–5 with shots of wheat grass, spirulina, echinacea.

Fresh and Wild

Wholefood shop

194 Old Street, EC1V 9FR
Tel: 020–7250 1708
Open: Mon–Fri 9.30–19.30, Sat 10.30–17.30
Tube: Old Street

Large wholefood store selling a huge range of take–away snacks, organic fruit & veg, herbs, veggie/vegan wine and beer, cosmetics, toiletries, books, vitamins and herbal remedies.
Above the store is the Open Centre, which has alternative therapies, workshops and talks.

Rye Wholefoods

Wholefood store and vegan cafe

35a Mydletton Street (off Rosebery Ave)
Tel: 020–7278 5878
Open: Mon–Fri 9.00–18.00, Sat 10.00–17.00
Tube: Angel

Hot dishes, sandwiches/ wraps, soups, and mixed salads for eat in or take–away £1.10–2.85.

Fruit & Veg Stall

Liverpool Street Station
Open: every day all day when the tube is
Tube: Liverpool Street

By the ticket barriers going into the underground in the mainline station.

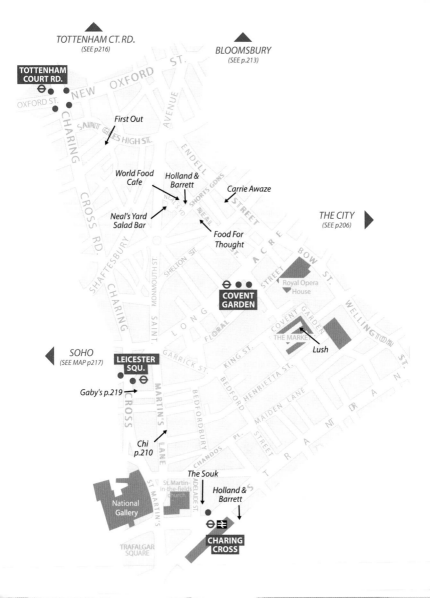

TOTTENHAM CT. RD.
(SEE p216)

BLOOMSBURY
(SEE p.213)

THE CITY
(SEE p206)

SOHO
(SEE MAP p217)

TOTTENHAM COURT RD.

First Out

World Food Cafe

Holland & Barrett

Carrie Awaze

Neal's Yard Salad Bar

Food For Thought

COVENT GARDEN

Royal Opera House

THE MARKET

Lush

LEICESTER SQU.

Gaby's p.219

Chi p.210

The Souk

St. Martin-in-the-fields church

Holland & Barrett

National Gallery

TRAFALGAR SQUARE

CHARING CROSS

OXFORD ST.

NEW OXFORD ST.

OXFORD ST.

SAINT GILES HIGH ST.

CHARING CROSS RD.

SHAFTESBURY AVE.

MONMOUTH ST.

SHELTON ST.

SHORTS GDNS

NEAL ST.

ENDELL STREET

BOW ST.

WELLINGTON ST.

LONG ACRE

FLORAL ST.

COVENT GARDEN

GARRICK ST.

KING ST.

BEDFORD ST.

HENRIETTA ST.

MAIDEN LANE

STRAND

ST MARTIN'S LANE

CHANDOS PL.

ADELAIDE ST.

CHARING CROSS RD.

ST MARTIN'S

BEDFORDBURY

Covent Garden

Carrie Awaze

Omnivorous sandwich shop

27 Endell Street WC2
Tel: 020-7836 0815
Open: Mon-Fri 10.30-20.00, Sat 12.00-18.00, Sun 10.30-20.00
Tube: Covent Garden

Omnivorous Indian and international take-away with stacks for veggies and vegans.

6 vegan and 21 veggie sandwiches £2.50-3.25 take-away, £2.50-3.80 eat in, such as "Brown Bomber" onion bhajia with hummous and salad.

Filled jacket spud £5.95-6.25 such as "Arne Street" with dhal and onion bhajia, or with veg curry and cashews. Main meal £7.95 such as vegetarian or vegan thali, curry and rice, or Hyderabadi korma with veg and fruit.

Chi

Vegan Chinese buffet restaurant

55 St Martin's Lane WC2
Tel: 020-7836 3434
Open: Mon-Sat 12-23.00, Sun 12-22.00
Tube: Leicester Square, Charing Cross

Fill up at the West End's best value restaurant on stir-fry vegetables, tofu, mushrooms and several kinds of fake meat dishes like black bean "chicken" and sweet and sour "pork" balls. All you can eat £5 before 5.30pm, then £6 afterwards and all day Sunday. Take-away £3 or £4 for a large box.

No credit cards.

First Out

Gay & lesbian vegetarian cafe

52 St Giles High St WC2H 8LH
Tel: 020-7240 8042
Open: Mon-Sat 10-23.00, Sun 11-22.30
Tube: Tottenham Court Rd

Smart, modern and very popular gay and lesbian vegetarian café with international menu and basement bar.

The soup of the day is always vegan for £3.50. Range of platters such as mezze with dips and pitta bread for £4.50. On Sundays they do brunch.

For main course you could try the veg chilli or veg curry, pies, bakes, or nachos from £4.95-5.45. Smoking only in the bar downstairs. Visa, MC.

They have party evenings and Friday night is 'Girl Friday' or women's night with men as guests.

Food For Thought

Vegetarian/vegan restaurant

31 Neal Street WC2H 9PR
Tel: 020-7836 9072 /0239
Tube: Covent Garden
Open: Mon-Sat 12-20.30, Sun 12-17.00

Extremely popular veggie take-away and café on fascinating Neal Street in a vaulted basement.Menu changes daily, main dish examples include: Ethiopian Wat; Middle Eastern mezze; Carri coco curry; Malay sambal; shepherdess pie; satay and tofu noodles; roast Mediterranean veg with polenta; mushroom stroganoff; cauliflower & peanut arial; sir-fry veg.

The evening menu from 5pm is slightly different with many different ingredients on a big plate, for £6.00 to £6.50.

Neal's Yard Salad Bar

International vegetarian cafe and restaurant

2, 8–10 Neal's Yard WC2H 9DP
Tel: 020–7836 3233
www.nealsyardsaladbar.co.uk
Tube: Covent Garden, Tottenham Court Rd.
Open: Every day 8.30–21.00
till 22.30 in summer

Brazilian vegan owned vegetarian wholefood café downstairs with tables inside and out, and a restaurant upstairs. Vegan, wheat and yeast free clearly marked. Six breakfasts 08.30–12.00 £2.75, £3.85, £6.05 from toast to full English with everything.

Daily specials £8.25–10.50 such as Brazilian feijoada of black beans, soya meat, rice, finger tapioca, fried banana, farofa and pumpkin; spaghetti bolognese with minced soya meat.

Juices and shakes, soyaccino £2.20. beer £3.85, sangria £3.85, and house wine £3.85 (bottle £15.50).

The Souk

Omnivorous Arabian restaurant

8 Adelaide Street WC2N 4HZ
(opposite Charing Cross Station next to St Martins Church market)
Tel: 020–7240 2337
Tube: Charing Cross
Open: Mon–Fri 08.00–19.00,
Thu till 20.00, Sat–Sun closed

This Moroccan / Mediterranean take-away/snack bar serves really good vegan wraps such as hummous, falafel and salad, bean and salad wraps, hot spicy sweet potato wraps, stuffed vine leaves, plus one vegan salad – all ready wrapped or sold in little containers to take away.

World Food Cafe

International vegetarian restaurant

First Floor, 14 Neal's Yard WC2H 9DP
Tel: 020–7379–0298
Tube: Covent Garden, Tottenham Court Rd.
Open: Mon–Fri 11.30–16.30, Sat –17.00

Upstairs international wholefood vegetarian restaurant, overlooking Neal's Yard. Meals from every continent £6.85/£7.95 could be Turkish meze; West African sweet potatoes in creamy groundnut and cayenne sauce; and a Mexican platter.
Fresh fruit juice £2.25, fresh lime soda £1.95, herb teas or barleycup £1.50, cafetiere £1.55. They have soya milk. Minimum charge £5.00 at lunchtime and all day Saturday.

Holland & Barrett

Health food shop

21 Shorts Gardens, Covent Garden
Tel: 020–7379 0298
Open: Mon–Sat 10–19.00, Sun 11–17.30

Big shop by the entrance to Neal's Yard, with take-away pasties and rolls.

Unit 16, Embankment Shopping Centre, Villiers Street
Tel: 020–7379 0298
Open: Mon–Fri 08–19.00,
Sat 9–18.00, Sun 11–18.00

Down the side of Charing Cross station with lots of take-aways and snacks.

Lush Covent Garden

Cruelty-free cosmetics

11 The Piazza, Covent Garden WC2E 8RB
Tel: 020–7240 4570.

Cruelty-free cosmetics, 70% vegan.

Noho is the name given by landlords and estate agents to the mainly residential areas north of Oxford Street.

The main attraction in Bloomsbury is the gigantic (and free!) British Museum.

Euston station is the departure point for trains north. Next to it is Drummond Street which is full of Indian restaurants.

Marylebone (between Oxford Street in the south to Madame Tussaud's and Regents Park in the north) has two new up-market vegetarian restaurants, of which Eat & Two Veg has been getting rave reviews.

Tottenham Court Road is an electronic and computer haven with two bargain Chinese vegan buffet restaurants.

Alara

Wholefood store & vegetarian cafe

58 Marchmont Street WC1N 1AB
Tel: 020–7837 1172
Tube: Russell Square
Open: Mon–Fri 9.00–18.00, Sat 10–18.00

Help yourself to 100% organic salads and hot food, 85p per 100g, such as chickpea salad and gluten–free veg curries. Microwave on premises. Organic, gluten–free and sugar–free cakes.

Freshly made organic juices £1.89 small, £2.69 large, such as orange, apple, carrot with ginger. Cockails £2.39–2.79 such as apple, beetroot and carrot. Smoothies £2.99–3.99, can be with rice or soya milk.

Stacks of vegan and organic produce in several aisles, including Swedish Glace vegan ice–cream and frozen foods.

Vegetarian's Paradise

Vegetarian Indian restaurant

59 Marchmont Street WC1N 1AP
Tel: 020–7278 6881
Open: Every day 12–15.00, 17.00–24.00
Tube: Russell Square

Indian vegetarian restaurant offering real value for money with a lunch time buffet for £4.50 per adult.

Hot starters, £2.10–£2.50, include stuffed potato cakes with spicy chick peas. Cold starters like pani poori – hollow wholewheat pooris served with tamarind and dates, spicy sauces and boiled chick peas for £2.45.

Mains from £3.50 for curries or £3.95 for a plain dosa; thalis from £4.95. Bring your own alcohol, no corkage charge.

Chutneys

Vegetarian Indian restaurant

124 Drummond Street NW1 2HL
Tel: 020–7388–0604
Open: Mon–Sat   12.00–14.45,   18–22.30, Sun 12–22.00
Tube: Euston, Euston Square

Eat as much as you like buffet from 12 noon to 2.45pm every day for £5.95, Sunday all day.

There are 16 starters such as bhel poori, £2.20 to £3.00.

Main courses include nine kinds of dosa £2.80–4.85, 11 curries £2.50–3.40. Plenty of whole wheat breads, pickles; salad and rice from 90p.

Thalis start at £3.95. If you are really hungry try the excellent Chutney's deluxe thali for £7.95 with dhal soup, 4 curries, pillau rice, chutneys, chappatis or pooris and dessert.

Diwana

Vegetarian Indian restaurant

121–123 Drummond Street NW1 2HL
Tel: 020–7387 5556
Open: Mon–Sat 12–23.30, Sun 12–22.30
Tube: Euston, Euston Square, Warren Street

They offer an eat as much as you like lunch buffet 12–14.30 every day for £6.50 which has different dishes daily, and also a full a la carte menu all day.

Lots of starters such as dahi vada chick peas £3.00, masala spring rolls £3.50. Thalis £5.50–7.75.

Lots of dosas £5.50–5.95 and vegetable side dishes like bombay aloo and aloo gobi £3.80–4.20.

Diwana are not licensed but you can bring your own with no corkage charge. There is an off licence next door.

Ravi Shankar

Vegetarian Indian restaurant

133–135 Drummond Street NW1 2HL
Tel: 020–7388 6458
Open: Mon–Sat, 12–22.45 (last orders 22.00)
Tube: Euston, Euston Square

Set 3 course meal £7.85, two courses
£6.55, or have a dosa or curry £5.15–
5.60.
On a Monday they serve cauliflower
potato curry for £4.50, Tuesday is veg
biriyani with curry for £4.25, and each
day the specials are different. Sat £4.75,
Sun £4.55.
Wine £7.95 bottle, £1.80 glass. Most
cards accepted.

Gi Gi Hut

Chinese vegan buffet restaurant

339 Euston Road NW1 3AD
Tel: 020–7387 5450
Tube: Warren Street
Open: every day 12–22.00

Oriental serve yourself buffet, as much
as you like for £5, or take-away boxes
£3. (Formerly called CTJ)

Health Food Centre

Health food shop and take away

11 Warren Street NW1
Tel: 020–7387 9289
Tube: Warren Street, Euston, Euston Square
Open: Mon–Fri 8.30–18.30, Sat 12–16.00

London's biggest range of veggie and
vegan sandwiches, such as (fake)
chicken and salad; lentil burger and
houmous with salad; date, walnut and
banana; veggie burger and hummous;
veggie BLT. All £3 for two which is
stunning value for central London.
Lots of cakes, some sugar free or

suitable for vegans like date crumble.
The juice bar has combos like apple,
ginger and orange for £1.30 medium,
£1.99 large. Energy drinks like spirulina,
echinacea or guarana £2.50. Vegan fruit
smoothie £1.40.

Nutri Centre

Cruelty-free cosmetics and food

7 Park Crescent W1N
Tel: 020–7436 5122
www.nutricentre.com
Open: Mon–Fri 9–19.00, Sat 10–19.00
Tube: Regents Park, Great Portland St

In the basement of a natural health
centre, this shop sells mainly supplements and body care products, plus a
few foods like pasta
There is a big books section with a
separate telephone: 020–7323 2382.
They have an impressive mail order
books catalogue.

Chai Pani

Vegetarian Indian Rajasthani Marwari
restaurant

64 Seymour Street W1H 5BW
Tel: 020–7258 2000 / 3444
Tube: Marble Arch
Open: Every day 12–14.30 (weekends till
16.30), 18.00–22.30, Tea room 15.00–17.00

The menu includes 10 thalis £6.20
including vegan, wheat-free and
London's only low-calorie thali; 8
starters £3.50 such as sabudana vada
(potato and sago patties); 17 curries £7;
12 Kadhi lentil based dishes £5; lots of
breads £3.50 and rices £5 including
khichadi, a kind of porridge dish made
by cooking rice with lentils, which goes
well with a spicy curry.
Typical Rajasthani drinks such as
Thandai, or Shikanji Indian style
lemonade, plus beer and wine.

Afternoon tea includes Indian sweets and savouries served with juices.

The basement dining room houses Indian artefacts for sale.

MC, Visa and Amex.

Eat & Two Veg

British and International Vegetarian restaurant

50 Marylebone High St (north end) W1U 5HN
Tel: 020-7258 8595
www.eatandtwoveg.com
Tube: Baker Street
Free parking from 6.30pm and all day Sun.
Open: Mon-Sat 08.00-23.00, Sat 9.00-23.00, Sun 10.00-22.30

Continental or full English veggie breakfast £1.50 to £7.50, served till noon Mon-Fri and till 2pm at weekends. Lunch and dinner menu includes soups; 12 main courses such as Lancashire hot pot and Schnitzel; sandwiches such as satay soya protein in peanut sauce; and burgers (served hot with coleslaw and fries or wedges) for £7.50.

Only a couple of the dishes on the menu appear to be vegan but in fact vegan versions of almost any dish can be arranged.

Half a dozen British desserts £5 include vegan fruit crumble, and they have Swedish Glace ice-cream.

MC, Visa, Diners, Amex.

Woodlands Marylebone

Vegetarian Indian restaurant

77 Marylebone Lane (off Marylebone High St.) W1U 2PS
Tel: 020-7486 3862
www.woodlandsrestaurant.co.uk
Tube: Bond Street, Baker Street
Open: every day 12-15.00, 18-23.00

Nine varieties of dosa (vegetable stuffed pancake, made from rice and wheat)

from £4.25-4.50. Their specialty is uthappam or lentil pizza, with coconut, tomato, green chilli for £5.95. 10 curries £4.50-£5.95. Many rice dishes such as pilau, lemon or coconut, £4.25. 7 desserts with some unusual ones like Jaggary dosa: a crepe filled with sugar cane and cardamom £3.95; and Sheera – cream of wheat with nuts, raisins and ghee £3.50. MC, Visa, Amex, Diners.

Bean Juice

Cafe and juice bar

10a St Christopher's Place W1
Tel: 020-7224 3840
Open: Mon-Fri 7.30-19.30, Sat 10.30-18.30, Sun 11.00-18.30
Tube: Bond Street

Mostly vegetarian cafe and take-away up a small alley opposite Bond Street tube. Fresh juices, smoothies, coffees, milk/soya shakes sandwiches and salads, cookies, brownies and home-made coconut cake, some vegan.

Holland & Barrett

Health food shop

78 Baker St, London W1M 1DL
Tel: 020-7935 3544
Open: Mon-Fri 8.30-18.00, Sat9.3-17.30
Tube: Baker Street

Medium size branch with some take-away food.

Unit C12, West One Shopping Centre, corner of Davis Street and Oxford Street
Tel: 020-7493 7988
Open: Mon-Fri 8-19.00, Sat 9-19.00, Sun 11-17.00
Tube: Bond Street

Larger than usual selection of take-away savouries including sandwiches and vegan pastries and pies.

Oxford Circus

Rasa

Omnivorous South Indian restaurant

6 Dering Street (off Oxford Street)
Tel: 020–7629 1346
Tube: Oxford Circus, Bond Street
Open: Daily 18–23.00, Mon–Sat 12–15.00

One floor of this two storey restaurant is vegetarian. A la carte menu includes four starters, £4.25; two soups £4.25; three types of dosas £9.95; six main courses all £6.25; and five side dishes £5.25, such as vegan cheeraparippu curry with fresh spinach.

Finish off with a vegan banana dosa £3.50 or mango sorbet £2.75

The take-away Rasa Express lunchbox £2.95 is excellent value. 12.5% optional service charge. MC, Visa and Amex.

Tottenham Court Road

Planet Organic

Organic wholefood supermarket and vegetarian cafe

22 Torrington Place WC1A 7JE
Tel: 020–7436 1929
Open: Mon–Fri 9–20.00, Sat 11–18.00, Sun 12–18.00
Tube: Goodge Street

The deli/cafe at the front has hot and cold dishes and salads, mostly vegan, for take-away or eat in at the tables by the tills and outside. Box of food £3, £4 or £5. Cakes and flapjacks, more of which are now dairy-free. Lots of juices and smoothies £2.50–3.00.

The shop sells 20 types of tofu and tempeh, fake meat, every kind of pasta you can imagine and some you can't (spelt, quinoa).

Huge section devoted to health and body care, including vitamins, herbs, tinctures, floral essences, homeopathy, aromatherapy oils, shampoos and conditioners, sun cream.

They have magazines and books including Vegetarian Guides.

Joi

Vegan Chinese buffet restaurant

14 Percy Street off Charlotte Street W1
Tel: 020–7323 0981
Open: Mon–Sat 12–22.30, Sun, 13–22.00
Tube: Goodge Street, Tottenham Court Rd

Chinese vegan buffet restaurant specialising in fake meats. Eat-as-much-as-you-like buffet £5 daytime, £6 evening and Sunday. Choose from chow mein, sweet and sour veg "pork" balls, soya chicken, fake beef, crispy seaweed, fried aubergine, spring rolls, tofu and much more.

Wai

Vegan Chinese buffet restaurant

32 Goodge Street W1
Tel: 020–7637 4819
Open: Every day 12–23.00
Tube: Goodge Street

Same as Joi (above).

Peppercorn's

Wholefood shop

2 Charlotte Street W1
Tel: 020–7631 4528
Open: Mon–Fri 9–18.00, Sat 11–18.00
Tube: Goodge Street

Take-away and macrobiotic specialities from around the world, some organic, with lots of vegan options including Mexican bean slices, vegetarian rotis, country pies, vegetarian sushi, spinach filo pastries, tofu parcels, rice rolls, organic hummous, cottage pies, veggie sausages, rice and curry. Most dishes, snacks and cakes have ingredients displayed.

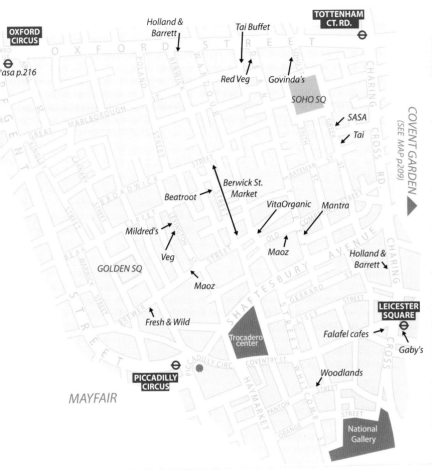

TOTTENHAM CT RD
(SEE p216)

OXFORD
CIRCUS

°asa p.216

Holland &
Barrett

Tai Buffet

TOTTENHAM
CT. RD.

OXFORD STREET

Red Veg

Govinda's

SOHO SQ

SASA

Tai

COVENT GARDEN
(SEE MAP p209)

MARLBOROUGH

Berwick St.
Market

Beatroot

VitaOrganic

Mantra

Mildred's

Maoz

Veg

Holland &
Barrett

GOLDEN SQ

Maoz

Fresh & Wild

SHAFTESBURY AVENUE

LEICESTER
SQUARE

Falafel cafes

Gaby's

Trocadero
center

PICCADILLY
CIRCUS

Woodlands

MAYFAIR

National
Gallery

Soho

Beatroot

Vegetarian/vegan cafe

92 Berwick Street,W1V 3PP
Tel: 020-7437 8591
Open: Mon-Fri 9-21.00, Sat 11-21.00, Sun 12-19.30

Point to whatever you fancy from 16 hot dishes and salads and they'll fill a box for you, small £3.15, medium £4.15 or large £5.15. Choose from, for example, tomato walnut and spinach pasta, spicy Moroccan tangine and all kinds of salads. Soup with bread £2.40.
Mostly vegan cakes and cheesecake £1.50-1.90. Fresh juices, soya-fruit smoothies £1.60-£2.20, teas £1.10 and filter coffee £1.40.

Govinda's

Vegetarian Indian restaurant & cafe

9/10 Soho Street W1V 5DA
Tel: 020 020-7437-4928
Open: Mon-Sat 12-20.00

Popular Hare Krishna place, with some fast food, next door to their temple. 10 main course dishes, but the best value is the 7 dish all-you-can-eat buffet £5.95. Happy hour 7pm-8pm £4.95. No eggs, garlic or onions used.

Mantra

Indian vegetarian restaurant

48 Dean Street, W1D 5BF
Tel: 020-7439 6868
Open: Mon-Fri 13-22.00, Sat 14-23.00
www.mantrasoho.com

Food made to order as spicy or bland as you like. Starters £2.95-5.50, mains £5.50-9.99 include fake meat. Desserts include vegan gulab jambu. Bar downstairs. Smoothies. OK for vegans. Average price £8. 20% discount for Vegetarian Society or with this book.

Mildred's

Vegetarian restaurant

45 Lexington Street, W1
Tel: 020-7494 1634
Open: Mon-Sat 12.30-23.00

Stylish restaurant and take-away with hip young clientele to match, serving modern European cuisine with some Asian influences, such as burger with fries £4.70; or energizing detox salad with tofu £4.90. Desserts include vegan chocolate and nut pudding with mocha sauce £4.25. Fully licensed.

Red Veg

Vegetarian/vegan cafe & take away

95 Dean Street, Soho W1V 5RB
Tel: 020-7437-3109
Open: Mon-Sat 12-22.00

Burgers, hot dogs, four kinds of falafels, three bean wrap, pastas, Noname nuggets, stuffed vine leaves £2.85-3.55. Fries or spicy potato wedges, stuffed jalapeno peppers, breaded mushrooms £1.45-1.95.

SASA Thai

Vegan Chinese buffet

6 Greek Street, Soho W1D 4DE
Tel: 020-7734 3888
Open: every day 12-23.00

All you can eat buffet £5 before 5pm, £6 evening and all day Sunday. Wine £11 bottle, £2.50 glass. Saki £6 small bottle. Juices £1.50-£2. Teas £1.

Tai

Vegan Chinese buffet restaurant

10 Greek Street, Soho W1V 5PL
Tel: 020-7287 3730
Open: every day 12.00-23.00

All you can eat buffet, as many trips as you like for £5, or £6 in the evenings and all day Sunday. £3 or £4 for a take-away box. Spring rolls, tofu, stir-fry veg, salad and soya meats. Cash only

Tai Buffet

Vegan Chinese buffet restaurant

3-4 Great Chapel Street, off Oxford Street W1
Tel: 020-7439 0383.
Open: every 12.30-21.30

Same as Tai (above).

Veg

Vegan Chinese buffet restaurant

41 Lexington Street, W1F 9AJ (corner Beak St)
Tel: 020-7287 9620

The newest all you can eat buffet.

Maoz

Vegetarian falafel cafe

43 Old Compton St, Soho W1
Open: Mon-Thu 11-01.00, Fri & Sat -02.00
Sun 11-24.00.
also at 4 Brewer Street, Open 11-01.00

Cafe specialising in fantastic falafels in pitta, £3-£3.50. Self-serve salad bar with large choice of tahini and salads.

VitaOrganic

Vegan Oriental and raw restaurant

74 Wardour Street, Soho W1
Open: daily 12-22.00. www.vitaorganic.co.uk

Super-healthy food, nothing heated about 100 degrees C, curries cooked by steaming or with high oleic oil, lots of raw food and sprouts. See page 228 for other branch..

Woodlands

Vegetarian South Indian restaurant

37 Panton St, (off Haymarket) SW1Y 4EA
Open: every day 12-22.45
Tel: 020-7839 7258

Lunchtime all-you-can-eat buffet on weekdays for £6.99

Gaby's

Omnivorouus Mediterranean cafe

30 Charing Cross Rd (by Leicester Square)
Tel: 020-7836 4233
Open: Mon-Sat 9-24.00, Sun 12-21.00

Stacks of veggie and vegan eat-ins and take-aways for great prices.

Fresh & Wild Soho

Wholefood supermarket & veggie cafe

71-75 Brewer Street W1R 3SL
Tel: 020-7434 3179
Open: Mon-Fri 8-21.00, Sat 9-20.00,
Sun 11.30-18.30, Bank hols 12-19.00

Heaps of take-aways, salad bar and juice bar/cafe with seating and organic fruit and vegetables.

Berwick Street Market

Outdoor fruit and veg market

Open: Mon-Sat 09.00-18.00

Bargains in £1 bowls and a nuts vendor.

Holland & Barrett

Health food shop

65 Charing Cross Road
Open: Mon-Sat 10-20.00, Sun 11-18.00

123 Oxford St. Open: Mon-Fri 08.30-19.00,
Sat 10-19.00, Sun 12-18.00

London

East London has a real vibrancy to it. Although not the most prosperous part of London, the upside is that it's a lot cheaper than the north and west, and the rich cultural mix and a number of friendly vegetarian restaurant choices make it a wonderful place to live.

Victoria Park is deceptively big and you can lose yourself completely, and momentarily forget that you're in a massive city. The area is also great if you're a cyclist. The canal provides a lovely traffic-free route all the way to Hoxton, Angel or King's Cross to the west and Limehouse and Docklands to the south.

For bargain hunters, Roman Road Market (Tue, Thur, Sat) is a must. The focus is on clothes, shoes and household goods but a few stalls sell extremely inexpensive fruit and vegetables. Don't miss the excellent olive stand where the Turkish owner insists that you try everything first.

The London Buddhist Centre offers meditation classes and nearby are two Buddhist run restaurants, a cafe and a wholefood store plus the gift shop Evolution.

Green Street is full of Asian shops run by Sikhs, Muslims, Hindus, Buddhists, even Hare Krishnas, selling henna, incense and clothes.

East London

Chawalla

Vegetarian Indian restaurant

270 Green Street, Forest Gate E7 8LF
Tel: 020–8470 3535
Open: Every day 11.00–21.00
Tube: Upton Park

Indian vegetarian restaurant with South Indian, Gujarati and Punjabi food. Eat for around £7 a head. They have some unusual dishes such as spicy masala potato chips garnished with lime juice, cassava chips with tamarind sauce and lentil and rice pancakes.

Ronak Restaurant

South Indian restaurant and take-away

317 Romford Road, Forest Gate E7 9HA
Tel: 020-8519 2110
Open: Tue–Sun   12–21.00
Tube: Stratford, Upton Park, Forest Gate BR

Masala dosa £4, thali with two curries £7.50.   Lots of snacks like bhel puri, samosas, kachori. Sunday all day there is an eat-as-much-as-you-want buffet for £4.50 with five kinds of curries. Desserts include vegan halva and monthar (made fom chickpea flour). No credit cards.

Sakonis Vegetarian

Vegetarian Indian and Chinese restaurant

149–153 Green Street, Forest Gate E7 8LE
Tel: 020-8472-8887
Open: Winter: Tue–Sat 12–21.30, Sun 12–21.30 / Summer: open half hour later, closed Mon (except bank holiday then closed Tue)
Tube: Stratford, Upton Park, Forest Gate BR

One of three London vegetarian South Indian restaurants that also offer some Chinese dishes.

Lunch buffet 12–3pm £5.99 + 10%, so £6.59. Dinner buffet 7–9.30pm (Sat from 6.30pm, Sun from 6pm) £8.69.

Gallery Cafe

Vegetarian cafe and restaurant

21 Old Ford Road, Bethnal Green E2 9PL
Tel: 020-8983-3624
Open: Mon–Fri 8.30–15.00, Sat 10.20–17.0
Tube: Bethnal Green, then short walk

Cosmopolitan vegetarian café run as a co-operative by Buddhists.   Outside umbrella seating in summer on the flower filled south facing terrace.
A different home made soup each day £2.40. Turkish meze starters or filled bagels £1.30–£1.80. Three salads each £1.50. Main course meze £5.30. Hot dishes £4.80 such as Spanish tortilla, casserole or stew, or pasta, sometimes vegan.
Cheques and Visa, MC accepted on orders over £5.

Thai Garden

Omnivorous Thai restaurant

249 Globe Road Bethnal Green E2 0JD
Tel: 020-8981 5748
Open: Everyday 18–23.00, Mon–Fri 12–15.00
Tube: Bethnal Green

Over 40 vegetarian dishes of which many are vegan. Intimate dining on two floors, the staff are friendly and attentive.
Sample Gang phed ped yang jay, consisting of Thai aubergine, mock duck, pineapple, tomatoes, grapes, bamboo shoots and sweet basil leaves in a red curry with coconut cream. Lard na is fried rice noodles, mushrooms, mixed veg and black bean sauce was also very filling. All major credit cards.

Globe Town

Wild Cherry

Vegetarian restaurant

241 Globe Road, Bethnal Green E2 0JD
Tel: 020-8980 6678
Tube: Bethnal Green
Open:Mon 11-16.00, Tue-Fri 11-19.00,
Sat 10-16.00

Cooperatively run vegetarian restaurant, which has a light, spacious feel to it, combined with elegant décor and a secluded garden out back.

Start with soup of the day or a huge range of salads. For mains there is always a vegan option or two, such as aubergine and courgette pilau plus salad £5.25; or veg with spicy & fruity peanut sauce and rice £4.95.

Wide range of homebaked cakes, including vegan, sugar-free and wheat-free, such as banoffee pie £2.85, carrot cake or chocolate brownies.

Saturday all day breakfast includes pancakes and freshly squeezed juices.
Non-smoking. All major credit cards.

Hackney

Pogo Cafe

Vegan cafe-restaurant

76a Clarence Road, Hackney E5 8HB
Tel: 020-8533 1214
www.pogocafe.co.uk
Train: Hackney Central BR
Open: Wed-Sat 12.30-21.00 (last order)
Sun 11-21.00, Mon 12-18.00

New 100% vegan, fair trade, mostly organic, cooperatively run cafe with comfy sofas, a children's corner, wooden floors, walls adorned with local art, spot lighting and cool music.

Full British Sunday vegan breakfast £5 from 11am features French toast, scrambled tofu, potatoes wedges, special beans and broccoli.

Main courses £5-5.75 such as curried black-eyed bean ragout with couscous, pitta salad and yoghurt dip; Feijoada Brasileira (black beans, vegan sausages, sundried tomato) served with stir-fried cabbage, wholemeal rice and farrofa (stir-fried manioc flour).

The best vegan cakes and cheesecake in London, £1-£2, cookies, muffins, some gluten/wheat or sugar free. And vegan ice-cream! Lots of smoothies and shakes. Bring your own wine, off license 5 doors down, £1 corkage.

Non-smoking. No credit cards. Children welcome, high chair.

Leytonstone

Chandni

Vegetarian Indian restaurant

715 High Rd, Leytonstone E11 4RD
Tel: 020-8539 1700
Tube: Leytonstone
Open: Everyday 17.00-midnight
(last orders 22.30)

Newly refurbished Indian vegetarian restaurant with a few Chinese and African dishes. 85% vegan.

17 mains £2.50-5.50 such as vegetable kofta curry, vegetable makhan wala, Punjabi dal fried, rajma masala and vegetable shahi korma.

Chandni special thali £6.50.

25 starters £1.50-4.50 including vegetable cutlets with potato chips and chutneys, Delhi chat masala mogo chips and kachori.

Lots of alcohol. Five house wines £6.50-8.00 bottle, £1.70-2.20 glass. Champagne from £17.50 half bottle up to £160 for a bottle of Cristal. (the favourite of MTV hip hop stars) Beers including Cobra from £1.50-1.70 (33cl) to only £2.30 (500cl), a lot less than you'd pay in many places.

North London has stacks of places to eat vegetarian and vegan. Stoke Newington is one of the best areas to live if you're into cruelty free living. Stoke Newington Church Street has a huge Fresh & Wild store and lots of great restaurants of which the Keralan Indian Rasa is our favourite.

Gateway to north London, home of Prime Minister Tony Blair and some cracking vegetarian eateries, Islington is a somewhat swanky shopping area that's great for designer gifts, antiques and bargain non leather jackets in Chapel Market.

Islington offers amazing value for a veggie night out. Diners converge from all over to meet their friends at Indian Veg Bhelpuri House for the cheapest all-you-can-eat buffet in London.

For a 100% vegan Chinese feast you need to visit Tai Buffet opposite Angel underground. A few doors to the left is their vegan dumpling and noodle restaurant.

Golders Green has lots of Jewish grocery stores full of dairy-free ice-cream, cakes and chocolate.

Although not a destination high on any tourist itinerary, Holloway has the North's finest vegetarian restaurant: Peking Palace. You may want to make the special journey up here just for a taste of vegan heaven.

North London

Crouch End

Haelan Centre

Huge wholefood shop

41 The Broadway Crouch End N8 8DT
Tel: 020-8340 4258
Open: Mon–Thu, Sat 9–18.00, Fri 9–18.00,
Sun 12–16.00
Tube: Crouch Hill, Hornsey BR

Large independent wholefood shop in hip Crouch End.

Ground floor is food, including organic fruit & veg, large fridge/ freezer section with several types of vegan cheese, ice–creams and a selection of veggie foods. Well stocked fresh take–away food with vegan options, sushi, pancakes, pies and cakes. Herbs, teas, amazing amount of dry wholefoods and pulses and a good selection of seaweeds and oriental sauces.

The second floor is an Aladdin's cave of non–food items which always smells lovely.

Finchley

Rani

Vegetarian Gujarati and South Indian restaurant

7 Long Lane, Finchley N3 2PR
Tel: 020-8349 4386
Tube:Finchley Central
Open: Mon–Sat 18.30–22.00, Sun 13–15.30
then 18–22.00

There are 12 main dishes such as bhindi fried okra, delicately spiced and slow cooked with whole baby potatoes and onions at £5.40.

Some dishes have an African influence such as akhaa ringal, Kenyan aubergine slit and pressed in spices, ground peanuts and fresh coriander and cooked with potato.

Excellent breads – the essential accompaniment to Gujarati food. Don't miss the mithi roti, a sweetened lentil mix with cardamon and saffron, parceled in unleavened dough, sprinkled with poppy seeds and roasted.

No eggs and only vegetable ghee.
MC, Visa, Amex.

Finsbury Park

Jai Krishna

Vegetarian Gujarati and South Indian restaurant

161 Stroud Green Road, Finsbury Park N4 3PZ
Tel: 020-7272 1680
Open: Mon–Sat 12–14.00, 17.30–23.00
Tube: Finsbury Park

There is a wide range of veg and vegan starters such as pakoras, katchori (lentils in puff pastry) for £1.80.

Dosas and curries, £4.50; and thalis £6.75. Try the coconut and lemon rice, or brown rice. There are lots of special dishes such as pumpkin curry £3.25.

Corkage £1.25 bottle of wine, 30p a bottle or can of beer, and there's an off license opposite.

Cash or cheque only.

Golder's Green

CTV

Vegan Chinese buffet

22 Golders Green Rd NW11 8LL
Tel: 020-7794 0848
Open: Every day 12.00–22.00
Tube: Golders Green

Mouthwatering eat–as–much–as–you–like buffet for £5 £6 after 5.30pm and on Sunday. Take–out box £3 or £4.

You can fill up on chow mein, crispy aubergine, spring rolls, Singapore noodles, Thai curry rice, sweet and sour won ton, and black beans hot pot.

Unlimited Jasmine tea £1. Detox, organic green or ginseng tea £1.50.

Golder's Green

Pita

Falafel cafe

98 Golders Green Road NW11 8HB
(corner of Hoop Lane)
Tel: 020–8381 4080
Open: every day1 1–23.00
Tube: Golders Green

Green herby or yellow spicy falafels with hummous £3.25, plus other nice take-aways. A few seats. It's by the railway bridge that goes over the main road, next to Baskin–Robbins.

Holloway

Peking Palace

Vegan Oriental restaurant

669 Holloway Road N19 5SE
Tel: 020–7281–8989
www.thepekingpalace.com
Tube: Archway
Open: Mon–Fri 12.00–15.00, 18.00–23.00,
Sat–Sun 18.00–23.00

London's biggest vegan menu, with 115 options. The décor is modern, bright and decorated with deep reds and ochre inspiring a lavish feeling.

Take–away buffet Mon–Fri £3 small, £4 large, or one large plate eat in £4.95. Half portion for children £2.50.

18 appetizers £3.00–4.80 like Peking dumplings and asparagus tempura.

The main course menu is divided into soya meat, tofu dishes, and curries. Try the sizzling soya beef steak Peking style which is very filling for £5.00, fried soya fish in black bean sauce with olive £4.80, or Kung Po soya king prawn for £5.00. 7 kinds of tofu dishes such as big braised tofu steak in black pepper sauce on a bed of cabbage £4.40. Fake fish steaks and even vegan fish and chips with a big plate with two pieces of fake fish with mushy peas and grilled tomatoes £6.80. Also deluxe vegan cheeseburgers.

Desserts include several flavours of vegan ice–cream £3.25, toffee and banana with ice–cream, or rambutan stuffed with pineapple in lychee syrup. MC, Visa

Islington

Indian Veg Bhelpuri

Vegetarian Indian restaurant

92–93 Chapel Market, Islington N1 9EX
Tel: 020–7837 4607
Tube: Angel
Open: Every day: 11.00–23.00

Best value veggie restaurant in London with a great bargain all–you–can–eat-buffet for £2.95 and has 3 types of rice, 2 curries, onion bhaji, poori, 3 sauces and lentil dhal.

Fresh vegan lassis in different flavours, £2.15. Juices 99p. 14 kinds of organic fruit juice in cans £1.65. Now serving alcohol: beers 330ml £1.99, 500ml £2.95, 710ml £3.95 and wine from £6.95 bottle, £1.95 glass.

They use vegetable oil not butter ghee. MC, Visa.

Tai Buffet

Vegan Chinese buffet

13 Islington High St, Islington N1
Tel: 020–7837 7767
Tube: Angel
Open: every day 12–24.00, Fri–Sun till 01.00

Yet another new Chinese vegan eat–as–much–as–you–like buffet, right opposite Angel tube station.

£5 daytime, £6 evening, or £3 for a take–away box.They have a vegan noodle and dumpling bar two doors down at number 11.

Kentish Town

Bumblebee

Wholefood & macrobiotic shop

30, 32 and 33 Brecknock Road N7 6AA
Tel: 020-7607-1936
Open: Mon-Sat 9.00-18.30, Thurs till 19.30
Tube: Kentish Town

Three shops with a massive selection of wholefoods, health foods, organic produce, macrobiotic foods and a bakery section. Enormous selection of vegan and organic wines and beers, probably the biggest in London.
Takeaway foods and lunches 11.30-15.00 £1.75 standard, £3.20 large.

King's Cross

Tony's Natural Foods

Vegan organic cafe, shop and juice bar

10 Caledonian Road, Kings Cross N1 9DU
Tel: 020-7837 5223
Tube: Kings Cross
Open: Mon-Fri 9-15.00

Hot food £2.80 small take-away (£3.20 eat in), £4.50 large (£5.20); salads; sandwiches £2.25 and hemp flour baps; and cakes £1.25.
Spirulina and fruit smoothies £2.50 with freshly made nut and hemp seed milk. Medicinal cannabis and herbal remedies clinic attached. They also offer relex-ology, energy healing and Japanese massage. Clinic open Mon-Fri 10-18.00, Sat-Sun 11-17.00.

Muswell Hill

Queens Wood

Vegetarian cafe

42 Muswell Hill Road, Highgate Wood,
London N10 3JP
Tel: 020-8444-2604
Tube: Highgate
Open: Sat-Sun10-18.00close 17.00 winter

In the Cue Environmental Centre in Highgate Wood, once a woodkeeper's cottage, where you can eat on the verandah or sit inside.
Starters and appetisers £3.50 such as carrot and coriander soup with bread, and olive or mushroom paté on toast.
Main dishes with salad £4.90-5.90, could include pasta bake, chickpea and broccoli curry, falafel with pitta bread, shepherd's pie, hot pot, or tortilla wrap.

Tai Buffet

Vegan Chinese buffet

271 Muswell Hill Broadway, Muswell Hill N10
Tel: 020-8442 0558
Open: Every day 12-12.30
Tube: Highgate or East Finchley then bus

See Islington branch (previous page)

Stoke Newington

Fresh and Wild

Wholefood supermarket and vegetarian cafe & juice bar

32-40 Church St, Stoke Newington
Tel: 020 7249 0344
Tube: Stoke Newington BR, Bus 476 from Angel or Bus 106 from Finsbury Park
Open: Summer Mon-Sat 18.30-22.45,
Sun 9-20.30;
Winter Mon-Sat 9-21.00, Sun 10-20.00

Serve-yourself salad bar, deli section with hot food, and a section for cakes and coffee. Ingredients are clearly labelled and usually one is vegan.

227

Big selection of organic fruit, veg, herb plants, wine, beers and ciders, toiletries, aromatherapy oils, supplements and herbal remedies.

Well stocked range of books on many subjects adjacent to the toiletries counter. There is a small bulletin board at the front of the shop for local events.

Stoke Newington

Rasa

Vegetarian Indian restaurant

55 Church Street, Stoke Newington, N16 0AR
Tel: 020-7249 0344
Tube: Stoke Newington BR or Bus 476 from Angel station
Open: Sun–Thu 18–22.45, Fri–Sat 18–23.30

The atmosphere is relaxed with classic Indian music in the background, and. dishes that don't seem vegan can be veganized.

Starters £2.75–£3.00 such as banana boli: plaintain slices battered in chickpea flour, seasoned with black sesame seeds and served with peanut and ginger sauce. Main courses feature a large dosa selection and over nine curries from £5.00.

MC, Visa, Amex, Diners.

West Hampstead

VitaOrganic

Vegan organic Asian and raw food restaurant and juice bar

279c Finchley Rd, West Hampstead NW3 6ND
Tel: 020-7435 2188
Tube: Finchley Road, Frognal BR
Open: Mon–Sun 12–15.00, 18–21.00

Lovely oriental atmosphere with Chinese lanterns, bamboo and friendly staff. It is especially ideal for those on a wheat free, food combining, raw or macrobiotic diet.

Self-serve buffet for £6.90 includes raw vegetables, seaweed soup, teriyaki, tempura, and spicy curries.

A la carte options include stroganoff, orange masala sprouted dal, and steamed moussaka.

West Hendon

Rajen's

Vegetarian Indian restaurant and take–away / sweet mart

195–197 The Broadway, W. Hendon NW9 6LP
Tel: 020–8203 8522
Open: Mon–Sun 11–22.00
Restaurant Mon–Fri 12–15.00,
Sat–Sun 13–22.00

They specialize in an eat as much as you like buffet thali which costs £5 on weekdays and £6.50 on the weekend. The a la carte menu has all the usual Indian snacks such as bhel poori, kachori, dosas, and curries.

Soft drinks only. MC, Visa over £10. No smoking. Children welcome, high chairs.

Close to where the start of the M1 and Edgware Road meet the North Circular Road. Free car park at the back.

South London's top area is Clapham and Battersea, well endowed with green open spaces, a theatre, plenty of shopping and a fine variety of veggie-friendly eateries.

Cicero's, in the middle of Clapham Common, is South London's only vegetarian park café. It also makes an unusual private party venue. Battersea Rice (formerly Sayur Mayur) has unfortunately closed but you'll find plenty to eat at the giant Fresh & Wild wholefood supermarket or Jasmin Oriental restaurant.

Not far from Clapham is Brixton, with its street market, Brixton Academy for rock gigs, and Bruno's restaurant.

Waterloo, by the River Thames, is close to the London Eye, Festival Hall, Gabriel's Wharf (a fun place by the river to meander if you like craft shops and bars), the IMAX surround cinema, the National Theatre, National Film Theatre, Royal Festival Hall, Hayward Gallery, the Young Vic and Old Vic theatres, and of course Waterloo Station itself – gateway to the continent. But where can a hungry veggie eat? Waterloo has only one truly veggie eating place, Coopers. It's not open in the evening, but don't despair, tasty veggie and vegan food can be found elsewhere in the vicinity and for a reasonable price, including Tas, a veggie-friendly Turkish restaurant with dolma and falafels, with live guitar music.

For tourists and tennis fanatics in the Wimbledon area, Service Heart Joy is a bright and tranquil vegetarian cafe on Hartfield Road. Alternatively, pop into Health Zone Ltd for snacks to take with you.

230	Brixton, Clapham, Crystal Palace
231	Greenwich, London Bridge, Norbury, Selhurst
232	Streatham, Tooting, Vauxhall
253	Waterloo, Wimbledon

South London

Brixton

Bruno

Italian vegetarian restaurant

424 Coldharbour Lane, Brixton SW9
Tel: 020–7738–6161
Tube: Brixton
Directions: Turn left out of Brixton tube, walk past the bus stops and turn left at KFC. It's just past a noodle bar.
Open:Mon–Wed 11.30–17.00,
Thu–Sat 11.30–23.00
(Kitchen closes 15.00 and 22.00 but keeps serving except mains and pasta)

Cafe Pushkar is under new ownership but still a great veggie restaurant. The standard menu chagnes every six weeks with salads, pasta, bangers and mash, couscous. Soup £3.50, panini £4 with salad. Pasta and salad small £3.50, large £5. Bruno's burger £4 with salad, £6 with chips and chutney. Specials could be stir–fry, curry, laksa, £6. Vegan cakes include chocolate, carrot & walnut, £2.50 with soya dessert.
House wine £3 glass, £8.50 bottle, organic £11–12. No smoking. MC, Visa. Children welcome, high chair.

Clapham

Cicero's

Vegetarian park cafe

2 Rookery Road, Clapham Common,
Clapham SW4 9DD
Tel: 020–7498 0770
Tube: Clapham Common
Open: Every day 10–18.00, Summer 10–16.00, Winter closed Mon

All day full veggie breakfast £5.50, add 50p for a (soya) capuccino.
Starters £3.50 such as sushi with dipping sauce, Taj Mahal soup and Moroccan stuffed aubergine with red pepper sauce.
Main courses £6 such as char grilled tofu with peanut sauce and aubergine moussaka.
Sandwiches, can be made with ciabatta, £2–3.75. Veggieburger special £6.

Jasmin Restaurant

Omnivorous Chinese restaurant

50 Battersea Rise, SW11 1EG

Several tofu and vegetable dishes.

Fresh and Wild

Organic wholefood supermarket

305–311 Lavender Hill, SW11 1LN
Tel: 020–7585 1488
Open: Mon–Fri 9–20.00, Sat 9–19.30,
Sun 11–18.00
Tube: Clapham Junction

Organic supermarket with a huge range of organic produce, fruit and veg, take–away, remedies and books.
Café, juice bar and deli with seats and tables. The café has heaps of organic hot and cold food made daily by the in–store chefs. Salad bar small £2.99, medium £3.25, large £3.99.

Crystal Palace

Domali

International cafe bar restaurant

38 Westow Street, Crystal Palace SE19 3AH
Tel: 020–8768–0096
Open: Mon–Tue 9.30–18.00, Wed–Sun 9.30–23.00
Train: Crystal Palace BR, Gypsy Hill BR
www.domali.co.uk

Veggie breakfast served until 6pm, includes muesli, veggie bacon and sausages £1.90–5.90.
Lunch specials include wild mushroom paté with farmhouse bread, olive oil and mixed leaf garnish £3.90

Toasties £3.90 include veggie sausage with mustard and tomato, or veggie salami with roasted pepper.

Coffee and juice bar with soya smoothies, double juices £2.20, singles £1.60. Add a shot of St. John's Wort, echinacea, gurarana or milk thistle for 40p.

Local artists' work is exhibited and is for sale. There IS A DJ on Sunday nights.

Greenwich

Greenlands Health

Health food shop

Unit 3a, Greenwich Craft Market
Greenwich SE10 9HZ
Tel: 020–8293 9176
Open: Mon–Sun 9.30–18.30
Tube: Greenwich

Health food store with all vegetarian take-away pies, pasties, snacks £1–3.75. Sandwiches from £1.79, salads £1.79. Also cakes and health drinks.

London Bridge

Borough Market

Covered food market

Between Stoney Street and Bedale Street, SE1
Open: Fri 12–18.00, Sat 9–16.00
Tube: London Bridge

An astounding array of stalls with exotic foods from around the world. If you want a great foodie day out or you need something unusual like truffles to impress your dinner gusts, no other market comes close. Plenty of organic normal fruit and veg too.

Norbury

Shahee Bhelpoori

Vegetarian Indian restaurant

1547 London Road, Norbury SW16 4AD
(opposite Norbury BR Station)
Tel: 020–8679 6275
Train: Norbury BR
Open:every day 12.00–14.30, inc bank holidays 18–23.00, Sun lunch 12.00–15.00

13 hot and cold starters £1.85–3.05 such as vegetable kebab. 20 side orders from £2.25 include vegetable kofta at £2.95.

Main courses from £2.95 include dosas from £2.95 and thalis £4.50–6.95.

10% discount to Vegetarian or Vegan Society members. Visa, MC.

Croydon Vegans meet here, see local contacts, and the local MP comes here for bhel poori.

Selhurst

Pepperton UK

Vegetarian restaurant

25 Selhurst Rd SE25 5PT
(opposite the Selhurst Arms)
Tel: 020–8683 4462
Tube: Selhurst BR, buses 75, 157
Open:Tue–Sat 10–22.00, Sun 12–20.00

The red front of this licensed vegetarian/vegan restaurant and contemporary art gallery makes it unmissable. Main courses are no more than £6.50 such as almond and vegetable fried rice with spinach dhal; wild rice with vegetable curry. Jacket potato with beans £2.50, with selection of cooked toppings £5.50.

Wholemeal Cafe

Wholefood vegetarian restaurant

1 Shrubbery Road, Streatham SW16 2AS
Tel: 020–8769 2423
Open: Every day 12.00–22.00 (except bank holidays)
Tube: Streatham BR, Streatham Hill BR

Wholefood veggie restaurant with Thai, Indian, Mediterranean and world cuisine. Large vegan selection. Typical dishes include garlic mushrooms with pitta £3.25; guacamole and warm pitta £3.25, or soup of the day £2.50, usually vegan.

Main dishes £2.5–6.50 include homity pie, hot bake of the day, casserole of the day, red Thai curry, spinach and mushroom crumble.

Kastoori

Vegetarian Gujarati restaurant

188 Upper Tooting Road, Tooting SW17 7EJ
Tel: 020–8767 7027
Tube: Tooting Broadway
Open: Mon–Tue 18.00–22.30, Wed–Sun 12.30–14.30 18–22.30

There is an east African influence to this vegetarian Indian Gujarati restaurant which doesn't use eggs.

12 curries, 8 vegan. You could try the Kastoori kofta – mixed vegetable balls, roasted aubergine curry, or a potato curry with the chef's sauce £4.75–5.25. Kastoori family specials include Kasodi – sweetcorn in coconut milk with ground peanut sauce; or kontola curry – a crunchy mountain vegetable cooked with garlic sauce.

Milan

Vegetarian Indian restaurant

158 Upper Tooting Road, Tooting SW17 7ER
Tel: 020–8767 4347
Tube: TootingBec, Tooting Broadway
Open: Mon 11–21.30, Tue–Thu 10 – 21.30, Fri–Sat 9–22.00, Sun9–21.30

Three thalis, £4.95–£7.95. Milan special thali has a vegan option for £7.95 with millet loaf, roast aubergine, moong, rice and papadum. All the usual parathas, nan, dahl, pickles.

Bonnington Cafe

Vegetarian wholefood restaurant

11 Vauxhall Grove, Vauxhall SW8 1TA
Tel: 020–7820 7466
www.bonningtoncafe.co.uk
Tube: Vauxhall
Open: Every day 19.00–23.00

Historically a large squatter community thrived here. Nowadays there are as many Mercs as 2CVs. Run on a cooperative basis with a different cook preparing the food each night from their own repertoire, so there is no set menu. The atmosphere is very laid back and it's great value as you can get a three course meal for £10.

Thursday is vegan night.

Coopers

Vegetarian cafe and deli

17 Lower Marsh SE1
Tel: 020–7261 9314
Tube: Waterloo
Open: Mon–Fri 08.30–17.30

Family run vegetarian cafe, deli and
health food store with excellent and
imaginative vegan rolls and sandwiches
to take away or eat in such as veg
sausage and pickle or Swiss herb paté.
Better than other sandwich bars for
quality and size of fillings. Savouries
such as potato and onion bhaji, veg and
sunflower rissole, carrot and onion
cutlet, chickpea roti, various kebabs,
vine leaves, humous and cottage pies,
salads and soups.

They normally have a choice of 5 cakes
daily like chocolate and walnut, carrot
and coconut, apple and sultana, at least
one is vegan.

The shop has lovely breads, organic
beers and ciders.

Tas

Omnivorous Turkish restaurant

33 The Cut, Waterloo SE1 8LF
Tel: 020–7928 1444
www.tasrestaurant.com
Tube: Waterloo
Open: Every day 12.00–23.30

Anatolian restaurant that received the
Time Out Best Vegetarian Meal Award
2000. Almost all starters (meze) are
veggie. The menu has a veggie section
with 10 main dishes £6.55–7.45 such
as patlicanli: grilled aubergine with
tomatoes, peppers and couscous.

Service Heart Joy

Vegetarian cafe

191–193 Hartfield Road, Wimbledon
SW19 3TH
Tel: 020–8542 9912
Tube: Wimbledon
Open: Mon–Thu 08.00–17.00, Fri   08.00–
21.00, Sat 9–17.00

Colourful vegetarian café and take-
away, well worth the walk from
Wimbledon station to the end of
Hartfield Road.

Cooked breakfasts from beans on toast
£2.35 up to brunch £5.45 which
includes vegetarian bacon and sausage.
Pancakes £3.95, all with maple syrup,
include blueberry; banana and walnuts;
Balinese style coconut milk, coconut
and banana.

Panini or wholemeal sandwiches £2.70–
3.40; salads £2.45–5.45; soup of the
day with bread £2.50; and Indian hot
dishes £3.95–5.95.

Health Zone Ltd

Health food shop

30 Wimbledon Hill Road, Wimbledon
SW19 7PA
Tel: 020–8944–1133
Open: Mon–Fri 9.30–19.00, Sat 9.30–18.00,
Sun 11–17.00
Tube: Wimbledon

Much more than your average health
food shop.

They stock a wide range of veggie and
vegan foods, many organic, supplements and organic body–care products.
Also a few veggie/vegan sandwiches,
falafel in pitta, pasties, pies, salads such
as couscous, from £2 upwards and a
gluten–free range. Vegan ice–cream.

Yoga and pilates equipment. Wide
selection of books on health,
magazines, CD's.

LONDON South

Hammersmith might at first glance seem like a huge roundabout under a giant flyover. However as well as being an important conference and business centre, there are fabulous walks by the peaceful Thames, some great British pubs, and the Riverside Studios for arty cinema and theatre. Nearby Shepherds Bush Green has the Bush Theatre where many top music acts perform.

There are terrific vegetarian dining possibilities. The Gate and Blah Blah Blah are two of London's longest established international vegetarian restaurants. Sagar is an Indian vegetarian restaurant. 222 at 222 North End Road is a superb new gourmet vegan restaurant with a lunchtime buffet and, unlike many vegan restaurants, also serves alcohol.

West London

Chelsea

Organic Cafe

Vegetarian English and Thai cafe

The Auction Rooms, 71 Lots Road,
Chelsea SW10
Tel: 020-7351 7771
Open: Sun 10.00-18.30
Tube: Fulham Broadway

Veggie cafe at the back of an auction room offering a very different Sunday out. It's inside the auction rooms where antiques are being sold, and it cannot be seen from the street.

Thai-influenced main courses £4; salad £3; or main course and salad £6.

Organic sandwiches. Soup £3 with organic bread.

Organic teas, coffee and alternatives £1. Freshly made real fruit juice.

Organic cakes, some vegan, such as chocolate almond £1.90, flapjacks or brownies £1.20. Cash only.

Fulham

Planet Organic

Wholefood supermarket and vege-tarian cafe

25 Effey Road, Fulham SW6
Tel 020-7731 7222
Open: Mon-Fri, 8.30-20.30, Sat 10-18.00, Sun 12.00-18.00
Tube: Fulham Broadway

The groceries section has all organic fruit and veg. Health and bodycare has qualified nutritionists and a herbalists to explain the vitamins, herbs, tinctures, floral essences, aromatherapy and homeopathy. Lots of books about health and bodycare.

The vegetarian café section is open throughout the day and all ingredients come from the shop. Small box £2.25, medium £4, large £5. Small platter £5.50, big one £7. All organic cakes, 50% vegan.

Juice bar with smoothies £3, juices £2.60-2.80. Cappuccino £1.75, and three kinds of soya milk including vanilla.

Two Two Two

International gourmet
vegan restaurant

222 North End Road W14 9NU
Tel: 020-7381 2322
Tube: West Brompton, West Kensington, Fulham Broadway
Open: every day 12-15.30 17.30-22.30

Starters £3.25-4.50 include avocado with tomato sauce and vegan cream; or black eye bean and tofu pate pancake with tomato chunks and cream sauce.

Main courses £7.50-10.50 such as marinated organic tofu baked in oat crumbs on tomato wholemeal spaghetti.

Desserts include organic vegan ice-cream, tofu cheesecake and pancakes with warm vanilla and chocolate sauce, £2.95-4.50. Visa, MC. Fully licensed.

Hammersmith

Blah Blah Blah

Vegetarian restaurant

78 Goldhawk Road,
Shepherds Bush W12 8HA
Tel: 020 8746 1337
Open: Mon-Sat 12.00-14.30, 19.00-23.00
Tube: Shepherds Bush

Five main courses £9.95 such as Thai green curry with basmati rice and fruit salsa; vegetable pie and chips with onion gravy .

No booze so bring your own (£1.25 corkage per person). No credit cards.

Hammersmith

The Gate

International vegetarian restaurant

51 Queen Caroline St,
Hammersmith, London W6 9QL
Tel: 020-8748 6932. Tube: Hammersmith
Open: Mon-Sat 12.00-15.00, 18.00-23.00
Menus at www.gateveg.co.uk
Book at least 2 days ahead at the weekend:
hammersmith@gateveg.co.uk

Top class restaurant set in an artist's studio with modernist leanings. Nine starters, most vegan or can be, £2.25-£5.50. Mezze platter £12.50 (serves 2) with a selection of all starters. Mains, 4 vegan or vegan option, £10-11.75, such as wild mushroom rosti, mussamen curry, aubergine teriyaki, tortillas, pasta of the day. Seasonal specials like the autumn 6 course fungi menu £35.

7 desserts £3.95-£6, 2 or 3 vegan or vegan option such as apple and black-berry charlotte.

House wine £10.50 bottle, £3 glass. Children welcome, high chairs. MC, Visa. Smoking allowed.

Sagar

Vegetarian Indian restaurant

157 King St, Hammersmith W6
Tel: 020-8741 8563
Open: Mon-Fri 12-14.45 17.30-22.45,
Sat-Sun 12-22.45
Tube: Hammersmith

South Indian vegetarian restaurant near the Town Hall. Thali set meal £11.45 with starters, curries and dessert. Visa, MC, Amex.

Kingsbury

Jays Pure

Vegetarian restaurant

547 Kingsbury Road NW9 9EL
Tel: 020-8204 1555
Tube: Kingsbury
Open: Every day 12.30-23.00

International menu, cooked with sunflower oil, so many dishes are suitable for vegans.

Indian mains are all under £6.00 and include vegetable biriyani and Hyderabad masala dosa.

The Mexican dishes £3-6 include burritos with picante sauce.

They also make Chinese curries such as baby corn with mushroom Szechuan style and Thai dishes like green curry, £3-£5.

Rose

Vegetarian Asian restaurant

532-534 Kingsbury Road NW9 9HH
Tel: 020-8905 0035
Freephone 0800-583 8905
Open: Everyday 12-22.30
Tube: Kingsbury

North and South Indian and Chinese vegetarian restaurant and take-away. Buffet lunch every day 12-15.00, £4.99. No alcohol. No smoking. Children welcome, high chairs. MC, Visa.

Gayatri Sweet

Vegetarian take-away

467 Kingsbury Road, Kingsbury NW9 9DY
Tel: 020-8206 1677
Open: Mon-Fri 10.30-18.30, Sat 10-18.30,
Sun 9.00-16.00
Tube: Kingsbury

Indian vegetarian take-away. 46 dishes £7-£8 per kilo. Savouries like samosas

45p, bhajias, dhokra, kachori. Sweets include barfis, pendas, ladoos, chevda (Bombay mix).

LONDON West

Knightsbridge

Wagamama

Omnivorous Japanese restaurant

Lower Ground Floor, Harvey Nichols
109–125 Knightsbridge
Tel: 020–7201 8000
Open: Mon–Sat 12.00–23.00, Sun 12–22.00
Tube: Knightsbridge

Omnivorous fast food Japanese noodle bar with over nine veggie and vegan dishes.

Ladbroke Grove

Portobello Wholefoods

Vegetarian restaurant

Unit 1,2 66 Portobello Road Ladbroke Grove W10 5TY(Junction with Cambrige Gardens or Acklam Rd, just under the Westway)
Tel: 020–8968 9133
Open: Mon–Sat 9.30–18.00, Sun 11–17.00
Tube: Ladbroke Grove

They pack all their own dry products like nuts, dried fruit, grains and beans, and make their own muesli. Organic fruit and veg. Non-dairy cheeses and ice-cream.

Notting Hill

Fresh and Wild

Organic supermarket and vegetarian cafe

210 Westbourne Grove, Notting Hill W11 2RH
Tel: 020–7229–1063
Open: Mon –Fri 8.00–21.00, Sat 10–20.00, Sun 10–19.00
Tube: Notting Hill Gate (7 min)

Huge wholefood and organic super-market on three floors with a staggering array of foods from all over the world, lots of fruit and veg, wines and beers, take–away snacks, remedies, bodycare and books.
Salad and hot food bar changes every day, £1.50 per 100g. Try a shepherd's pie, coconut dahl or a daily chef's special such as nut roast.
Organic sandwiches just under £2.
Juice bar and smoothies £2.99, £3.99.

Planet Organic

Organic supermarket
and vegetarian cafe

42 Westbourne Grove W2 5SH
(Queensway end)
Tel: 020–7727 2227
Open: Mon–Sat 9.30–20.30, Sun 12–18.00
Tube: Bayswater

Load up here with every kind of veggie food and heaps you never even knew existed. 15 aisles makes this one of the largest retailers of organic foods, alcoholic and non–alcoholic drinks, environmentally friendly household goods including Ecover.
Health books section includes Veggie Guides.
Vegetarian hot food and salads bar £2.25–5.00, eat in or take–away.

Portobello Market

Market

Portobello Road, W11
Open: Mon–Sat 8.00–18.30 not Thu pm
Tube: Ladbroke Grove, Notting Hill Gate

Gigantic market, competing with Walthamstow for the title of longest in Britain, with antiques at the south end, fruit and veg in the middle and clothes and household tat at the top.

The Grain Shop

Vegetarian bakery and take–away

269a Portobello Road, Notting Hill W11
(In Portobello market, opposite Tavistock Rd)
Tel: 020–7229–5571
Open: Mon–Sat 9.30–18.00, Sun 11–16.30
Tube: Ladbroke Grove

Vegetarian take–away and bakery that uses organic flour. 16 hot dishes, 13 of which are suitable for vegans, like tofu stir–fry, veg curry or ratatouille, as well as fresh salads. Small £2.25, medium £3.65, large £4.60.
Specialist breads and cakes for allergy free diets, also gluten–free pastries and sugar–free items.

Greens Foods

Health food shop and take–away

11–13 Strutton Ground
off Victoria Street SW1P
Tel: 020–7222 4588
Open: Mon–fri 8.30–17.30
Tube: St James's Park

Midway between Victoria Station and the House of Commons, near Buckingham Palace and St James's Park, where you could take some of their food for a picnic. Take–away sandwiches, curries, salads, pasta dishes, Mediterranean, Thai and Middle Eastern. Vegan cakes.
Lots of supplements, herbals, homeopathic, sports and nutrition, essential oils and flower remedies.

Holland & Barrett

Health food shop

Unit 15, Victoria Place Shopping Ctr,
Buckingham Palace Rd SW1W 9SA
Tel: 020–7828–5480
Open: Mon–Fri 8.00–20.00, Sat 9.00–19.00,
Sun 11.00–17.00
Tube: Victoria

At the back of Victoria rail station upstairs in the shopping centre, handy for stocking up on the way to the National Express and Eurolines coach station. There is a Sainsbury's supermarket opposite.

Revital Health Place

Health food shop

3a The Colonnades,
123–151 Buckingham Palace Rd SW1W
Tel: 020–7976–6615
Open:Mon–Fri   9.00–19.00,   9.00–18.00
Tube: Victoria

Health food shop between Victoria coach and train station with macrobiotic foods and a large range of sea vegetables. Also vegan desserts, pasties, pizza and cakes. Nelsons products and lots of books. Organic cosmetics, herbs and supplements. A great place to stock up before a coach journey. Nutritionist based at shop on Wednesdays.

Sabras

South Indian Gujarati restaurant

263 High Road, Willesden Green NW10 2RX
Tel: 020–8459–0340
Tube: Willesden Green, Dollis Hill.
Close to Willesden bus garage.
Open: Tue–Sun 18.30–23.30,
last orders 22.30

75% organic South Indian and Gujarati restaurant, with some North Indian dishes too.

7 starters, all vegan, £3.50; 10 kinds of dosa £3.50–6.50; and all kinds of Indian vegetable and lentil dishes £4.90–5.50 like Kashmiri kofta.

Two of the four desserts are vegan, either chilled mango pulp or puran-poli, a mini chupati filled with sweetened Toover dal, enriched with nutmeg, cloves and cardamon, £3.50.

Praise for previous editions of 'Vegetarian London'

"For people living in or viisiting the capital, this book is more important than the A–Z." – The Vegetarian Society

"You'll have no trouble finding nosh with this remarkably thorough guide to everything vegetarian in London." – Tony Banks MP

"From Wood Green to Wimbledon, the book is a comprehensive catalogue of the best restaurants, shops and tourist attractions in the capital." – The Big Issue

"The most striking thing about this hand-sized guide to all things animal friendly is its appeal to non-vegetarians." – The Big Issue

"This well laid out guide … tells you where to buy cruelty-free cosmetics, leather-free clothing and even lists dozens of organisations where you can meet people who want to enjoy a fun lifestyle that is not at the expense of animals." – Traveller Magazine

"A feast of food for under six pounds." – BBC Vegetarian Good Food

See page 201

SOUTH

Counties

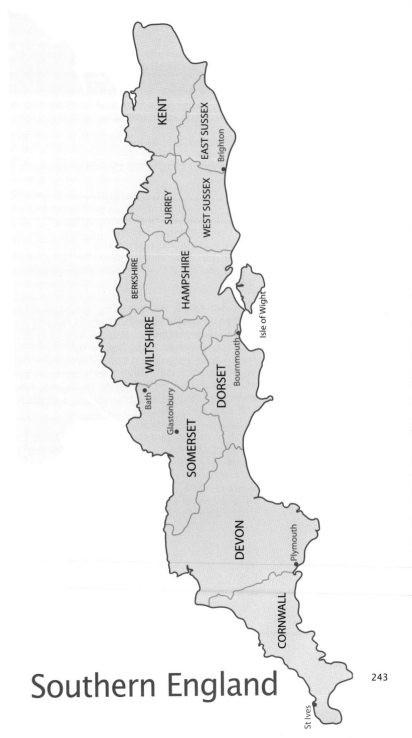

KENT

EAST SUSSEX

Brighton

SURREY

WEST SUSSEX

BERKSHIRE

HAMPSHIRE

Isle of Wight

WILTSHIRE

DORSET

Bournmouth

Bath

Glastonbury

SOMERSET

DEVON

Plymouth

CORNWALL

St Ives

Southern England

243

In Reading be sure to fill up in Café Iguana, or at the vegetarian Sweet Masala.

One of the biggest tourist attractions in England, Windsor Castle, is in Berkshire. Nearby you can enjoy an Asian lunch in Misugo or Nell Gwynns.

If you've got kids in tow, a trip to Legoland (be sure to take a lunch as they only offer omnivorous junk food) or a visit to the River Thames may be on the itinerary.

But there is much more! Challenging and very accessible walking routes and cycling paths cover the entire county. For the leisurely, there is a gentle walking route along the Thames, and the Kennet and Avon Canals. Better still, why not rent a boat and see if from a totally different perspective!

Bracknell Forest is perfect for mountain-biking, with its extensive network of tracks ranging from easy to highly technical. You can hire bikes at the Lookout, opposite Coral Reef leisure pool (great for a sauna afterwards), both of which are sign-posted in Bracknell. Either pack a picnic, or cycle all the way through the forest to Bagshot where there are a couple of curry houses, a chip shop, and a excellent Indian take away.

North of Reading are the Chiltern hills which have plenty of woodland footpaths and bridleways. For a one-way cycle, try planning a route between train stations, such as Oxford, Goring, or Pangbourne, where you can wander over to Garland's Organic Shop afterwards for veggie refueling. Don't forget to bring a good map for navigating.

Berkshire

Sultan Balti House

Omnivorous Indian restaurant

7 Great Hollands Square, Great Hollands,
Bracknell RG12 8UX
Tel: 01344–303 331
Fax: 01344–303 332
Open: Daily 12.00–14.00 & 18.00–23.30

If you are unfortunate enough to be
stuck in Bracknell, be vegan and need
something to eat, this is your best bet.
Most of the main curries on the menu
have a vegetarian version specified, and
there is the usual range of vegetable
side dishes. They will check what is
dairy–free and egg–free on request,
which is most of the vegetable dishes.
The Sultan is tucked away on a housing
estate on the north west side of
Bracknell, so follow signs to "Great
Hollands".

Le Shanghai

Omnivorous Oriental restaurant

32 Church Street
Caversham, Reading RG4 8AU
Tel: 0118–947 2097
Open: every day 18–23.00, 12–14.30

Omnivorous Thai, Cantonese, Szechuan
and Singapore restaurant in the north
part of Reading, with a special vegetarian dish on the menu every week.
You could spend £13.50 each on a
bespoke feast where you just ask for
"everything without eggs, dairy and
MSG." You can also specify the
spiciness level. Good place for a
romantic meal or to impress relatives.
Jeans are fine, but it's a nice place to
dress up for. They have high chairs.

The Spice Oven

Omnivorous Indian restaurant

2–4 Church Street
Caversham, Reading RG4 8AT
Tel: 0118–948 1000
Open: Mon–Sun 12–14.30, 18–23.00

The usual variety of Indian dishes,
including some unusual ones. They may
prepare a vegan version of masala dosa
(rice pancakes, stuffed with potatoes,
vegetables, and spices) on request. The
Thursday buffet nights are busy.

Alderborne House

Omnivorous bed and breakfast

Alderborne House, Hungerford, RG17 0LL
Tel: 01488–683228
www.honeybone.co.uk
pat@honeybone.co.uk

Veggie– and bicycle–friendly B&B on the
edge of an Area of Outstanding Natural
Beauty, in a quiet location and backing
on to open countryside. Two singles
and two twin rooms from £20 per night
per person. Vegetarian and special diets
catered for. A choice of breakfasts is
served in the conservatory dining room
which has panoramic views of the local
countryside. A short walk from the town
centre, railway station and the Kennet
and Avon Canal.

Kathmandu Kitchen

Omnivorous Indian/Nepalese
restaurant

55–59 Whitley Street, Reading RG2 0EG
Tel: 0118–986 4000
Open: every day 12.00–14.20, 18.00–23:30

Large modern Indian and Nepalese
restaurant seating up to 100. Close to

Cafe Iguana

Vegetarian restaurant

Reading's only vegetarian restaurant with an internationally influenced, vegan friendly menu and a cocktail bar upstairs. They do vegan melting Cheezly, mayo and Swedish Glace, so ask for these, even if they are not specified on the menu.

11 St Marys Butts
Reading
Berkshire
RG1 2LN

Starters from £2.75–£4.50 such as garlic and herb wedges, and soup of the day. A range of organic salads are available, like beetroot and courgette. Mains, £6–£8.50, including vegetarian tahitas with organic salads and spinach and mushroom risotto.

Tel: 0118-958 1357

Open:
Sun-Mon 11.00–17.00,
Tues–Sat 11.00–23.00

They try to source locally and use organic produce as much as possible. Everything is freshly cooked on the premises. Fair Trade coffees and teas, and organic vegetarian wine are on the menu. They can cater for special diets. Separate smoking section. Visa, MC.

Cocktail bar upstairs Tues–Sat 17.00–23.00

Global Cafe

Omnivorous cafe and bar

Omnivorous global café-style restaurant and bar (with 30 kinds of beer including unusual foreign ones) close to the Oracle shopping centre. 75% of the main menu is vegetarian and around half the hot dishes vegan. They use as much Fair Trade and organic produce as possible, and sell it in the adjoining World shop. Average price for a meal £5–6.

35–39 London Street
Reading
Berkshire
RG1 4PS

Tel: 0118-958 3555

Fax: 0118-958 4357

Different specials every day, eg. falafel platter or Mexican chilli. Sandwiches £1.95–2.50. Desserts £3–4.

www.risc.org.uk

theglobalcafe@risc.org.uk

Soya cappucinos. Smoke free area till 20.00, then it gets a bit smoky. There is a £2 cover charge after 10pm Fri–Sat and booking is advised Thu–Sat night. Parties can be arranged. No credit cards. Children welcome before 8pm; wheelchair/pram access to whole dining area.

Open:
Tue –Thu 12–23.00,
Fri till 24.00 Sat 01.00;
stop serving food at 22.00
then it's a bar

Reading University and popular with Hunt Sabs due to its friendliness, good value and wide choice for vegans. Eat as much as you like buffet on Mondays.

Pizza Express

Omnivorous pizza chain

56 St Mary's Butts, Reading RG1 2LG
Tel: 01189–391 920
www.pizzaexpress.co.uk
Open: Mon–Sat 11.30–24.00,
Sun 11.30–23.00

This branch is extra special for vegans and veggies. It does not say so on the menu, but it stocks a wide range of Redwood's vegan products, including super melting Cheezly, which is completely dairy-free, Cheatin' Ham and Cheatin' Pepperoni.

Shakeaway

Milkshake chain

4 Union St, Reading RG1 1EU
Tel: 01189–583 858
www.shakeaway.com
Open: every day

Huge range of flavours of milkshakes, including 30 vegan ones made from organic soya milk, and vegan ice-cream.

Sweet Masala

Vegetarian Indian deli and take-away

435 Oxford Road, Reading RG30 1HG
Tel: 0118–958 6668
Open: Mon–Sat 9.30–20.30, closed Sun

According to the local Vegan Society contact, this is by far the best place for vegans and veggies in Berkshire. The food is delicious, staggeringly good value and everyone goes back again and again. Food from all over India including South and Gujarati. Most of the savoury snacks are vegan, as are the daily changing curries £2.50, rice £1.25 and specials such as dosas, idlis. They sometimes use TVP. There are a few seats if you want a coffee or a quick snack.

Wagamama

Omnivorous Japanese restaurant

Riverside Level, The Oracle, Reading RG1 2AG
Tel: 0118–951 1599
www.wagamama.com
Open: Mon–Sat 12.00–23.00, Sun 12.30–23.00

Please see entry under Manchester for details of menu.

World Shop

Fair Trade shop

RISC, International Solidarity Centre,
35–39 London Street,
Reading, RG1 4PS
Tel: 01189–586 692

Fair Trade shop and book shop. Most products are vegetarian but not vegan. Range of foods and drinks includes coffee, teas, flapjacks, rice and pasta.

Pangbourne

Garland's Organic Shop

Wholefood shop

6 Reading Road
Pangbourne RG8 7LY
Tel: 01189–844 770
Open: Mon–Sat 9–17.00

People travel from Reading to this amazing shop for its range of hard to find vegan foods like tempeh, hemp pesto and hemp ice-cream. They also sell vegan sandwiches and various prepared foods in their chiller cabinet.

Magic Chef

Omnivorous Chinese restaurant

102 High Street, Slough SL1 1HL
Tel: 01753-571 818
www.placetoeat.co.uk/magicchef.htm
Open: Mon-Sat: 12.00-14.30, 18.00-23.30
Sun & Bank Holidays: 18.00-23.30

Chinese restaurant with large and exciting veggie menu utilizing fake meats. All but one of the veggie dishes is vegan. You could try delicious satay "king prawns" on skewers with peanut sauce £5.50, seaweed £3.20, veggie Szechuan chicken £4.60, "duck" with cashew nuts in a yellow bean sauce £4.80, and stir fried mixed vegetables with a sweet and sour sauce £3.50. Major credit cards accepted. Fully licensed.

Nell Gwynns

Omnivorous Chinese restaurant

6 Church Street,
Windsor SL4 1PE
Tel: 01753-850 929

Offers an extensive vegetarian menu, including mock meat dishes: braised Szechuan bean curd, garlicky vegetarian lamb with mange tout and fried rice. Most dishes cost £4.50

Misugo

Omnivorous Japanese restaurant

83 St. Leonards Road, Windsor SL4 3BZ
Tel: 01753-833 899
khy@yeung.biz
Open: Mon-Thur 17.30-22.30, Fri & Sat 17.30-23.30

About 18 vegetarian options on the menu.

Spice Route

Omnivorous Indian restaurant

18A Thames Street,,Windsor SL4 1PL
Tel: 01753 860 720
info@spice-route.com
http://www.spiceoven.co.uk

Omni-adventurous Indian restaurant with a strong touch of class. It's down a small pedestrian alley just off where the High Street turns into Thames Street, by the castle.

Only a few months after Thames Valley Veggies suggested having more vegan dishes and marking up special diets on their menu, have they developed a menu which does. Mains £4.50-£8.95 include stir-fried tofu, channa masala and tofu shish kebab.

MC, V, DC, Amex and Switch.

Holland & Barrett

Health food shop

22 High Street, Bracknell RG12 1LL
Tel: 01344-455 313

69 High Street, Maidenhead SL6 1JX
Tel: 01628-789 622

105a North Brook Road, Newbury RG14 1AB
Tel: 01635-552 218

2 Union Street, Reading RG1 1EU
Tel: 0118-950 7825

58 The Broad Street Mall, Reading RG1 7QE
Tel: 0118-957 2787

Unit 2 Queensmere Centre, Slough SL1 1DB
Tel: 01753-694 355

Cornwall

DEVON

Plymouth

Torpoint

Bude

Launceston

Whitsand
Bay

Loee

Camelford

Liskeard

Lostwithiel

Fowey

Eden Project

Tintagel

Wadebridge

Bodmin

St Austell

Falmouth

Padstow

Falmouth Bay

Newquay

Truro

Penryn

Helston

Coverack

St. Agnes

Redruth

Cambome

Mullion

Hayle

Mount's
Bay

St Ives

St Michael's
Mount

Lelant

Penzance

St. Buryan

St Just

Land's End

Cornwall

Whether you visit the fishing villages of the northern Cornish coast, the lovely beaches of Penzance, the artistic enclave of St. Ives, or the awe-inspiring cliffs of Lizard Peninsula, you will be met with warm smiles and delicious vegetarian food all over the pleasant county of Cornwall.

Search for the legendary sites of King Arthur, Lancelot and Merlin in Treknow, where Michael House offers vegan/vegetarian bed and breakfast at affordable prices. Further along the north is the backpacker surfing capital of Newquay where you can enjoy the sauna and pool at Woodlands Hotel, an omnivorous hotel and restaurant that caters well for vegetarians and vegans.

Nearing the tip of England is the relaxed, Mediterranean-style St. Ives. A perfect escape from the hustle and bustle of most cities, this town has vegetarian lodgings and cafes. Choose to stay at Making Waves for scrumptious vegan chocolate brownies, Boswednack Manor for a farmhouse feel, or The Great Escape for its harbour views.

The nearby Coast B&B at Carbis Bay is convenient for an art gallery, rooms overlooking the sea, and the Bean Inn, Cornwall's newest vegetarian restaurant which is making a grand reputation for itself.

Round "the shoe" of England, passing windy Land's End, and arrive at Penzance. This pretty town has Archie Brown's Cafe and wholefood store, and Sancreed House which offers vegetarian B&B, self catering, spiritual healing and reflexology. Wisteria Cottage in St Buryan is a lovely new veggie B&B in an 18th century cottage.

Mount Pleasant Farm in Roseland Peninsula is convenient for Heligan Gardens and the amazing domes of the Eden Project, one of Britain's greatest tourist attractions.

Lizard Peninsula has rugged cliffs and you can take a boat ride to one of the quiet little coves. Stay in Lanherne vegetarian B&B in the peaceful village of Mullion

Wisteria Cottage

New vegetarian and vegan guest house on the edge of a small village, central to everywhere on the Land's End peninsula. Quiet, informal and friendly in an 18th century village cottage. There's no chintz though the cottage décor has occasional whimsical touches. Omnivores welcome but will be fed exclusively veggie.

Three double rooms, two of which can be converted to twins, £17-22 per person. Single person supplement £6-11 depending on season.

Breakfast includes porridge, vegan sausages, mushrooms, tomato, tofu, rice cakes, rye and wholewheat bread, fresh fruit, juices, etc soya milk used. Menu varies. They have vegan margarine and muesli, soya milk and yoghurt.

Evening meal available by prior arrangement. They are not open to non-residents.

A local pub and village shops (including post office) are only two minutes walk away, and there is a regular circular bus service between Penzance, St. Buryan and the whole peninsula. There are two exclusively vegetarian restaurants/cafes 5 miles plus health food shops. Many other restaurants offering veggie dishes. See their other web site www.vegetariancornwall.co.uk

The cottage is close to the clifftop Minack Theatre (4 miles), Land's End, museums, art galleries and gardens. Nearby are Penzance, St Ives, St Just, the South West Coast Path, many ancient sites, arts, family attractions, woodland walks, and a choice of stunning beaches. The Eden Project is only a day trip away (1 hr by car). For detailed information see their web site: Discovering West Penwith www.westpenwith.com

TV, hairdryer, tea/coffee making in rooms.

Vegetarian B&B

Wisteria Cottage
Penzance Road
St Buryan
Cornwall TR19 6DZ
England

Tel: 01395 264944

www.wisterianet.co.uk
enquiries@wisterianet.co.uk

Train Station: Penzance 5 miles, buses and taxis available

Open: most of the year including Christmas, New Year and bank holidays

Directions: Take the A30 from Penzance towards Land's End for 3 miles, turn left at Catchall on to the B3283 (signposted to St. Buryan and the Minack), continue 2 miles to St. Buryan. Wisteria Cottage is the fouth house on the right as you enter the village.

Parking: available

Children welcome but no high chairs yet.

No pets, but they have a shy cat on the premises.

No smoking throughout, but there's a sin bin in small conservatory in the garden.

Disabled note: difficult staircase

Michael House

This is a one hundred year old house at the top of a valley, looking down to the sea, in the sleepy village of Treknow. There are en suite double and twin rooms at £29.50 per person per night (children under 10 £14.50). A deposit of £29.50 required.

All food is locally sourced where possible and much is grown in the organic garden on site. Breakfast comprises of fruit juice, muesli, home-baked bread and a full cooked English breakfast. They have vegan margarine, soya milk, soya yogurt and vegan muesli. Please let them know in advance if you are vegan or have other dietary requirements.

A three course dinner is offered for £15.50 and may include roasted tomato soup, asparagus and mushroom gratin, with new potatoes and broccoli, filo pastry tarts with apple and pear, almonds amaretto and fruit coulis. Dinner is served on one long candle-lit table and has a dinner party atmosphere. They are open to non-residents for dinner and they sell organic vegan wines and beers. Packed lunches are available.

Michael House is in the heart of King Arthur country and a walk along the Cornish coastal path to Tintagel castle and Merlin's Cave is not to be missed. It is a ten minute walk to the beach at Trebarwith Strand which is popular with both surfers and families. Surfing equipment and bicycles can be hired by the day.

Further afield are the historic and mysterious Bodmin Moors and the National Trust maintained Old Harbour of Boscastle. The Eden Project is an hour drive away.

There is a TV lounge. Fair trade tea and coffee making facilities are in the rooms.

Vegan/vegetarian bed and breakfast

Trelake Lane
Treknow
near Tintagel
Cornwall PL34 OEW

Tel: 01840-770 592

www.michael-house.co.uk

Email:
info@michael-house.co.uk

Train: Bodmin Parkway, 21 miles

Open: All year

No smoking throughout

Directions:
From the A39, the village of Treknow is one mile south of Tintagel.
From the A39 Bude to Wadebridge Road, take the B3263 (Camelford to Tintagel) stretch until you reach Trewarmett.
As you go through the village on your left hand side is a small garden centre which is followed by a left hand bend. Immediately following this corner is an unmarked lane to the left. This is Trelake Lane and goes down into the village of Treknow. Michael House is on your right just before the church on the left.

Parking: plenty available

10% discount for those staying 5 nights or more.

Pets welcome if well-behaved £5 per night

SOUTH Cornwall

Coast B & B

This combined vegetarian restaurant, therapy centre, art gallery and B&B with stunning sea views, is owned by local artist and photographer Katrina Slack and hypnotherapist Gail Richards.

All rooms are en suite, and include 6 doubles, one twin and one family priced £25-£30 per person. Some rooms are available for £22 out of season. Single occupancy £35.

Start the day with cereal or fruit then a full English vegetarian or vegan breakfast, courtesy of the Bean Inn vegetarian restaurant and cafe. Please state in advance if you are vegan or have other dietary requirements. Vegan margarine, milk, muesli and sausages can be made available.

Lunch and evening meals are available at the in-house Bean Inn (see page 261) and include smoked tofu with mustard mash and roasted vegetables. Starters and desserts are priced separately. Non residents are also welcome, but best to book. All meals are served in the restaurant.

Enjoy coastal walks, and dining outside in their garden with wild flowers and palm trees.

St Ives is a beautiful Cornish town and has a Tate Gallery, Barbara Hepworth, RSPB reserves, sites of special scientific interest, trips to the Scilly Isles, surfing, diving, swimming, and day trips to the Eden Project or the Lost Gardens of Heligon.

All rooms have tea and coffee making facilitites and TV. Hair dryers are availabale. Most rooms have fabulous sea views.

Vegetarian bed and breakfast & restaurant

St Ives Road
Carbis Bay
St Ives
Cornwall TR26 2RT

Tel: 01736-795 918

www.coastcornwall.co.uk
info@coastcornwall.co.uk

Train: Carbis Bay 1/4 mile. Can collect or there are taxis.

Open: all year

No smoking throughout

Directions: A38, follow signs to St Ives, through Lelant into Carbis Bay. Big white building with blue shutters on left before the Tesco roundabout.

Children welcome, can provide travel cots and high chairs

No pets

5-10% discount given to members of Vegan and Vegetarian Society, Viva!, PETA, Animal Aid and people with this book.

No credit cards yet

Parking for 7 cars

The Great Escape

Veggie B&B run by two women, located five minutes from the harbour and the centre of St. Ives. There are four double ensuite rooms (two with harbour views) priced at £24–£30 per person per night.

Begin your morning with a glass of freshly squeezed orange juice, cereal, fresh fruit and soya yoghurt. Follow with a cooked breakfast of hash browns, veggie sausages, grilled tomatoes, fried mushrooms, baked beans, home baked rolls, toast and preserves and tea or coffee.

No evening meal is offered but most of the restaurants in St. Ives serve veggie food.

The clean sandy beaches, resident artists and little cobbled streets of St. Ives combine to create an enticing Mediterranean style resort.

You can go swimming or surfing at one of the four beaches nearby, or for a scenic walk along the South West Coastal Path.

Other attractions include Hepworth Gardens and the Tate Gallery, which displays work by St. Ives based artists. There are several other galleries, studios and craftshops.

The Great Escape is a short walk from St. Ives Leisure Centre which has an ozone treated swimming pool and a fully equipped fitness suite.

Tea and coffee making facilities, televisions and CD players in the rooms.

Vegetarian bed and breakfast

16 Park Avenue
St. Ives
Cornwall
TR26 2DN

Tel: 01736–794 617

www.g-escape.freeuk.com

Train station:
St. Ives, 1/2 mile

Open: all year

Directions:
From St. Ives station turn right onto St. Andrews Street, then left onto Street-an-pol, right onto Tregenna Place, then left onto Gabriel Street and left again onto Park Avenue.

Parking: on street and a car park 100m away

Dogs welcome

No smoking throughout

SOUTH Cornwall

Boswednack Manor

Vegetarian bed and breakfast

Zennor
St. Ives
Cornwall
TR26 3DD

Tel: 01736–794 183

Train station:
Penzance or St. Ives,
6 miles, then bus or taxi.
Collection is sometimes possible.

Open: Easter–early October

Directions:
One mile west of Zennor on the St. Ives to Land's End coast road B3306.

Parking: available

5% discount to members of the Vegetarian Society, Vegan Society or people presenting this book for stays of three nights or more

Children welcome

Cot and high chair

No smoking throughout

A self-catering cottage is also available for four people

Spacious granite farmhouse on the north coast of the Land's End Peninsula, over-looking Gurnard's Head – one of the wildest promontories in Cornwall.

Boswednack Manor has five rooms. One single, one twin and one family at £19–£21 per person; and two double ensuite rooms (one with sea views) £22–£24 per person. It is set in a three acre organic small holding and private nature reserve. A meditation barn is open to all, and they run occasional yoga and other retreats during the year.

Breakfast is juice, cereal and fresh fruit followed by potato waffles, mushrooms, tomatoes, toast and tea, coffee or herbal tea. Soya milk, vegan margarine and vegan muesli are provided. Dinner is not offered but there are veggie restaurants in St. Ives and Penzance.

The lounge has a piano and a library of local interest and history books. Free walk leaflets and available. Rooms have tea and coffee making facilities. There is also an outdoor chess board.

Treryn Dinas, one of Cornwall's ancient cliff castles, is here. There are many walks such as the South West Coast Path amongst the unspoilt scenery of the moors and coast. You can also see stone circles, standing stones and quoits. Near Zennor lies a unique cromlech.

Many attractions are nearby St. Ives, Penzance and Marazion such as sandy beaches, schools for windsurfing and surfing, indoor pools, gardens, galleries, museums, nightclubs, restaurants, shops and summer festivals.

Making Waves

Victorian terraced house in a quiet lane overlooking St. Ives Bay, just above semi-tropical gardens. There is one double room at £22–£24 per person, one twin at £24–£26 per person, and a double/family room with a view at £30 per person. Extra adults in family room £16; extra child under sixteen £14; and under four years free.

Sit inside or out for your delicious vegan breakfast of muesli or cereal, fruit salad and soya yoghurt with freshly extracted juice or a milkshake, followed by a fry-up with toast and toppings and filter coffee.

A three course organic dinner can be provided by arrangement for £16.50. It could be warm tempeh and mung bean salad, followed by kebabs with peanut sauce, then chocolate and pecan brownies with ice cream. Food is free from hydrogenated fats and GM ingredients. Any special diets are catered for – let them know in advance.

The town centre and harbour are a two minute walk and all St. Ives' beaches are within a ten minute stroll. It is an artistic community and you will find many galleries around town. Other attractions include ancient Pagan monuments, St. Michael's Mount, Land's End, Seal Sanctuary or the Lost Gardens of Heligan. Activities include surfing, kite flying, diving, walking and cycling. Lots of pubs, night clubs and restaurants serve veggie/ vegan food and there is a vibrant live music scene.

Making Waves has a small experimental veganic forest garden with a variety of edible flowers, fruits and herbs. The guest lounge has a TV, musical instruments, music system and books. Tea and coffee making facilites and washbasins in rooms. They have a cot and high chair.

Vegan/organic guest house

3 Richmond Place
St. Ives
Cornwall
TR26 1JN

Tel: 01736–793 895

www.making-waves.co.uk
simon@making-waves.co.uk

Train Station: St. Ives, 1/2 mile, then taxi or collection is possible.

Open: March–October and New Year's Eve

Directions: Follow the A30 through Cornwall, then the signs to St. Ives. Descending into St. Ives from Carbis Bay, turn right at Porthminster Hotel downhill into St. Ives. Follow to the right at Barclays Bank, then first left into Market Place. Turn left again at New World Chinese. Making Waves is 50 metres up Richmond Place on the right.

Parking: available

5% discount to members of Vegan Society, Viva!, Animal Aid, PETA and Vegan Organic Network.

10% discount for stays of six nights or more (excluding June–August).

No pets and no smoking.

Secure bicycle storage.

Mount Pleasant Farm

Omnivorous B&B with veggie owners on an organic small holding. There are four ensuite rooms: one single, two doubles and one family at £21–£27 per person. There is a £6 single supplement.

Wake in the morning to porridge with sesame seeds and fruit compote or crispy tofu with mushrooms and tomatoes. Veggie sausages, vegan muesli, vegan margarine, soya milk and soya yoghurt are all available.

A substantial one course dinner is available by request three days a week for £9. Dinner is always veggie or vegan and could be a home made pie, pastie, burger or nut loaf with seasonal salad and home grown potatoes. All the food is local and organic where possible and most of their vegetables are home grown. Special diets are catered for with prior notice.

Mount Pleasant Farm is an excellent base for walks through beautiful scenery. It is on the eastern edge of the Roseland Peninsula and just a mile from the coastal footpath where wildlife abounds. There are three unspoilt beaches nearby, the closest is a mile away and ideal for children.

The famous Heligan gardens are three miles away and the Eden Project is nine miles away.

Alternative therapies are available. Bike hire offered.

Children are welcome and they have a cot and high chair. There are tea and coffee making facilities, televisions and wash-basins in the rooms. No smoking throughout.

Omnivorous bed and breakfast

Gorran High Lanes
St. Austell
Cornwall
PL26 6LR

Tel: 01726–843 918

www.
vegetarian-cornwall.co.uk
jill@mpfarm.vispa.com

Train station:
St. Austell, 8 miles, then get a bus to Mevagissey where they will collect you.

Open:
end March–end October

Directions:
Take the road from St. Austell to Mevagissey. After ascending a steep hill past Pentwan beach, you come to a cross roads. Take the turning on your right, sign posted 'Gorran'. Follow this road. You will pass Heligan on your left and after three miles, at a phone box, you will see the Mount Pleasant Farm tourism sign on your right. Follow further signs from here. Please take care not to enter the drive of their neighbours at Mount Pleasant House.

Parking: plenty available

5% discount to members of the Vegetarian Society, Vegan Society and people presenting this book if staying for three nights or more.

Lanherne

Veggie and vegan bed and breakfast set in the village of Mullion, on the west coast of the beautiful Lizard Peninsula. The views across the village towards Mount Bay are spectacular. There are three rooms, one double, one twin and one family room. All cost £23–£25 per person and have showers and washbasins. Two have panoramic views. Children 5–13 are half price; under 2, free.

Help yourself to a breakfast buffet of cereals or porridge, juice and fruit, then tofu, onion, mushrooms and dill on toast. Or have a full cooked breakfast of veg sausages, nut rissoles or bean burgers with grilled tomatoes, baked beans, mushrooms and scrambled tofu with toast. Vegan margarine, soya milk, rice milk, vegan muesli and soya yoghurt available. Rice cakes and spelt bread can be supplied for those with wheat allergies.

A two course meal is £12. The long menu includes Red Dragon Pie with fresh veggies, Savoury Nut Roll with roast potatoes, fresh veggies and gravy, and Vegetable Pie with new potatoes and broccoli. Dessert could be Kathy's pudding of the day or fresh fruit salad with soya cream or ice cream. Bring your own wine.

The Lizard Peninsula is an unspoilt area of outstanding natural beauty with wooded valleys, ancient hedgerows, rugged cliffs and sandy coves. With some of the best beaches in West Cornwall, the cliff top views are tranquil and breathtaking. Boat trips from Mullion Cove are available, whilst guided birdwatching can be arranged.

Rooms have tea and coffee making facilities, water filters, TVs and clock radios. Guests are welcome to roam the large gardens.

Redruth

Vegetarian bed and breakfast

Meaver Road
Mullion
Helston
Cornwall
TR12 7DN

Tel: 01326–241 381/
0786–762 0083

www.cornishspirit.co.uk
kathlanherne@aol.com

Train Station: Redruth 20 miles, then two buses or collection can be arranged

Open: all year

Directions: Head for the M5 and A30. Exit A30 at Scorrier/Helston. When you approach Helston, follow the Lizard sign, then the sign to Mullion. The right hand turn to Mullion is Meaver Road.

Parking:
available in grounds

Discounts on stays of five nights or more

No smoking throughout

Cot available

Special diets catered for

Lostwithiel

Talbot Lodge

Vegetarian bed & breakfast

2 Duke Street, Lostwithiel, Cornwall PL22 0AG
Tel: 01208-0871184
Email: julietamblin@btconnect.com

£30 single occupancy, £50 double, for women and couples. Organic local food. Also business English and French classes available. Some Italian, Spanish, German and Cornish spoken.

Newquay

Woodlands Hotel

Omnivorous hotel and restaurant

Pentire Crescent, Newquay TR7 1PU
Tel: 01637-852 229
www.newquayaccommodation.co.uk/
woodlands
Open: Mar-Oct (inclusive)

There are fifty-four rooms: 11 singles, 23 doubles and 20 twins, all ensuite and all with breathtaking views. Rates are £30-50 per person.
Breakfast includes veggie sausages, hash browns, beans and toast. Vegan margarine, soya milk and vegan muesli are available.
A four course dinner is included in the room rate and may start with vegetable pate or hummous, followed by soup of the day and pasta pesto or a vegan cutlet for the main course. Vegan desserts include apricot crumble with soya cream.
Although close to the beaches, the hotel has its own sauna, solarium and outdoor swimming pool.

Helston

The Top House

Omnivorous pub

The Lizard, nr Helston TR12 7NQ
Tel: 01326-290 974
Open: Mon-Sun Lunch 12-14.30,
Evening meal 18.30 (Sun 19.00)-21.00

Omnivorous restaurant with vegetarian dishes from £5.95, and vegan meals always on their specials board. Licenced. Separate smoking and non-smoking section. Visa, MC.

Padstow

Waves Cafe

Omnivorous restaurant

Higher Harlyn, St Merryn, Padstow
Tel: 01841-520 096, 520096
www.cornwall-online.co.uk
Open: irregular hours

Good selection of veggie food in a restaurant on a caravan site. Eat for around £10. New pizza menu in 2005.

Penzance

Sancreed House

Vegetarian B&B and self catering

Sancreed, Penzance TR20 8QS
Tel:01736-810 409
claredyas@madasafish.com
www.sancreedhouse.com

Vegetarian B&B offering single rooms for £25 and doubles for £35. Not en suite. Veggie evening meals are offered for £6. S/C is offered at £80 pw for one person or £60 pppw with reduced rates for the unwaged. Therapies are also offered: spiritual healing, animal healing, reflexology, kinesiology, counselling, massage, astrology charts and transits, regression therapy and art therapy. Prices range from £5-£30.

Archie Brown's Cafe

Vegetarian cafe and wholefood shop

Bread Street, Penzance TR18 2EQ
Tel: 01736-362 828
Open: Mon–Sat 09.30–17.00 closed Sun
Also most Friday nights from 19.00, booking essential.

Vegetarian wholefood café and art gallery which caters well for vegans. Mains from £4.50 such as homity pie. They have some vegan home-made cakes, and vegan ice cream. House wine is £9 a bottle. No smoking inside. Visa, MC accepted. A 10% discount is offered for Vegetarian Society members. The entrance to this upstairs cafe is in Archie Brown's Health Food Shop.

Yam Parlour Vegetarian Restaurant

Vegetarian Restaurant

36 Causewayhead, , Penzance, TR18 2ST
Tel: 01736 366740
www.vegetariancornwall.co.uk
Open: 10–16.00, 19–22.00

Friendly cosy atmosphere with mellow music and big choice of home made food. Average £4.50-8.50, e.g. toritilla stuffed with veggie bacon, avocado, sweet chilli sauce and salad. Fresh juices. Visa. No smoking except at tables outside. Disabled facilities. Bring your own wine. Car park opposite. Children welcome.

Archie Brown's

Health food shop

Old Brewrey Yard, Bread Street
Penzance TR18 2EQ
Tel: 01736-362 828
Open: Mon–Sat 9.00–17.30, closed Sunday

Wholefood and vitamins shop with take-away food that's made in Archie

Brown's Cafe upstairs. Also a chiller cabinet and small deli counter.

The Granary

Wholefood & fruit/vegetable shop

15D Causeway Head, Penzance TR18 2SN
Tel: 01736-361 869

General vegetarian wholefood store. All bread is vegan and freshly baked. There is a weekly delivery of organic bread. The chiller cabinet is well stocked with dairy and vegan foods, including veggie/vegan ice-cream, cakes and vegan flapjacks and savouries.

St Ives

The Bean Inn

Vegetarian cafe

St Ives Road, Carbis Bay, St Ives TR26 2RT
(in the Coast B&B, page 254)
Tel: 01736-795 918
info@coastcornwall.co.uk
www.coastcornwall.co.uk
Open: May–Sept
Fri–Sun 12–15.00, Wed–Sun 18–22.00.
Rest of the year best to ring for details, more open than not especially on public holidays.

80% vegan. Healthy breakfasts (best to book as often full if B&B full), lunches £5.85 large or £4.25 light, sandwiches, afternoon teas, picnic hampers and take-aways with chill bags for the beach, Sunday Roasts, evening meals £7.45 mains, £3.25 starters and desserts. Bring your own wine, corkage £1 bottle, 50p beer and soft drinks. No smoking except in garden. Cheque or cash only. Children welcome, 2 high chairs.

St Ives

Good Health

Wholefood shop

Tregenna Place, St Ives
Tel: 01736–794 726
Salad bar 799 868
Open: Mon–Sat 9–17.30, closed Sun

Central vegetarian wholefood shop opposite Spar, with a take–away salad bar (omnivorous) at the front which can also cater for vegans. £2 for a three scoop salad, £3 for five; sandwiches and split big rolls also from £2. Chilled drinks, snacks etc.

Truro

The Feast

Vegetarian restaurant

15 Kenwyn Street, Truro TR1 3BU
Tel: 01872–272 546
Open: Mon–Sat 10–17.00, closed Sun.
Last weekend of month open for themed evening.

Vegetarian world food restaurant with a tea garden and huge selection of Belgian fruit, white, blonde and chimay beers. They have starters from £2.90, 4 vegan; salads £3.60–£4.80; and mains include savoury and sweet pancakes which can be made vegan, jacket potatoes, sandwiches, dish of day £4.50. Desserts feature enticing soya ice creams and cakes made on premises. They will cater for diabetic and gluten free diets. No smoking throughout. No credit cards.

Wadebridge

Elixir Health Foods

Wholefood shop

47 Molesworth Street, Wadebridge PL27 7DR
Tel/Fax : 01208–814 500
info@elixirhealth.co.uk
www.elixirhealth.co.uk

Independent healthfood shop, with good range of supplies, including ready to eat vegan items. Also has potions which the website focuses on.

Holland & Barrett

Health food shop

48 Market Street, Falmouth
Tel: 01326–319 327

3 Market Place, Penzance
Tel: 01736–331 855

13/14 Aylemer Square, St Austell
Tel: 01726–73548

1 Francis Street, Truro
Tel: 01872–272 991

Devon

Fern Tor

Veggie and vegan guest house set in over twelve acres of grounds. There is one double room with a door opening onto the patio garden and one twin room, for £22 per person per night. There is also one double/twin with a private lounge, for £27 per person. All have ensuite bathrooms.

You will be well looked after by the vegan proprietors, one of whom is Cordon Vert trained. Breakfast starts with a selection of stewed or fresh fruit with cereal, home made granola or porridge, followed by a full cooked breakfast of vegan sausages, bacon, tomatoes, mushrooms, beans, potatoes and home made bread. Eggs are from their rescued hens. Soya milk, soya yoghurt and vegan margarine are available. A two course dinner is offered for £12 and a three course dinner for £15. Bring your own wine, no corkage charge.

The evening meal could be garlic mushrooms, followed by cabbage parcels on a bed of red peppers, and FernBocker Glory for dessert. Organic veg and their own produce is used whenever possible. Special diets are catered for with advanced notice. Packed lunches available.

You could have a holiday just relaxing in their five acres of grassland along the Little Silver River which is overflowing with wild-flowers. The remaining land is used for their rescued animals and organic gardens.

Explore the beaches, moors and other attractions of the North Devon Coast, Exmoor and Mid Devon. Exmoor National Park is a 20 minute drive and Dartmoor National Park is within an hour's drive.

Vegan/vegetarian guest house

Meshaw
South Molton
Devon EX36 4NA

Tel and Fax:
01769–550 339

www.ferntor.co.uk
veg@ferntor.co.uk

Train Station: Kings Nympton, 6 miles, then they will collect you.

Open: all year

Directions: on B3137, 4 miles south of South Molton, between villages of Alswear and Meshaw. Look out for a large stone wall.

Parking: available

Children welcome
Cot and high chair

Pets welcome

No smoking throughout

Cycle hire available locally

Lounge with log fire. Rooms have TV, radio and tea and coffee making facilities.

10% discount to members of Viva! and League Against Cruel Sports.

10% discount on stays of five nights or more and bargain breaks available Nov–March.

Fern Tor

Vegetarian & Vegan Guest House

Relax in our 12 acres,
or explore
Exmoor, North & Mid-Devon.

En-suite, non-smoking rooms.
Children & pets welcome.
Cordon Vert host.

Meshaw,
South Molton, Devon, EX36 4NA

Tel/Fax 01769 550339
email: veg@ferntor.co.uk
http://www.ferntor.co.uk

Dart Villas B&B

Newly refurbished Georgian house in a quiet and peaceful hillside location at the edge of Totnes in a quiet cul de sac, with lovely views overlooking the town and the Dart valley and castle, yet close to the bustling centre. 1 double, 2 doubles en suite (one with bath, one with shower), 1 twin, £24–35 per person. Single person is £27.50, £35 or £40 depending which room. A family room for 2 adults and 2 under 12's can be made by connecting a double and twin, £100.

Cooked or continental breakfast with a choice of fresh fruit salad, muesli, cereals, croissants, porridge, yoghurt, sausages, fried garlic tomatoes and mushrooms, juices. Organic food is used where possible.

Totnes is a lovely Elizabethan market town. Highlights include the castle ruins and the steep and characterful Fore St. There are markets Friday and Saturday and many shops sell designer clothes, hand-made soaps and cosmetics, local arts and crafts and ethnic gifts from around the world. It's the best place in Devon for vegetarian food, see pages 282–3, with cafés where you can chill out and watch the world go by.

Totnes lies between Dartmoor and the beautiful coast. There are many beaches and walks or cycle rides along the breathtakingly beautiful Dart valley towards Sharpham and beyond. You can enjoy traditional villages and old-world pubs, plus the delights of English Riviera seaside towns Torquay (good for nightclubbing), Paignton and Brixham. You can also do mountain biking, kayaking, climbing and caving. Other attractions are the South Hams, National Trust and English Heritage treasures, museums and churches, two steam railways, Buckfastleigh Abbey and Butterfly Farm and Otter Sanctuary, and riverboat trips to the historic naval town of Dartmouth. Plymouth and Exeter are less than an hour's drive.

Organic vegetarian B&B

3 Dart Villas
Totnes Down Hill
Totnes
Devon TQ9 5ET
England

Tel: 01803-865895

www.dartvillasbb.co.uk
(map and pictures)
mounivk@yahoo.co.uk

Train: Totnes 10 minutes walk, on the main line rail serving the West Country including Exeter and Plymouth through to Penzance. They can collect you from the station.

Open: all year

Directions: Totnes is 6 miles from the A38 Expressway between Exeter and Plymouth. On the main line rail service serving much of the West Country including Exeter and Plymouth through to Penzance.

Parking: three spaces in front of the house

Special diets catered for (there are health food shops in Totnes)

No smoking

Children welcome, cot, high chair

No dogs (they have cats)

No credit cards

Tea and coffee making in rooms. Hairdryer available.

Ansteys Cove Hotel

Omnivorous hotel owned by a lifetime vege-tarian, set in one of the warmest climates in Britain. There are nine rooms, all with ensuite bathrooms. Single rooms £34 per night, doubles and twins £65-£70 per room, or treat yourself to the Penthouse four-poster suite for £85 per night. Ask about the arrival gifts that can be added to your room to surprise your partner.

At breakfast help yourself to fruit juice, cereals, fruit, toast and preserves, tea and coffee. Follow with a full cooked breakfast of veggie sausages, smoked sliced tofu, baked beans, tomatoes, mushrooms, hash browns and fried bread. Soya milk, vegan muesli and vegan margarine are also available.

A two course meal is offered for £12 or three courses for £15. You must book in advance. Starters include soup of the day and mixed pepper pudding with a spicy tomato sauce, both served with home made bread. A sorbet is then served to cleanse your palate before the main course which could be baked aubergine, veggie mock fillet of 'sole' stuffed with chives and celery, vegetable curry with rice and pickle, or Cornish Starry Gazy pie. Desserts include Helston Pudding and spicy apple pie served with soya cream. Proprietor/ Chef is Cordon Vert trained, so expect something delicious.

Set amidst spectacular unspoilt scenery and within walking distance of award winning beaches. Good public transport to all attractions in Torquay, as well as South Devon and Dartmoor National Park. Beautiful coastal walks in the area.

All rooms have satellite TV, direct dial phone, hairdryer, alarm clock radio and tea and coffee making facilities. They also run certified courses in food hygiene.

Omnivorous hotel

327 Babbacombe Road
Torquay
Devon TQ1 3TB

Tel: 01803-200 900
Freephone:
0800-028 4953

Fax: 01803-211 150

www.torquayengland.com
info@torquayengland.com

Train Station: Torquay, 1.5 miles, then bus or taxi.

Open: December-September (inclusive)

Directions: Take the A3022 Riviera Way. Go straight on at roundabout. Go left at the traffic lights by Courts Store into Hele Road B3199. At the roundabout, turn left for Teignmouth Road. At the next roundabout turn right for St Marychurch B3199. Head towards Babbacombe going straight on through the next round-about. Follow road through St Marychurch Village. The hotel is one mile on the right just pass Babbacombe Pottery.

Veggie and vegan wines

No pets

No smoking

Parking: available

TV lounge and two bars

Devon

Cuddyford

Set in rural Dartmoor National Park, this B&B has two rooms, one double (which can be converted into a family room) and one twin for £20 per person per night (and thereafter £18.50 per night). The twin room has views of the Woodland River Valley with Dartmoor on the horizon.

Breakfast begins with fruit from the garden, either stewed or fresh, cereal and juice and is followed by veggie sausages, veggie rashers, beans, tomatoes and pancakes. Vegan margarine, soya milk and soya yoghurt are available.

Dinner is offered from £10 and begins with soup or salad, then a curry or pasta, and a dessert, which can be vegan. There is a kitchenette for the use of guests where you can make a packed lunch. Organic fruit and vegetables are grown on the property.

Cuddyford is well situated for exploring Dartmoor with its mysterious stone circles, the Dart Valley and the South Devon coast line. There are white water sports on the River Dart, beaches with sailing and coastal footpaths.

Nearby there are steam trains, a sports hall with a gym and shops selling arts and crafts.

Alternative therapies are available locally.

Tea and coffee making facilities in the shared kitchen. All rooms hold some books, and a television is in one of the rooms.

Ashburton

Vegetarian bed and breakfast

Rew Road
Broadpark
Ashburton
Devon TQ13 7EN
England

Tel: 01364-653 325

Train Station:
Newton Abbott, then 20 minute bus or taxi ride.

Open:
all year, except Christmas

Directions: Follow the A38 from Exeter or Plymouth. Turn off into Ashburton. Continue down the main street until you reach the Golden Lion. Opposite the hotel you will see Roborough Lane. After half a mile turn left at a cross roads into Rew Road. Cuddyford is the fourth house on the right.

Parking: off street parking

No smoking throughout

Children welcome

High chairs available

Pets by arrangement

Enstone Guest House

Small friendly guest house with a vegetarian proprietor. It's situated in a peaceful garden at the end of a residential cul-de-sac, adjacent to the River Sed, with the park beyond.

There are four rooms: one single, one twin, one double and one family. Prices are reduced in the low season and range from £17–£22 per person per night. Cheaper weekly tariffs and child rates are available.

Breakfast begins with fruit, juice and cereal with soya yoghurt followed by veggie sausages, baked beans, tomatoes, mushrooms and hash browns. Soya milk and vegan margarine are available.

Dinner is £8 and could be spaghetti veg bolognaise, soy protein pie with three veggies, followed by fresh fruit or stewed fruit with soya ice cream. Special diets are catered for with advance notice.

Enstone Guest House is only a few minutes walk to the centre of Sidmouth, a charming and tranquil resort town. It offers a cinema and a theatre. There are lots of nice walks by the river and along the cliffs and it's a ten minute walk to the beach. There's a donkey sanctuary nearby.

The guest lounge has a television. There are TVs and tea/coffee making facilites in the rooms.

Omnivorous guest house

Lennox Avenue
Sidmouth
Devon EX10 8TX
England

Tel: 01395–514 444

Train Station: Honiton, 8 miles, then bus or taxi or collection is possible by arrangement

Open: April–September (inclusive)

Directions:14 miles from Exeter off the A3052

Parking: available on site

10% discount given to members of the Vegetarian Society and people presenting this book

Children aged three and over welcome

Cot and high chair available

Credit cards accepted

No smoking throughout

SOUTH Devon

269

Little Burrows

Little Burrows is set in a large garden in a secluded corner of Dartmoor, the largest area of wilderness in the South of England. There is one double room in the house for £25–£27 per person per night. Or you could stay in one of their self contained wooden cabins for £25–£27 per person B&B, or self catering £20–£22 per person. There is also a caravan which can sleep four people for £17 per person or £22 with breakfast.

Begin the day with fruit juice, fresh organic fruit, home made muesli or cereal and home made breads with a selection of crisp-breads. In winter, try cooked porridge or fruit compot. They have soya yoghurt, soya milk, vegan margarine and a wide selection of dry and fresh herb teas.   Dinner is available for £12 and could be home made spicy lentil pie with leafy green veggies, baked root veg, fresh mixed salad and herb sauce, followed by Swedish soya ice cream with fresh raspberries. All food is organic. Special diets catered for.

Both proprietors are artists and enjoy making improvised music. There is an art and a professional recording studio and tuition is available. Little Burrows is a peaceful haven overlooking the moors. The surrounding area is full of rock strewn rivers, stone circles, wild ponies and woodland walks. It's a truly magical place to explore. Chagford is three miles away and has interesting shops, pubs, a pool and a vegetarian cafe. Two miles away is South Zeal with a shop selling organic produce, pubs and a cyber cafe.

There is a wood–burning sauna, with massage and healing by arrangement, and group creative retreats with meditation, dreamwork and creative painting classes.

Throwleigh

Vegan/vegetarian B&B and self catering retreat centre

Shilstone Lane
Throwleigh
Devon EX20 2HX
England
Tel: 01647-231 305

www.organicaccommo dation.com
www.sacredartstudio.com
www.fireflystudios.co.uk

kristin@organic accommodation.com

Open: all year
Train Station: Exeter St. Davids 15 miles then bus

Directions: From Exeter take A30 towards Okehampton. At first roundabout take left exit into Whiddon Down, then second left signposted Throwleigh. Turn immediately right into road signposted Throwleigh 2 miles. Take second left in village centre (at Church steps). After 200 metres, park next to house on the left in lay-by. Little Burrows is 20 metres down drive at side of this house.

No smoking throughout

Parking: available

Bike and tent hire available
Animals welcome
Children welcome

Lounge with TV. Tea and coffee making facilities, and TV's / music system in the rooms and cabins.

10% discount on stays of seven days or more

Lower Norris House

Vegetarian guest house

Built on an ancient site, this guest house is set in beautiful countryside overlooking a tranquil valley with streams and woodland. There are three rooms: one double ensuite at £30 per person per night, one double/twin and one single/twin both at £25 per person. The doubles can be used as family rooms.

North Huish
Totnes
Devon TQ10 9NJ
England

Tel and Fax:
01548–821 180

Breakfast can be fruit, fruit juice and cereal, veggie sausages, beans, tomatoes, mushrooms and toast.

Train Station: Totnes, 7 miles, then collection is possible

Open: all year

An evening meal is £12.50 and might be a nut loaf, stuffed peppers, vegetable crumble, or vegetable curry or lasagne. Special diets are catered for. Organic produce is used where possible. The house is supplied by natural spring water.

Directions: From the A38, take the South Brent/ Avonwick exit (B3210) and follow signs to Avonwick. Pass under the A38 and turn left. After a mile turn right just before garage, then take first turning left by the phone box. Drive for about one mile. After entering North Huish take second turn on right, following signs for Coombe House. Pass the cottages on the left, then take first right. Lower Norris House is at the bottom of the hill on the left just before the bridge. Cross the cattle grid, and keep right at the top of the drive.

There are many local attractions and walks within easy reach. The village of South Brent is nearby, also Shipley Bridge with water-falls and wildlife. Dartmoor National Park is ten minutes drive. Walkers, cyclists, bird-watchers and artists will love it here. Buck-fastleigh is a short drive east, where you can make a tour of the historic Benedictine Abbey, famous for its tonic wine. Visit the Butterfly Farm and Otter Sanctuary, or take a steam train to Totnes.

The house has a spacious lounge with a TV and both rooms have a log fire. Stunning views of the valley can be enjoyed from here. Relax and unwind in the friendly surroundings. Aromatherapy massage, reflexology and spiritual healing are available by request.

Parking: plenty available

Children welcome and they have high chairs

Well behaved pets accepted by arrangement

Tea and coffee making facilities are in the rooms.

Smoking in garden only

10% discount to people presenting this book

SOUTH Devon

271

The Old Forge

Bed and Breakfast in an ancient stone creeper clad building within easy walk of the river and town centre. There are ten rooms: five double ensuites, one double with private bathroom and two twin ensuites at £28–£32 per person per night; plus two family rooms for around £112 per room per night for four people. (Price depends on the age of children).

Start the day with a choice of fruit juices, fruit and cereal, a cooked feast of veggie sausages, tomatoes, mushrooms, baked beans, potato waffles or hash browns, and wholemeal toast, washed down with a variety of teas and coffees. Soya milk and vegan margarine are available. Breakfast can be served in rooms by arrangement. Dinner is not included. Dave, the co-proprietor, is apparently an excellent chef.

There is an old blacksmith's prison cell on the property which is now a listed building, and a coach arch which leads to a walled garden. In Totnes there are markets on Friday and Saturday, many interesting shops, a steam train, castle, museum and cruises on the river.

Attractions in the area include Dartmoor National Park, English Riviera beaches, many castles, National Trust properties and beautiful gardens. There is good night life in Torquay, and Dartmouth, Kingsbridge and Salcombe are all within easy reach. The Eden Project is 1 1/2 hours drive away.

The whirlpool spa in the conservatory is screened by climbing and rambling flowers. Tea and coffee making facilities, televisions and hairdryers are in the rooms.

They have a bronze Green Tourism Award (South Hams District Council for Environmental Excellence).

Totnes

Omnivorous bed and breakfast

Seymour Place
Totnes
Devon TQ9 5AY
England

Tel: 01803–862 174

Fax: 01803–865 385

www.oldforgetotnes.com
enq@oldforgetotnes.com

Train Station: Totnes, 1/2 mile, then taxi

Open: all year

Directions: M5 to Exeter, A38 to Buckfastleigh/Staverton/Totnes exit A384. Follow signs to Totnes town centre. Turn right at big roundabout (at Safeway petrol station). At mini roundabout by Seven Stars Hotel, turn left over town bridge, then second on left. You will see a brown tourist board sign. Go straight on down hill into Totnes. Turn left.

Parking: available

Children of all ages welcome

Cots and high chairs available

Limited disabled access

No smoking throughout

Credit cards accepted

Riverbank Hotel

Attractive seventeenth century hotel situated on the bank of the River Lowman, with garden seating overlooking the river. There are one twin, one double and one family room, all ensuite, at £45 per room per night or £30 for single occupancy.

For breakfast choose from a selection of cereals and fruit followed by cooked tomatoes, beans, veggie sausages, fried potatoes and garlic mushrooms. Vegan margarine and soya milk are available. You can have breakfast in your room if you feel like being spoilt.

Dinner is offered in the cafe for £4–£5 and could be spicy pumpkin and coconut curry with rice, or polenta with Mediterranean roasted veggies. All food and cakes are freshly made. They have vegan ice-cream and vegan cakes. House wine £2 per glass or £7.50 for a bottle. Beer is £1.20.

The cafe is sometimes open to non-residents in the evenings for special events.

Tiverton is a historic market town on the rivers Exe and Lowman. There is a swimming pool, castle, cinema and markets. The town is not far from Exmoor and Dartmoor where there are plenty more attractions.

Riverbank Hotel offers massage, reflexology and aromatherapy. They offer internet access and a locked shed to store bicycles.

Rooms have tea and coffee making facilities and televisions.

Vegetarian hotel and restaurant

45 Gold Street
Tiverton
Devon EX16 6QB
England

Tel: 01884–254 911

www.riverbankhotel.co.uk
shirleyfield@talk21.com

Train Station: Tiverton Parkway, 7 miles

Open: all year

Restaurant open:
Tue–Sat 10.00–17.30
Sun–Mon closed

Directions: M5 to A361 to first turning for Tiverton. Follow signs for town centre and go past the Esso garage on the left.

Parking: limited

Children welcome

Cot and high chair available

Dogs welcome by arrangement

Smoking in garden only

SOUTH Devon

273

Southcliffe

Southcliffe is in the village of Lynton, which is a short distance from the picturesque harbour of Lynmouth. There are eight rooms, all with ensuite facilitites: six doubles and two twins for £23–£27 per person per night. Two of the doubles have balconies with views over Lynton and the surrounding Exmoor hills.

The breakfast menu has several vegetarian options, including a full cooked veggie or vegan breakfast.

Dinner is available on request and could be cashew and mushroom layer bake, almond risotto or rigatoni. There is also a good selection of local pubs and restaurants with veggie options nearby.

Southcliffe is set in some of the finest coastal scenery in the country. Lynton and Lynmouth have been known for many years as 'England's little Switzerland'. There is an incredible variety of scenery within a few square miles of the guest house.

A five minute walk from Southcliffe will take you to an unusual furnicular railway which links the twin villages of Lynton and Lynmouth. Take a boat cruise along the Heritage Coast with its nesting colony of seabirds. Drive only a short way and you will be in the heart of Exmoor. Spot the wild red deer roaming in the heathered hills and wooded valleys. Visit the Doone Valley, setting for the novel Lorna Doone by R.D Blackmore.

Tea and coffee making facilities. TV's and hairdryers in the rooms.

AA four diamonds and English Tourist Council four diamonds silver award.

Omnivorous guest house

Lee Road
Lynton
North Devon EX35 6BS
England

Tel: 01598–753 328

www.southcliffe.co.uk
info@southcliffe.co.uk

Train Station: Barnstaple, 20 miles, then bus

Open: March–October incl.

Directions: the house is opposite the post office on Lee Road

Parking: available

No children under 13

No pets

Credit cards accepted

No smoking throughout

Sparrowhawk Backpackers

This is the only strictly vegetarian hostel in the U.K. Sparrowhawk is situated in the centre of a small Dartmoor town, fourteen miles uphill and west of Exeter. Private room with double bed available for £30. The self-contained dorm is a beautifully converted stone stable with fourteen dorm beds upstairs for £12 per person. The dorms can be divided by curtains. Children stay for £7 per night.

There is a fully equipped strictly vegetarian kitchen to make your meals in. An organic veggie box is available with a couple of days notice. Fairtrade tea and organic coffee are provided free and if the mood takes them, the veggie proprietors Alison and Darren might make cakes and flapjacks. Local shops sell organic and wholefood supplies. Vegetarian meals are available in nearby pubs and cafes.

Situated within the Dartmoor National Park, with open moorland nearby, it is a great place to walk and cycle. There are Magnificent Tors, stone circles and burial sites of ancient civilisations to be explored. You'll see wild ponies and buzzards in your explorations. There are year round guided walks and talks organised by the National Park. More info at www.dartmoor-npa.gov.uk

Moretonhampstead is a small town and has a few shops, cafes, pub, a solar heated pool, recreation fields and footpaths leading to the moors. Bike hire is available. The third week in August is carnival week. The Eden Project is 1-2 hours drive away, or visit the Steward Community Woodland to see sustainable living in practice – dedicated vegan eco-warriors living in 32 acres of woodlands. (www.stewardwood.org)

Moretonhampstead

Vegetarian hostel

45 Ford Street
Moretonhampstead
Devon TQ13 8LN
England

Tel and Fax:
01647–440 318

www.
sparrowhawkbackpackers
.co.uk

Train Station: Exeter, Okehampton 12 miles, then get a direct bus no. 359 or 82

Open: all year

Directions:
From Exeter, take B3212. From M5, take J31 to A30 Okehampton. Moreton-hampstead is signposted a couple of miles on. More-tonhampstead is on cross roads of A382 and B3212. Sparrowhawk is on Ford Street going towards Chagford. Park in the car park and walk down.

Parking: available nearby

Families, groups and individuals welcome

Secure bicycle storage

Smoking outside only

SOUTH Devon

The Whiteleaf

Omnivorous hotel in a comfortable 1930's house standing in its own gardens near the North Devon Coastal Path. Croyde Bay is a couple of minutes walk across the dunes. There are five rooms: three doubles, one twin and one family all with their own private facilites. The doubles and twin cost £29–£36 per person per night and the family is £90–£105 for the room. Cheaper rates for longer stays.

A veggie breakfast could be cereal followed by tomatoes, mushrooms, baked beans and veggie sausages with toast.

A vegetarian dinner is always available. A la carte costs approximately £23 for three courses and is cooked by the co–proprietor and qualified chef, David. Fresh local produce is used. The restaurant is licensed and open to non residents. House wine is £2.75 per glass or £11.25 per bottle. Beer is £2.30. All diets are catered for, please advise when booking.

Croyde village is two minutes away with its thatched cottages, inns and tea rooms. A stream runs along the main street. The town of Georgeham is nearby with its 13th century church as well as the bustling village of Braunton, reputedly England's largest village.

The area has many natural attractions such as the beach, forests and remote moorlands. Golf, surfing, walking, bird watching and sea trips are some of the activities that could keep you amused during your stay.

All rooms have radios, televisions, tea and coffee making facilities, fridges and hair dryers. There is a guest lounge.

Braunton

Omnivorous hotel and restaurant

Croyde
Braunton
North Devon EX33 1PN
England

Tel: 01271–890 266

www.thewhiteleaf.co.uk

Train station: Barnstaple, 12 miles, then bus or taxi

Open: all year
(except 25–27 December)

Directions: from junction 27 on the M5, take the A361 North Devon Link Road through Barnstaple to Braunton. Turn left at traffic lights in Braunton. Keep straight on through Faunton into Croyde. Whiteleaf is on the left hand side opposite Bayview Farm.

Parking: available

Restaurant open 7 days: Breakfast 08.00–10.00, dinner 19.00–21.00 (Sun eve, residents only)

Dogs welcome with well behaved owners at £3.50 per day

Children welcome

All major credit cards accepted, except American Express

Smoking in some areas

Life Dynamic

Vegetarian organic B&B and retreat

Langford, North Bovey, Dartmoor, TQ13 8RH
Tel: 0845–330 4033
info@lifedynamic.com
www.lifedynamic.com
Open: All year, not Xmas holidays

Double rooms and family room with two pine bunk beds, £25 per person, children under 12 half price. Organic gourmet vegan living raw foods are their speciality, or cooked vegan and vegetarian options. Evening meal £12, child £6. Hearty packed lunch £7. Children of all ages are welcome and there's a toy box in the kitchen. Reflexology, health kinesiology and life coaching available by appointment, £30. No smoking inside. Dogs on leads at all times.

Avalon Guest House

Omnivorous guest house

Vicarage Road, Sidmouth EX10 8UQ
Tel: 01395–513 443
owneravalon@aol.com
www.avalonsidmouth.co.uk

Omnivorous B&B, but caters well for veggies and vegans. Best to say in advance if you're vegan or veggie. Can provide soya milk. RAC 4 Stars. Double and twin rooms, including one with 4 poster bed. All en suite with tea and coffee making in rooms, colour TVs, alarm clock radios and hair dryers. No children or pets. No smoking throughout.

Southcote

Omnivorous bed and breakfast

Southcote, Bridgetown Hill, Totnes TQ9 5BN
Tel: 01803–862 157
Fax: 01803–868 543
joe@direct–mortgages.info
Open: April – October

Detached house 5 minutes walk from Totnes and the river Dart. One family room en suite, one twin en suite, one double with bathroom next to it, all £25–30 per person. Min 2 nights stay. One of the proprietors is a watercolour artist and her pictures are on the walls, framed and unframed prints and cards are for sale. Cooked breakfast on request, just say if you are vegan on booking. Child in family room add £5–10. Children welcome, no high chair.

SOUTH   Devon

Ashburton
Moorish

Omnivorous wine bar/cafe

11 West Street, Ashburton TQ13 7ED
Tel: 01364–654 011
jgjandhil@btopenworld.com
Open: Tues–Sat 10–14.30 & 18.00–22:30,
Sun 11.00–14.00 & 19.00–22.00

Licensed cafe/restaurant with Mediter-ranean influences. The tapas selection includes vegan choices. The menu changes regularly and the chef uses local produce. Children are welcome until 9.00pm and high chairs are available. The veggie cooked breakfast is £4.50, tapas £3.50 each or a taster plate of 3 £5.50. Drinks include hot or cool ginger beer £1.80, San Miguel lager £2.40. Luscombe's cider and juices (all vegan).

The Ark

Wholefood shop

38 East Street, Ashburton TQ13 7AX
Tel: 01364–653 020. the-ark@clara.co.uk
Open: Mon–Fri 9–17.30, Wed & Sat–16.00

Independent vegetarian wholefood shop, including a wide range of fresh and chilled produce. They stock most vegan dairy products, except ice-cream, and a wide range of toiletries. About 50% organic, including fresh bread, fruit and vegetables.

Axminster
Total Liberation

Vegetarian shoe shop

c/o Lyme Leisure, South Street, Axminster EX13 5AD. Tel/Fax: 01297–631 1133
www.total-liberation-footwear.com
axevegans@yahoo.co.uk
Open: Mon–Sat 9–17.00, Sun closed.
Sometimes closed Sat if at a show.

Ganesha

Health food shop

Simpson House, South Street, Axminster
Tel: 01297 33957
Open: Mon–Sat 9–17.00

Take-away samosas, pasties, bhajias, and sosrolls.

Brixham
The Garret Cafe

Vegetarian cafe

Beach approach, The Strand, Brixham TQ5 8JL
Tel: 01803–882 610
Open: Mon–Sun 08.30–17.30,
some nights later, phone to check

Home cooked food, locally produced. Soups are vegan and cost £1.95 with a roll. Mains such as veggie stir fry with noodles or potato skins with chilli, are £3.75. There is always a vegan dessert, such as banana fritters, £1.75, and sorbets. Visa, MC accepted.

Chagford
The Courtyard Cafe

Vegetarian cafe

76 The Square, Chagford TQ13 8AE
Tel: 01647–432571
Open: all year Mon–Sat 9–17.00, closed Sun

Nearly all organic. Soup and bread £3. Different dishes daily including one or two vegan meals and one wheat free. Lots of cakes and pies. Mug of tea £1.10, pot £1.25 for one, £2.40 for two. All kinds of herbal and Rooibosch tea. Cappuccino £1.40. Big bulletin board with what's going on in the area and they double as the Tourist Information Centre for Dartmoor. Newspapers to read. About 3 miles from Sparrowhawk Backpackers hostel.

Cranks

Vegetarian cafe

Cider Press Centre, Shinners Bridge
Dartington TQ9 6JB
Open: Mon–Sat 9.30–17.00
Tel: 01803–862 388
www.cranks.co.uk
also Sundays Easter–December

This sole surviving branch of the famous veggie chain of restaurants is set in a crafts centre within the grounds of Dartington Hall. All foods made fresh and daily on premises without preservatives and additives. They are open for breakfast and always have vegan and gluten free dishes. Soups are £3.30 with organic bread, main dishes £4.95–£6.50 such as Thai curry and various homemade burgers. Garden for al fresco dining. No smoking. Visa, MC.

Herbies

Relaxed, unpretentious bistro–style veggie restaurant.
Starters £1.80–£3.50 include dhal with chapatis, soup of the day, provençal mushrooms, paté, hummou and, various types of bread. Snacks are £1.95–£4.25, such as nut & beanburgers, stir–fry, jacket potatoes and wraps.
Main courses £5.75–£6.50 such as homity pie, pizza, vegan spinach and mushroom lasagne, or courgette, mushroom and polenta flan. Items marked V on the menu may be vegan, but you need to make sure. Cakes, desserts and ices are listed on the blackboards.
Drinks for 90p–£2.25 such as mineral water, juices, organic cola and ginger cordial. Coffees from £1.10. Organic wine £2.60 a glass or £11.95 for litre bottle. Lagers and beers from £2.40, alcohol–free beer £2.25.

Coolings

Omnivorous bistro & wine bar

11 Gandhi Street, Exeter EX4 3LS
Tel: 01392–434184
Email: coolings@southdevoninns.co.uk
Open: Mon–Sat 10–23.00, Sun 10–22.30

Bistro/wine bar in the city centre. Always a hot veggie dish £6.50 and four salads £5.60 for a big bowl. Vegan food available, though not every day. Calling ahead is advised.

SOUTH Devon

Vegetarian restaurant

15 North Street
Exeter
Devon EX4 3QS

Tel: 01392–258 473

Open:
Mon–Fri 11–14.30,
Sat 10.30–16.00.
Tue–Sat 18–21.30.
Closed Sun.
(end times are for last orders)

Children's portions

High chairs

Small smoking area

Visa, MC

Kingsbridge

The Ring O'Bells

Omnivorous pub

West Alvington, Kingsbridge TQ7 3PG
Tel: 01548–852 437
Open: Meals 11–14:30 & 17.00–21:30pm

An independent restaurant where George, the chef/patron, wants it to be like dining in your own home without the cooking or washing up to do. There's a vast menu, which includes several vegetarian and vegan options. Starters: melon coulis £4.95, or avocado salad with tomato & garlic dressing & pan fried mushrooms £4.95. Mains: sweet and sour vegetable stir fry, vegetable curry, pasta Roma, all for £6.95. No vegan puds beyond fruity things.

Mybridge

Nature's Larder

Wholefood shop

10 Glanvilles Mill, Ivybridge PL 21 9PS
Tel: 01752–894 197
Open: Mon–Fri 9.00–17.30 Sat 9.00–17.00

Friendly independent omnivorous wholefood shop. They have frozen or chilled pies & pasties to take away and ready meals. Dragonfly tofu only 99p. Therapy centre upstairs.

Newton Abbot

The Country Table

99% vegetarian restaurant

12 Bank Street, Newton Abbot, PQ12 2JW
Tel: 01626–202 120
www.thecountrytablecafe.co.uk
Open: Mon–Sat 08.30–16.30;
first Sat of month 19.30–22.00 (reserve)
Closed Sun & Bank Holidays

Wholefood café, restaurant and take-away. Breakfast snacks £3.65. Soups £2.95, salads £2.85 or £3.85, Italian panini (incl. gluten free pannita) from £3.75. Mains at £4.95 are homemade and change daily such as spicy parsnip & lentil pie or bean & tomato bake. Vegan and gluten free diets catered for. Desserts from £1.45 with vegan apricot or date slices, and Swedish glace ice-cream £2.30. Soya milkshakes. No smoking throughout. No credit cards. 10% discount to Vegetarian and Vegan Society members.

Plymouth

Nutters

Vegetarian restaurant by day, omnivorous bistro by night

2 Haye Rd South, Elverton,
Nr Plymouth PL9 8HJ
(on the Kingsbridge Road 3 miles out of town, the route to the country and beaches)
Tel: 01752–481 117
Open: M on–Sat 10.30–16.00,
Thur–Sat 19–23.00 (Wed for groups)

Lunch £4.25 main, substantial soup and roll £3.50. Evening meal starter £3.50, main £7.95 such as spicy vegetable chili and rice. Lots of home made desserts £3.50, can be made vegan if you let them know. No smoking. Children welcome, no high chairs. BYO, no corkage. MC, Visa.

Plymouth Arts Centre

Vegetarian restaurant & take-away

Plymouth Arts Centre, 38 Looe Street PL4 0EB
Tel: 01752–202 616
www.plymouthac.org.uk
Open: Mon 10.00–17.00,
Tue–Sat 10.00–20.30, Sun closed
(lunch 12–14.00, evening meal from 17.00)

Close to the historic Barbican, based in an arts centre with a gallery and an independent cinema. Baked potato

Veggie Perrin's

Gujarati vegetarian (80% vegan) restaurant and takeaway.

Starters £1.55–£2.50 include samosas, bhaji, kachori, stuffed puri etc. Lots of veg curries £3–£4.95, even "korma sutra" on request. Rice from £1.50 and all those scrummy breads and the English ethnic delicacy, chips.

They have various desserts (vegan choices include mango sorbet, doughnuts and carrot halva) and a big selection of Indian and world beers. A glass of house wine is £2, bottles £7.95 and up.

Take–away: 20% off a la carte prices. They also do catering for events and summer festivals.

Indian vegetarian restaurant & take away

97 Mayflower Street, Plymouth, Devon

Tel: 01752–252 888
Fax: 01752–220 808

www.veggieperrin.com

Open: Mon–Sat 12.00–14.00, 18.00–22.00, closed Sun except for private functions

Visa, MC

No smoking

SOUTH   Devon

from £1.95. Filled wraps (Mexican, Satay veg) £3. Mains £4.10 such as mango, veg and coconut curry. Vegans always have plenty to choose from. World cooking night once a month. Vegetarian house wine £1.85 glass, £9.30 bottle. No smoking. Children welcome, high chair. MC, Visa (50p surcharge). Parties catered for and outside catering. 20% student discount on Tuesday evenings.

Tooleys

Omnivorous Chinese take away

The Ridgeway, Plympton, Plymouth PL7 2ZN
Tel: 01752–342211
Open: Mon–Sat 17.30–22.30, closed Sun

Chinese take–away. They used to have a huge separate vegetarian menu, but now they've combined it with the meat menu which leads to the meat–eaters choosing more veggie dishes, £3.20–£4.40. The cook is a pure Buddhist.

From 10–14.30 it's an ordinary English café run by other people with sand–wiches and Chinese food for veggies.

The Salcombe Coffee Company

Omnivorous cafe/bistro

73 Fore Street, Salcombe TQ8 8BU
Tel: 01548–842 319
Open: daily 9.00–17.00, Easter–Oct also 17:30–21.00 Thu–Mon

Friendly coffee shop and cafe in the day and informal bistro at night. Spinach, sundried tomatoes, & black olive panninis for £3.95. Vegetarian soup is nearly always vegan, £2.75 with choice of bread & olive oil. Specials are often vegetarian, such as roasted veg on tomato couscous or spinach mushroom & pinenut pasta £6.95. Soya or rice cappuccino £1.45.

Tiverton

Reapers

Health food shop

18 Bampton Street, Tiverton EX16 6AA
Tel: 01884–255 310
Open: Mon–Sat 8.30–17.00

Organic fruit and veg, tofu, vegan cheese and ice-cream. Pasties, flapjacks, cakes (including vegan ones). Baby section with environmentally friendly nappies, Ecover refills. Supplements. A homeopath and a herbalist operate from the shop by appointment.

Torquay

Cafe Toree

Omnivorous cafe

Teigmouth Rd, Torquay TQ1 4DZ
Tel: 01803–315 780,College 01803–400 700
Open: Mon–Fri 9.00–15.00

Aabout 50% vegetarian, mostly organic, in a community college. The people making the food are on a course. Quiche and salad £2.50, home made soup £2 with roll, baked potatoes with fillings. Cup of tea or coffee under £1. No smoking. No credit cards. Children welcome but no high chairs.

Totnes

Fat Lemons Cafe

Organic vegetarian wholefood cafe

1 Ticklemore Court, Ticklemore Street, Totnes TQ9 5EJ. Tel: 01803–866 888
Open: Mon–Sat 9.00–17.00

One of the hot daily specials is vegan, such as tofu kebabs with mango salsa, or vegan paella and salad, £5.95. Wheat and yeast-free options, raw and other special diets catered if pre-booked. Sometimes there is a vegan cake. Soyaccino £1.20.

282

Bistro 67

Omnivorous bistro

67 Fore Street, Totnes TQ9 5NJ
Tel: 01803–862 604. www.bistro67.co.uk
Open: Mon–Sat 12.00–21/22.00 last orders

Omnivorous bistro with 1/3 of the menu vegetarian. Can adapt items for vegans. No smoking. Visa, MC, Amex. Licensed. Children welcome.

Willow Vegetarian Garden Restaurant

Vegetarian restaurant & take away

87 High Street, Totnes TQ9 5PB
Tel: 01803–862 605
Open: Mon–Tue, Thu 10–17.00;
Wed , Sat 10–22.00; Fri 9–22.00
Sun closed, open most bank holidays

Menu changes daily. Four mains, which include one or two vegan, such as blackeye bean bake or savoury tofu flan £4.50–6.50 (with mixed salads £5.25–7.20). Filled jacket potatoes £4.50. Soups with roll and scone £3.50. Filled rolls £2.05. Evening starters £1.95–3.95 such as dips, soup, garlic bread (can be vegan); mains £6.75–8.20 include Indian and Caribbean dishes.

Champions of the south–west for vegan desserts £2.50–2.95 including fruit slice with Tofutti or soya dream, 3-layer gateau, Chocolate Forest ice-cream special (Tofutti, slices of banana, blueberry sauce), lots of vegan cakes and brownies.

Lots of wines and beers. House wine £2.25 glass, £8.50–9.00 bottle. Children are seriously welcome, family room with toys and books, high chair. No smoking inside, ok in the gorgeous garden. Cash or cheque only.

Barrel House

Omnivorous restaurant

59a High St, Totnes TQ9 5PB
Tel: 01803–863000
Open: Sun–Wed 9–18.00, Thu–Sat 9–23.00

Cafe downstairs, resaurant upstairs.
After a misspent night, veggie cooked
breakfast till 4pm £4.50. Ratatouille
£4.50, veggieburger, salads and soups.
Licensed. Kids welcome, but no U–18's
after 6pm. Fireplace, lots of character
Smoking area upstairs. MC, Visa.

Brioche

Omnivorous cafe

49 High St, Totnes TQ9 5NP
Tel: 01803–864463. Open: Mon–Sat 9–17.00

Vegan soups, salads, sandwiches.
Specials are always vegan like roast
Mediterranean veg £4.50.

Greenlife

Wholefood shop

11–13 Fore St, Totnes. Tel: 01803–866 738.
www.greenlife.co.uk/shop
Open: Mon–Sat 9.00–17.30

Wide range of toiletries and potions,
including sunscreen and toothpaste.
Discounts for senior citizens and
students on special days.

Sacks Wholefoods

Wholefood shop

80 High St, Totnes. Tel: 01803–863 263
Open: Mon–Sat 9.00–17.30 (Wed from 10)

Organic veg,. Vegan Swedish Glace and
choc–ices. Sausages, tempeh. Toiletries.
Notice boards of local events, classes,
services and practitioners.

Apothecary Now

Vegetarian apothecary

83 High St, Totnes. Tel: 01803–866 882
Open: Tue–Sat 10–17.00, Mon in summer

Handmade skin care products,
shampoos and soaps, produced by
small companies using no animal
testing. Many products are vegan and
are clearly labelled.

Seeds Bakery & Health

Omnivorous bakery

22 Duke St, Dartmouth. Tel: 01803–833 200
Open: Mon–Sat 9.30–17.00

19 High St, Exmouth. Tel: 01395–265 741
Open: Mon–Sat 9.30–17.00

35 High Street, Totnes. Tel: 01803–862 526
Open: Mon–Sat 9.00–17.00

Daily home–baked veggie take–away
items such as filled rolls £1.65, pasties
90p, vegan fruit slice 95p.

Holland & Barrett

Health food shop

92 High Street, North Cotes, Barnstaple
Tel: 01271–328 295

16 Waterbeer Street, Guildhall, Exeter
Tel: 01392–277 194

16–18 Princesshay, Exeter
Tel: 01392–251590

58 Cornwall Street, Plymouth
Tel: 01752–661 822

Unit 2, 36 Royal Parade, Plymouth
Tel: 01752–661 076

35 Fore St, Tiverton. Tel: 01884–256 690

28 Union St, Torquay. Tel: 01803–212 215

Dorset

Cowden House

Cowden House is set in its own three acres of land in the beautiful Cerne Valley, and offers spacious accommodation for up to six guests. There are four rooms: one double and one twin at £23 per person per night, one double ensuite at £25 per person, and one twin ensuite at £24 per person. All rooms have lovely views.

Breakfast is a choice of cereals, fruit salad and fruit juice followed by a full cooked veggie breakfast if desired, or simply toast or fresh bread with various spreads and jams. Soya milk, vegan muesli, vegan margarine and veggie sausages are available.

Dinner is offered for £14.50 and could be bruschetta followed by Moroccan tofu and aubergine casserole with cous cous salad, then a dessert of fruit crumble and vegan ice cream. They are open to non residents for dinner.

Cowden House is on the edge of Godmanstone, a tiny unspoilt village. You can walk up a farm lane and off into the hills and go for miles away from roads.

The house is ideal for individuals or for small groups who wish to stay for a period with a particular theme, such as a painting weekend or personal growth work.

Dorset has dozens of picturesque villages to explore, beautiful gardens and historic houses to visit, plus a spectacular coastline. The west of the county is completely rural and to the east are Poole and Bournemouth – great centres for shopping, night life and clean sandy beaches.

Tea and coffee making facilities in the rooms and a television in the lounge.

Vegetarian bed and breakfast

Frys Lane
Godmanstone
Dorchester
Dorset DT2 7AG
England

Tel: 01300–341 377

www.cowdenhouse.co.uk

Train station: Dorchester, 5 miles, then bus ot taxi or collection is possible

Open: all year, except Christmas

Directions: Cowden House is five miles north of Dorchester, just off the A352. Frys Lane is the first left on entering Godmanstone.

Parking: available

One dog is welcome

Children welcome

High chair available

No smoking throughout

SOUTH Dorset

285

Bournemouth

Glenvale

Vegetarian B&B

14 Gardens View, East Cliff, Bournemouth,
Dorset, BH1 3QA. Tel: 01202 553769.
www.glenvale-vege.co.uk

1 mile from Bournemouth town centre,
opposite the Green Flag awarded
Knyveton Gardens and 10 mins walk
from train and coach stations. Double,
two twins (one with fridge), two singles,
all with central heating, basins, colour
TV, tea/coffee. Organic food used
whenever possible and vegans catered
for by arrangement. No smoking.

St. Antoine Guest House

Omnivorous guest house

2 Guildhill Road, Southbourne,
Bournemouth BH6 3E7. Tel: 01202-433 043
Email: kathden@kathden.fsnet.co.uk

St. Antoine is set on a quiet road only a
few minutes walk from the beach.
There are five rooms: one single, two
doubles and two family ensuites at
£20-£22 per person per night.
Start your day with cereal and fruit juice
followed by veggie sausages,
mushrooms, tomatoes and toast with
home made preserves. Soya milk and
vegan margarine are available.

Wessex Tales

Vegan restaurant

20 Ashley Road, Boscombe,
Bournemouth BH1 4LH
Tel: 01202-309 869
t.west@onetel.net.uk
www.geocities.com/vegetarian_restaurant
Open: Tue-Sat 11.30-14.30,
Fri, Sat evenings 19-22.00

World food menu with mostly organic
food. Starters £2.00-£2.50 such as
garlic mushrooms on onion and herb
bread. Mains include nut roast, and
masala dosa £5 day, £7.50 evenings.
Desserts include Swedish glace vegan
ice-cream and cakes £2-£3 such as
chocolate, or orange and lemon.
Wine £9 bottle, £1.90 for a glass. Vegan
ales. Non smoking. Cash or cheque
only.

The Salad Centre

Vegetarian cafe

667 Christchurch Road,
Boscombe, Bournemouth BH7 6AA
Tel: 01202-393 673
Open: Mon-Sat 10.00-17.00

Vegetarian cafe, £3.85 for main course
such as lentil moussaka or ratatouille
with brown rice. Vegan desserts include
apple pie £1.95, cakes and ice-cream.
Freshly squeezed juices, shakes, soya
milk available. Not licensed. Children
welcome, no high chair. No smoking.
MC, Visa.

The Falafel Restaurant

Omnivorous restaurant

218 Holdenhurst Rd, Bournemouth BH8 8AX
Tel: 01202-552277
Open: Sun-Thu 12-14.00, Sun-Fri 18-22.00.
Closed Fri eve, Sat all day.

50% of the food here is veggie. Vegan
falafels take-away £2.75, eat in £5.45.
Lots of salads, hummous, peppers in
olive oil.
Desserts include apple pie, baklava with
syrrup they make themselves (not
honey), non-dairy ice-cream.
Fully licensed, house wine 12 bottle, 3
glass. Children welcome, high chairs.
No smoking. MC, Visa.

Shakeaway

Milkshake chain

7 Post Office Road, Bournemouth BH1 1BB
Tel: 01202–310 105
www.shakeaway.com

Huge range of flavours including 30 vegan ones made from organic soya milk and/or vegan ice-cream.

Walnut Grove

Omnivorous restaurant

25 Durngate Street, Dorchester DT1 1JP
Tel: 01305–268 882
Open: Mon–Sat 9.30–17.00, Sun (in summer only) 9.30–16.00

Omnivorous restaurant with a third of the menu vegetarian. Friendly and will try and adapt items for special dietary needs. Gourmet evenings held once-monthly (call for dates). Will also open evenings for private parties and functions for 15 people or more. Non smoking. No credit cards.

Poole

Clipper Restaurant

Omnivorous restaurant

The Dolphin Centre, Poole BH15 1SS
Tel/fax: 01202–683 334
Open: Mon–Fri 9.30–17.00, Sat 9.00–17.15

At the top of the shopping centre, this omnivorous restaurant offers an extensive vegetarian selection. Big salad bar with salads from £1.85, many without dressings and suitable for vegans. Jacket potatoes with fillings. Visa, MC.

Southbourne

Earthfoods

Organic wholefood shop + take-away

75 Southbourne Grove, Southbourne
earthcures@vegemail.com
Tel: 01202–422 465
Open: Mon–Sat 9–18.00

SOUTH Dorset

Much more than just an organic wholefood shop, all vegetarian or vegan, GM free. Fresh fruit and vegetables. Range of take-aways including raw food items. Chemical and cruelty free cosmetics, toiletries, household products such as paints and brushes, hemp tiles, wall paper and glue – all vegan.

Weymouth

No. 21 Vegetarian Restaurant

Vegetarian restaurant

21 East Street, Weymouth DT4 8BN
Tel: 01305–767 848
Mobile: 07979–885 685
cafe2021@hotmail.com
Open: Mon–Sun midday–late, bookings taken

Starters £3.95, lunch from £5.95 and evening meal £7.95 from 6.30 to 7.30pm then £10.25 Main dishes may be sweet potato African stew or spicy nut roast. Desserts from £4.25 include vegan apple crumble or pecan tart. Non smoking, except in garden. No credit cards. Offer 10% discount to Vegetarian and Vegan Society members and also to members of Greenpeace and Friends of the Earth. Children welcome, high chair available. Bring your own alcohol.

Helens Famous Wholefoods

Wholefood shop

61 St Mary Street, Weymouth DT4 8PP
Tel: 01305–777 261
Fax: 01305–848 017
Open: Mon–Sat 8.30–17.30

Holland & Barrett

Health food shop

23 The Arcade, Bournemouth
Tel: 01202–297 713

14 Gardens Way, Bournemouth
Tel: 01202–553 769

54 South Street, Dorchester
Tel: 01305–251 857

25 Kingland Terrace, Poole
Tel: 01202–649 291

West Road, West Lulworth, Wareham
Tel: 01929–400 592

33 St. Mary's Street, Weymouth
Tel: 01305–766 485

Vegetarian Guides – Links

Don't travel abroad without checking locally
compiled vegetarian websites. Here's a small selection.

Americas
www.vegetarianismo.com.br/guia/guia.html – Brazil
www.veghawaii.org
www.bayareaveg.org/ug – San Francisco

Asia
www.i-v-s.org – Indonesia
www.jpvs.org/p2/eat1.html – Japan Restaurants (Japanese)
www.vegetarian-society.org – Singapore

Australasia
www.veg-soc.org – Vegetarian Australia

Europe
www.vegan.at – Austria
www.vegetarian.be – Belgium
www.budaveg.com – Budapest
www.vegetariani.it – Italy
www.veganstockholm.se/lang_eng – Stockholm
www.vegetarismus.ch – Switzerland

International
www.ivu.org – International Vegetarian Union
www.FreeTranslation.com – Paste blocks of text for translation

Nutrition & Recipes
www.veganoutreach.org
www.vegsource.com
www.vegweb.com
www.fatfreevegan.com

Great Travel Sites
www.whichbudget.com – European cheap flights
www.nationalrail.co.uk – British trains
www.eurolines.com – Coach travel in Europe
www.nationalexpress.com – Coach travel in Britain
www.megabus.com – Ridiculously cheap coach travel

www.vegetarianguides.co.uk/links – mapping the world for veggies

East Sussex Brighton

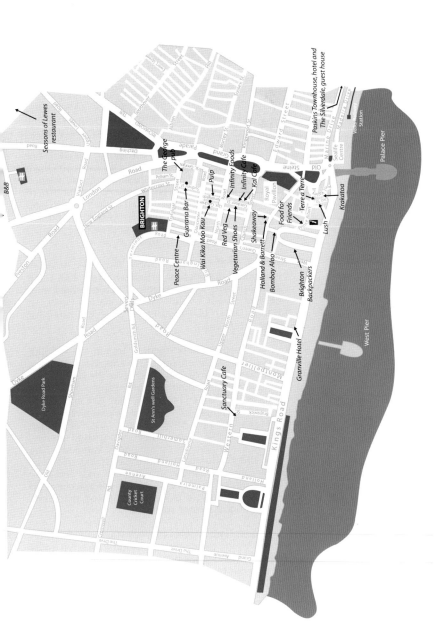

Seasons of Lewes restaurant

B&B

BRIGHTON

The George Pub

Guarana Bar

Peace Centre

Wai Kika Moo Kau

Pulp

Red Veg

Infinity Foods

Infinity Cafe

Kai Cafe

Vegetarian Shoes

Shakeaway

Holland & Barrett

Bombay Aloo

Food for Friends

Terre a Terre

Krakatoa

Lush

Brighton Backpackers

Sanctuary Cafe

Granville Hotel

Paskins Townhouse, hotel and
The Silverdale, guest house

Station

Sealife Centre

Royal Pavilion

Dyke Road Park

St Ann's well Gardens

County Cricket Court

Palace Pier

West Pier

Kings Road

Brighton rivals London and Edinburgh as being the best city in the UK for veggies and vegans. However, Brighton's small centre means you'll never be more than five minutes walk from a veggie restaurant. It offers the city excitement of clubs, pubs, restaurants and theatres but it's by the sea and only a short cycle ride to the countryside. There is a thriving arts scene and a vibrant student, veggie and gay population.

Brighton is an ideal day trip from London, but everyone knows it, so to avoid the crowds come on a weekday. You'll find restaurant and bar staff friendlier and there'll be no need to fight for a table. There are vegetarian restaurants for all budgets, cafés and take-aways, the veggie pub The George, and the decadence of Terre à Terre gourmet vegetarian restaurant.

To really chill out, come for a few days. Veggie-friendly accommodation includes hostels, B&B's and the luxurious Granville Hotel. If you do come on a weekend, book your accommodation well in advance. Most guesthouses in Brighton cater for veggies and vegans.

You could spend hours getting lost in the winding alleys of The Lanes exploring the shops and drinking in the bars. North of Church Street is the slightly less touristy bohemian quarter, North Laine. You'll find plenty of second hand clothing, New Age and record shops in amongst trendy cafés, expensive clothes stores and gadget shops. Don't miss Vegetarian Shoes, the animal friendly shoe shop (closed Sunday) and the collectables shop Snooper's Paradise. The Peace and Environment Centre has stacks of books on environmental and animal rights issues and eco-friendly gifts. If you're dying for a soyaccino and aren't near a veggie place, rest assured that most cafés in Brighton have soya milk.

It's almost impossible to walk through Brighton without seeing the distinctive Oriental inspired Royal Pavilion. It was built between 1815 and 1822 as a villa for Prince George (future George IV) to have lavish parties. It's well worth a visit and is open daily from 9:30am–5pm. Entry is £5.95 or £4.20 for seniors, students and unemployed with relevant ID. Family tickets £9.45 (one adult) or £15.40 (two adults). Brighton's Museum and Art Gallery on Church Street has paintings, furniture and ceramics, including some valuable Art Deco and Art Nouveau. Some people come just to see Salvador Dali's famous Lip Sofa. Entry is free and it's open Tuesday to Saturday 10am-5pm, Sunday 2pm-5pm, closed Mondays.

If you fancy a spot of exercise and some breath-taking scenery, cycle along the coast to the town of Rottingdean, or a bit further to Saltdean, stopping for a quick bevvie in one of the pubs on the seafront before heading back.

There are also water sports, ten pin bowling and an ice skating rink. Kids love Brighton for the beach with its paddling pools and play equipment and the Palace Pier with funfair rides and candyfloss. Further west towards Hove is the disused listed West Pier, which has been destroyed by numerous fire over the years.

During the three weeks of Brighton Festival in May there is even more music, theatre and comedy than usual. The Fringe events are worth seeing too and often feature local talent.

Getting there: From London's Victoria Station, Brighton is a fifty minute train ride. There is a fast train every half an hour every day, except for peak times and Sundays when it takes about one and a half hours. There's also a train that goes through King's Cross, Blackfriars and London Bridge but it's slow. Phone National Rail Enquiries for information and times on 08457 484950. If you want to try getting to Brighton for only a quid, www.megabus.com. Most guesthouses are a walk or short taxi ride from the station. Once you're in Brighton you don't need a car. It's much better to leave it at home, as parking is hard to find and expensive.

The Granville Hotel

Omnivorous hotel with restaurant

124 Kings Road
Brighton
East Sussex BN1 2FA
England

Tel: 01273–326 302

Fax: 01273–728 294

www.granvillehotel.co.uk
granville@brighton.co.uk

Train station: Brighton, 1/2 mile, then walk or get a bus or taxi.

Open: all year

Directions:
The Granville is on the sea front opposite the West Pier.

Parking: limited

Children welcome and they have facilities like high chairs.

Pets welcome.

Smoking in designated areas only.

Televisions and tea and coffee making faciities in the rooms.

Treat yourself to luxury and comfort at the this hotel, set on Brighton's sea front opposite the Pier. Each of the twenty four ensuite rooms are decorated in their own distinctive style and offer a choice between sea views and tranquil north facing accommodation. Doubles are £37.50–£77.50, twins £37.50–£57.50 and family rooms, £30–£50 per person per night. Some rooms have jacuzzis and four poster beds. One room has a water bed.

Begin your day with a delicious veggie breakfast in bed which could consist of cereal and organic fruit juice followed by veggie sausages, veggie rashers, organic baked beans and tomatoes with toast. Soya milk, soya yoghurt, vegan margarine and vegan muesli are all available. The food is guaranteed to be free of GM content and additives and they use organic produce.

The beach is just across the road where there is a basketball court, paddling pools and several bars and nightclubs. The working pier with its fun fair rides is a ten minute stroll and a six screen cinema is only five minutes walk away.

The separately operated basement restaurant, Tables 88, is international omnivorous and has three veggie dishes but not vegan. Lunch Tue–Sat 12.30–14.30, Sun 12–17.00. Dinner Mon–Thu 18–22.00, Fri–Sat till 23.00, closed Sun evening. £5.95 for lunch. Dinner £15 for two courses, £25 for three, excluding wine. Tel 01273–323888.

There are lots of nearby veggie restaurants and cafes in Brighton, such as Food for Friends and Terre a Terre, as well as many bars, pubs and nightclubs.

Rozanne Mendick B & B

Vegetarian bed and breakfast in a large family home close to the centre of Brighton. There are three rooms; one single, one double and one twin all costing £25 per person per night.

Wake in the morning to a delicious veggie or vegan breakfast which could consist of fresh and dried fruit, fruit juice, cereal or muesli and soya yoghurt followed by soya sausages, mushrooms, tomatoes, baked beans, toast and more if requested. Vegan margarine, soya milk and vegan muesli are all available.

No evening meal is offered but you certainly won't go hungry in Brighton! There are lots of veggie cafes and restaurants and even a veggie pub in town. Just take a look at the Brighton restaurant section in this book. If you fancy going on a picnic, there are several health food shops around town where you can get tasty snacks.

The town centre is a fifteen minute walk away with its many shops, pubs and clubs.

The sea front is a twenty minute walk where you can enjoy strolls on the beach watching the sunset, or go on the fun fair rides on the pier.

Tea and coffee making facilities, and a television are in the rooms.

Vegan/vegetarian bed and breakfast

14 Chatsworth Road
Brighton
East Sussex BN1 5DB
England

Tel: 01273–556 584

r_mendick@yahoo.co.uk

Train station:
10 minute walk north of Brighton station, near Seven Dials, bus or taxi

Open: all year

Directions: Ten minutes walk north of station, near Seven Dials

Parking: on street

Children of any age welcome, but no baby facilities

No pets

No smoking throughout

Paskins Town House

An omnivorous hotel with a vegetarian proprietor in a grade II listed building. Others will soon follow in the steps of Paskins – it has purposefully put aside the prosaic for its own beliefs. It is not smart or imposing or fancy, just a little chic, graciously hospitable and genuinely green in outlook. Extending across two fine-looking town houses the hotel is just yards from the beach.

The 19 rooms are lovely, the odd four-poster room, some rooms mildly eccentric; all are colourful, eclectic and palpably comfortable and clean. £35 to £60 per person per night for ensuite rooms. There are a few budget rooms at £30 per person.

There is a pleasant sense of fun – the Art Nouveau reception is a joy to enter, hallways are full of colourful theatre prints and the Art Deco breakfast room is a delight, as is the huge choice of breakfasts. In fact it's worth travelling to Brighton for: organic tomatoes sprinkled with oregano or organic mushrooms with a grind of sea salt, freshly baked croissants. Vegetarians are treated royally with many individual home made dishes on the menu. Soya milk, home made marmalade and vegan margarine, organic porridge, organic muesli, half a dozen each of fruits, cereals and juices. The tables groan. Many will tell you it is the best vegetarian breakfast anywhere in England. Much of the food is organic or where possible, sourced from local farms. On top of that the coffee, tea and chocolate in the rooms is Fair Trade, the cosmetics in the room free of animal testing.

You are close to the centre of things including the beach and lots of veggie restaurants within walking distance.

A very special town house hotel with a fully licensed lounge and terrific value.

Omnivorous hotel

18/19 Charlotte Street
Brighton
East Sussex BN2 1AG
England

Tel: 01273-601 203
Fax: 01273-621 973

www.paskins.co.uk
welcome@paskins.co.uk

Train station:
Brighton, then bus or £3 taxi ride

Open: all year

Directions:
Arrive at the Palace Pier and proceed with the sea on your right towards Newhaven. They are ten minutes walk from the pier.

Parking: on street

10% discount to members of the Vegetarian Society, Vegan Society and people presenting this book.

Facilities include high chairs

Children up to 11 get 50% discount if sharing with two adults

Pets welcome

Smoking permitted in rooms and some other areas

Rooms have TV's, direct dial telephones and some really original locally baked biscuits.

RAC Four Diamonds Award

Brighton Backpackers

Backpackers hostel

76 Middle Street, Brighton BN1 1AL
Tel: 01273-777 717
www.brightonbackpackers.com
stay@brightonbackpackers.com
Train Station: Brighton, ten minutes walk
Open: all year

A fun place for international travellers and students in the centre of town near the sea with a relaxed and friendly atmosphere. Four to eight beds in each mixed or single sex room £12 per person (from £13 summer). Weekly £70-80. Two or three double rooms on the sea front with ensuite bathrooms £30. No meals provided but there is a kitchen for you to cook your own stuff. In front of the hostel are water sports facilities, including windsurfing and sea canoes. The social area has a hi-fi, satellite tv, bar and pool table. Internet access, and there are lockers. 24 hour access. No children or pets. Smoking allowed in some areas

Kai Organic Cafe

Vegetarian organic cafe & take-away

52 Gardner Street, Brighton BN1 1UN
Tel: 01273-684 921
Open: Mon-Sat 9-17.30, Sun 10.30-17.00

The only cafe in Brighton we know of to be certified by the Soil Association. Wide selection of vegetarian, vegan and wheat free dishes. There are a few tables downstairs, but if you can get a table upstairs by the window, it's a great place to watch the world go by. There are a couple of outside tables, but on Saturday the street is pedestrianised and as many as twenty people can sit outside.
Counter service and pick and mix. The long counter has cakes, soups and salads on display. There is a drinks fridge also.
All soups and salads are vegan. Soup with bread £3.45, large bowl with extra bread £3.85. Mezze plate of hummous, roasted vegetable salad, Greek salad (vegans ask for no feta), marinated olives and warm pitta bread. Daily specials. Lots of cakes. Cappuccino £1.80. Soya milk available.
High chair. MC, Visa. No smoking.

Krakatoa

Oriental vegetarian & fish restaurant

7 Pool Valley, Brighton BN1 1NJ
Tel: 01273-719 009
Open: every day 11-23.00

Veggie dishes are cooked separately and most are vegan or can be made so. For the best experience, ask to sit upstairs where there is Asian style seating with cushions and low tables. Good for either a party or a cosy intimate dinner.
Starters £4.90 such as Sulawesian coconut and corn soup with tofu and bean sprouts; Indonesian spring rolls with sweet chilli sauce; crispy vegetable and sweet potato fritters; steamed or grilled Japanese gyoza vegetable dumplings; Hanoi rice paper rolls.
Mains courses £6-9 such as Indonesian yellow rice with tofu and sweet potato curry, pergedel, tempeh goreng and spicy stir fried vegetables; Pad Thai; Gado Gado; Japanese Bento Box of miso soup, rice, noodles, tempura, teriyakii marinated tofu and Java curry; stir-fried udon noodles with wakame seaweed, tofu and bean sprouts; green vegetables stir fried with tofu, fragrant spices and garnished with basil; Massaman curry.
Wine £11-13 bottle, £2.90 glass. MC, Visa. Smoking allowed, except in smoke free room. 10% service charge. Gluten and wheat free diets catered for.

Bombay Aloo

Eat as much as you like at Bombay Aloo for only £4.95. It's open late on Friday and Saturday nights so it's the place to head for those post pub munchies. Monday to Friday 3.15-5.15pm are happy hours when you can stuff yourself for only £3.50.

There is heaps to choose from and it's all delicious. There are always six curries, like Tarka Dal, Swede and Mushrooms, Vegetable Dhansak, Chickpeas Aloo, Saag Aloo and Mixed Vegetable Curry. There are many accompaniments including pakoras, onion bhajees, naan bread, pappadums, samosas, pilau rice, mixed salad, onion salad, as well as dips and pickles. Vegans won't have a problem here as there are usually at least four vegan curries. Just ask one of the friendly staff to show you what's suitable.

You don't have to pay any extra for a dessert as they always have a fruit salad and a pudding as part of the buffet. If you want a dessert from the menu, it's £2.50.

There is a separate menu with cooked to order items, but it hardly seems worth it when the buffet is such good value. If you have any special requests, they can sometimes make something for you, providing they have time.

House wine is £1.95 per glass or £8.95 per bottle. Beer is £1.40 for a half pint or £2.60 for a pint. Coffee and soft drinks £1.20.

For kids they have high chairs and the buffet costs £3.95.

When the restaurant is busy, they open the upstairs, which has lots of extra seating and a second buffet. They can take large group bookings.

Ship Street

Vegetarian Indian buffet restaurant

39 Ship Street
Brighton
East Sussex BN1 1AB
England

Tel: 01273-776 038/
01273-771 089

Train Station: Brighton,
15 minutes walk

Open: every day
Sun-Thu 12.00-23.00
Fri-Sat 12.00-24.00

People presenting this book pay £4.45 instead of £4.95 for buffet

Licensed

MC, Visa

No smoking, except in smoking area

Infinity Foods Cafe

Gardner Street

Vegetarian organic
co-operative cafe

50 Gardner Street
Brighton
East Sussex BN1 1UN
England

Tel: 01273-670 743

www.infinityfoods.co.uk

Train Station: Brighton,
10 minutes walk

Open: Mon–Sat
10.00–17.00
Sun opening imminent

Global cuisine

Licensed

Large noticeboard of local
holistic events

Accepts major credit
cards, over £5

High chairs for kids

Baby changing facilities

No smoking throughout

They have an area of forest
planted to offset carbon
dioxide produced by the
cafe

Most products are Fair
Trade and Eco friendly, and
they recycle

All food is locally sourced
and freshly prepared on
premises

Recently refurbished veggie Co-op devoted to organic and natural food and drink. They are committed to offering GMO-free food with 99% organic content. All fruit, vegetables, grains and pulses are 100% organic. Choose freshly made cakes and salads from the beautiful display counter or choose hot food from the blackboard. Chefs specials available from the kitchen too.

Soup of the Day (always vegan, wheat-free and gluten-free) is £3.25, or £2.65 to take away with extras like sliced wholemeal or rye bread. The most popular soups are pumpkin, coconut and coriander, and tomato, lentil and fresh basil.

There is a choice of five fresh vegan salads daily with three dressings – tahini and lemon, mustard vinaigrette, and roasted seeds. Salads could be Chinese marinated tofu salad, leafy green salad with red pepper and watercress, rice salad with almonds and cherry tomatoes, or coleslaw salad. Small £2.10 eat in or £1.75 take away, medium £4/£3.35, large £5.95/£4.85.

Main meals change daily and are often vegan, £5.95/£4.85, such as polenta with roasted vegetables and tomato and herb sauce; or green or red Thai curry; and dahl with rice. Millet slice £2.95/£2.60 served with fresh tomato and herb sauce.

Most desserts are vegan, sugar free, wheat-free and gluten-free, like date and apricot flapjacks £2/£1.70. Polenta, lemon and almond cake, vegan chocolate cake and various tofu cheesecakes, are all £3/£2.50.

Most special diets are catered for. Vegan margarine, soya milk and soya cappuccinos are available.

Red Veg

The first and only veggie fast food restaurant in Brighton is situated in the North Laine, a few shops up from Vegetarian Shoes. It's perfect for a quick meal on the run, but it's also a great place to sit and relax, as the decor and furniture are much more comfortable than most fast food outlets.

They say: 'No lentils and no meat, no pain and no suffering, no hassle, no exploitation and no competition. More people are concerned with health, more people care about the world and about what they eat, meat is less and less popular, we need an alternative, we need an alternative tasty food fast. Red Veg provides vegetarian fast food. It's different and affordable with a global menu from independently created recipes.'

Try a RedVeg or Chilli or MushroomVeg or Hickory smoked veg burger for £2.85 (very tasty and 'meaty). Vegwurst vegetarian hotdog £2.85, with caramelised red onions £2.95. NoName nuggets £3.55. Falafels are £3.85 and now come in coriander and parsley, sesame or chilli. Fries £1.05 medium serving, £1.45 large. Spicy potato wedges £1.75. Spicy baby corn firesticks £1.85. Stuffed jalepeno peppers £1.95. Breaded mushrooms £1.75. All items can be made vegan.

Soft drinks £1.95 to £3.35 for an organic beer. £1.50 for coffee. Soya milk available.

No GM ingredients used. They develop all their own products. Veggie proprietor.

Check out the other branch next time you're in London, 95 Dean Street (Tel: 020–7437 3109), Soho, just off Oxford Street near Virgin Megastore.

Gardner Street

Vegetarian fast food

21 Gardner Street
Brighton
East Sussex BN1 1UP
England

Tel: 01273–679 910

www.redveg.com

Train Station: Brighton, 5 minutes walk.

Open: every day 11.00–21.00

Global Cusine
Fast food to eat in or takeaway.

Licensed

High chair for kids.

No Credit Cards

No smoking throughout

The George

Don't expect your usual pub grub at the George, one of the best places to eat in Brighton. It's at the bottom of Trafalgar Street, only five minutes walk from the station. The cosy interior is filled with chunky dark wooden tables and chairs. Dramatic abstract paintings adorn the walls. Order drinks and food from the bar, then sit in the busy area nearby, or at a quieter table in one of the many nooks. In summer relax in the beer garden, which is covered and heated during the colder months. In winter they have open fires.

Light meals include Soup of the Day £3.25, Nachos £5.95. Salads £5.65. Side Salads are £2.60. Main meals include George Tapas (enough for two) £110.95. The menu changes seasonally but they always keep a few favourites like Bangers and Mash £5.95, and Hot Sausage Baguette £4.45. Check the blackboards for daily specials which include a dessert of the day for £2.75. On Sundays the menu changes, but always has Nut Roast. Sunday evenings from 18:30 pizzas (some can be made with vegan cheeze) are served to a pub quiz (turn up, billed as 8.30, may start later).

The draught cider and several draught lagers are vegan. Pints of lager £2.65–£2.85; house wine £2.50 for 175ml glass, £3.50 for 250ml and £10.25 for a bottle. Fair Trade organic coffee £1.25; cappucino £1.40; hot chocolate £1.30; tea 80p. Drinks with soya milk 5p cheaper.

Most of the menu is vegan or can be made vegan with soya milk, vegan margarine, mayonnaise, ice cream and cheese.

Vegetarian pub/restaurant

5 Trafalgar Street
Brighton
East Sussex BN1 4EQ

Tel: 01273–681 055
Fax: 01273–696 752

Train Station: Brighton, then five minute walk.

Open: every day
Mon–Thu 12.00–23.00, last food orders 21.30.
Fri–Sat 12.00–23.00, last food orders 20.30.
Sun 12.00–22.30, food served 12.30–18.00 then pizzas 18.30–21.30 (can be vegan cheese)

Children welcome until 7pm. High chairs and kiddy sized food portions

Dog friendly

Credit cards accepted

Smoking allowed, except in no smoking area

Special diets catered for. All the food is completely home made. No GM ingredients used.

25% discount on food to members of Viva!
10% discount on food to members of the Vegetarian Society, Vegan Society, Animal Aid, PETA and people presenting this book.

Some veggie and vegan staff.

Terre a Terre

Vegetarian restaurant

Terre à Terre is known throughout Brighton and beyond for its innovative cuisine. You'll feel truly spoilt dining here. Come for the evening, relax and enjoy the friendly efficient service and fabulous food. The restaurant is large and spacious, seating over a hundred people. It has a vibrant, modern feel and is perfect for either a large party or a cosy candlelit dinner for two. They have made a big move towards local and seasonal produce. Vegans well catered for and they will do you a three course raw meal with a couple of days notice.

Starters include soup of the day with bread for £5.50, or Rizola Mechoui spice rolled fried rice patties, crammed with palm hearts and Masai Mara stuffing, served with Moorish slaw, tarragon mint and flat leaf parsley soft grain chop, finished with macadamia mayonnaise, Argan oil and mulberry caper hash £6.95. If you can't decide, try the gorgeous Terre à Tapas, a taste around the menu in miniature, for £14.95 (enough for two, or one very hungry diner). Salads starter £6.95, main £11.75.

There are 6 or 7 main courses from £11.75–13.25, such as Takka D'Otta consisting of Rassam dhal, Froo Froos (steamed basmati with smoked tofu, saffron, mustard oil) and aloo tikki stuffed with green tomato and fat date chatni, served with tamarind relish and capsicum sas vermicelli, mango taza salad (mango, cucumber spaghetti, fried split peas) finished with nariyal hot toddy, ginger joos ice and amchoor mango naan filled with cashew and sultana maraba.

Two of the six desserts £6.95 are vegan and they're good ones such as fried coconut and pear rice castles or banana fritters rolled in pistachio pink pepper powder, served with fresh pineapple carpaccio. Little boxes of regular or vegan truffles £5.95 flavoured with rum or Chipotle chilli infused with ouzo.

71 East Street
Brighton
East Sussex BN1 1HQ
England

Tel: 01273–729 051
Fax: 01273–327 561

Train Station: Brighton, 15 minutes walk.

www.terreaterre.co.uk
(full menus and more, you can register for monthly newsletter)

Open:
Mon closed
Tue 18.00–22.30
Wed–Fri 12.00–15.00, 18.00–22.30
Sat & Sun 12.00–22.30
These are subject to change, please refer to the website above

Global cuisine

Licensed

High chairs, toys, and kids' menu available.

All credit cards accepted

No smoking throughout

Book early for evening meals, especially at weekends.

Outside catering for weddings and parties.

Fantastic, all vegetarian organic and predominantly vegan wine list, beers, spirits, digestifs. Fair trade coffees.

The Guarana Bar

Juice bar and retail shop

Europe's only Guarana Bar is in Brighton's North Laine. Based on Brazilian guarana bars and Dutch coffee shops, it's the place to find natural energy drinks, safe and legal herbal highs, power nutrients and aphrodisiacs. It's a friendly and relaxed gallery space with a chilled out vibe. If you are a guarana novice, ask the well informed staff for advice.

136 Sydney Street
Brighton
East Sussex BN1 4EP
England

Tel/fax: 01273-621 406

Guarana is made from sun dried seeds of a Brazilian bush, Paullinia Cupana, and is a natural pick-me-up and aphrodisiac. It gives you a natural high and acts as a general tonic for well-being.

www.goguarana.com
ejk@guarana.demon.co.uk

info@goguarana.com

Train Station: Brighton,
10 minutes walk

Choose from a wide range of freshly made hot and cold drinks like Hot Guarana Punch £2 or Guarana Vitamin Shakes and Smoothies – your favourite juice mixed with guarana powder and crushed ice from £2.50. All slushies are available with wheatgrass or spirulina. There are lots of drinks to choose from in the fridge too, including Gusto Original with Chinese herbs, Brazilian guarana, ginseng and kolanut £1.80, Guarana Brahma – the national soft drink of Brazil £1, or Black Booster, an energy drink from Holland with a refreshing cola taste £1.50. Drinks can be made to your specifications.

Open: every day
Mon-Sat: 10.30-18.30
Sun: 12.00-18.00

10% discount to people presenting this book

Non alcoholic juice bar with New Age retail

Not licensed

Most credit/debit cards accepted, except Amex.

Smoking allowed

Two tables outside.

You can purchase herbs to take home with you, like guarana in capsule, powder or tincture, catuba, marapuama, St. Johns wort, kava kava, echinacea and a wide range of Rainforest Botanicals and herbal highs. They also sell chill out CD's,magic mushrooms, gifts, smoking paraphernalia and Vegetarian Guides' books.

Soya milk available for soyaccinos and soya smoothies.

SOUTH Brighton

Wai Kika Moo Kau

Extensive menu with 7-8 fresh daily specials such as penne pasta in olive oil with cherry tomatoes, courgettes and olives; spicy Moroccan aubergine, spinah and chickpea curry, £6.50-6.95.

Snacks such as chips, garlic bread, toasties, nachos, hummous bagel £1.50-£4.25,

Lots of salads, vegetables,

Wide range of burgers such as veggie, chilli, red bean and nut, £4.95 to 6.50 with chips and a side salad.

Desserts £2.25-3.95 including vegan cakes, sticky tofu pudding and custard, pancakes, chocolate

Freshly squeezed juices £2. House wine £10.50 bottle, £2.50 glass.

Kensington Gardens

Vegetarian cafe

11a Kensington Gardens, Brighton BN14AL

Tel: 01273-671 117

Train Station:
Brighton, 5 minutes walk

Open:
Mon-Fri & Sun 9.00-18.00,
Sat 9.00-19.00

Children welcome, kids menu, two high chairs.

Smoking and non-smoking areas and outside area.

MC, Visa, Amex

Food For Friends

Vegetarian restaurant

17-18 Prince Albert Street, Brighton BN1 1HF
near the sea front
Tel: 01273-202 310
Open: every day, 11.30-22.15 (last orders)

Nice ambience and chilled out vibe. Soup and bread £2.35, medium salad £3.90, hot dishes £4.95-£6.95. Vegans dishes prepared separately to avoid mix-ups. Cocktails, organic and vegan wines available. No smoking except in designated area. Gluten free and nut free diets catered for. All major cards accepted if spending over £5. 10% discount off eat-in for members of Vegetarian Society, Vegan Society and Viva!

Shakeaway

Milk shake chain

8 Bond Street, Brighton, BN1 1RD
Tel: 01273-711 179
www.shakeaway.com

Milk shake chain with huge variety of flavours, including 30 vegan ones which are made from organic soya milk and/or vegan ice-cream.

Holland & Barrett

Health food shop

105 London Road, Brighton
Tel: 01424-696209

66-68 North Street, Town Centre.
Tel: 01424-746 343

Infinity Foods Co-Operative

Wholefood shop

25 North Road, Brighton BN1 1YA
Tel: 01273-603 563
www.infinityfoods.co.uk
Open: Mon–Sat 9.30–18.00, Sun 11–16.00

Vegetarian and vegan shopping heaven! this excellent wholefood shop has almost every veggie and vegan delight you could think of like vegan fetta, veggie sausages and burgers, fishless fish cakes, vegan organic ice creams and chocolates including Booja Booja. Also organic fruit and vegetables, freshly baked bread (from their bakery) and eco-friendly cleaning products and toiletries. If you've got enough dosh, you could do all your shopping here. Is this what meat eaters feel like in Sainsbury's?

Lush

Cruelty-free cosmetics

41 East Street, Brighton BN1 1HL
Tel: 01273-774 700
www.lush.co.uk
Open: Mon–Sat 9.00–18.00, Sun 11.00–17.00

You can smell Lush before you even walk through the door. It's full of gorgeous hand made body and skin care products made with natural ingredients. Many of the products are vegan. You'll find soaps, bath bombs, shampoos, conditioners, hair treatments, moisturisers, massage bars, chocolate face masks and more. 80% of products are non-preserved, eg. in solid or "chilled" form.

Peace and Environment Centre

Ethical shop

39–41 Surrey Street, Brighton BN1 3PB
(In Brighton Eco Centre opposite train station)
www.bpec.org. info@bpec.org
Tel: 01273-766 610
Open: Tue–Sat 10.00–18.00

Ethical resource centre selling goods from organisations promoting peace, justice, and environmental issues, as well as from Fair Trade importers. Great place to pick up a gift for a friend. They stock stationery, greeting cards, books, journals, tea, coffee and crafts. If you join the Peace and Environment Centre, you can borrow books from their comprehensive library and use their computer services for a small charge.

Vegetarian Shoes

Vegetarian shoes & accessories

12 Gardner Street, Brighton BN1 1UP
Tel: 01273-685 685
www.vegetarianshoes.com
info@vegetarianshoes.com
Open: Mon–Sat 10.00–17.30,
Closed Sun and public holidays

You may have ordered your shoes from them already by mail order, but while you're in Brighton, make sure you check out the shop. They don't just sell shoes and boots either. You can also get belts, jackets, bags, T-shirts and wallets.
Check out their web site before coming or call for a catalogue. If they're down to the last pair of what you want, you can try them on and they'll send you your shoes as soon as they're ready.

East Sussex

Sanctuary Cafe

Relax and be sanctified in this unique cafe spanning three floors of a distinctive Brunswick building. It's arty, eclectic, comfortable and friendly. After a recent refurbishment, there are now sofas upstairs where you can enjoy art work exhibited by local artists.

Order your meal from the counter, while drooling over the wide selection of gorgeous cakes, of which about half are vegan. Their menu includes Toasted Bagels £2.75 and freshly baked baguettes, with hummous and a salad garnish. Jacket Potatoes with a selection of 8 fillings from £3.20, includes salad. The salads are delicious and can be a meal in themselves. A large costs £5.25. Hummous and warm pitta with salad, and pate, such as aubergine, tarragon and lime, and salad are £4.75. Soup of the Day served with bread is £3.75 and could be carrot, parsnip or lentil and mushroom. Daily specials could include vegan Pad Thai with spicy peanut dressing for £6.50, Wraps with courgette, aubergine and mushrooms in a garlic and basil tomato sauce with salad for £6.75. A delicious veggie/vegan roast is served on Sundays. House wine is organic and vegan, £2.80 per glass or £11 per bottle. Beer £2.50 and coffee £1.70. A huge slice of delicious vegan cake is £2.50 and could be Carrot and Orange, Lemon and Poppyseed or Coffee and Walnut. Freshly squeezed organic juices also available.

Downstairs is The Cella, a funky and intimate venue for regular live music, poetry, performance and creative innovations. Also available to hire for parties.

For table service add 10%. Soya milk for soyaccinos and smoothies.

Vegetarian and fish cafe

51–55 Brunswick St East
Hove
East Sussex BN3 1AU
England

Tel: 01273–770 002

Cella enquiries/Fax: 01273 770006

www.sanctuarycafe.co.uk
info@thesanctuarycafe.co.uk

Train Station:
Brighton or Hove

Open: every day
9.00–23.00

Global Cuisine

High chairs
Children's portions

Licensed

Credit cards accepted

No smoking throughout

SOUTH East Sussex

307

Alfriston

Dacres

Omnivorous bed and breakfast

Alfriston BN26 5TP
Tel: 01323–870 447

Spacious twin ensuite in a pretty country cottage with beautiful gardens. In a lane, signed 'To Alfriston Tennis Club', off the High Street.. From £27.50 per person per night, and self-catering rates are by agreement. There is a full kitchen for self caterers. Organic breakfasts include vegetarian and vegan meals and can be enjoyed in the garden on sunny days. No children and no pets. Parking available. No smoking throughout.

Rye

Flackley Ash Hotel

Omnivorous hotel

Peasmarsh, Rye TN31 6YH
Tel: 01797–230 651
Fax: 01797–230 510
www.flackleyashhotel.co.uk
www.bw–flackleyashhotel.co.uk

This Best Western is set in a Georgian country house hotel close to the historic town of Rye and the castles and gardens of Sussex and Kent. Ideal for country and seaside walks. All 45 rooms are ensuite and have satellite televisions, telephones, hair dryers and coffee/tea making facilities. £66–£91 per person per night. Special diets are catered for if you let the staff know in advance.
Gym, sauna, swimming pool. Dogs welcome by prior arrangement. Children welcome and stay for free if sharing with two adults. Smoking area. Parking available.

Seaford

The Silverdale

Omnivorous guest house

21 Sutton Park Road, Seaford BN25 1RH
Tel: 01323–491 849
Fax: 01323–891 131
Open: all year
www.mistral.co.uk/silverdale/silver.htm
Email: silverdale@mistral.co.uk
Train Station: Seaford, four minutes walk

Eight rooms: two doubles £14.50–£21.50 per person per night; two double ensuites, £17–£27.50 pppn; four–poster ensuite £20–£30 pppn; conservatory ensuite £22–£32.50 pppn; and two family rooms £12.50–£25 pppn. Three course evening meal £12. Coeliacs catered for. Disabled access, category three. Children and pets welcome. Smoking allowed in some rooms and the bar.

Hastings

Heaven and Earth

Vegetarian cafe

37e Robertson Street, Hastings TN34 1SL
Tel: 01424–712 206
Open: Mon–Sat 10–17.00, Sun 11–16.00
Closed Sun in winter

Café with counter service. All food is home made. Always vegan options and salad bar is entirely vegan. They also do vegan pizza, £1.60, and vegan cakes, £1.30–£2.10. Children are welcome.

East 2 West

Tel: Hastings 01424–429 092
Mobile 0794 616 6396

Vegetarian catering service only.

Holland & Barrett

Health food shop

21 Queens Road, Hastings TN34 1QY
Tel: 01424-427 253

Trinity Wholefoods

Wholefood shop

3 Trinity Street, Hastings TN34 1HG
Tel: 01424-430 473
Open: Mon-Sat 9.00-17.30

Seasons of Lewes

Vegetarian organic cafe

199 High Street, Lewes BN7 2NS
Tel: 01273-473 968
Train Station: Lewes, five minutes walk
Open: Tue-Sat 9.30-17.00, Sun-Mon closed

Using local and seasonal produce, 2/3 of the menu is vegan. Starters like soup with bread £3, salad bowl £3. Mains around £5.50. Cakes £1.50 (one usually vegan) and fruit crumbles too. Homemade vegan ice cream. Not licensed, but you can bring your own wine. Gluten free and wheat free diets catered for. No credit cards. No smoking. Outside catering for weddings, buffets etc. Frozen individual meals for take away.

Salad Bowl

Omnivorous cafe

21 High Street, Seaford BN25 1PE
Tel: 01323-890 605
showellb1@aol.com
Open: Mon-Sat 9.30-15.00

Omnivorous cafe with veggie main courses £3.50-3.95, though quite cheesey. Soya milk available.

Wealden Wholefoods Cafe

Vegetarian cafe and shop

High Street, Wadhurst, East Sussex TN5 6AA
Tel: 01892-783 065
www.wealdenwholefoods.co.uk
Cafe: Mon-Sat 09.00-16.30 (last orders)
Sun closed
Shop: Mon-Sat 9-17.15 (Wed & Sat -17.00)

Vegetarian organic wholefood café with take-away home-cooked soup and rolls too. Run by a cooperative with an emphasis on organic, fair traded, locally produced foods.

Savoury dishes include Homity pie, spinach pie, lentil and buckwheat slices and nut loaf croquettes. Salads change daily and are buffet style, £1.20 small, £2 large. Homemade cakes and (vegan) ice cream is served.

Coffee is £1.60 for a cafetiere that holds one and a half cups and £2.50 for one that holds two and a half cups. Soya milk is available. Organic house wine £2.20 glass, £5 for 1/2 bottle; beer £3 pint.

Everything purchased in the shop can be served in the cafe.

Small outside seating area for 4-6 people.

Hampshire

The Barn

The only exclusively vegetarian guest house in the New Forest, a recently refurbished Edwardian house offering a restful stay with easy access for walking, cycling and visits to the south coast. One double en suite (bath/shower) and one twin en suite (shower), £24–£28 per person. £10 single supplement.

Breakfast includes cereals, DIY muesli, scrambled tofu, vegan sausages, tomato, beans, mushrooms and toast. Vegan margarine and soya milk are available.

Evening meal at 6.30pm is available for £14. Starter could be hummous with red pepper or crudtes, or lentil soup; main course such as Mediterranean Vegetable Tian or carrot nut roast with steamed seasonal veg; desserts include apple crumbe with (soya) cream, champagne rhubarb fool, chocolate tofu cheesecake or T hai black rice pudding slathered in coconut cream sauce; followed by tea or coffee. Bring your own alcohol, no corkage.

The dining room has armchairs, a music system, books, games and a piano.

The New Forest enclosures are only 5 minutes walk away. Of the many different walks, one starts just across the road. The Barn is on a cycle route for safe access to an endless variety of rides.

The nearby town of Boscombe has a vegan restaurant, Wessex Tales, and The Salad Centre vegetarian wholefood restaurant. Southampton is a 10 minute drive or 30 minutes on the cycle route. The coast is 20–30 minute drive or 1 hour by bike.

Rooms have tea and coffee making facilities, hairdryer and colour TV.

Vegetarian/vegan guest house

112 Lyndhurst Road
Ashurst
Hampshire SO40 7AU

Tel: 023–8029 2531
Mobile 07791 990 351

www.veggiebarn.net
info@veggiebarn.net

Train:
Ashurst New Forest – 500m. They can collect you.

Open: all year

Directions:
From M27, take Junction 3 onto M271. At the round-about at end of M271, follow signs to Bournemouth (A35, second exit). The Barn is 2.5 miles along A35, on right hand side. Look out for white gates 200m before a pedes-trian crossing.

Parking available

Under cover secure cycle storage. You can try their tandem.

Children welcome, some toys and games available

No smoking throughout

Pets welcome

Cash or cheque only

10% discount to Viva! members or if you arrive by bike

SOUTH Hampshire

Romsey Accommodation
The Cricketers
Omnivorous bed and breakfast

Top Green, Lockerley,
Romsey, Hampshire, SO51 0JP
Tel: 01794-341 947
john.clark@TheCricketersBnB.co.uk
www.thecricketersbnb.co.uk
Open: Open most of the year

Reluctantly omnivorous B&B, run by
vegetarians John and Pat Clarke who
warmly welcome other veggies. Double
£50 per room, double en suite £60.
Notice needed if you have a special diet,
or are a vegan. Located in a spacious
family home with countryside views and
ample parking. Open fires are available
in the dining room and guest lounge
providing a cosy atmosphere in the
winter months.

Southsea Accommodation
Hamilton House B&B
Omnivorous bed and breakfast

95 Victoria Road North
Southsea, Portsmouth PO5 1PS
Tel/fax: 023-9282 3502
www.hamiltonhouse.co.uk
sandra@hamiltonhouse.co.uk
Train station: Portsmouth and Southsea, 1/2
mile then bus no. 17 stops outside the house,
or get a taxi for £3.

There are nine rooms: two doubles and
two twins at £24–£27 per person per
night, three double ensuites and two
twin ensuites for £27–£30 per person,
and two family rooms for £25 per
person.
Veggie sausages, vegan muesli, soya
milk, vegan margarine and soya
yoghurt are all available on request.
Hamilton House has a booklet which
guests can use that will get you 20–50%
off entry tickets for the local attractions.

All rooms have a television, clock,
hairdryer and tea/coffee making facilities. There is a television lounge.
Children welcome, and reduced rates
are available. Parking on street; no
smoking throughout.

Havant
Red Mango
Omnivorous cafe

Havant Arts Centre, East Street, Havant
Tel: 02392-480 113
www.havantartsactive.co.uk
Open: Mon–Sat 9.00–16.00

Veggie-friendly cafe in a relaxed arts
centre, offering Chinese, Greek,
Indonesian, Italian, Mediterranean,
Mexican, Thai and South Indian influenced cuisine. They cater for special
diets such as gluten-free, wheat-free,
and vegan.
Starters include soups and sandwiches
at £2.75, various salads with cous cous,
beans, potato and pasta: £1.85 for
small, £3.55 for large.
Quiches or bakes cost £4.25 for a slice.
They carry organic wines, vegan ice
cream, mayonnaise, margaine, and
soya milk.
Their bar is open in the evenings, Mon-
Sat 18.00–23.00.

Sweet Joe Pye

Wholefood shop

31 St. Thomas Street, Lymington SO41 9NE
Tel: 01590–672 931
Open: Mon–Fri 9–17.30, Sat 9–13.00

Located at the top end of the High Street near Waitrose, away from the tourist strip. A wide range of natural, vegetarain skincare products and snack foods, but no take aways.

The Bran Tub

Vegetarian & vegan take away

20 Lavant Street, Petersfield GU32 3EW
Tel: 01730–267 043
Open: Mon–Sat 9–17.30 (Thu –17, Sat –16)

GM free veggie shop with take away pasties, cashewnut rolls, etc. They also have vegan ice creams like choc ices and Cornettos. There is now a clinic above the shop that offers 14 different alternative therapies.

Pizza Express

Omnivorous pizza restaurant

Gunwharf Quays, North Promenade, Portsmouth, PO1 3TA. Tel: 0239 2832939
Open: every day 11.30–24.00

GNC

Health food shop

48a Kingswell Path, Cascades Portsmouth
Tel: 023–9285 1552.
Open: Mon–Sat 9–17.30

Stocks food supplements, vitamins and minerals.

Scoltocks Natural Foods

Health food shop

1 Market Place, Ringwood
Tell: 01425–473 787
Open: Mon–Sat 9–17.00

Carries veggie and vegan freezer, soya cheeses, cereals, grains, nuts, herbal teas and vitamin supplements.

Country Kitchen

Vegetarian restaurant

59 Marmion Road, Southsea PO5 2AX
Tel: 023–9281 1425
Open: Mon–Fri 9.00–17.00, Sat 8.00–17.00

Vegetarian restaurant. Soup from £2.25 and bakes and mains at £4.15, such as vegan shepherd's pie or vegetable korma with rice. Cakes from 95p with gluten–free and vegan choices. No smoking. No credit cards. Children welcome, high chairs. Bottle of wine £9, glass £2.70.

Allsorts Psychic Cafe

Vegetarian cafe

22 Carlton Place, Southampton
Tel: 02380–23 7561
www.allsorts–psychic–cafe.com
Open: Wed–Sat 10.30–17.00,
Fri & Sat 19.00–late

Veggie cafe selling soup and savouries. Most of the cakes are vegan. They have soya milk for tea, coffee and coffee substitutes. 10% discount for Viva! and Southampton Vegetarian & Vegans Society members.

Bella Italia

Omnivorous pizza & pasta restaurant

107 Above Bar, Southampton SO14 7FH
Tel: 023–8022 7664
Open: every day 12–22.30, Fri–Sat –23.00,
Sat–Sun from 10.00 for breakfast

Bella Italia

Omnivorous pizza & pasta restaurant

19 Hanover Buildings, Southampton SO14 1JX
Tel: 023–8033 9215
Open: Sun–Thu 12–22.00, Fri–Sat 12–23.00

Near the city centre and footbal ground.

Koh I Noor

Omnivorous Indian restaurant

2 Portswood High Street, SO17 2WE (by Bingo)
Tel: 02380–58 4339
Open: every day 12–14.30, 18–24.00

Food from all over with a good vegetarian selection, vegan friendly as they
use vegetable oil. Lunch £5.95 for three
courses, evening a la carte £8.50–£14
per head. All desserts are dairy based.
House wine £7.95, £2.30 glass.
Children welcome, no high chairs.
Smoking section. MC, Visa.

Pizza Express

Omnivorous pizza restaurant

31 Oxford St, Southampton SO14 3DS
Tel: 023–8049 9090
Open: every day 11.30–24.00

Vegan pizza bases, can be without
cheese.
The Olive Tree at 29 Oxford St (Tel
02380–343 333) and Blah Blah Blah at
40 Oxford St (Tel 02380–225 727) also
have veggie dishes, but not vegan.

Shakeaway

Milkshake chain

24 Bargate Centre, Southampton SO14 2YD
Tel: 023–8033 2155
www.shakeaway.com

Milkshake chain with huge range of
flavours including 30 vegan ones made
with organic soya milk and/or vegan ice
cream.

Winchester Health Food Centre

Health food shop

Sheridan House, 41–42 Jewry Street,
Winchester
Tel: 01962–851 113
Open: Mon–Fri 9.15–17.00, Sat 9.15–17.45

GM–free products and some organic
fruit and vegetables. They have a chiller
cabinet for take away food.

Holland & Barrett

Health food shop

17 Mayfair House, Hollins Walk, Basingstoke
Tel: 01256–346 170

233 Fleet Road, Fleet
Tel: 01252–625 671

240 Commercial Road, Portsmouth
Tel:02392–825 416

27 Southampton Row, Ringwood
Tel: 01425–483 950

18 East Street, Southampton
Tel: 023–8021 1859

33 High Street, Winchester
Tel: 01962–843 194

Kent

Copperfields

Vegetarian guest house

11 Queens Road, Broadstairs, Kent CT10 1NU
Tel: 01843–601247
www.copperfieldsbb.co.uk
enquiries@copperfieldsbb.co.uk
Tourist info www.broadstairs.gov.uk

Great stopover on the way to France in this restored Edwardian house in a charming seaside town 40 minutes from Dover. Two doubles and a twin/double (superking), all ensuite, £60–70 per room. Special rates at Easter, Xmas and New Year. Full vegetarian breakfast. Candlelit evening meal at 6.30pm £17.50, mostly organic with vegan options. Menus on website. Small secluded garden with patio and swing. Bicyble lockup and drying room. Children 12+ welcome. 4 diamonds English Tourism Council.

The Canterbury Environment Centre

Vegetarian cafe

St Alphege Lane, Canterbury CT1 2EB
Tel: 01227–457 009
www.cusk.org.uk   cantenv@talk21.com
Centre open: Tue–Sat 10.00–16.00
Cafe open: Sat 10–16.00

Vegetarian café in the Canterbury environment centre, in a medieval church. Most food is vegan. Nothing over £2.70. Jacket potatoes , bakes, salads. No smoking. No credit cards. Children welcome, high chair. Licensed.

Cafe des Amis

Omnivorous International restaurant

93 St Dunstan Street, Canterbury
Tel: 01227–464 390
Open: Mon–Thu 12–22.00, Fri–Sat 12–22.30, Sun 12–21.30

Busy omnivorous restaurant with modern Mexican and French influences. Main courses range between £6.95–£14.95. They always have vegetarian options and can adapt items for vegans, such as garlic mushrooms, bean and spinach enchilladas, roast vegetable tostada, aubergine and mushroom burrito. Near Westgate Towers. Smoking section. Visa, MC. Children welcome, four high chairs. House wine £9.95 bottle, £2.45–3.50 glass.

Tapas En Las Trece

Spanish omnivorous restaurant

13 Palace Street, Canterbury CT1 2DZ
Tel: 01227–762 637

Classic Spanish tapas bar in a historic street, recommended by Canterbury Environment Centre.

The Goods Shed

Farmers market and omnivorous restaurant

Station Road West, Canterbury CT2 8AN
Tel: 01670–514 414
Open: Tue–Sat 10–19.00, Sun 10–16.00

In the Victorian railway goods shed at Canterbury West. A market sells organic vegetables and freshly baked breads and the omnivorous restaurant always offers a few vegetarian options.

Canterbury Wholefoods

Vegetarian cafe and wholefood shop

1–2 Jewry Lane, Canterbury
Tel: 01227–464 623
www.canterbury-wholefoods.co.uk
Shop: Mon–Sat 9–18.00, Sun 11–17.0
Café: Mon–Fri 11–15.00, Sat 10–16.00

Vegetarian cafe above a wholefood co-op shop. Eat in the licensed café for no more than £5, which caters for vegans and special diets. No smoking. Visa, MC. Children welcome, high chairs.
Fresh bread baked daily, pasties, sosage rolls, flapjacks, cruelty free toiletries, organic fruit and vegetables, and free delivery service in Kent if your order is worth £30 or more.

Health House

Health food shop

116 High Street, Chatham ME4 4BY
(opposite Argos)
Tel: 01634–409 291
Open: Mon–Sat till 9–17.30, closed Sun

No longer a vegetarian cafe in this shop, but they have take–away pasties (mostly vegan), bhajias, spring rolls.

The India Restaurant

A dozen vegetarian and vegan dishes but they can prepare a vegetarian version of any other traditional Indian dish with prior notice. No butter ghee though vegans should watch for butter in the breads.

Starters £2.95 include vegetable or tomato soup, samosa, onion pakora. Main courses include vegetable biryani with pillau rice mixed with vegetables, £5.50. Vegetable side dishes £2.50 such as spinach, mushroom bhajia, okra, cauliflower, potatoes with peas, Bombay aloo, plain or Tarka daal (lentils), chana masala (chick peas). Green salads £1.75. Rice dishes from £1.60. If you're heading for France through the tunnel, get in the mood with French ratatouille provençale with tomatoes, courgettes, aubergines, garlic and basil £5.25.

Desserts, £1.75–2.25, such as lemon sorbet. Tea or coffee £1. Irish (with whiskey), French or Calypso coffee £2.95.

Omnivorous Indian restaurant

1 Old High Street
Folkestone, Kent CT20 1RJ
(near the ferry terminal)

Tel: 01303–259 155

Open: Tue–Sat 18.00–22.00
Fri, Sat also open 12–14.00

French, German, Hindi, Urdu, Bengali, and English spoken.

Menu in French and English.

MC, Visa

Holland & Barrett Restaurant

Vegetarian cafe & shop

80 Sandgate Road, Folkestone CT20 2AA
Tel: 01303-243 646
Open: Mon-Sat 9.30-17.00

Wholefood vegetarian cafe and take away in a Holland & Barrett shop. Selection of 6 salads 50p-£2.70. Bakes, jacket potatoes, etc. £1-£2.10. For that sweet tooth, they have fruit tarts, and cheesecakes £1.25-£1.55. No smoking throughout. Cash or cheque only.

Blackthorn Trust Cafe

Vegetarian cafe

Blackthorn Medical Centre, St Andrew's Road
Maidstone, ME16 9AN
Tel: 01622-725 585
www.blackthorn.org.uk (no menu)
info@blackthorn.org.uk
Open: Mon-Fri 10-15.00, lunch 12-14.00

Vegetarian café based behind a medical centre. Soup from £1.50. Mains (many vegan) from £4 such as shepherd's pie, bolognaise, ghoulash, Mediterranean casserole. Desserts from £2 but usually dairy except fruit salad. Can cater for coeliacs and other special diets on request. No smoking. No credit cards. Children welcome, two high chairs. No alcohol.

Brockhill Country Park

Vegan/vegetarian cafe

Sandling Road (nr Saltwood and Hythe)
CT21 4HL
Tel: 07798-752 555
Open: Easter-Halloween every day 10.30-17.30; park open every day but Xmas 9-19.00 or dusk

Amazingly good value vegetarian café in a 54 acre park which includes a lake, children's play area and a beautiful valley. Great location for getting take away and having a picnic.

Mexican or Tandoori bean burgers £1.50 in a bun with salad. Avocado salad £2.80, garlic bread £1.50, Greek salad (can be with vegan cheese), chips and even veggie sausages with chips and beans. Organic wholewheat pasta £1.80. Soups in Spring and Autumn 80p with a roll.

Swedish Glace and Tofutti ice-cream which they make cornets from. Tea 40p, coffee 60p, fruit juices.

Take the Junction 11 off the M20 but beware that the cafe is poorly sign-posted. Aim for Saltwood, not Hythe, or you'll miss it.

Wagamama

Omnivorous Japanese restaurant

54-58 Mount Pleasant Road,
Tunbridge Wells TN1 1RB
Tel: 01892-616 514
www.wagamama.com
Open: Mon-Sat 12-23.00 Sun 12-22.00

See Manchester entry for menu.

Welling

Pili Pili

Vegetarian Indian restaurant

Welling, Kent DA16 1TH
Tel: 020–8303 7636
Open: Tue–Sun 12–15.00, 18–22.00, Fri–Sat
till 23.00, Mon closed (except bank holidays)

New vegetarian Indian restaurant, midway between Greenwich and Dartford. Much of the food is vegan and they can make non–vegan items with soya milk on request.

Over 30 bites £1.95–4.50 include uttapam lentil pizza, dosas, dhokla rice and lentil pancake, lentil doughnuts, pani puri, bhel puri, chilli corn on the cob, potato fritters, idli, samosas, sev puri, spring rolls. Main specials inclide potato curry with daal bhajia £4.50, mushroom pitta pocket £5.50, vegetable sizzler £7.50. Indo–Chinese soups and dishes such as Hakka o Szechuan noodles with veg £3.95, sweet and sour veg £4.50.

Whitstable

El Loco

Omnivorous Mexican restaurant

Oxford Street, Whitstable
Tel: 01227–771914
Open: Tue–Sat 19–22.30, last orders 22.00

Mexican restaurant at the site of the old veggie restaurant, Beanies. Vegans can have a vegetarian burrito for £7.50 with lots of vegetables like aubergines plus beans, and all cooked with sunflower oil – just ask them to leave the cheese out. House wine from £9.95 a bottle. Smoking allowed but they'll seat non–smokers nearer the door. Visa, MC, Amex. Children welcome, no high chairs.

Holland & Barrett

Health food shop

87 High Street, Ashford TN24 8SQ
Tel: 01233–620 392

41 High Street, Canterbury CT1 2RY
Tel: 01227–787 861

Unit A, 203 High Street, Chatham ME4 4BG
Tel: 01634–830 735

38 High Street, Deal CT14 6HE
Tel: 01304–371 664

35 Biggin Street, Dover CT16 IBU
Tel: 01304–241 426

8 St. Georges Centre, Gravesend DA11 0TA
Tel: 01474–321 838

Hempstead Valley Shopping Centre
Hempstead Valley, Gillingham
ME7 3PB
Tel: 01634–375 796

Unit 345, Dukes Walk, Chequers Centre
Maidstone ME15 9AS
Tel: 01622–765 277

10 The Centre, Margate CT9 1JG
Tel: 01843–228 131

13 –15 The High Street, Ramsgate CT11 9AB
Tel: 01843–852 568

96 High Street, Sittingbourne ME15 6AJ
Tel: 01795–476 664

Unit 11, Swanley Shopping Centre
Swanley BR8 7UB
Tel: 01322–666 910

23 Mount Pleasant Road,
Tunbridge Wells TN1 1NT
Tel: 01892–533 077

19 Calverly Road, Tunbridge Wells TM1 1LS
Tel: 01892–539 287 .

Middlesex

Chai

Vegetarian Chinese restaurant

236 Station Road, EdgwareHA8 7AU
Tel: 020–8905 3033
Tube: Edgware
Open: Mon–Fri 12–14.30, 18–23.30
Sat 12–15.30, 18–23.30, Sun 12.00–23.30

Almost entirely vegan, Buddhist owned, with a bar. Astonishing range of fake meats and lots of other dishes. The ideal night out for both reluctant and avid vegetarians, with 153 items on the menu. Lunch buffet Mon–Sat £4.50, Sun (12–4pm) £6.90. 2 set meals £12 or £15 per person. Wine £2.50 glass, £9.50–14.50 bottle. MC, Visa. Smoking area at back.

Natraj

Vegetarian Indian take away

341 Northolt Road, South Harrow
Tel: 020–8426 8903
Tube: South Harrow
Open: Mon–Tue, Thu–Sat 10–19.30, Sun 10–16.30, closed Wed

Indian vegetarian take away with plenty for vegans. Regular take away box of curry (most vegan) is £2.50–£3.50. Box of half curry and half rice £2–£3.

Sakonis

Vegetarian Indian &
Chinese restaurant

5–8 Dominion Parade, Station Road, Harrow
Tel: 020–8863 3399
Open: Sun–Thu 12–21.30 (last entry),
Fri–Sat till 22.00, Wed closed

Same menu as Wembley branch. Buffet 12–3pm £6.50 + 10%, so £7.15 eat in (no take–away), 6.30–9.30pm £8.99 +

10%, i.e. £9.89. The buffet is a combination of the whole menu with 20 to 25 items including starters and 3 desserts. No alcohol. No smoking. Children welcome, 7 high chairs.

Supreme Sweets

Indian vegetarian take away

706 Kenton Road, Kenton, Harrow HA3 9QX
Tel: 020–8930 1274
Tube: Kingsbury
Open: Mon–Fri 10–19.00, Sat 9.30–19.00, Sun 8.30–17.30, closed Wed

Sweets and savouries like bhajias £7 per kilo, samosas and pakoras from 40p. Also frozen samosas, kachoris and spring rolls. 75% of items are vegan, but butter ghee in sweets. Catering for weddings and parties, they prepare for you to collect but deliver on orders over 100 people.

Swadisht

Vegetarian Indian take–away

195 Streatfield Road, Kenton, Harrow
Tel: 020 8905 0202
Open: every day 12.30–22.30
Tube: Kenton Road

New Indian vegetarian restaurant. A la carte, four people could have two courses for £30. No smoking, no alcohol. Children welcome, two high chairs. MC, Visa.

Bodywise Health Foods

Health food shop

249 Station Road, Harrow
Tel: 020–8861 3336
Open: Mon–Sat 9–18.00
Tube: Harrow-on-the-Hill

Very well stocked plus supplements and complementary health practitioners.

Hounslow

Revital

Wholefood shop

154 High Street, Hounslow
Tel: 020-8572 0310
Open: Mon–Sat 9–17.30, closed Sun

Wholefood store near Heathrow airport with take–away sandwiches, pies, pasties, salads and burgers, some of which are vegan.

Kenton

Ram's Gujarati Surti Cuisine

Gujarati vegetarian restaurant

203 Kenton Road
Tel: 020-8907 2022
Tube: Kenton Road, 5 mins
Open: Tue–Sun 12–15.00, 18.00–23.00

Around £8.99 for a thali with starter such as bhajias, papodoms, two curries, three djipatis, dal and dessert. They use butter ghee, but vegetable ghee is available. Desserts include vegan halva. Milkshakes can be made with soya milk. Wine £2.10 glass, £9.20 bottle. Beer 330ml £1.50, 660ml £3. No moking. Wheelchair access and toilet. Visa, MC. Very child friendly, high chairs.

Rayners Lane

Kathiyawadi

Gujarati vegetarian restaurant

434 Rayners Lane, Harrow HA5 5DX
Tel: 020-8868 2723, 020-8868 9885
Tube: Rayners Lane
Open: Mon–Fri 17–23.00, Sat–Sun 12–23.00

Average £10 for a good meal. Licensed. Children welcome, high chairs, MC, Visa. Smoking area.

Southall

Shahanshah

Vegetarian North Indian restaurant

60 North Road, Southall UB1 2JL
Tel: 020-8574 1493
Tube: Ealing Broadway, Southall BR
Open: Every day 10–20.00

North Indian restaurant, take away and sweet centre with 50% of their ingredients organic. Starters £1–£1.25 such as two samosas or pakoras. Main meals £5. They use butter ghee but will cater for vegans if requested. Outside seating. Alcohol and smoke-free. Cash and cheque only.

Twickenham

Gaia Wholefoods

Wholefood shop

123 St. Margarets Road, Twickenham
Tel: 020-8892 2262
Open: Mon–Fri 9.30–19.00, Sat 9.30–17.00

Wholefood shop selling fresh organic fruit and vegetables, Japanese macrobiotics, organic bread. They stock body care, eco cleaning products and gluten free ranges. Also some vegan take-aways like pastries.

The Healthy Harvest Food Store

Wholefood shop in gardening centre

Squires Garden Centre, 6 Cross Road Twickenham (between Twickenham and Hampton Court)
Tel: 020-8943 0692
Open: Mon–Sat 9.30–17.30, Sun 10–17.00

Usual foods plus serve yourself wholefoods. Vegetarian pasties and flapjacks. Swedish Glace ice-cream.

Chetna's

Vegetarian restaurant & take-away

420–422 High Road, Wembley
Tel: 020-8903 5989
www.chetnassweetmart.co.uk
Tube: Wembley Park, Wembley Central
Open: Tue–Fri 12–15.00 and 18.00–22.30,
Sat and Sun 13.00–22.30

Specialise in Indian snacks, dosas, simple curries and pizzas. Starters such as bhelpoori, pani poori from £2.50. 3 types of thali. Some food doesn't have onions or garlic. Lots of dosas under £5. Pizza £5.90–£7.20 (can be without cheese). Desserts but nothing vegan. Minimum charge £5.50 per person. MC, Visa, Amex. Children welcome, 5 high chairs.

Chowpatty

Vegetarian Indian restaurant

234 Ealing Road, Wembley, Middlesex HA0 4QL
Tel: 020-8795 0077
Tube: Alperton, Wembley Central
Open: Mon–Sat 10.00–22.00

Named after Mumbai's famous beach, this is a new vegetarian restaurant where prices are low and the variety good. Lunch thali £3.99 . Starters, £1.45–£2.95. South, East or North Indian main courses £2.75–£4.95, such as rajma chawal (red kidney beans with rice) from Punjab in the north, idli and dosas from south India, or Indo-Chinese offerings in the form of noodles or Chinese idli. Lemon or coconut rice £1.99. Drinks from £1.25, with sweet or salted lime soda at £1.95. Beers £2.75. House wine £6.95 for a bottle.

Jashan

Vegetarian Gujarati Indian restaurant

1–2 Coronet Parade, Ealing Road, Wembley
Tel: 020-8900 9800
Open: Mon–Fri 12–15.30 and 18.00–23.00,
Sat–Sun 12–23.00

The menu has 13 different sections and stacks of veggie snacks and some Chinese dishes. Specialities include bharwan bhindi, pakoda kadhi or jeera aloo for £3.50. Then there are 'treasures of the Nawabs': subzi pulao or saade chawal for £3.95 each. "Tangy bites" include aloo tikkiya chaat or karol baug ke samose at £3.95. Mumbai Express section has a Bombay burger for £3.25. Many cold drinks like fresh coconut water and fresh lime juice with soda water. Outside seating in summer. An alcohol and smoke-free zone. Children welcome, high chairs.

Maru's Bhajia House

Indian cafe

230 Ealing Road, Alperton, Wembley
Tel: 020-8903 6771
Tube: Alperton, Wembley Central
Open: Mon–Thu 12.30–20.30, Fri–Sun 12.30–21.30

Kenyan Asian cuisine since 1976 with bhajias of course, samosas, maize and assorted snacks. The Maru bhajia has always been the main dish, made from potato slices mixed with gram (chickpea) flour fried with spices, with their special tamarind sauce. Asian film stars fill up here on pani puri, kachori and vada. £3.40 for a portion, £6.80 for a double portion. It gets very busy at lunch and weekends.

SOUTH Middlesex

Naklank Sweet Mart

Vegetarian Gujarati cafe & take-away

50b Ealing Road, Wembley HA0 4TQ
Tel: 020-8902 8008
Open: Mon-Sat 10.30-19.00, Sun 12-19.00

---

39 different sweets and savouries, samosas, pakoras, and 20 kinds of bhajia. Curries from £2.50 and mostly vegan. Two tables inside. Children welcome. Alcohol and smoke free. Ouside catering service.

Sakonis

Vegetarian Indian snack bar, take-away & sweet shop

127-129 Ealing Road, Wembley
Tel: 020-8903 9601
Tube: Wembley Central, Wembley Park
Breakfast: every day 08.00-11.00
(weekend 9-11.00)
Open: Sun-Thu 12-22.00, Fri-Sat 12-22.30
close half an hour earlier in winter

Over 100 Gujarati, North Indian and Chinese dishes. Buffet south Indian breakfast weekdays £3, weekends £3.50, eat as much as you like.
Buffet lunch every day 12-16.00, eat as much as you like for £5.99. 10% eat in charge added to bill.
Buffet dinner every day 19-21.30, £7.99 + 10%. A la carte starters £1.50-£3.95, mains £3.50-£6.50.
Lots of sweets, fruit shakes and fresh juices from £2.75, including fresh coconut water. Take-away Indian sweet shop too.

Sarashwathy Bavans

South Indian vegetarian restaurant

549 High Road, Wembley HA0 2DJ
Tel: 020-8902 1515
Open: Mon-Sun 12.00-23.00
Tube: Wembley Central
www.sarashwathy.com

New and popular place with some Indo-Chinese choices too. Starters, £1.75-£5.25, mains from £3.95 with large selection of dosas, idli and noodles. Fresh juices from £1.95. Free delivery within a 3 mile radius (minimum order of £12) and outside catering.

Tulsi

South Indian vegetarian restaurant

22/22A Ealing Road, Wembley HA0 4TL
Tel: 020-8900 8526
Open: Tue-Fri 11.00-15.00, 18.00-22.30
Sat-Sun 11.00-22.30, Mon closed
Tube: Wembley Central
tulsirestaurant@yahoo.co.uk

South Indian plus some Indo-Chinese food. Idli, dosas, even noodles dosa, from £3. Soups from £2.50. Vegetable dishes from £3.70 and fried rice, noodles and chow mein from £4.

Woodlands

Vegetarian Indian restaurant

402a High Road, Wembley
Tel: 020-8902 9869
Tube: Wembley Central, Wembley Stadium
Open: every day12-15.00 and 18.00-23.00
www.woodlandsrestaurant.co.uk

Within walking distance of Wembley conference centre. Same menu as central London (page 215) though a bit cheaper. House wine £10 bottle, glass £2.25. Beer 330ml £2.75, 660ml £5.35. Children welcome, 2 high chairs. No smoking. MC, Visa, Amex.

Africana

Indian vegetarian restaurant

224 Ealing Road, Wembley
Tel: 020-8795 2455
Open: every day 13–22.00
Tube: Wembley Central

You know it's good when it's full of
Indian people! 20 starters £2–2.50.
Thalis £5.50–7.50. Curries £3.50–4.00
with rice or paratha. Desserts £2–3. Soft
drinks and juices 90p–£3. Also take-
away frozen samosas, spring rolls etc.

Holland & Barrett

Health food shop

22–24 College Road, Harrow
Tel: 020-8427 4794
Open: Mon–Sat 9–17.30, Sun 1–17.00

13 King Street, Twickenham
Tel: 020-8891 6696
Open: Mon–Fri 9–20.00,
Sat 10–20.00, Sun 11–20.00

21, Wembley Square, High Road, Wembley
Tel: 020-8902 6959
Open: Mon–Sat 9–17.30, closed Sun

Glastonbury Somerset

Glastonbury is another world. Another world where everybody seems a little bit kinder and more sensitive. Vegetarian, vegan, organic, earth-friendly, cruelty-free, fairly traded are terms that are not merely acknowledged as being in existence (but only really relevant somewhere else), here people genuinely support, embrace and LIVE these and other ethical life-choices!

Glastonbury is magical. And not just because of Arthurian legends or claims of the first Christian church or culdee (similar to wattle and daub hut) being built on the site where the Abbey now stands or belief in the Holy Grail resting within the Chalice Well. Glastonbury's particular magic is much, much older and it continues to draw modern and ancient pilgrims of all belief-systems and none. You'll see posters for meditation, yoga and events or try asking the friendly people at Enlightenment, the Buddhist shop half way up the High Street.

THINGS YOU MUST SEE: The Tor, The Red Spring, Chalice Well and Gardens, Glastonbury Abbey.

Everywhere serves vegetarian and vegan food. Most of the veggie cafes are shut at night so we've included ethnic restaurants and pubs with food recommended by readers.

Interestingly enough, most people immediately associate Glastonbury with Michael Eavis' legendary 'Glastonbury Festival', which in fact takes place in a field 6 miles away!

If you can't get into our listed veggie accommodation, try: www.glastonbury.co.uk or Glastonbury Tourist Information Tel: 01458-832 954
Email: glastonbury.tic@ukonline.co.uk

Bath is the other big destination in Somerset, with the Roman Baths and the Abbey the top tourist spots. There are some good eateries and a veggie pub. If you can't find anywhere to stay cheaply, Bristol is only half an hour away by bus.

Shekinashram

Shekinashram is a spiritual community based on a commitment to living Truth through self-inquiry and self-honesty. There is a smoke, caffeine, alcohol, sugar and drug ban. Please do not bring any of these substances with you here.

B&B is offered in 2 double rooms and one twin at £25–£27 pppn or dormitory £18. A yurt is available.

The community follows a raw food diet and offer breakfast and lunch accordingly. Hemp milk and banana smoothie with spirulina, fruit and vegan muesli for breakfast. Raw food lunch (open to non-residents) is offered at 1.30pm (book by midday) for £6 and may be tahini, hummous, seed pate, green salad, marinated seaweed, ceasar salad, avocado or tomato and olive salad with dressing.

The Centre offers holistic therapies such as reiki, aromatherapy, altai massage, remedial and Indian Head massage, vortex healing, acupressure, reflexology and spiritual counselling for £30 per hour. Longer blocks are possible at £7.50 per extra 15 mins. There is also a sauna available to guests, £4 and outside visitors for £4.50. It is also possible to book a healing break for one or two nights at a cost of £70 pn inclusive of all food, one healing session per day and sauna use. You can come for meditation classes or saunas if staying elsewhere in Glastonbury.

The centre also takes in volunteers sometimes as and when needed, phone to ask for details.

There are lots of veggie and vegan cafes and restaurants in Glastonbury as well as new age shops. The Tor, Challace Well and Glastonbury Abbey are nearby.

Organic vegan holistic centre

Dod Lane,
Glastonbury,
Somerset, BA6 8BZ

Tel: 01458–832 300/
0845–456 9330

info@shekinashram

www.shekinashram.org

Train:
Castle Cary ,15 miles by bus or taxi

Open: All year
All day til 22.30

Children welcome though no facilities for babies

No pets

Directions: Go up Glastonbury High Street (top of hill) turn right at T junction, second left onto Dod Lane, private drive on right as the Lane bends left.

Parking available

Credit cards accepted

No smoking throughout

Apple B&B

Vegetarian bed and breakfast

25 Norbins Road, Glastonbury BA6 9JF
Tel: 01458–834547
www.glastonbury.co.uk/accommodation
/apple. applebnb@ukonline.co.uk

1 double en suite, 1 double, 1 twin, £25 per person, from £35 single. Organic continental vegetarian breakfast. Parking. Cycle lock up. AA 3 diamonds.

The Barn

Vegetarian bed and breakfast

84b Bovetown, Glastonbury BA6 8JG
Tel: 01458–832 991. Open all year.

Organic vegetarian bed and breakfast, that welcomes vegans. Two twins and one single, all en suite, £28 per person. Quiet and secluded with wonderful views. Non-wheat cereals and muesli, local stewed fruit, toast, croissants, local and home-made jams, local apple juice. On the Tor side of the town. No smoking. Cash and cheque only.

Ploughshares – The Fisher King Centre

Vegan detox centre

54 Roman Way, Glastonbury, BA6 8AD
Tel: 01458–831 182.
www.ploughshares.co.uk
Train: Castle Cary, 40 mins drive, can collect
Open: all year, except Easter and Christmas

One double, one twin and one single room available at £15 per person per night, and including a light breakfast. £750 per week per person for cleansing programme, includes all therapies, supplements, organic fruit and vegetables, and a meal at the end of the week. There is a beautiful garden and a guest lounge to relax in, a sauna and a medi-tation/treatment room. A maximum of three people are there at a time, so you will receive very individual treatment.

Tordown

Vegetarian guest house

5 Ashwell Lane, Glastonbury BA6 8BG
Tel: 01458–832 287. Fax: 01458–831 100
michael@tordown.com. www.tordown.com

Vegetarian guest house on the southern slopes of Glastonbury Tor, a haven of tranquility. 7 rooms: twin, family, single with shared bathroom £25 per person; double, twin en suite £26–28, family ensuite with kitchen £30; single en suite £25. 75% extra for double for one person. No smoking. Visa, MC. Pets by appointment. Spa and pool.

Blue Note Cafe

Vegetarian cafe

4 High Street, Glastonbury
Tel: 01458–832 907
Open: every day 9.30–17.00, longer at Easter

At the bottom of the high street.. Soup £2.95, main meals £5.75, chips £1.95. Beers £2.20–2.50. Wine £2.40 glass, £9 bottle. Children welcome, high chairs. Non smoking.

Rainbow's End Cafe

Vegetarian cafe

17a High Street, Glastonbury
Tel: 01458–833 896
Open: every day 10–16.00

Look for a board on the High Street, just below St. John's Church. Walk down the little alleyway and there it is. You will find some very nice hot dishes, fresh salads and cakes with some seating outside in an enclosed garden. Predominantly vegetarian with plenty for vegans.

Elaichi Tandoori

Omnivorous Indian restaurant

62 High Street, Glastonbury
Tel: 01458-832 601
Open: every day 12-14.30, 17.30-23.00
including bank holidays

Vegetarian dishes recommended by Indians who've stayed at The Barn.

Heaphy's

Omnivorous organic creperie

16 Market Place, Glastonbury
Tel: 01458-837 935
Open: every day 8-17.00

Organic creperie with dairy and gluten free options. Licensed.

Hawthorns Hotel

Hotel, pub and restaurant

8 Northload Street, Glastonbury
(near the bottom of the High Street)
www.hawthornshotel.com
Tel: 01458-831 255
Food: Mon-Thu 18.30-21.30 (last orders)
Fri-22.00, Sat 11-22.00, closed Sunday.

Vegetable pakoras £3.50, roasted aubergine and tomato salad with couscous £3.95. Mains stir fry beancurd and veg with noodles £8.25, gallo pinto beans and rice stir-fried with garlic, onion, tomato, coriander; all veg dishes served with mixed salad. Desserts are mostly dairy. Vegetable curries £6.50 for a plate of two different ones. Smoking and no smoking rooms and a

Cafe Galatea

Vegetarian and vegan café which is also an internet café and art gallery. They have a varied and extensive menu and source locally and organically as much as possible.

Soup, £3, salads from £5.50. Mains start at £5.50 for lunch and £8 in evenings and include pizza (with option of vegan cheese), pasta bakes and aviyal, a South Indian dish of stir-fried vegetables with spices.

In the evenings they do a mezze plate with assorted popular dishes and have an a la carte menu.

Speciality coffees, soya lattes and barley-cinos. All wines and beer are organic. Wine £10 per bottle, lager £2.50 for 500ml, beer £2.75 for 500ml.

Live music evenings and weekends, when it's best to book.

Glastonbury

Vegetarian cafe & art gallery

5a High Street
Glastonbury
Somerset BA6 9DP

Tel: 01458-834 284

www.cafegalatea.co.uk

Open:
Wed-Sun 10.45-21.00
(Fri Sat till 22.00 last orders)

Licensed

Non smoking

Visa, MC

Disabled access

Special diets catered for

patio. Children welcome, high chairs. MC, Visa. House wine £2.95 glass, £3.95 large, £10.95 bottle.

Gigi's

Omnivorous Italian restaurant

2–4 Magdalene St,Glastonbury BA6 9EH (Opposite the gate of the Abbey grounds, by the Growing Needs bookshop.)
Tel: 01458–834612
Open: Tue–Fri 18–22.45,
Sat–Sun 12–14.30, 18–23.00

Cheerful Italian restaurant.

Market House Inn

Omnivorous Pub with food

,12 Magdalene Street, Glastonbury
Tel: 01458–832 220
Open: every day

Egon Ronay listed.

The Mitre Inn

Omnivorous pub with food

27 Benedict Street, Glastonbury
(Near the bottom of the High Street)
Tel: 01458–831 203
Food: every day 12–14.00, 18–21.00ish (Sun from 19.00)

Several vegetarian mains £6.25 such as char–grilled veg pasta or teriyaki veg and noodles, though vegans may be better off at the Hawthorns. Children welcome, high chair, and there's a no smoking room. House wine £2.35–2.85 glass, bottle £9.70. MC, Visa.

The Wholefood Store

Wholefood shop

29 High Street, Glastonbury
Tel: 01458–831 004

Stone Age

Crystal shop

2–4 High Street, Glastonbury
Tel: 01458–835 514

Beautiful, beautiful crystal shop.

The Speaking Tree

Spiritual bookshop

5 High Street, Glastonbury
Open: every day 9–18.00

Fantastic range of books on all matters spiritual, from herbalism to witchcraft, massage to permaculture.

Enlightenment

Meditation shop

40 High Street, Glastonbury BA6 9DX
Tel: 01458–830250
http://web.onetel.com/~naturalearthling /structure.htm

Tibetan singing bowls, horns, bells, statues, thangkas, prayer flags, protection banners, incense, books and more..

Natural Earthling

Fair Trade and yoga shop

38 High Street, Glastonbury BA6 9DX
Tel/Fax: 01458–830 250
www.naturalearthling.com

From their Fair Trade tailoring shop in Nepal, bags, clothing, slippers, quilts and cushions made from fabrics including linen, organic cotton, oriental satin brocades and hand– woven hemp. Upstairs is a room available for meetings, meditations and sessions. You can arrange a massage from Kay, a shiatsu with Simon or a Satsang with Narayan, Brendan or Linda, or rent it for your own activity.

Lavender House

Vegetarian owned omnivorous B&B in Bath. There are five rooms: one single with private bathroom £52-60 per night, three double ensuites and one twin ensuite £80-£95 per room per night. Discounts are available for longer stays.

Imaginative veggie and vegan breakfasts include three-seed bread with vegan pesto, vine tomatoes, avocado and mozzarella, and fried potatoes, or field mushrooms stuffed with cous cous, veg and herbs. Standard cooked veggie breakfasts with veg sausages are also on the menu. Vegan margarine, soya milk, home made vegan muesli and soya yoghurt are all available.

Organic home grown produce used when possible. Special and gluten-free diets are catered for. There is a veggie restaurant, cafe and pub in town and several other restaurants cater for vegetarians.

Everyone comes to Bath to see the Roman Baths. At the Thermae Bath Spa, which open in 2005, you can take the natural spring water and have thirty different therapies. A qualified therapist, one of the owners, can advise on treatments. Many other attractions include the Royal Crescent, the Jane Austen Centre, Assembly Rooms and Costume Museum, Beckfords Tower, Postal Museum, American Museum and the Sally Lunn Oldest House and Museum (1482), Victoria Park Botanical Gardens and the Prior Park Landscape Gardens. Bath has many beautiful walks in its vicinity like the Bath Skyline walk and the Kennett and Avon Canal walk. There is much to explore in the area around Bath, such as Cheddar Gorge.

The guest lounge has a TV, video and CD player. Rooms have TV's and tea and coffee making facilities.

Omnivorous guest house

17 Bloomfield Park
Bath
Somerset BA2 2BY
England

Tel: 01225-314 500

Fax: 01225-448 564

www.lavenderhouse-bath.com
lavenderhouse@btinternet.com

Train Station: Bath Spa, 1.8km then bus, taxi or collection is possible

Open: all year

Children over eight only or non walking babies

No pets

No smoking throughout

Directions: From A36 ring road, take A367 Wells Road, then fork right into Bloomfield Road and take the second right turn into Bloomfield Park

Parking: available on and off road

Locked garage available and secure storage for bicycles

Marlborough House

Impressive stone Victorian house with spacious and elegantly furnished rooms close to the city centre of Bath. There are seven rooms, comprising of double ensuites at £65– £95 per room per night, twin ensuites and family rooms at £75– £105 per room per night. Children are £10 per night. A single person in any room is £55– £85 per night.

Breakfast could begin with cereal and soya yoghurt, followed by vegan pancakes or veggie sausages, breakfast potatoes and sauteed mushrooms. Soya milk, vegan muesli and vegan margarine are available.

Dinner is available for £18 as part of Christmas and New Year packages and also on special request. Specialising in world cuisine, all food is organic. Vegans, diabetics and the allergy sensitive are happily catered for. Bath serves vegetarians and vegans well.

Marlborough House is situated close to Queen Square, the heart of Bath, and at the edge of Royal Victoria Park. All the sites are within walking distance, like the Roman Baths, Assembly Rooms, Museum of Costume, the Jane Austen Centre and the Royal Crescent Circus. The Marlborough House is a perfect base for exploring other nearby historical sites, such as Stonehenge, Wells, Glastonbury, Lacock, Castle Comber, Cheddar and Longleat. There are also many beautiful walks nearby.

Rooms have telephones, TV's, tea and coffee making facilities, a variety of herbal teas, with homebaked cookies and complementary sherry.

Vegetarian guest house

1 Marlborough Lane
Bath
Somerset BA1 2NQ
England

Tel: 01225–318 175

Fax: 01225–466 127

www.marlborough-house.net
mars@manque.dircon.co.uk

Train: Bath Spa, 3/4 mile, then bus or taxi

Open: all year

Cots and high chairs available

Pets welcome

Directions: From M4, take the Bath exit #18 (A46 to Bath), through the green hills surrounding Bath. Get in the correct lane to exit towards Bath again. The roundabout leads to the A4. Keep on this road through Bath as if heading to Bristol. You will drive around Queen Square (a small green) which joins up with the Upper Bristol Road (the A4 again). Pass a string of B&B's. Just after some pedestrian lights, with a Vauxhall Dealer on your left, is Marlborough Lane.

Parking: sometimes available, three spaces

No smoking throughout

Credit cards accepted

Poplar Herb Farm

Veggie B&B situated rurally on the Somerset Levels, an area renowned for its abundant wildlife. There are three rooms: one double shower ensuite at £20 per person per night, one twin and one family room at £18 per person per night.

Breakfast begins with juice, fruit, soya yoghurt and cereal followed by a cooked feast of veggie sausages, mushrooms and tomatoes with home made bread and spreads, washed down with tea or coffee. Soya milk, vegan muesli and vegan margarine are available.

Dinner is offered by request for £10 and could be carrot and coriander soup, followed by nut fritters, home grown salad and herbed potatoes, finished with a dessert of apricot fool. There are excellent veggie restaurants in nearby Glastonbury and several local inns serve veggie food.

Poplar Herb Farm is a 2 1/2 acre nursery and organic smallholding. Enjoy the serenity of the herb gardens and nursery or meet the rescued animals.

The farm is an excellent base for a walking or cycling holiday in the unspoilt Somerset countryside. Seven miles away is historic Glastonbury, with its famous Tor and Abbey Ruins. There are fascinating caves in Cheddar and Wookey Hole, twelve miles away, and numerous coastal resorts and attractive villages to explore.

They have a meditation room which guests can use. Astrological consultations or personal tuition in astrology or meditation can be arranged. Tea and coffee making in rooms.

Burtle

Vegetarian bed and breakfast

Burtle
nr Bridgwater
Somerset TA7 8NB
England

Tel: 01278-723 170

Email:
richardfish@lineone.net

Train Station: Bridgwater or Highbridge, 9 miles, then taxi from Bridgwater

Open: all year

Children welcome

Cot and high chair available

Well behaved pets welcome by prior arrangement

Directions: Take the A39 from Glastonbury. After approximately 7 miles turn right (left if coming from Bridgwater) at the sign for Edington and Burtle into Holy Well Road. Upon arriving at Burtle, turn right at the junction by the Church. Poplar Herb Farm is the first property on your left.

Parking: available off-road

No smoking throughout

Demuths

Vegetarian restaurant

2 North Parade Passage, Off Abbey Green
Bath, BA1 1NX
Tel: 01225-446 059
us@dermuths.co.uk
www.dermuths.co.uk
Open: Every day 10-22.00 (Sat till 23.00, Sat
from 09.00), closed every day 17.30-18.00

Vegetarian dishes from all around the world, half of them vegan and clearly marked, including the desserts. Menus change every month. 12 entrées £1.75-4.95 such as soup, hummous, guacamole, roasted squash, pumpkin and nachos. Fabulous main courses £5.95-8.50 day, £11.75 evening. Vegans, who get a lousy deal in the dessert department in many vegetarian restaurants, will think they've landed in heaven. House wine £11.75 a bottle or £3.15 a (large) glass.

Metropolitan Cafe

Vegetarian cafe

15 New Bond Street, Bath, BA1 1BA
Tel: 01225-482 680
www.bloomsburystore.com/cafe/
Open: Mon-Fri 9.30-17.00, Sat 9-17.00, Sun
11-16.00

Vegetarian café in the shopping area near the Abbey, above Bloomsbury crafts shop and opposite The Gap clothing store. Take-away style food like wraps, ciabattas, sandwiches and bruschetta. Average £3.95 for a sandwich, £4.95-£5.95 for a wrap and ciabatta. Some vegan, organic food. Smoothies and milkshakes (can be soya) around £2.95. Cup of tea £1.30-£1.45. Children's menu, one high chair. No smoking. Visa, MC.

The Porter

Vegetarian pub

15 George Street, Bath, BA1 2EN
Tel: 01225-424 104
www.theporter.co.uk
info@moles.co.uk
Open: Mon-Sat 11.00-23.00, Sun 12-22.30

Vegetarian pub. Friendly atmosphere, with outside seating on a quaint side street. Many dishes are under £5, including traditional pub food like Veggie Sunday Roast Dinner/Lunch. The menu is varied and half vegan, with cashew nut curries, ratatouille, Trinidadian casseroles and homemade soups. Ciders and beers are vegetarian. Small glass of wine £2.80, large £3.95, bottles 11-£12.80. Beer £2.50-£2.90 for a bottle. Smoking permitted. Visa, MC. Mon-Thu evening live music, Sun evening is comedy and there are DJs on Fri and Sat nights.

Tilley's Bistro

Omnivorous restaurant

3 North Parade Passage, Bath
Tel: 01225-484 200
www.tilleysbistro.co.uk
Open: Mon-Sat 12.00-14.30, 18.30-23.00

Restaurant specialising in French and English cuisine with an extensive vegetarian/vegan selection. Lunch set menu, £7.50 for 2 courses, £9.50 for 3. At dinner there is a separate a la carte vegetarian menu. Starters include ciabatta with six varieties of olives £6, avocado salad £6, and a spread of Greek appetizers £11. Mains could be Satay Brochettes with Aniseed Tofu £8.50, Wild Mushroom Pancakes £8.50, and Thai red curry £9. Separate smoking section. Visa, MC.

Bath

Shakeaway

Milkshake chain

3 Beau Street,, Bath BA1 1QY
Tel: 01225-466 200. www.shakeaway.com

Huge variety of flavours, including 30 vegan ones made from organic soya milk and/or vegan ice-cream.

Frome

Garden Cafe

Vegetarian cafe

16 Stony Street, Frome BA11 1BU
Tel: 01373-454178
Open: Mon-Thu Sat 9-18.00; Sun 11-16.00;
Fri 9-21.00, ring for late opening other days

Mains from £5.50 such as cashewnut and bean patties with salads, pitta and hummous; korma curry with organic basmati, popadums and chutneys.
Cakes, none vegan, from £2, but they do have soya ice-cream. (Soya) cappuccino £1.65. House wine £10 bottle, £2.50 glass.
Lovely walled courtyard at back. No smoking except in garden. Small children's play area (for controlled children – this is not a creche!), high chairs. No credit cards. Private hire evenings. Outside festival catering.

Frome Wholefoods

Vegetarian wholefood shop

8 Cheap Street, Frome
(in the centre by the cenotaph)
Tel: 01373-473334
Open:Mon-Wed & Fri 9.30-17.30,
Thu -17.00, Sat 9-17.00

No chilled take-away but there is vegan stuff like flapjacks, sweets, crisps, chocolate.

Taunton

Lotus Flower

Omnivorous Thai restaurant

89 Station Road, Taunton
Tel: 01823-324 411
Open: Tue-Sat 18-23.00, closed Sun-Mon

11 vegetarian dishes. Set meal £18.50 per person with three starters, soup, four mains, two rices. Three course take-away £33 for two people. House wine £10.50 bottle, £2.60 glass. Children welcome, no high chair. One side is no smoking though some people might. MC, Visa, Amex, Diners.

County Stores

Health food shop & take away

52 North Street, Taunton
Tel: 01823-272 235
Open: Mon-Sat 8.30-17.30

Food shop with a health food section. There's a deli counter that sells sandwiches, breads, cakes (but not vegan). Make a picnic with bread, salads and smoked cherry tomatoes in oil from the deli, and add vegetarian pates from the shop such as chickpea and olive, mushroom and tarragon, sweet tomato with lentil and basil.

Country Harvest

Health food shop

8 The Courtyard, St. James Street, Taunton
Tel: 01823-252 843
Open: Mon-Fri 9.30-17.00, Sat 9.30-13.30

The Good Earth

Vegetarian restaurant

4 Priory Road, Wells BA5 1SY
Tel: 01749-678 600
Open: Mon-Sat 09.00-17.00 closed Sunday

Licensed vegetarian restaurant and take-away in a wholefood store and gift shop. Salads from £2.90. Main meals from £4.75 such as ratatouille, mushroom and spinach stroganoff and jacket potatoes. Courtyard for outside eating and conservatory. No smoking. Visa, MC.

Holland & Barrett

Health food shop

42 Stall Street, Bath
Tel: 01225-330 812

Unit 20, Angel Place Centre, Bridgwater
Tel: 01278-452 567

6 Station Road, Clevedon
Tel: 01275-342 049

5 Old Market Centre, Paul Street, Taunton
Tel: 01823-274 347

22 High Street, Wells. Tel: 01749-677 665

19 Meadow Street, Weston Super Mare
Tel: 01934-620 020

Surrey

Wooded hills, sandy heathland, and chalky downs provide the diverse landscape of Surrey, the county that begins at London's southwestern edge.

Criss-crossed by bridleways and paths, there are plenty of ways to pursue active adventures in Surrey. Start in Haslemere for an eight-mile walk through Greensand Way, across the heathlands of Hindhead Common to the summit of Gibbet Hill. Or head for the hills for a spectacular walk along The North Downs Way National Trail between Gomshall and Dorking, which offers spectacular views of lush, green countryside. You will need to take the bus or train from Dorking to Gomshall, and start the walk at Colekitchen Lane opposite the Compasses pub on the A25. For a snack, head for Blubeckers, Gomshall's best veggie-friendly restaurant.

A good way to enjoy Surrey is to spend a day at Hampton Court Palace, the magnificent Tudor residence of the infamous King Henry VIII. Take the bus R68 to and from the Palace from Richmond train or tube station. Finish the day with a bang at one of Richmond's many cafes: Tide Tables, Hollyhock and The Green Cafe. Croydon has the terrific Veggie One restaurant, with fake meats and authentic Chinese dishes on the menu.

Another tourist attraction is Kew Gardens, a sprawling 300 acres of botanical gardens and two beautiful 19th century greenhouses, located near Richmond. The site is easily accessible from London, just take the Metropolitan tube line to the Kew Gardens stop. Oliver's Wholefood Store is conveniently located near the station, providing tasty take-aways.

For a more relaxing holiday, simply find a river-boat cruise sailing up the Thames in Kingston-upon-Thames, and drift away. You can enjoy lunch along the river, at the Riverside Vegetaria, or pick up Japanese treats at Wagamama. If you are short on time, you could pop into Food For Thought for snacks.
To get away from it all, Claridge House is a Quaker centre retreat in the small village of Dormansland.

Claridge House

Quaker centre standing in two acres of beautiful gardens in the small Surrey village of Dormansland. There are twelve rooms; three singles at £50 per night and nine twins at £50 per person per night. Prices are for full board which includes all meals. You will get a £10 reduction if only B&B is required. A mid week break (Mon–Fri) with full board £98–160 per week.

A light breakfast is served and includes a selection of cereals, muesli, soya yoghurt and fresh bread. Gluten free and vegan muesli is available, as well as soya milk and vegan margarine. Dinner is a main course with vegetables followed by a dessert. What is served depends on the dietary needs of guests. Let them know when booking if you are vegan or on a special diet.

Courses are run at weekends on a variety of subjects. The house is open to anyone who is seeking healing, rest or renewal as the emphasis is on spirituality, not on religion. This unique centre offers a sanctuary away from the stresses of every day life or it could act as a bridge between hospital and home.

The house is well situated for exploring the surrounding areas of Surrey, Sussex and Kent. There are more than a dozen National Trust and private properties and gardens open to the public within easy reach. There are also miles of attractive walks in the immediate vicinity.

Two guest lounges and a Quiet Room. Rooms have washbasins and tea and coffee making facilites. Good disabled access to four ground floor rooms, two of which are purpose built. No TVs.

Vegetarian guest house & retreat centre

Dormans Road
Dormansland
Lingfield
Surrey RH7 6QH

Tel: 01342–832 150

Fax: 01342–836 730

www.claridgehouse.quaker.eu.org

Email: welcome@claridgehouse.quaker.eu.org

Train Station: Lingfield, 1 mile, then bus or taxi, or they can pick up with prior notice.

Open: all year

Directions:
From M25: leave at Junction 6 (A22) following signs to East Grinstead. At Blindley Heath turn left to Lingfield on B2029.
From M23: leave at Junction 10 (following signs to East Grinstead. At the second roundabout turn left to Lingfield (B2028).
From Lingfield: about 1/2 mile out of Lingfield. past the racecourse on your right, you will go under a bridge. About 1/4 mile after the bridge, fork right along Dormans Road. Claridge House is situated on the left just before the 30mph sign.

Parking: available

No children or pets.

No smoking throughout

Camberley

Tekels Park

Vegetarian guest house & study centre

Tekels Avenue, Camberley, Surrey, GU15 2LF
Tel: 01276–23159
Fax: 01276–27014
Open: all year, except Christmas
www.tekelspark.co.uk
ghouse.tekels@btclick.com
Train Station: Camberley, one mile

Theosophical Society owned guest house with twenty two rooms comprised of singles, twins and doubles, from £35 per person per night. Evening meal with advanced notice, from £8 for one course. Children by arrangement. No pets. Disabled access. No smoking.

Croydon

Pizza Express

Omnivorous pizza chain

3 South End, Croydon CR0 1BE
Tel: 020-8680 0123
www.pizzaexpress.co.uk/rest/rd200.htm
Open: Daily, 11.30–24.00

Vegan–friendly pizza chain. This branch offers Redwood's melting Cheezly and Cheatin' ham available on request when booking. Child–friendly with high chairs.

Shakeaway

Milkshake chain

1150 (1st Floor), Whitgift Centre, Croydon CR0 1XB
Tel: 020-8686 3222
www.shakeaway.com

Milkshake chain with huge range of flavours, including 30 vegan ones made with organic soya milk and/or vegan ice-cream.

Gomshall

Blubeckers

Omnivorous restaurant

Gomshall Mill, Gomshall, Surrey GU5 9LB
Tel: 01483–203 060
www.blubeckers.co.uk
gomshall.blubeckers@btopenworld.com
Open: every day 12–14.30,
17.30–22.00 (Fri–Sat –22.30)

Omnivorous restaurant with at least half a dozen vegetarian main dishes from £10, some of which can be made vegan. No vegan desserts. Smoking section. House wine £9.95 bottle, from £2.65 for a glass. For children, high chairs, balloons and crayons! Some outside seating. Credit cards ok. Big white building on the A25, between Guildford and Dorking.

Guildford

The Beano

Vegetarian lunch restaurant

1st floor, Guildford Institute, University of Surrey, Ward St, Guildford GU1 4LH (off North St, opposite the library)
Tel:01483–562 142
Open term time: Mon–Fri 10–14.00, lunch 12–14.00, also first Sat in the month 12–14.00.

Home made vegetarian and vegan food, e. Soup £2.10, main meals £2.95 such as Spnish chickpeas ratatouille, butter-bean bake. Desserrts £2.10 include apricot, banana and almond syllabub or apple and rhubarb crumble. No smoking. Children welcome, high chairs. House wine £1.70 glass, about £8.50 bottle. Art exhibitions on the walls. Can get extremely busy. You can also visit the historic library in the same building.

Guildford

Wagamama

Omnivorous Japanese restaurant

25–29 High Street, Guildford GU1 3DY
Tel:01483–457 779
www.wagamama.com
Open: Mon–Sat 12–23.00 Sun 12.30–22.00

See entry under Manchester for menu details

Kingston–upon–Thames

Riverside Vegetaria

Vegetarian restaurant

64 High Street, Kingston–upon–Thames
Tel: 020–8546 7992
www.rsveg.plus.com
Train: Kingston BR
Open: Every day 12–23.00 (Sun to 22.30)

Superb riverside vegetarian restaurant by the Thames. In warm weather you can eat under the sky. 70% vegan including some awesome desserts. Starters £4.25–£5.50. Main dishes £6.50–£8.50 include masala dosa, tofu marinated in teriyaki sauce, mushroom and lentil bake; all served with veg, salad and/or rice. Organic and vegan wines. 10% discount for Vegetarian and Vegan Society members. Booking advised for weekends and outside.

Shakeaway

Milkshake chain

15 Thames Street, Kingston KT1 1PJ
Tel: 020–8392 0092
www.shakeaway.com

See Croydon for details. (previous page)

Wagamama

Omnivorous Japanese restaurant

16–18 High Street, Kingston–upon–Thames
Tel: 020–8546 1117. www.wagamama.com
Train: Kingston BR
Open: Mon–Sat 11–23.00, Sun 12.30–22.30

Omnivorous fast food Japanese noodle bar with at least nine veggie and vegan dishes. See entry under Manchester for menu details.

Food for Thought

Wholefood shop

38 Market Place, Kingston KT1 1JQ
Tel: 020–8546 7806
Open: Mon–Sat 9–17.30

Wholefood shop with plenty of staples like dried fruit, nuts, seeds, pulses etc. plus supplements, aromatherapy, skin-care ranges and homeopathic remedies.

Richmond

Tide Tables

Vegetarian cafe

2 The Archways, Richmond Bridge, Richmond
Tel: 020–8948–8285
Train: Richmond BR
Open: every day, daylight hours. Phone ahead in winter as they close if weather is bad.

Under the arch of a bridge near the town centre, with beautiful views of the Thames, a riverside terrace and outside seating in summer. Open for breakfast, lunch and tea. Vegan soup, spinach pastie with salad, stuffed focaccia, falafels and vegan shepherdess pie with salad, from £2.20 to £5.90. Handmade organic cakes. Hot and cold drinks and free corkage. Child and dog friendly, high chairs. Smoking outside. No cards.

The Green Cafe

Vegetarian cafe

29 The Green, Richmond TW9 1LX
Tel: 020-8332 7654
Open: every day 9-18.00

Similar to Tide Tables, on picturesque, historic Richmond Green tucked behind the main high street, with outside seating. This one is more of a specialist juice bar. Smoothies £3, fresh fruit and veg juices £2.50, wheatgrass available. Always have soya milk. Also salads, stuffed pitta, soups. Very child friendly but no high chairs as less seating. Smoking outside only. No cards.

Hollyhock Cafe

Vegetarian cafe

Petersham Road, Richmond TW10 6UX
Tel: 020-8948 6555
Train: Richmon BR
Open: Easter-Autumn half term, every day, daylight hours. Closed in Winter.

In the middle of a park overlooking the Thames. Breakfasts, salads, baked dishes, juices, smoothies, (soya) cappuccino. Very child frindly, high chairs, parents sit on the verandah while kids play on the grass.

Oliver's Wholefood Store

Wholefood shop

5 Station Approach, Kew Gardens, Richmond
Tel: 020-8948 3990
Tube/train: Kew Gardens
Open: Mon-Sat 9-19.00, Sun 10-19.00

Veggie and vegan sandwiches, pastries, salads, seaweed rice snacks and wraps. Organic fruit and veg. Vegan wines. Nutritionist and beauty therapist, regular lectures in-store.

Santok Maa's

Vegetarian Indian restaurant

848 London Road, Thornton Heath
Tel: 020-8665-0626
Train: Thornton Heath, Norbury
Open: Thu-Tue 12-22.00. Closed Wed.

North and South Indian vegetarian restaurant and take-away, with some Chinese dishes that use Indian spices like stir-fries. Nearly 100 veggie and vegan dishes. Starters average £2.95, main courses £3.95 and rice £1.75. Desserts from £1.50 but no vegan ones. Bring your own wine, £1 per person corkage. Special offer on Monday, all food half price excluding dessert and take-away. Visa, MC, Amex.

Swad

Vegetarian Gujarati Indian restaurant

850 London Rd, Thornton Heath CR7 7PA
Tel: 020-8683 3344
Open: Mon-Fri 9-21.00, Sat-Sun 10-22.00

Buffet £5-6 12-15.00. Wine £8-10. Children welcome, high chair. No smoking. MC, Visa. Outside catering up to 2,000 people.

SOUTH Surrey

Holland & Barrett

Health food shop

19 Grace Reynolds Walk, Camberley
Tel: 01276–64043

---

185 High Street, Dorking
Tel: 01306–889 654

1098-00 The Mall, Whitgift Centre, Croydon
Tel: 020–8681 5174
Open: Mon–Sat 10–17.30, Thu until 20.00,
Sun 11–17.00

Unit 44, Ashley Centre, Epsom
Tel: 01372–728 520Open: Mon–Sat 9–17.30,
Sun 10–16.00

Unit 3, Friary Centre, Guildford
Tel: 01483–537 207

12–13 Apple Market, Kingston
Tel: 020–8541 1378
Open: Mon–Fri 9–17.30, Sat 9–18.00, Sun
11–16.30

---

68 High Street, Reigate
Tel: 01737–248 260

50a George Street, Richmond
Tel: 020–8940 1007
Open: Mon–Sat 9–17.30, Sun 11.30–16.30

---

213 High Street, Sutton
Tel: 020–8642 5435
Open: Mon–Sat 9–17.30, Sun 11–16.00

---

13 King Street, Twickenham
Tel: 020–8891 6696

---

27 Wolsey Walk, Woking
Tel: 01483–772 978

Unit 20, The Swan Shopping Centre,
Leatherhead
Tel: 01372–378 682

Unit 20, Swan Shopping Centre, Leatherhead
Tel: 01372–378 682

---

50 London Road, Morden
Tel: 020–8685 0375

This county has a prime location, perched on the southern shore of England, overlooking the beautiful English Channel. The very veggie-friendly Brighton is an absolute must-see in nearby East Sussex, but if you have more time, a side trip to either Arundel or Chichester is recommended.

Arundel, in the southwestern corner of the county, has a grand castle with a gothic interior jam-packed with Van Dyck, Gainsborough, and Reynolds paintings. Entrance is £11 for adults, or £6.50 to stroll the grounds only. If you come to Arundel, you can dine in Pizza Express, an omnivorous pizza chain in a beautiful historic building.

Chichester, further west, was founded by the Romans and by following the city walls and Roman street plan, you can enjoy a relaxing walk. For more history, head to Chichester Cathedral where you can see the Roman mosaics uncovered during restoration works, and a stunning stain glass piece by Chagall. St. Martin's Organic Tea rooms offers traditional high tea – veggie style – to visitors to this neck of the woods. For an inexpensive casual lunch, try Cafe Paradiso. They serve simple, light lunches for most special diets, and is quite inexpensive.

West Sussex

Arundel

Pizza Express

Omnivorous pizza restaurant

33 High St, Arundel, W Sussex BN18 9AG.
20 minute walk from Arundel station on the
Victoria to Portsmouth train line. Off the A27
Tel: 01903 885 467
Open: 11.30–23.00

This vegan–friendly pizza restaurant is
in a Grade II listed building with
exposed wooden breams and a 15th
century painting on the olde worlde wall
and views of other historic buildings
including the Gothic cathedral.

Chichester

St. Martin's Organic Tearooms

Organic tea rooms

3 St. Martins Street, Chichester
Tel: 01243–786 715
www.organictearooms.co.uk
Open: Mon–Sat 9–18.00

Wholefood tearoom selling English food
in the attractive Chichester town centre,
near the cross. All veggie cuisine, apart
from one salmon dish. There are several
types of vegan soup, priced around £4,
including broccoli, mushroom, and
tomato. Salads, potato cakes, and
sandwiches are also offered.
Drinks include freshly squeezed jjuiced,
vegan smoothies, coffees, and hot
chocolate. Soya milk is not available,
but they have organic oat milk and
make 'oataccinos'.
The menu clearly lists all ingredients
and amount of calories for individual
dishes. All food is low in fat.

Cafe Paradiso

Vegetarian cafe

9 Priory Lanes, Northgate, Chichester
Tel: 01243–532 967
Open: Mon–Sat 9–17.00

Vegetarian cafe with salads, from £3.85
eat in, £2.60 take–away. Mains £4.50–
5.50, such chili, curries. falafels. Cater
for vegans and coeliacs. Licensed. No
smoking throughout. Cash and cheque
only.

GNC

Health food shop

66 South Street, Chichester PO19 1EE
Tel: 01243–532775

Holland & Barrett

Health food shop

17 London Road, Bognor Regis
Tel: 01243 830354

71 Church Walk, Burgess Hil
Tel: 01444–242 724

19 North Street, Chichester
Tel: 01243–778 898

Unit 6, County Mall, Crawley
Tel: 01293–565 913

Swan Walk, West Street, Horsham
Tel: 01403–274 353

123 The Street, Rustington
Tel: 01903–784101

The Isle of Wight

Just below Southampton and Portsmouth, in the centre of the south coast of England, is the Isle of Wight, the perfect escape from the mainland.

The entrance to this island is Cowes, at the northern tip. Queen Victoria and Prince Albert spent most vacations here after purchasing the magnificent residence Osbourne House, of which she said "It is impossible to imagine a prettier spot." After Albert's death in 1861, Queen Victoria moved here to mourn, until her own death in 1901. Admission is £8.50 adults, £6.40 concessions, £4.30 children, family ticket (2 adults and 3 children) £21.30. Reduced rates for viewing the grounds only.

Passenger and Car Ferries

Wightlink: Portsmouth to Ryde/Fisbourne and Lymington to Yarmouth
National rate 0870 582 7744
Portsmouth 02392-827 744
www.wightlink.co.uk

Red Funnel: Southampton to Cowes
023-8033 4010
www.redfunnel.co.uk

Hovertravel: Southsea to Ryde (foot passengers only)
Southsea 02392- 811 000
Ryde 01983-811 000

Island Line: railway from Ryde to Shanklin
Ryde 01983-811000
Southsea 023-9281 1000

General Information about the Island
www.islandbreaks.co.uk
01983-813 818

Brambles

A warm, friendly welcome from John and Angela awaits you at the Isle of Wight's only vegan bed and breakfast. Brambles is set in a quiet location only five minutes walk to miles of sandy beaches. All four bedrooms are ensuite: two twin for £25 per person per night; two double £24 per person, one of which can also be a family room. Single occupancy is £28. Cheaper rates may be available for week-long stays.

Breakfast begins with fresh fruit juice, cereal with soya or rice milk, soya yoghurt and fresh or dried fruit, followed by French bread or toast, and warm scones or soda bread with a selection of preserves. A cooked breakfast is available for £3.50 and could be veggie sausages, marinated mushrooms, tomatoes and toast. Various teas, coffee and Barleycup are available.

Dinner is available by request for £12.50 and could be potato wedges with Scoralia dip, followed by Special Occasion Tofu with basmati rice and fresh green salad. For dessert, there is Chocolate Orgy Pudding. Bring your own wine. Open to non-residents for dinner too. They can also make you a packed lunch for £4.50 which includes sandwiches, fruit juice or flavoured soya milk, fruit and a flapjack. 50-100% of the food is organic.

Shanklin town centre is only five minutes from Brambles, and has many interesting shops and a lively theatre. It is an ideal location for ramblers and cyclists who will enjoy the magnificent countryside.

Tea and coffee making facilities, televisions, clock radios and hairdryers in the rooms. The guest lounge has a remote controlled TV.

Vegan bed and breakfast

10 Clarence Road
Shanklin
Isle of Wight PO37 7BH
England

Tel: 01983-862 507

freespace.virgin.net/
brambles.vegan

Email: vegan.brambles
@virgin.net

Train Station: Shanklin, five minutes walk

Open: May-Sept

Directions: for foot passengers travelling from Portsmouth via Wightlink or from Southsea via Hovertravel, the Island's railway runs from Ryde through to Shanklin

Parking: available on road

Adults only

No smoking throughout

No pets

10% discount given to members of the Vegetarian Society, Vegan Society, Viva!, PETA, Animal Aid and people presenting this book, for stays of one week or more

Cowes

Cowes Health Food

Health food shop

8 High Street, Cowes. Tel: 01983–282 070
Open: Mon–Sat 9–17.00

Prime Foods

Health food shop

62 High Street, Cowes.
Tel: 01983–291 111
Open: every day 11–18.00, sometimes later
and around the clock during Cowes week.

Freshwater

Dimbola

Vegetarian tea rooms

Dimbola Lodge Museum, Terrace Lane,
Freshwater PO40 9QE
Tel: 01983–756 814
www.dimbola.co.uk
Open: Tue–Sun 10–17.00, also Mon in school
holidays

Light meals around £5 such as soups,
chips, cakes (some vegan) and veggie
specials. No alcohol. No smoking. Visa,
MC. Dimbola Lodge is the former home
of one of the first Victorian lady photog-
raphers. The centre contains galleries, a
camera museum, studio, dark room,
and they run courses. Admission £4
adults, under–16 free. You don't have to
go in to use the tea rooms.

Godshill

Godshill Organics

Health food shop

Yard Parlour, Newport Road, godshill
Tel: 01983–840 723

Newport

Quay

Mostly vegetarian cafe

Quay Arts Centre, Sea Street, Newport PO30
8BD. Tel: 01983–530055
Open: Mon–Sat 9.30–16.30, evenings if
events on, closed Sun

Vegetarian or vegan main course
£4.95–6.25 such as nut roast. Cakes
include vegan date oatie and flapjacks.
House wine £9.25, glass £2.50.
Children welcome, high chairs. MC,
Visa over £10. No smoking.

Ralph's Health Foods

Health food shop

64–65 St. James Street, Newport
Tel: 01983– 522 353 / 528 627
Open: Mon–Fri 8.30–17.30, Sat –17.00,
closed Sun

Lots of vegetarian pasties, plus Swedish
Glace and Tofutti vegan ice–cream.

Ryde

Beijing Palace

Omnivorous Chinese restaurant

Appley Rise, Ryde PO33 1LE
Tel: 01983–811 888
Open: Daily 12.00–14.30, 18.00–24.00

Vegetarian and vegan dishes include
Peking spring rolls £2.20, Szechuan
Kung–Po bean curd £4.30, sweet & sour
veg £4.20, vegan fried rice noodles.
Children welcome, high chairs.

Holland & Barrett

Health food shop

52 Upper St. James Street, Newport
Tel: 01983–522 121

1 High Street, Ryde. Tel: 01983–565 257

Wiltshire is a relatively unknown county, which is surprising considering that it is home to one of the most magical and mysterious wonders of the world, Stonehenge. But Wiltshire'se allure does not end there, it also has Silbury Hill, Europe's largest man-made prehistoric mound, and Britain's largest burial chamber, the West Kennet Long Barrow. In the summer months crop circles appear in the fields.

The county is dominated by the beauty of nature: rolling hills, valleys and picturesque stone cottages cover the landscape. More than half of the county has been designated an Area of Outstanding Natural Beauty. The Kennet and Avon Canal makes an excellent circular route for exploring on foot or bicycle and you can enjoy the hospitality of Bradford Old Windmill, a veggie-friendly bed and breakfast in a quiet corner of Bradford-on-Avon.

If you have time to linger in Wiltshire, a tour of Salisbury is highly recommended. The towering spires of Salisbury Cathedral and the ancient hillfort, Old Sarum, will not fail to impress. Pop into Salisbury Health Foods if you need a snack, or a treat – they sell a variety of vegan ice creams.

If all this sight-seeing make you ravenous, be sure to visit the National Trust's Circle Restaurant in Avebury, which serves vegetarian lunches with a little piece of history, literally! The building is actually made from the same sarsen stone as nearby Stonehenge.

Wiltshire

Bradford Old Windmill

Bed and breakfast in a converted windmill hidden away amongst the trees with a vegetarian proprietor. There are three rooms, all double ensuites from £69–£109 per room per night. All have their own unique features such as the Damsel room with its queen sized water bed and whirlpool bath, the round bed in the round Great Spur room and the Fantail suite with its spectacular views.

Of their seven breakfast choices, six are vegetarian such as devilled mushrooms on wholemeal muffins. Soya milk and vegan margarine are available. 95% organic.

Dinner is offered for £22 per person on most nights and will be a veggie adaption of a recipe collected from Mexican, Thai, Nepalese, Gambian or Jamaican cuisine. 80% organic. Nearby Bath (eight miles away) also offers restaurants serving plenty of veggie food.

Bradford on Avon is an unspoilt town with many charms, like secret courtyards and overflowing gardens viewed from narrow alleyways between weavers' cottages and clothiers' mansions.

Nearby attractions include the Kennet and Avon canal, the cities of Bath, Glastonbury and Wells, Cotswold villages, the stone circles of Avebury and Stonehenge, Wookey Hole caves and the Forest of Dean.

Curl up on the sofa in the circular lounge and enjoy a log fire on cold winter nights.

Televisions and tea and coffee making facilities are in the rooms.

Omnivorous bed and breakfast

4 Masons Lane
Bradford on Avon
Wiltshire BA15 1QN
England

Tel: 01225–866 842
Fax: 01225–866 648

www.
bradfordoldwindmill.co.uk
vegbritain@
bradfordoldwindmill.co.uk

Train station: Bradford on Avon, 1/4 mile, then taxi.

Open: March–December (incl.)

Directions: On A363 from north find mini roundabout by Castle pub. Take Masons Lane down hill towards town centre. Turn left after fifty metres into private unsigned drive immediately before and beside first roadside house.

Parking: available

Children over six years are welcome

No smoking throughout

Visa, MC

The National Trust Circle Restaurant

Vegetarian restaurant

High Street, Avebury SN8 1RF
Tel: 01672–539 514
www.nationaltrust.org.uk
Open: April–Oct every day 10–18.00; Oct–
Mar every day 10–16.00; Closed Xmas Day

Vegetarian and vegan restaurant in a 19th century stable block built of the same sarsen stone as the adjacent megalithic stone circle. Menu changes every month, with main courses £5.25–£5.95 including salad. Soup and roll, £3, is always vegan and gluten free. Fruit wine, beer and the usual hot beverages. One highchair. Wheelchair access and disabled toilet.

Devizes

The Bistro Cafe

Daytime vegetarian cafe,
evening omnivorous restaurant

7 Little Brittox, Devizes SN10 1AR
(just off the market place)
Tel:01380–720043
Bistro: Tue–Sat 19–21.30 ish (last orders)
Cafe: Mon–Sat 10–15.00

It's a vegetarian cafe by day, an omnivorous bistro by night that caters for veggies and vegans, run by cookery-writer and tv chef Peter Vaughan (the Dinner Doctor on Channel 5).
Falafels with organic pitta £5.95. Vegetarian sausages and mashed celeriac and caramelised red wine sauce £6.95. Evening omnivorous 2 course menu £17, 3 courses £21.95, always a couple of vegan and veggie dishes.
Desserts £4.95 including many vegan such as warm banana and lemon cake with raspberry soya ice–cream, tarte tatin with cinnamon soya cream, marinated strawberries with rosehip syrup and sorbet.

Vegan house wine £3.95 glass, £12 bottle. No smoking. Children welcome, high chairs.
Private dining room for parties of 14–24 any night with prior booking, great for parties.

The Healthy Life

Vegetarian natural foods shop

4 Little Brittox SN10 1AR
Shop open: Mon–Sat 9–17.30

Specialising in wholefoods, local and fair trade produce, artisan breads used in the bistro. Environmentally friendly household products. Home brew kits. Greengrocer next door. MC Visa.

Marlborough

Applebys

Vegetarian cafe

5 Old Hughenden Yard,
Marlborough SN8 1LT
Tel: 01672–515 200
Open: Mon–Sat 8.30–17.00

Vegetarian café with hot lunches £6.50 or cold lunches with salad £5.30. Also on offer, quiches, soups £2.80, sandwiches £2.80–£3.90 and salads £3.75. Teas £1.20 pot, cappuccino and lattes, £1.50. Cakes are £1.40–£2.50. Children's sandwiches, 2 high chairs. No smoking. Visa, MC accepted.

The Swan Inn

Omnivorous pub

Wilton, Near Marlborough SN8 8SS
Tel: 01672–870 274

Homely and friendly pub with a choice of vegan dishes and a nice outside seating area. You can make it a stop on the circular walk

SOUTH Wiltshire

353

Yummy Express

Chinese take-away

127 South Western Rd, Salisbury
(right by the railstation)
Tel: 01722–411422

Veggie options include several beancurd dishes, mixed veg in black bean sauce, Kung Po veg, stir-fried broccoli in garlic, vegan pancake rolls, Singapore fried noodles (can be without egg). You can get a 2-person meal like spring rolls, a couple of main dishes and a couple of plain rice portions for under £13.

Anokaa

Omnivorous Indian restaurant

60 Fisheron Street, Salisbury, SP2 7RB
Tel: 01722–414142

Excellent up-market new Indian restaurant and takeaway. Portions aren't huge, but the flavour is fantastic. Some vegan options include baby augergines with a peanut and sesame sauce served with saffron rice £8.25; Ramish, asparagus and broccoli with sweetcorn and green chillies, with steamed rice £8.50; Aloor Bhaigon, new season baby potatoes and aubergine with fruity sauce and fresh spices, with saffron rice. Indian runner beans in spices and spinach £3.10. Excellent tandoori roti bread (without melted butter). Small smoking section.

Shah Jahan

Omnivorous Indian restaurant

111–113 South Western Rd, Salisbury
Tel: 01722–328120

A more regular but nevertheless high quality Indian restaurant. Main dishes are cooked in vegetable oil, but breads and rices may use butter ghee. They will do vegetarian versions of the common main dishes even though not listed, e.g. vegetable Ceylon, Madras. Take-aways are good value, free popadums and usually a free side dish (make sure it's veggie though!)

They do good chapattis and will happily do Tandoori roti (ask for no added butter if vegan) even though they are not on the menu. Smoking allowed.

Pizza Express

Omnivorous pizza restaurant

50 Blue Boar Row, Salisbury SP1 1DA
Tel: 01722–415 191
Open: every day 11.30–24.00

Chang Thong

Omnivorous Thai restaurant

14 Ox Row, Market Square,
Salisbury SP1 1EU
Tel: 01722 328923
Open: 12–14.00, 18–23.00

New restaurant where Berli's vegan place used to be. Children welcome. Smoking allowed.

Salisbury Health Foods

Wholefood shop

15 Queen Street, Salisbury
Tel: 01722–335 965.
Open: Mon–Sat 9–17.30

Wholefood shop with lots of take away foods including vegan Clives pies, vegan ice-cream, cakes and Redwood range. They also carry gluten free foods, supplements, chiller and frozen foods and dairy-free produce.

Salisbury also has two organic fruit and veg stalls on the market every Tuesday, as well as an organic bread stall. Some of these are also in the Saturday market.

Wiltshire SOUTH

Parasol

Omnivorous Chinese restaurant

97 Commercial Road, Swindon SN1 5PL
Tel: 01793-533188
Open: Mon-Sat 12-14.30, 17.30-23.30
Sun 12-22.00

A welcome find in one of the worst cities in Britain to be a vegan without a kitchen. Vegetarian set menu £13.90 for three courses or go a la carte. House wine £9.50 bottle, £2.60 glass. Take-away 25% discount for cash. MC, Visa. Non-smoking section.

Pizza Express

Omnivorous pizza restaurant

5 Bath Road, Old Town, Swindon SN1 4AS
(follow signs for Old Town from M4 or A419)
Tel: 01793 484 300
Open: 11.30 to 24.00 most nights

In the Old Town, 15 minutes walk from the town centre. Live jazz Wednesday 8-10pm.

GNC

Health food shop

16 The Plaza, Swindon SN1 1LF
Tel: 01793-520385

Holland & Barrett

Health food shop

9-10 The Brittox, Devizes
Tel: 01380-722 025

59 Silver Street, Salisbury
Tel: 01722-324 064

1a, 17 Brunel Shopping Centre, Swindon
Tel: 01793-521 235

Unit 15, The Shires, Trowbridge
Tel: 01225-776 056

Unit 1, Market Place, Warminster
Tel: 01985-847 965

SOUTH Wiltshire

The Channel Islands

The fascinating Norman style farmhouses, narrow winding lanes and French street names of the Channel Islands reflect an intricate history that links the two great nations of France and Britain.

Located just off the coast of France, these islands have technically been British since 1066, though not officially a part of the United Kingdom. The weather proves it! They have a pleasant climate, and the beaches are excellent for summer vacations.

The bigger island of the two, Jersey has an excellent omnivorous restaurant, The Green Olive, that takes care of vegans and veggies. For a fancy night on the town in St. Helier, try Lido's Wine Bar and Bistro.

The other big island, Guernsey, has one particularly veggie-friendly restaurant, Roberto's in the capital of St. Peter Port. The main attraction here is the home of Victor Hugo, Hauteville House.

For maps, pictures, and transportation guides, try the tourist information centres:

Liberation Square, St Helier, Jersey JE1 1BB
Tel: 01534-500 700
Fax: 01534-500 808
E-mail: info@jersey.com
www.jersey.com

VisitGuernsey, PO Box 23, St Peter Port, Guernsey, Channel Islands, GY1 3AN
Tel: 01481-723 552
enquiries@visitguernsey.com
www.visitguernsey.com

Guernsey

Roberto's

Omnivorous restaurant

1 Trinity Square, St. Peter Port GY1 1LP
Tel: 01481–730 419
Open: Tue–Sun 12–13.30, 18–22.00

Some vegetarian dishes like pancakes or pasta for £7.25.

Hansa Wholefoods

Wholefood shop

20 Fountain Street, St. Peter Port, Guernsey
Tel: 01481–723 412
Open: Mon–Sat 08.00–17.00

Some wraps to take–away.

Hansa Wholefoods

Wholefood shop

South Side, St Sampsons, Guernesey
Tel: 01481–249 135
Open: Mon–Sat 09.00–17.30

Jersey – St Helier

The Green Olive

Omnivorous restaurant

1 Anley Street, St. Helier, Jersey JE2 3QE
Tel: 01534–728 198
Open: Tue–Fri 12–14.30
Tue–Sat 18–21.30 (kast irders)

About a third of the menu is vegetarian and some vegan. Lunch starters include marinated mixed olives, £2.95, soup of the day £3.75. Four salads in small or large sizes £3.25–£5.50. Ciabatta sandwiches with a side salad from £4.95. Loaded potato bake with your choice of filling served with side salad £4.95–£5.50.

Lunch main courses e.g. char–grilled veg and wild mushroom pesto pasta £8.95; oven baked samosa with butternut and sunblushed tomato served on chive mash £10.95 (vegan). The evening menu offers the lunch starters and four veggie mains, such as the aubergine boat. Specials are also available and change regularly.

Desserts £4.95 include vegan summer fruits pudding.

House wine £3 glass, £10.95 a bottle. Over 20 more wines from around the world, or champagne £39.95. Beer £2.75, coffee £1.30, cappuccino £1.95 (no soya milk).

10% service charge evenings. Separate room for smokers. Visa, MC. Children welcome, no high chairs.

Lido's Wine Bar & Restaurant

Omnivorous brasserie

4–6 Market Street, St. Helier JE2 4WY
Tel: 01534–722 358
Open: Mon–Sat 12–16.00; Mon–Thu & Sat 18–21.00, bar Mon–Sat 10–23.00 with pastries and afternoon tea

Up–market wine bar and brasserie which can do lunches later than most Jersey places. They always have a couple of veggie dishes, but with notification they'll cook anything as everything is made fresh from scratch. Starters £5–£6. Main courses £9–9.50 such as pasta mushroom ravioli. All desserts are dairy based. House wine £2.65–2.95 glass, £11.50–13.00 bottle. It's located in a pedestrian precinct so you can sit out in the sun in the heart of the town. There are lots of business folk for weekday lunches, but it gets quieter at night. You'll find the Victorian food market next door, open Mon–Sat dawn until 17.30, Thursday till 14.00. Smoking throughout. Children welcome, high chairs. MC, Visa, Amex.

Pizza Express

Omnivorous pizza restaurant

59 Halkett Place, St Helier, Jersey JE2 4WG
Tel: 01534–733 291
Open: 11.30–00.00

OK it's a chain, but they are a good bet for veggies and can do pizzas without cheese for vegans.

Bella Italia

Omnivorous Italian restaurant

10–12 York Street
St Helier, Jersey JE2 3RQ
Tel: 01534–725478

Some vegetarian dishes, can be vegan.

Leaders Health Food

Wholefood shop

The Arcade, Bath Street/Halkett Street
St. Helier JE2 4WJ
Tel: 01534–871 588
Open: Mon–Sat 9–17.00

Picnic and self–catering heaven, this veggie health food shop has organic foods, dried fruits and nuts, soya milk and vegan ice cream. No take away or fresh vegetables.

Carob Sandwich Bar

Omnivorous sandwich bar
and health food shop

19 Quennevais Precint, La Route de Quen-
nevais, St Brelade, Jersey JE3 8FX
Sandwich bar tel: 01534–490887
Shop tel: 01534–741 648
Sandwich bar open: Mon–Sat 08–14.30
Shop open: Mon–Sat 9–17.30

On the west side of the island, near the airport. Sandwich bar also has salads, cakes, vegan things from £2.50. Shop has flapjacks, vegan chocolate and ice-cream, soya dessert, supplements, bodycare, household products.

Pizza Express

Omnivorous pizza restaurant

91 La Route de la Baie,
St Brelade, Jersey JE3 8EF
Tel: 01534–499 049
Open: 11–23.00

In the middle of St Brelade's Bay with views of the beach and a sliding glass roof for summer.

WEST

Counties

Staffordshire

Shropshire

Birmingham

Worcestershire

Warwickshire

Herefordshire

Gloucestershire

Oxfordshire

Bristol

Western England

Bristol

Most people know Bristol for Isambard Kingdom Brunel's Clifton Suspension Bridge and SS Great Britain, the first steam powered iron ship in the world, two beautiful and very different cathedrals, or its long list of homegrown talent including Wallace and Gromit, Massive Attack and Portishead. Travellers see the city as a an excellent base for exploring the West. Being close to Wales, Bristol makes for an excellent stopover between Bath or Stonehenge, and Newport or other Welsh destinations.

Bristol is electric: museums, shopping, arts and the vibrant nightlife combine to create a fresh vibe so that art connoisseurs, theatre-lovers and concert-goers are spoilt for choice.

Vegetarians will find fabulou cuisine readily available, for instance at Cafe Maitreya, the winner of the Vegetarian Society's Gourmet Vegetarian Restaurant of the Year in 2004. In the centre your best daytime bet is Royce Rolls cafe in St Nicholas Market. You can get falafels most evenings on the waterfront opposite the Watershed. Heading up Park Street, near the City Museum on the Triangle and Queen's Road are the new Krishna's Inn restaurant and Fresh & Wild organic supermarket and veggie cafe.

For convenient accommodation consider the Arches Hotel, not far from the centre. If you fancy the peace and quiet of a residential neighbourhood, Basca House offers sophisticated stays in a beautiful Victorian home one mile from the city centre.

Arches Hotel

Vegetarian guest house with ten rooms: three singles at £27.50–£34.50 per night, one double £48.50, one double ensuite £56, one twin £51, one twin ensuite £58.50 and three family rooms £67–£74.50 per night.

A continental breakfast is included, however a vegetarian or vegan full cooked breakfast is available for £2.50–£3 and could be veggie sausages, tomatoes, beans and fried bread. Vegan muesli, vegan margarine, soya yoghurt, rice and oat milk are all available.

Dinner is not offered but there are several restaurants nearby serving veggie food. The owners can advise you where to go.

Bristol's attractions include Brunel's suspension bridge, two cathedrals, museums, several theatres and concert halls, as well as the waterfront and marina. There are lots of parks, terrific shopping, and the Georgian city of Bath is easily reached by car, bus or train.

Tea and coffee making facilities, televisions and washbasins are in the rooms.

Nearby are Harvest wholefood shop at 11 Gloucester Road and the vegetarian restaurant One Stop Thali Cafe in Montpelier.

Montpelier

Vegetarian guest house

132 Cotham Brow
Cotham
Bristol BS6 6AE
England

Tel and Fax:
0117–9247 398

www.arches-hotel.co.uk
ml@arches-hotel.co.uk

Train station: Bristol Temple Meads, 2km, then bus or taxi.

Open: all year, except Christmas and new year.

Directions: 1km north up A38 (from Broadmead) turn left at first mini roundabout. Hotel is 100m on left.

Parking: on street

Children over 6 welcome

Pets welcome with prior notice

MC, Visa, Diners

No smoking throughout

Basca House

Elegant Victorian house retaining many original features. The house has a peaceful atmosphere and is situated in a quiet tree lined street in a residential area, but is only one mile from the city centre. There are two single rooms from £27 per night, one single ensuite from £35 and two twin rooms from £45 per room per night.

There is an excellent veggie/vegan spread for breakfast including fresh fruit, fruit juice, cereal or muesli and soya yoghurt followed by veggie sausages, baked beans, mushrooms and herbed tomatoes with wholemeal bread and home made preserves. As one of the proprietors is Indian, a more adventurous breakfast may also be offered which includes spicy potatoes and dahl. Vegan muesli, vegan margarine and soya milk are available.

Dinner is not offered but there are numerous restaurants in town offering veggie food. Bristol offers a lively night life with many clubs, theatres, music venues and pubs. During the day, take a look at the famous Clifton Suspension Bridge, the symbol of Bristol, and visit the Create Environment Centre, or one of the many cathedrals, museums or art galleries. You could explore further afield and visit the Cheddar Caves and Gorge or Wookey Hole in Wells.

Basca House is about five minutes walk from two yoga centres and a shop selling Indian clothing and artefacts. Scoopaway wholefood store is at 113 Gloucester Road.

All rooms have televisions, radio alarms and tea and coffee making facilities.

Bishopston

Omnivorous bed and breakfast

19 Broadway Road
Bishopston
Bristol
BS7 8ES
England

Tel: 0117-9422 182

Train Station:
Bristol Temple Meads,
1.5 miles, then taxi or bus

Open: all year, except Christmas to New Year period

Directions:
At the big roundabout by the bus station and Debenhams, take A38 Stokes Croft, signposted Redland/Cotham (this road has a building over it, go under the building). Continue on this road, go under the railway arches, bear right at next junction and just before Texaco petrol station turn left into Berkeley Road. Go up the hill and take the first left into Broadway Road.

Parking: on street with no restrictions

Children welcome

High chairs available

No smoking throughout

Cafe Maitreya

Vegetarian restaurant off the M32, very much into organic and fair trade with no GM. This is the kind of place Bristol has needed for years.

The menu changes regularly. Here are some examples:

Daytime menu till 3pm (week ends only) full English cooked veggie or vegan breakfast £5.25 or £5.95.

Lunch: soup £3.50, Bubble and Squeak, £4.50–£4.95, majoram rarebit £5.25, toasted brushetta £4.75, ciabatta sandwiches with various fillings, from £3 take away or £3.50 eat in. Maitreya Mezze £5.95, includes sourdough bread, olives and a choice of three side dishes from paprika/basil hummous, beetroot with walnut dressing, oven roasted veg and Moroccan spiced quinoa.

Evening menu: two courses for £13.45 and three for £16.95, excluding service. A 10% service charge is added to tables of more than 10 people. Start with soup, cauliflowers cornets, sauteed carrot and almond cakes, crisp nori roulade or watercress and hazelnut salad. Main courses include ravioli, saute brazil nut rissoles, summer pithivier or red chilli laksa. Desserts such as ginger cheesecake, baked raspberry spring roll and warm chocolate and pecan pudding. Dairy free cream available.

Freshly squeezed juices are £2.50 and smoothies £2.75–£3.20. Other drinks 75p–£2.60, soya milk is readily available.

All wines and beers are organic and most are vegan. House vegan wine £8.95 bottle white, £8.95 red, glass 250ml £3.25. Vegan beers and cider £2.25–2.75.

Easton

Vegetarian restaurant

89 St Mark's Road
Easton
Bristol BS5 6HY

Tel: 0117–9510 100

www.cafemaitreya.co.uk
thesnug@
cafemaitreya.co.uk

Open:
Tue–Sat 18.45–21.45
also Fri 11–15.00, Sat 11–16.00, Sun 11–17.00

Directions:
Near M32 Stapleton Road. From the city centre, go out along Old Market, head towards M32 but veer off onto Stapleton Road and cross over M32.
Take bus 48 or 49 from town, get off on Stapleton Road and walk down Berwick Road.

No smoking throughout

Visa, MC

Kids menu

Reservations advised evenings

Licensed with food only

Voted by Yaoh's Vegan Guide to Bristol as Best Restaurant for a Vegan Meal, and Best Vegetarian Restaurant in the UK by the Vegetarian Society.

Royce Rolls Wholefood Cafe

Vegetarian cafe

The Corn Exchange, St Nicholas Market,
Corn St BS1 1JQ. Tel: 0117-9824 228
Open: Mon–Fri 07.30–16.00,
Sat 09.30–16.00.

Friendly central vegetarian take–away with café seating too. Savoury snacks, tea, coffee, flapjacks and cakes. Filled rolls include brie and avocado, various cheeses, houmous with watercress and cucumber, and tomato with olive oil, organic sea salt on white overnight rise bread. Vegan and gluten free options available. Soya milk offered. Locally sourced ingredients. No smoking throughout. Cash only.

Falafel King

Vegetarian take–away

City Centre, opposite the Watershed arts centre. Tel: 07855 715676
Open: every day from midday:
Sun–Mon till 19.00 winter, 20.00 summer;
Tue –22.00, Wed–Thu–24.00, Fri–Sat –03.00

Falafels, hummous and pitta. Look for the purple trailer.

Big Banana Juice Bar

Juice Bar

21–22 St Nicholas Market, Corn St, Bristol
Tel: 0117-907 7804

Holland & Barrett

Health food shop

83 The Horsefair, BS1 3JP
Tel: 0117-9293 170

Unit 2 Odeon Development
Broadmead, City Centre BS1 3DN
Tel: 0117-926 0557

Krishna's Inn

Indian Vegetarian restaurant

4 Byron Place, Triangle South, Clifton,
Bristol BS8 1JT. Tel: 0117-927 6864
Open every day 12–15.00, 18–23.00,
Fri–Sat –24.00,

Brand new South Indian vegetarian restaurant and take–away with a bar.

Wagamama

Omnivorous Japanese restaurant

63 Queens Road,
Clifton, Bristol, BS8 1QL
Tel: 0117-9221 188
www.wagamama.com
Open: Mon–Sat 12–23.00, Sun 12.30–22.00

See entry in Manchester for menu.

Fresh & Wild

Organic supermarket & veggie cafe

85 Queen's Road BS8 1QS
Tel: 0117-9105 930
Open: Mon–Fri: 8–21.00, Sat 8–20.00,
Sun 12–17.00

Big wholefood shop with a great cafe and juice bar, by the Triangle.

Holland & Barrett

Health food shop

21 Clifton Down Shopping Centre
Whiteladies Road BS8 2NN
Tel: 0117-9738 188

Wild Oats

Wholefood shop

9–11 Lower Redland Road, Redland, Bristol
Tel: 0117-9431 967

Big shop. Specialists in macrobiotics.

WEST

Bristol

369

Blue Juice

Juice bar & vegetarian cafe/take-away

39 Cotham Hill, Cotham
Tel: 0117-9734 800
Open: Mon-Fri 08.30-16.00, Sat 9-16.00,
Sun closed

Juices, wraps and salads.

Tiffins

Omnivorous Indian take-away

151 St Michael's Hill (top end)
Tel: 0117-973 4834
Open: Mon-Sat 12-20.00, closed Sun and
some bank holidays

Always about seven veggie dishes, six
kinds of lentils, four or five pulses. £3
for a portion of veg curry, rice £1.50.

Earthbound

Organic health food shop

8 Abbotsford Road, Cotham
Tel: 0117-9042 260

Almost entirely organic health food
shop with 90% vegan produce.

One Stop Thali Cafe

Vegetarian Indian restaurant

12a York Road, Montpelier BS6 5PZ
Tel: 0117-9426 687
Open: every day 18.30-23.30

Located between Arches Hotel and the
city centre. Thalis with rice, dahl, curry
and salad are £6.50. Bring your own
alcohol.

Harvest

Wholefood shop near Arches hotel

11 Gloucester Road
Tel: 0117-9425 997

Riverside Garden Centre Cafe

Vegetarian cafe

Clift House Road, Southville, Bristol
Tel: 0117-966 7535 ext 64
Open: Mon-Sat 9.30-17.00 Summer (Winter
16.30), Sun 11-16.30

Vegetarian cafe inside a garden centre
by the river, near the away entrance of
Ashton Gate Bristol City socccer ground.
Salads, tapas, baguettes, home made
soup. Hot dishes £5.50 such as vegan
Mexican hotpot, bangers and mash.
Wide range of cakes and flapjacks
including vegan. Soya milk available for
lattes. Lots of fair trade products,
organic veg.

Bristol Vegan Fayre

Sat 10th - Sun 11th June 2006
10:00 - 18:00

at the L-Shed, Princess Wharf, Wapping Rd.
www.veganbristol.makessense.co.uk
www.yaoh.co.uk

Huge annual festival with dozens of
exhibitors, food demos, entertainers,
talks and the chance to have fun and
make friends. Come and meet Veggie
Guides here in person! Organised by
Bristol based hemp foods and vegan
cosmetics company Yaoh.

Gloucestershire

Cheltenham

Lawn Hotel

Vegetarian bed and breakfast

5 Pittvilee Lawn, Cheltenham GL52 2BE
Tel: 01242-526638

Listed Regency town house 5 minutes wak from the centre on the edge of a park. 2 singles £25–27, 2 single en suite £30–35, 2 doubles en suite £35–45 (one with four poster bed), 1 twin en suite £30 (or £35 single), all prices per person. Under 5 £5, 10–15 £10, baby free if you bring cot. Family room available with two Z-beds. TV in rooms, some with DVD. Art gallery and studio in drawing room. Local organic produce. English Tourism 4 diamonds. AA 4 diamonds.

Newland

Omnivorous Vietnamese and Chinese restaurant

119 The Promenade, Cheltenham
Tel: 01242-525346
Open: Mon–Sat 18–22.00, closed Sun

Set vegetarian menu £13 for veg spring roll and crispy seaweed followed by stir-fry beancurd, mixed veg with satay sauce, veg with cashewnuts, fried rice.

Indus Tandoori

Omnivorous Indian restaurant

226 Bath Road, Cheltenham
(5 minutes by car from the centre)
Tel: 01242-516676
Open: every day 12–14.30, 18–23.30
(Fri–Sat till midnight)

Lots of vegetarian starters £2.75–3.50. Mixed vegetable curry, masala, jalfrezi, chana masala, balti dishes such as mixed veg masala, mushroom, aloo £5.40–5.95. Sunday lunch buffet with many vegetarian dishes £7.95, children under 8 £3.95. Smoking and no smoking sections. MC, Visa. Children welcome, no high chairs. Wine £8.75–14.95 bottle, £2.40 glass.

Sala Thai

Omnivorous Thai restaurant

39 Rodney Road, Cheltenham
(off the High Street near Barclays and Lloyds)
Tel: 01242-232155
Open: Thu–Sat 18.30–22.30

Vegetarian set menu for two or more people £15 each: There are more dishes on the a la carte menu. Wine £9.99, glass £2.75. No smoking. MC, Visa. Not disabled friendly as it's in a basement with 130 year old stairs.
When this one's closed you can try Thai Bistro in Well Walk, near the Library and Museum. Tel: 01242-244 590.
There are also some pizza restaurants in Cheltenham. The Orange Tree vegetarian restaurant closed May 2005.

Cirencester

Organic Farm Shop and Cafe

Vegetarian cafe and omnivorous shop

Abbey Home Farm Burford Rd, Cirencester GL7 5HF, On B4425, 2 miles north of Cirencester. Tel: 01285-640441
Cafe: Tue–Wed 9–16.30, Thu–Fri 9–17.00, Sat 9–15.30. Shop: Tue–Wed 9–17.00, Thu–Fri 9–18.30, Sat 9–16.00
www.theorganicfarmshop.co.uk

Organic farm shop and cafe in an 1800 acre organic farm with 15 acre garden, lots of small wodlands, but beware they also have livestock. Veggie dishes use what's in season in the garden such as Thai green curry, fennel and lentil bake, spicy potato cakes with salsa. Always a vegan dish of the day. 4 or 5 salads such as quinoa, couscous, brown rice.

Organic wine £2.95 glass, £11 bottle. Local Arkell's ale £3.75 a bottle. Terrace. Well behaved children welcome, 2 high chairs and play area in garden. No smoking. MC, Visa.

The certified organic shop sells organic yoga and baby clothes, bed and table linen, beauty care and household products such as Bio-D, books.

Also a greenfield camp site, £2 per night per person, no tent charge. Tap and compost loo but no showers. Yurt for rent and simple one room hut with veranda by pond with woodburner and double room to rent – see website.

Gloucester Guildhall Cafe

90% vegetarian cafe

Guildhall Arts Centre, 23 Eastgate St, Gloucester GL1 1NS. Tel: 01452-396378
Open: Tue-Sat 10-15.00, closed Jul-Aug

Everything veggie and home made (except ham sandwiches). Soup and roll £2.25,. Mains £3.75-3.95 such as red beans and rice, pasta provencale, Mediterranean potatoes. (Toasted) sandwiches from £1.60. Jacket potatoes from £2.25. Hot chocolate fudge cake. Coffees but no soya milk. House wine £9 bottle, £2.30 glass. Children welcome, high chairs. No smoking. No credit cards (maybe Autumn 2005).

The Haus

Omnivorous pub-restaurant

56 Westgate Street, Gloucester GL1 2NF
Tel: 01452-525359
Open: bar food every day 10.30-21.30
www.thehaus.co.uk

Nice place to eat by the cathedral. Meaty restaurant but the bar food includes falafels, tempura vegetables, garlic mushrooms, panini.

Ruskin Mill Arts & Crafts

Organic cafe and craft shop

Old Bristol Road, Nailsworth GL6 0LA
Tel: 01453-837 537 www.ruskin-mill.org.uk
Open: Tue-Sat 10-16.00, Sun 11-16.00, bank holidays 15-18.00

Organic café, serving vegetarian and fish dishes for £4.80, with salad. Vegan and gluten free dishes available. No smoking anywhere in the centre. Cash and cheque only. Organic veg and craft shop open Tue-Sat 10-17.00. Gallery of contemporary local artists open every day 10-17.00, except Christmas day, and sometimes they have environ-mental exhibitions. For a list of regular events, see website.

Mother Nature

Vegetarian cafe

2 Bedford Street, Stroud GL5 1AY
Tel: 01453-758 202
Open: Mon-Sat 9-17.30, closed Sun

Vegetarian café which sometimes has vegan food. Fresh salads every day. Main meals from £4. They use organic fruis and vegetables. Soya milk is available. Non smoking. Visa, MC.

Holland & Barrett

Health food shop

37 Regent Arcade, Cheltenham
Tel: 01242-528 749

3 St. Michael's Buildings, Gloucester
Tel: 01452-311 281

24 Crickdale Street, Cirencester GL7 1JH
Tel: 01285-641068

Herefordshire

On the border with Wales, western Herefordshire is dominated by Welsh-sounding place names, glorious views of the nearby Brecon Beacons, Golden Valley and Black Mountains, and an abundance of veggie-friendly hosts in and around the Hay-on-Wye area.

At the western end of the Golden Valley is Haie Barn, a vegetarian bed and breakfast with spectacular views and ample walking opportunities. Explore the Brecon Beacons and Radnorshire Hills and the second-hand book shops in nearby Hay-on-Wye.

Stop in at Bredwardine Lodge, 8 miles from Hay-on-Wye, where you can opt for a spacious double or deluxe Oriental four-poster room.

In Hereford, a must-do is Cafe @ All Saints, a gourmet vegetarian restaurant in a restored medieval church.

Bramlea Bed & Breakfast

Small vegetarian bed and breakfast offering friendly personal service. There are three rooms: one single, one twin and one family all costing £20 per person per night.

Breakfast is fruit and soya yoghurt with a selection of cereals followed by a full cooked veggie breakfast. Special diets are catered for and they have soya milk, vegan margarine, vegan muesli and veggie sausages.

Dinner is not offered although may be arranged for single vegetarian or vegan females on request. Bramlea is a ten minute walk from the cente of Leominster where there are hotels, restaurants, pubs and cafes which offer vegetarian food. There is a selection of menus at the house and they can book a table for you. There are also a few health food shops where you can pick up picnic supplies.

Leominster has a medieval priory church and boasts many antique shops, gardens, National Trust Properties, specialist nurseries and historic buildings in the area. Local artists display and sell their works. The cities of Hereford, Ludlow and Shrewsbury are nearby as are the medieval villages of Woebley and Eardesland.

The bungalow is suitable for people with limited mobility (using a walking frame or stick). The narrow doorways make it unsuitable for wheelchairs.

Tea and coffee making facilities are available in the rooms. There is a TV lounge.

Winners of Green Business Award (Bronze) and Wildlife Action Award (Silver).

Vegetarian bed and breakfast

Barons Cross Road
Leominster
Herefordshire HR6 8RW
England

Tel and Fax:
01568-613 406

www.bramleabandb.co.uk
lesbramlea@netlineuk.net

Train station: Leominster, 1.5 miles, they will collect you

Open:
1 March to 31 October

Directions:
Bramlea is one mile from the centre of Leminster situated on the A44 towards Wales. They are directly opposite a Safeway super-market.

Parking:
three off street spaces

Children aged three and over welcome

Pets welcome

Smoking outside only

WEST

Gloucestershire

Bredwardine Lodge

Listed Victorian Gothic building built in 1857, formerly a school but now a family home and vegetarian bed and breakfast. There are two spacious rooms; one double at £50 per night and one family (with an oriental four poster bed) at £60 per night.

Breakfast is served in the library and is organic as far as possible.   A typical breakfast comprises juice, cereal or muesli, and fruits followed by tomatoes, mushrooms, baked beans, fresh coffee and a variety of teas. Rice milk, oat milk and soya milk is offered on request, as well as vegan margarine. Vegan breakfast is also available on request and special diets can be catered for.

Dinner is not usually offered but can be if specially requested.   The local pub serves home cooked meals with veggie options.

The house is set in a quiet garden amidst fields, hills and woodland.   Alongside the house is a public footpath and Bredwardine is on the Wye Valley walk. On the hill above the village is Arthur's Stone, a prehistoric burial chamber, from which there are splendid views of the Black Mountains and the Golden Valley. Five minutes down the hill is the River Wye. Bredwardine Bridge is popular in summer with people sun bathing, swimming, paddling and canoeing.

Bredwardine Lodge is eight miles from Hay-on-Wye, the second hand book town which has a literary festival each May. The ancient cathedral city of Hereford is twelve miles away.

Children are welcome and they have toys and a small cot-bed. No TV but there is plenty to read. No smoking throughout.

Vegetarian bed and breakfast

Bredwardine
Herefordshire HR3 6BZ
England

Tel: 01981-500 113

Train station:
Hereford, 12 miles

Open: all year

Directions:
On the edge of the rural village of Bredwardine off the A4352 between Hereford and Hay-on-Wye.

Parking: available

Children welcome

Toys provided

Arabic dance lessons and Tai Chi available in the old school hall

No smoking throughout

WEST Herefordshire

Haie Barn

Vegetarian bed and breakfast in a barn conversion at the western end of the Golden Valley. There is one double ensuite room with a king sized bed which may also serve as a twin (from £24 per person per night), and one double with private bathroom (£21-£25 per person). Single occupancy is £25-£30 per night.

Try the Big Barn breakfast of mushrooms, tomatoes, baked beans, a choice of six varieties of veggie sausages and potato wedges. Alternatively, there is always a daily special, for example buckwheat pancakes with fruit compote. There are always five other breakfasts available in addition to fruit, cereal and toast. Ingredients are sourced locally wherever possible. Vegan margarine and soya milk are available. Special diets are catered for. Let them know your needs when booking.

Dinner is £15 for two courses and £18 for three courses and could be carrot and orange soup, mushroom and chestnut cobbler with seasonal veg and for dessert, poached pears on a pastry bed. Nearby restaurants also cater for veggies.

The area boasts many walks including the Wye Valley walk and the Offas Dyke walk. For solitude explore the Brecon Beacons and Radnorshire Hills. Spend days at Hay-on-Wye browsing the many second-hand book shops, or visit the the historic city of Hereford. Lovers of gardens, historic houses, country churches, recreational walking and other outdoor activities will all find something of interest in the area.

There is a guest lounge. Rooms have bath robes, hair dryers, wash basins, TVs, radio alarms, and tea and coffee making facilities.

Vegetarian bed and breakfast

The Bage
Dorstone
Herefordshire HR3 5SU
England

Tel: 01497-831 729

www.golden-valley.co.uk
/haiebarn
goodfood@haie-barn.co.uk

Train station: Hereford,
16 miles, then bus or taxi

Open: March-end October

Adults only

No smoking throughout

Directions: On the B4348 you will pass the road sign for Dorstone, followed by a sharp left bend. Do not enter the village but continue on this road, passing St. Faith's church on your left, for 1 1/2 miles. Haie Barn is the first habitation on your left as you approach the hamlet of the Bage.

Parking: plenty of off road parking available

English Tourist Council Four Diamond & Silver Awards

Herefordshire Nature Trust Growing Green Tourism Silver Award

Green Tourism Business

The Old Post Office

Vegetarian bed and breakfast

Llanigon, Hay-on-Wye, Powys HR3 5QA,
Tel: 01497-820 008
www.oldpost-office.co.uk

Veggie bed & breakfast in an outstandingly beautiful area with the Brecon Beacons national park on the doorstep. Right on the Wales and Herefordshire border. Full details in the Wales section, page 458.

Oscars

Omnivorous restaurant

High Town, Hay-on-Wye HR3 5AE
Tel: 01497-821 193
Open: Mon-Sun 10.30-17.00

Omnivorous restaurant that typically serves 3 vegetarian main dishes daily, each at £7.50-8.00. They usually have something vegan or can adapt, but best to check. No smoking. Visa, MC. Licensed.

Hay Wholefoods

Wholefood shop

1 Lion Street, Hay on Wye
Tel: 01497-820 708
Open: Mon-Sat 9.30-17.30, Sun closed

Wholefood shop with some take away such as sandwiches, soup, salads, jacket potatoes, but you need to get there early. They also have vegan ice cream.

Nutters

Vegetarian restaurant

2 Capuchin Yard, Off Church Street
Hereford HR1 2LT
Tel: 01432-277 447
Open: Mon-Sat 9.00-18.00, Sun closed

Vegetarian restaurant with several vegan options, including 3 main dishes which start at £4.50. Soup £3.25. There is a large selection of home made cakes which also includes vegan choices 95p-£1.60. Wine is £1.95 for a glass with food. Non smoking, but outside area where smoking is permitted. No credit cards. Children welcome, high chairs.

Cafe 47 at Harveststore

Wholefood cafe and shop

47 Eign Gate, Hereford HR4 0AB
Tel: 01432-268 209
Open: Mon-Sat 9.00-17.30,
also pavement café March-Oct

Wholefood café and take-away, with 75% of the menu vegetarian. Always something vegan too, and they have soya milk. Sandwiches from £2.50, baked potato £3.75 to eat in, main courses such as curries £3.95, vegan burgers £2.50. The shop sells vegan ice-cream. Non smoking. Visa, MC. 5% discount to Vegetarian and Vegan Society members.

Salad Bowl

Health food shop

30 Union Street, Hereford HR1 2BT
Tel: 01432-355 712
Open: Mon-Sat 9.00-17.30, closed Sun

Lots of vegetarian dishes £2.10, mostly cheesey, but vegans could have baked potato and salad from £1.60.

WEST

Herefordshire

379

Cafe@All Saints

Bill Sewell's modern English veggie cafe is in an award winning refurbishment of a superb medieval church.

All food, even the bread, is freshly made on the premises. The menu changes regularly but always includes a hot special for around £5.65, such as pasta with roast Mediterranean vegetables or basil and puy lentils in a balsamic vinaigrette. Generally speaking, if the main course is vegan, the soup contains dairy products, and vice-versa.

Soup £2.45, such as spiced tomato comes with an olive oil roll or a slice of one of their breads.

Salad combination £3.65, contains mixed leaves, broccoli, carrots and mint with parsley, olive oil and lemon dressing; and wholegrain rice, puy lentils, herbs and fresh vegetables in a soy balsamic vinaigrette.

Sandwiches £3.50-4.10, such as roast mushroom and roast tofu, are made on their own breads baked each morning.

Cakes, tarts and puddings, 95p-£2.10 such as flapjacks, scones and brownies are available. Ask for vegan options.

Organic local apple juice, £1.25, freshly squeezed orange or pink grapefruit, £1.25, spring water or home made lemonade or elderflower cordial 95p.

Beer and cider £1.90-£2.50. Wine £2.55 glass, £8.75 bottle.

WEST

Herefordshire

Vegetarian gourmet cafe

All Saints Church
High St
Hereford
HR4 9AA

Tel: 01432 370 415

www.cafeatallsaints.co.uk
billgrub@aol.com

Mon-Sat
8.30-17.30,
closed Sundays

10 min. walk from Hereford station

No smoking

Licensed

Children's portions and high chairs

Outside seating area

Switch, Visa, MC

Fodder

Wholefood shop

26–27 Church Street, Hereford
Tel: 01432–358 171
Open: Mon–Sat 9–17.30, Sun closed

Veggie wholefood shop with take awy
sandwiches, pasties and Tofutti vegan
ice cream.

Holland & Barrett

Health food shop

1–2 Commercial Street, Hereford
Tel: 01568–614 147\

Organic Options

Wholefood shop

15a Broad Street, Leominster
Tel: 01568–612 154

Nitty Gritty

Wholefood shop

24 West Street, Leominster
Tel: 01568–611 600

Oxfordshire

Oxford, the quintessential college town, is a high priority for most visitors to England. It is one of the few places left in the country where you can still watch a procession of graduates draped in traditional gowns veering towards the Sheldonian Theatre or hear the sound of choristers singing Latin from the Magdalen Tower. Although some of the romanticism is tainted by big awkward tour buses, Oxford still holds a special allure. There are plenty of parks and colleges to pop into for peaceful sanctuary from the bustling centre.

To explore Oxford, try one of the many walking tours offered by the Tourist Information Centre, or grab a map and give it a go yourself. Blue Badge Guides leave the T.I.C. several times daily throughout the year and visit 19 places (fewer if colleges are closed, i.e. during the term). Tours last approximately 2 hours and the pace is leisurely. People using wheelchairs are welcome to join any tour.

Oxford University and City Tours: daily tours from the Oxford Information Centre at 11.00am and 2.00pm, with extra tours at busy times. £6.00 per adult and £3.00 per child (6–16yrs).

Inspector Morse Tours: Tours depart on Saturdays at 1.30pm. £6.50 per adult and £3.50 per child (6–16yrs) for a limited period. To confirm departures in advance phone +44 (0) 1865 726871.

Ghost Tours: Departing from the Oxford Information Centre, this tour of Oxford's ghoulish and gory past lasts for about one and a half hours. Tours operate on Friday and Saturday evenings at 8pm June–September, and 31 October (Halloween). £5 per adult, £3 per child (6–16yrs).

Christ Church Tours: Saturdays, leaving from the Oxford Information Centre. £7 per adult, £3.50 per child (6–16yrs).

Highfield West

Vegetarian bed and breakfast

188 Cumnor Hill, Oxford OX2 9PJ
Tel: 01865–863 007
highfieldwest@msn.com
Open: all year except Christmas and New Year

Two and a half miles west of the centre on the western edge of Oxford. One family room £85, if full; 1 double and 1 twin £60; 2 singles £35. All are ensuite except the singles which share a bathroom. No smoking house and garden. Cash and cheque only. Children welcome, high chair. Dogs by arrangement one at a time.

Cotswold House

Omnivorous bed and breakfast

363 Banbury Road, Oxford, OX2 7PL
Tel/Fax: 01865–310 558
Open: all year
Email: d.r.walker@talk21.com
Train Station: Oxford, 2 1/2 miles

Two single ensuites £52 and £58, two double ensuites and one twin ensuite £80 per room, and two family rooms £100 for three people.
Vegans catered for by prior request. Children six and over only. Parking available. No pets. No smoking throughout. MC, Visa.

Gables Guest House

Omnivorous guest house

6 Cumnor Hill, Oxford, OX2 9HA
Tel: 01865–862 153
Fax: 01865–864 054
www.oxfordcity.co.uk/accom/gables
Email: stay@gables–oxford.co.uk
Train Station: Oxford, 1 mile
Open: all year except Christmas and New Year

Two singles £38–£40 per night, two doubles and two twins £58–£64 per room per night, all with ensuite bathrooms. Special diets cater for, but you must specify at the time of booking. Children welcome. No pets. No smoking throughout.

Oxford Youth Hostel

Omnivorous hostel

2a Botley Road, Oxford, OX2 0AB
Tel: 01865–727 275/0870–770 5970
Open: all year
www.yha.org.uk
oxford@yha.org.uk
Train Station: Oxford, just behind the hostel

Twin rooms £46 per room per night, or £19.50 (£14.40 under 18's) per person per night in a four bed or six bed dorm. All rooms are ensuite. Dorms are segregated by sex unless filled with a group of friends. Lockers and hanging space are available.
Vegans and those on special diets can be catered for with advanced notice. Evening meals available, but they also have a self catering kitchen. Internet access. 24 hour access. Disabled access. Credit cards accepted. Smoking allowed in some areas.

Forge Cottage

Omnivorous bed and breakfast

East End, North Leigh, Woodstock OX8 6PZ
Tel: 01993–881 120
www.country–accom.co.uk/forge–cottage

B&B from £27 per person. One of the family members is vegan, so they always have dairy-free products and vegan sausages. Cooked breakfasts are served. Home grown organic fruit in the breakfast salad and home made jams.

Nature's Harvest

Health food shop

6 Castle Centre, Banbury, Oxon OX16 8LR
Open: Mon–Sat 9–17.00. Tel: 01295 253208

Health foods, alternative remedies, essential oils, but no take–away. Chiller with tofu and non–dairy ice–cream.

Oxford restaurants

The Magic Cafe

Vegetarian cafe

110 Magdalen Road, Oxford OX4 1RQ
Tel: 01865–794 604
Open: Mon–Sat 10.00–18.00, Sun closed

Spacious vegetarian café featuring cheerful décor and art exhibitions. Always vegan options available and you can have lunch for under £5. Non smoking. No credit cards. Great New Age bookshop next door. Live music Saturday lunchtime. Children welcome.

The Garden

Pub with vegetarian kitchen

at The Gardeners Arms pub
Plantation Road, Jericho, Oxford
Tel: 01865–559 814
www.thegarden-oxford.co.uk
Open: Wed– Fri 12–15.00, 17–21.00
Sat 12–21.00, Sun 12–18.00

All the food here is veggie, vegan dishes are marked (v) and most can be made vegan. Bar drinks may not be veggie or vegan, please check with bar staff. Ciabatta sandwiches £4.95 served with side salad and veggie and vegan burgers come with fries, toppings and dressings for £5.65. Various salads from £4.95–£5.95 and 9 mains including full English breakfast, Thai green curry, chilli non-carne and vegan vegetable korma, £4.95–£6.95.

Alpha Bar

Mainly vegetarian take–away

89 The Covered Market, Oxford OX1 4LU
Tel: 01865–250 499. info@alphabar.co.uk
Open: Mon–Sat 10.00–16.00, closed Sun

Mostly vegetarian take–away in the covered market. Sandwiches are £2.60–£2.90 according to the type of bread. All kinds of mostly vegan spreads, falafels, tofu and tempeh. Salads £2.90–£3.90 and sometimes soups in the winter. They serve organic drinks, and vegan cakes for £1, such as banana and apple muffins, brownies, sugar free sweets and vegan apricot flapjacks.

The Beat Cafe

Almost vegetarian cafe-bar

Little Clarendon Street, Oxford OX1 2HS
Tel: 01865–553 543
Open: every day 12.00–23.00 (Sun 22.30)

Almost completely vegetarian upstairs café with a bar downstairs, in a trendy street in posh Oxford. Food ranges from £3.50–4.00 and includes such dishes as curried rice salad, veg couscous, falafels, tortillas, burgers and veggie BLTs. Other dishes are soya dogs £2, fries with skins £2.50 and Covent Garden soup with baguette £3.50. Smoothies £2.95, juices £1.50 and lots of teas £1.60. Smoking throughout.

Chutneys Indian Brasserie

Omnivorous South Indian restaurant

36 St Michaels Street, Oxford OX1 2EB
Tel: 01865–724 241
Open: Mon–Sat 12–14.00, 18–23.00;
Sun closed

Near Gloucester Green coach station. Lots of veggie/vegan food. Licenced.

Meltz

Omnivorous cafe

8 St Michael's Street, Oxford OX1 2DU
Tel: 01865-202 016
Open: every day 10-22.00 or later

Omnivorous café that often stays open as late as midnight. Starters such as garlic bread, hummous, £2.25-3.75. Pasta or salad £7.

The Nosebag Restaurant

Omnivorous restaurant

6-8 St Michael's Street, Oxford OX1 2DH
Tel: 01865-721 033
Open: Mon-Thu 9.30-22.00,
Fri-Sat 9.30-22.30, Sun 9.30-21.00

Upstairs omnivorous café with several veggie and vegan dishes, over a Malaysian restaurant which also has veggie food. Dishes include soup with bread £3.50 and chickpea and roast aubergine provencale £6.75 with rice and green salad. Lots of cakes, two vegan including the pear crumble cake from the famous Cake Scoffer cookbook, the dessert bible of quite a few cafes. Beer £2.50, wine £8.50 for a bottle and £2.20 a glass. Non-smoking. Children welcome, six high chairs.

Uhuru Wholefoods

Wholefood shop

48 Cowley Road, Oxford OX4 1HZ
Open: Mon-Fri 10-18.00, Sat 9.30-17.30
Tel: 01865-248 249

Independent wholefood shop east of the city centre. Well stocked with a range of ethical products and very pro-vegan. Take-away counter with pasties etc, some of which are vegan.

The Crooked Billet

Omnivorous restaurant

Newlands Lane, Stoke Row,
Henley-on-Thames RG9 5PU
Tel: 01491-681 048
www.thecrookedbillet.co.uk
Open: Mon-Sat 12-14.30, 19-22.00,
Sun 12-22.00

Up-market restaurant, close to Reading, with a separate vegetarian menu. Lunch menu £12.95 for two courses or £15.95 for three. Evening anything up to £35 each with wine: starters £5.95-8.00, mains £12, desserts £5-6.80 though none vegan. House wine £12.95 bottle, £4-5 a glass. Smoking throughout. Well behaved children welcome but no reductions. Car park. Reservations recommended for evenings. Long hours at weekends if you want lunch at 4pm on a Sunday. Visa, MC.

Holland & Barrett

Health food shop

6 Golden Cross Arcade, Cornmarket Street
Oxford OX1
Tel: 01865-792 102

6 Suffolk House, Banbury Road,
Summertown, Oxford
Tel: 01865-552 523

100 London Road, Headington, Oxford
Tel: 01865-764 578

Unit 17, Westgate Centre, Oxford
Tel: 01865-249 219

6 Castle Centre, Banbury
Tel: 01295-277 909

Unit 15, The Square,
Templars Shopping Centre, Cowley
Tel: 01865-772 473

47 Market Place, Wantage
Tel: 01235-768 965

The main attraction in Shropshire is the Ironbridge Gorge, the group of villages that was instrumental in fueling the Industrial Revolution. This area, once a bed of coalfields, is now a sprawl of fascinating museums offering visitors a comprehensive industrial history of Great Britain. In addition, the surrounding countryside draws in crowds of walkers and hikers. Olivers vegetarian bistro in Ironbridge is a great place to eat out.

Ludlow, the site of the beautiful red sandstone Ludlow Castle, has a traditional open-air market every Monday, Friday and Saturday and a Local Producers Market on the second Thursday of each month. If you'd rather be pampered than picnic, head for the lavish Malayasian Nonya cuisine available to non-residents at Mynd House in the hamlet of Little Stretton, but be sure to book.

Shropshire

Vegetarian Guides – Links

www.vegetarianguides.co.uk/links

Don't travel abroad without checking the Links page of the
Vegetarian Guides' website. Here's a small selection.

Americas
www.vegetarianismo.com.br/guia/guia.html – Brazil
www.veghawaii.org
www.bayareaveg.org/ug – San Francisco

Asia
www.i-v-s.org – Indonesia
www.jpvs.org/p2/eat1.html – Japan Restaurants (Japanese)
www.vegetarian-society.org – Singapore

Australasia
www.veg-soc.org – Vegetarian Australia

Europe
www.vegan.at – Austria
www.vegetarian.be – Belgium
www.budaveg.com – Budapest
www.vegetariani.it – Italy
www.veganstockholm.se/lang_eng – Stockholm
www.vegetarismus.ch – Switzerland

International
www.ivu.org – International Vegetarian Union
www.FreeTranslation.com – Paste blocks of text for translation

Nutrition & Recipes
www.veganoutreach.org
www.vegsource.com
www.vegweb.com
www.fatfreevegan.com

Great Travel Sites
www.whichbudget.com – European cheap flights
www.nationalrail.co.uk – British trains
www.eurolines.com – Coach travel in Europe
www.nationalexpress.com – Coach travel in Britain
www.megabus.com – Ridiculously cheap coach travel

www.vegetarianguides.co.uk/links – mapping the world for veggies

Mynd House

Omnivorous hotel in a 1902 house in "Little Switzerland" in the quiet hamlet of Little Stretton, close to Church Stretton and Cardingmill Valley. The village has pubs and a thatched church.

All rooms en suite, and prices are per person: one single £40-50; 3 doubles £35-50, one with sitting room, a 4-poster bed and double bath spa; two twins £35-45; and one family room for £100-120. No single supplement except in deluxe rooms.

Cereals and cooked veggie breakfasts offered. They have vegan margarine, soya milk and yoghurt.

For residents the evening meal is £18, whilst non-residents can pre-book 3-courses for £20.50 and 2-courses for £17.50. They specialise in Western and Malaysian Chinese (Nonya) cuisine to add a touch of spice to your holiday. 5 starters, 3 vegan, include aubergine melts, Malaysian salad, Mediterranean vegetable tart, vegetarian 'duck' pancake; 5 mains, 3 vegan, such as claypot vegetables with shitake and chinese five spice, spinach and mushroom filo bundle, Mediterranean vegetables Wellington, mixed vegetables stir fried with rice noodles.

The hotel has a bar and the lounge has a cosy log fire for winter evenings. All rooms have remote control TVs, hairdryers, tea and coffee making facilities, and adjustable central heating.

Nearby attractions include Long Mynd National Trust, Shrewsbury with its abbey and Tudor buildings, Ludlow's 900 year old castle, 13th century Stokesay castle (English Heritage) and Ironbridge world heritage site. Outdoor activities range from walking the Shropshire hills to hillside golfing. Acorn wholefood restaurant and coffee shop in Church Stretton.

Omnivorous hotel

Ludlow Road
Little Stretton
Church Stretton
Shropshire SY6 6RB

Tel: 01694-722 212
Fax: 01694-720 163

www.myndhouse.co.uk
info@myndhouse.co.uk

Station: Church Stretton 1 mile, taxi available

Open: mid Feb to mid Nov plus Xmas and New Year for group bookings

Children welcome, but no high chairs

Pets welcome. One double room has direct access to the car park without passing through the main part of the hotel.

Open to non-residents for dinner Wed-Sat by prior reservation only

Directions: 2 hours from Birmingham, Manchester, Liverpool or Bristol. Main line train services connect Shrewsbury with Hereford stopping off at Church Stretton. The hotel is on B54, off A49, between Shrewsbury and Ludlow, 1 mile south of Church Stretton.

Credit cards accepted

Smoking only in the bar

WEST Shropshire

389

Llwyn Guest House

Omnivorous bed and breakfast

5 Llwyn Terrace, Beatrice Street,
Oswestry, Shropshire, SY11 1HR
Tel: 01691–670 746
llwyn_guesthouse@members.v21.co.uk
Open: All year

Old Victorian house. Double or twin (1–2 nights) £17.50 per person. Single occupancy (1–2 nights) £19.50. Children under 12 (1–2 nights) £11. Reduction of £1.50 per night if staying 3 nights or more. Special diets catered for – vegetarian and vegan are their speciality. They also do evening meals £6.50–7.00 (just say what you'd like, can be lighter) and packed lunches can be ordered in advance. Children welcome, cot, high chair. Dogs welcome. No smoking in public areas. No credit cards but cashpoint opposite or cheque.

The Haven

Omnivorous bed and breakfast

Frodesley, Nr Dorrington,
Shrewsbury, Shropshire, SY5 7EY
Tel: 01694–731 672
www.welcomingyou.co.uk/the-haven/

One double, one twin, £22 per person. Cater well for vegetarians with prior notice. They appreciate a few hints and tips from vegans and do a hearty breakfast spread as a result. Small self-catering cottage sharing the pretty orchard garden, sleeps four, £160–280 per week for the whole cottage. Children welcome, high chair, travel cot and toys. No smoking. No dogs. No credit cards.

Cinnamon Coffee and Meeting House

Vegetarian cafe

Waterloo House, Cartway, Bridgnorth
WV16 4EG
Tel: 01746–762 944
www.cinnamoncoffee.co.uk
Open: Mon–Fri: 10–18.00, Sat 10 –17.00

Fair trade, organic cafe serving sandwiches, soups and muffins and mains such as Keralan red lentil bake. Fresh juices and smoothies.
Baby food heated up on request. Large terrace with views over the Severn valley. No smoking inside. Books, magazines, newspapers, board games, toy box. Performance evenings listed on their website.
(NB Quaints Vegetarian Bistro in Bridgnorth is still listed on many websites but became a Thai restaurant in 2003.)

Acorn Wholefood Cafe

Omnivorous cafe

26 Sandford Avenue, Church Stretton
Tel: 01694–722 495
Open: Mon–Tue, Fri–Sun 10–17.00 and bank holidays. Wed–Thu closed.

Veggie dishes £5.55, nut roast with salad £4.55, jacket potatoes £3.20 with one filling. Desserts £2.75–4.00, including vegan crumble and wheat, dairy, gluten and sugar free cakes. 30 kinds of teas. Bring your own alcohol, 99p corkage. Well behaved dogs welcome, children on a lead (3 high chairs). Tea garden in good weather. Not suitable for wheelchair access as first floor.

Olivers Vegetarian Bistro

Vegetarian restaurant

33 High Street, Ironbridge, Shropshire TF8 7JR
Tel: 01952–433 086
Open: Tue–Thu 19–21.30, Fri–Sat 19–22.00,
Also Sat 12–15.00, Sun 11–16.30.
Closed Mon.

Vegetarian bistro with at least 50% of the menu vegan including desserts. All day veggie breakfast. Starters £4.45 such as roast pepper with white beans, pesto optional; fennel and four onion tartlet. Main courses £10.05 such as chickpea and lentil dhansak; wild mushroom and bilberry sausage with mustard mash and onion gravy; Moroccan spiced stew with couscous; Tuscan roast vegetables with parsnip rostis. Mains all served with mixed leaf salad and Oliver's own savoury Cajun style potatoes.

Vegan desserts £3.95 such as spiced peach crumble; toffee and banana sundae; mint iced layer with black cherry coulis. Swedish Glace vegan ice-cream available.

Weekend daytime menu is more snacky, for example veggieburgers from £3.90 with salad, Mexican burger £4.40 with chili and salsa, pasta Italiano £5.90. Toasted baguettes with any three fillings from 20 for £4.40, extra fillings 40p, with a side salad. Also filled baked potatoes from £3.30.

Lots of beers. Bottle of house wine £9.95, glass £2.75. Pot of all kinds of tea or coffee £1.25 per person. Soya milk available.

MC, Visa. Kids' portions, high chairs. No smoking except outside

Broad Bean

Health food shop

60 Broad Street, Ludlow SY8 1NH
Tel: 01584–874 239
www.broad–bean.co.uk
Open: Mon–Sat 9–17.00

Non–vegetarian wholefood store. A few samosas but try the nearby bakers for sandwiches. Organic wine, beer, cider. Supplements, homeopathic remedies, essential oils, water filters, flower remedies, toiletries and eco–friendly cleaning materials.

Myriad Organics

Health food shop

22 Corve Street, Ludlow SY8 1DA
Tel: 01584–872 665
Open: Mon–Fri 8.30–18.00, Sat 9–17.30

Organic fruit and veg, bread, wines. Deli counter with mostly vegetarian salad, vegan cheese, non–dairy ice–cream.

Harvest Wholefoods

Health food shop

by Glebe Farm, Lydham,
nr Bishops Castle SY9 5HB
Tel: 01588–638 990
Open: Mon to Sat 9–17.30

Organic fruit and veg, herbs, natural remedies, books, household products. A few veggie pasties.

WEST

Shropshire

Honeysuckle Wholefood Co-op

Wholefood shop

53 Church Street, Oswestry SY11 2SZ
Tel: 01691-653 125
www.honeysuckle-wholefoods.co.uk
Open: Mon–Sat 9–17.00

Local organic fruit and veg, herbs, household products, but no take-aways.

Goodlife Wholefood Restaurant

Vegetarian restaurant & coffee shop

Barracks Passage, 73 Wyle Cop,
Shrewsbury SY1 1XA
Tel: 01743 -350 455
Open: Mon–Fri 9.30–15.30, Sat 9.30–16.30

In one of historic Shrewsbury's passageways. Everything made fresh on site daily with local produce.
Soup is £2.20, add a roll for 50p. Daily specials such as spinach mousaka, chilli bean pot, chickpea tagine £2.80. Several kinds of nut loaf £2.50 for a big slice. Savoury potatoes £2.25, jackets £1.75, plus 80p per filling. Salad bar from £1.80 for two generous portions.
Desserts including vegan crumble from £2, scones and flapjacks, £1. Pots of tea £1.10, coffee cup £1, mug £1.10. Wine and beer £1.75 glass.

Wild Thyme Wholefoods Co-operative

Wholefood shop

1–2 Castle Gates, Shrewsbury, SY1 2AQ
Tel: 01743-364 559
Open: Mon–Sat 9.30–17.30

Organic fruit and veg, wheat free pastas, complementary medicines, household products. Gluten free pasties, samosas. Non-dairy cheeses and ice-creams.

Holland & Barrett

Health food shop

4 Butchers Row, Shrewsbury
Tel: 01743-272 016

3 The Square, Shrewsbury
Tel: 01743-272 016

Unit 34 Sherwood Street,
Telford Shopping Centre,
Tel: 01952-291 356

13 New Street, Wellington, Shrops TF1 1LU
Tel: 01952 243720

Staffordshire

Bolaka Spice

Omnivorous Indian restaurant

41 Stockwell Street, Leek
Tel: 01538-373 734

Indian restaurant with veggie and vegan options in this market town, well known for its antique shops. Award Winner International Indian Chef of the Year.

Breckles Wholefoods

Wholefood store

14 Stanley Street, Leek
Tel: 01538 387660

Usual range of vitamins and reasonably good range of dry, chilled and frozen foods. Also bread. Discount to Vegan and Vegetarian Society members.

Health Matters

Health food shop

21/23 The Strand, Longton
Tel: 01782 319333

Wholefoods, vitamins, herbal and homeopathic stuff. Handy for the Gladstone Pottery Museum and various factory shops such as Doulton and Port-meirion.

No.1 King Street

Omnivorous restaurant

1 King Street, Newcastle–under–Lyme
Tel: 01782-715 885

Describing itself as "fine dining", this place offers several vegetarian dishes including one vegan and others can be adapted.

Reubens

Omnivorous cafe

40 High Street, Newcastle–under–Lyme
Tel: 01782-627 699

Cafe in the centre of Newcastle–under–Lyme, a market town, the only place in the area to offer soya milk in drinks, though for 30p extra. They also have vegan panini. Bistro opening soon Thu-Sat nights.

The Arch

Omnivorous Chinese restaurant

Units 1– 3 The Mall, Brunswick St
Newcastle–under–Lyme ST5 1HF
Tel: 01782 630849

Omnivorous Chinese restaurant with a reasonable selection of vegetarian food, especially popular at weekends. You can request items not on the menu.

Boots Ltd Stores

Wholefood shop

5 Castle Walk, Newcastle, ST5 1AN
Tel: 01782 617463

Wholefood shop with with fresh and frozen veggie and vegan food, some chilled food, and lots of vitamins.

Health Rack

Health food shop

17 Castle Walk
Newcastle-under-Lyme
Tel: 01782 662045

Wholefood shop with with fresh and
frozen veggie and vegan food.

Passion of India

Omnivorous Indian restaurant

Snow Hill, Howard Place, Shelton ST1 4LY
Tel: 01782 266360
Open: Mon–Thu 12–14.30, 18–23.00;
Fri–Sat –23.30

Omnivorous Indian restaurant between
Hanley and Stoke in a student and
ethnic area, near the College of Further
Education. The food is 100% Indian with
an Arabic approach. The only Indian
restaurant in Staffs to get an AA Rosette
Award and win No.1 Taste of Staffordshire Awards 2002 and 2003.

Al Shafiq's Balti Centre

Omnivorous Indian restaurant

58 Church St, Stoke on Trent
Tel: 01782 410080

Reasonable choice for veggies for about
a fiver. Jug of cold table water brought
to you on arrival and you can bring your
own drinks.

Bauhinia

Omnivorous Chinese restaurant

Parklands,A34, Stoke on Trent
Tel: 01782 719709

Omnivorous Chinese restaurant outside
town with its own car park. Popular at
lunchtimes for business lunches. Piano
player in the evening.

Fortune Rendez-Vous

Omnivorous Cantonese restaurant

19–21 Broad St, Hanley, Stoke on Trent
Tel: 01782 271179

Omnivorous Cantonese restaurant with
reasonable veggie choice. The mock
duck is very ducky. Very bright inside.

Lazeez

Omnivorous Indian restaurant

The Cultural Quarter, 56 Piccadilly
Hanley, Stoke on Trent
Tel: 01782 261717

Stoke is blessed with lots of omnivorous
Indian restaurants but this is one of the
best, almost opposite the Regent
Theatre. A screen downstairs shows
Bollywood movie extracts.

Ria

Thai omnivorous restaurant

65 Piccadilly, Hanley, Stoke on Trent
Tel: 01782 264411

Omnivorous Thai restaurant in the
Cultural Quarter, with many veggie
dishes most of which are or can be
vegan.

WEST Staffordshire

395

Robertos

Italian omnivorous restaurant

25 Pall Mall, Hanley, Stoke on Trent
Tel: 01782 287410

One of many omnivorous Italian pasta and pizza places in Stoke, but this is our favourite, in the "Cultural Quarter." The vegetariana comes with olives and capers and dishes can be made up vegan without cheese on request. Around the corner is another Italian called Portofino.

Zest Bistro

Omnivorous restaurant

79 Broad Street, Stoke-on-Trent
Tel: 01782-285111

We've heard this restaurant caters well for veggies and vegans but as we go to press they were only doing party bookings and outside catering and catering equipment hire.

A B Wholefoods

Wholefood shop

75 Broad Street, Hanley, Stoke on Trent
Tel: 01782 219363

Wholefood store just outside the centre of town with West Indian and Chinese foods, woks, frozen patties, some vegetables.

Armstrongs Health and Herbal Store

Wholefood shop

22 Town Road, Hanley, Stoke on Trent
Tel: 01782 215417

Holland & Barrett

Health food shop

8 Underhill Walk Shopping Centre
Burton on Trent
Tel: 01283-740 078

Unit 21, Cannock Shopping Ct, Cannock
Tel: 01543 500046

41 Market Street, Lichfield
Tel: 01543-256 782

29 High Street,
Newcastle-under-Lyme
Tel: 01782-713 059

1 Goalgate Street, Stafford
Tel: 01785-252 758

8 Upper Market Square
Hanley, Stoke On Trent
Tel: 01782-266 126

Although much of Warwickshire is, from a veggie point of view, much ado about nothing, Stratford-upon-Avon is a main stop on the beaten tourist track. If you do pay a visit to Shakespeare's old home, the vegetarian proprietors at Parkfield will look after you well. Prepare yourself for a comfortable stay in their Victorian house and wake up to the smell of a full English breakfast in the morning. Stratford does not have a vegetarian restaurant, but after exploring the sights you'll still have plenty of choice at Hussain's Indian or Thai Kingdom.

Head through the sleepy villages of Warwickshire and the miles of gorgeous countryside to discover what inspired Shakespeare. When you reach the town of Warwick, take an hour to explore the castle, which is perched on a cliff overlooking the Avon river. It holds one of the finest collections of medieval armour and weapons in Europe, and also displays some priceless paintings by Rubens and Van Dyck. The Red Lion Inn on Station Road has a few veggie dishes and are happy to make something vegan.

In Rugby is the daytime vegetarian Summersault cafe.

Warwickshire

Parkfield

Omnivorous B&B in a Victorian house with a vegetarian proprietor. There are seven rooms: one single with a private bathroom at £30 per night, 3 double ensuites and two twin ensuites at £52 per room per night and one family ensuite at £20 per person per night.

For breakfast, start with cereal followed by pancakes and stewed fruit, or have a full cooked English breakfast of veggie sausages, beans, tomatoes and mushrooms with toast and preserves. Vegan margarine and soya milk are available.

Parkfield is only one hundred metres from the Greenways cycle path which connects with the Heart of England way.

The town centre, where there are Shakespeare Birthplace Trust houses and three Royal Shakespeare theatres, is only a ten minute walk away.

Nearby there is a teddy bear museum, river rides and many small restaurants and shops.

Stratford is also an excellent base for visiting the Cotswold Hills, Warwick Castle, Blenheim Palace, Coventry, Oxford, Birmingham and the National Exhibition Centre.

Don't be surprised if you come back as many of their customers do.

Tea and coffee making facilities, radio alarms and televisions are in the rooms.

Stratford Upon Avon

Omnivorous bed and breakfast

3 Broad Walk
Stratford Upon Avon
Warwickshire CV37 6HS

Tel/fax: 01789-293 313

www.parkfieldbandb.co.uk
parkfield@btinternet.com

Train station: Stratford upon Avon, 1/2 mile, then taxi

Open: all year

Directions: Take the B439 towards Bidford on Avon from Stratford town centre. Turn left into Broad Walk immediately before the first roundabout.

Parking: plenty available (own carpark)

Children over five are welcome

No smoking throughout

Visa, MC accepted

Leamington Spa

Rhubarb

Omnivorous cafe

50 Warwick Street, Leamington Spa CV32 5JS
Tel: 01926–425 005
Open: Tue–Thu 9–22.30, Fri 9–23.00, Sat 10–23.00

Three specials each day, around £6.50 such as Mexican wraps. They also have bagels, sandwiches, soup, nachos and cakes. some of their food is vegan, or can be adapted. Smoking is allowed everywhere. Cash or cheque only. The shop attached sells artifacts from all over the world.

Rugby

Summersault

Vegetarian cafe

27 High Street, Rugby CV21 3BW
Tel: 01788–543 223
Open: Mon–Sat 9–16.30, shop until 17.30

Entrees from £2.10, range of vegan and vegetarian salads from 90p per portion. Vegan and veggie mains from £5.25 with a changing menu daily. Desserts £2–£3.60, are all wholemeal, including vegan options. Everything is cooked on the premises, including the bread. Organic vegetarian wine is £2.35 a glass, £12.95 for a bottle. Pot of tea for one £1.50, coffee £1.40. No smoking throughout. Child–sized portions and high chairs available.

Stratford Upon Avon

Hussains

Omnivorous Indian restaurant

6a Chapel Street, Stratford Upon Avon
www.hussainsindiancuisine.co.uk
Tel: 01789–267 506
Open: every day 17–24.00, also Thu–Sun 12.30–14.30

North and South Indian omnivorous restaurant. £6.99 for a three course lunch, dinner is around £15 per head. A la carte dishes average at £6.45 each. House wine is £7.75 per bottle, £2 for a glass. Smoking and non–smoking sections. Children welcome. Parking outside. Visa, MC and Amex accepted.

Thai Kingdom

Omnivorous Thai restaurant

11 Warwick road, Stratford upon Avon
Tel: 01789–261 103
Open: Mon–Sat 12–14.00, 18–22.45

The bargain here is the £4.99 special lunch, popular with students and tourists, which offers vegetarian options like sweet and sour tofu with rice.
The vegetarian set menu is £19.99 with a starter, one choice of 5 mains with rice, dessert and coffee. Everything is cooked to order so they can make it vegan or nut–free. Also a la carte dishes. Smoking and non–smoking sections. House wine is £9.99 per bottle and £2.50 for a glass. Well behaved children welcome afternoon but not evening, no high chairs. MC, Visa, Amex Diners.

Warwick

The Red Lion Inn

Omnivorous restaurant

Station Road, Claverdon, Warwick CV35 8PE
Tel: 01926–842 291
Open: Mon–Fri 12–15.00, 18–23.00,
Sat–Sun 12–21.00

Typically has 3 vegetarian dishes on the menu, from £7.95, such as tomato and basil pasta, or baked butternut stuffed with tomato, potato and couscous. They are happy to adapt for vegans. Non smoking dining area. Children welcome, high chairs. MC, Visa.

399

Holland & Barrett

Health food shop

55 Warwick Street, Leamington Spa
Tel: 01926–421 775

2 Market Place, Nuneaton
Tel: 02476–352 649

36a High Street, Rugby
Tel: 01788–570 280

31 Bridge Street, Stratford upon Avon
Tel: 01789–269 893

20 High Street, Warwick
Tel: 01926–409 305

West Midlands

Sibila's

Veggie restaurant in holistic centre

The Watermarque, 100 Browning Street
Birmingham B16 8EH. (near Broad Street)
Tel: 0121–456 7633
Restaurant open: Mon–Thu 10.30–20.30 (last
orders), Fri–Sun 10.30–18.00. Centre open:
Mon–Sat 08.00–20.00, Sun 09.00–18.00
Treatments available from 09.30
www.bodyandbeing.co.uk
(see website for location map)

Vegetarian restaurant inside the new
Body & Being holistic health centre and
day spa with yoga studio. Almost
everything is organic. Over half the
dishes are either vegan or can be. Open
for snacks all the time, lunch 12.30–
14.30, and dinner from 18.30 Mon–
Thu. Main courses £5.50–8.00 such as
tempeh with ginger, veg and rice; spelt
and veg tortelloni with tomato and
fennel concassé. Cakes from £2,
flapjacks £1.20, vegan apple and fruit
strudel £3.20, and they have Tofutti
vegan ice-cream. Organic juices and
smoothies. NIA car park nearby.

Canalside Cafe

Omnivorous cafe

Canalside Cottage, 35 Worcester Bar
Gas St, Birmingham B1 2JU
Open: every day until late

Near the main entertainment area Broad
Street, on the tow path by the canal, in
an 18th century lock-keeper cottage.
Run by an animal rights activist. Veggie
soup, vegetarian burger £2.95, variety
of meals. Desserts such as summer
pudding or spotted dick with soya ice
cream or cream. Thick soya milk
shakes. Licensed for alcohol.

Natural Choice

Vegetarian cafe in a food court

Pavilion Central, High St, Birmingham B4 7SL
Tel: 0121–643 6096
Open: Mon–Sat 9–17.30, Sun 11–16.30

Sandwiches, baguettes, wraps, salads,
bakes and other vegetarian take-aways.
Juices and smoothies.

Rooty Frooty

Vegetarian restaurant

at The Custard Factory, Gibb Street, Digbeth,
Birmingham (5 mins walk from city centre, by
the coach station)
Tel: 0121 224 8458
Open: Mon–Thu 08–18.00,
Fri–Sat 08–22.30 (last orders), Sun closed

Self service buffet, large plate £4.80,
bowl £3. Also take-away, soup £2,
small box £2, medium £4, big £5.75.
Cakes including vegan, sugar-free and
sometimes wheat-free. Smoothies,
juices and wheatgrasss shots, organic
coffees, mocca, many teas. House wine
£2.60 glass, £12 bottle. Organic wine
£14, beer and spirits. Children
welcome, no high chairs. No smoking
day, small smoking area evening. MC,
Visa.

Soya Cafe

Omnivorous Oriental restaurant

Unit B106, The Arcadian Centre,
70 Hurst Street B5 4TD
Tel: 0121–683 8350
Open: Thu–Tue 12–22.00, closed Wed

Big on, you guessed it, soya! A la carte main courses with rice £6–7, such as tofu hot pots, stir fries, and tofu in chilli, lemongrass, and black bean sauces. 12–5pm set lunches £6.45 inc main, drink and dessert like soya dessert or fruit salad. Soya shakes and smoothies, soya sesame drinks, Chinese teas. Bring your own alcohol, 15% of overall bill for corkage. Children welcome, high chair. Smoking allowed. No credit cards.

Wagamama

Omnivorous Japanese restaurant

Edgebaston Street, Birmingham

See Manchester entry p.87 for details.

The Warehouse Cafe

Vegetarian restaurant & vegan shop

54 Allison Street, Digbeth,
Central Birmingham B5 5TH
(in Friends of the Earth building)
Tel: 0121–633 0261
Open: Mon–Sat 12.00–14.30.
Also some evenings on special occasions

Varied menu with a mixture of Indian, Mediterranean, Mexican, organic, Spanish, Thai and wholefood. Mains £1.95–£3.75. 60% vegan, including salads, ice cream and burgers. Always have soya milk. No smoking. No credit cards.
Downstairs is the One Earth vegan wholefood shop which also sells footwear, belts, candles, oils.

One Earth Shop

Vegan wholefood shop

54 Allison Street, Digbeth,
Central Birmingham B5 5TH
Tel: 0121–632 6909 and ask for shop
Open: Mon–Sat 10–17.00, closed Sun

Wholefoods, vegan, wheat–free, organic and Fairtrade goods, essential oils, cards, body care. Ethical Wares vegan shoes. Take–away pasties and cakes.

Natural World @The Health Store

Independent health food store

26 Great Western Arcade, Colmore Row,
Birmingham, B2 5HU
Tel: 0121–233–9931. Mail order and details:
www.healthfoodshop.co.uk

Organic veg, bread, vitamins, homeop–athy. Practitioners available include osteopath, herbalist, acupuncture, homeopathy, reflexology, sports therapy.

Birmingham – Handsworth

London Sweet Centre

Vegetarian Indian take away

104 Soho Road. Handsworth
Birmingham B21 9DP. Tel: 0121–554 1696
Open: Sun–Thu 9–20.00, Fri–Sat 9–21.00

Samosas and pakoras (with vegetable ghee), and lots of sweets.

Milan Sweet Centre

Vegetarian Indian take away

238 Soho Road, Handsworth B21 9LR
Open: Mon–Sun 10.00–19.45

Some vegan–friendly savouries and sweets.

403

Khazana

Vegetarian Indian/Chinese restaurant

12 Holyhead Rd, Handsworth B21 0LT
Tel: 0121-551 0908
Open: Tue–Fri 12–15.00, Sat–Sun 12–17.00;
Tue–Sun 18–22.00. Closed Mon.
www.khazanarestaurant.co.uk (menus)

Big new restaurant with South Indian, Punjabi, Gujarai, East African and Chinese food. A la carte, or lunch buffet £5.99, evening £9.99, children £2.99, £4.50. No smoking, no alcohol. Children welcome.

Pritam Sweet Centre

Vegetarian Indian take away

291 Rookery Road, Handsworth
Birmingham B21 9PS. Tel: 0121-551 5626
Open: every day 10–19.30

Take away savouries and sweets.

Sangam

Vegetarian Indian take away

334 Soho Road, Handsworth, Birmingham
Tel: 0121-523 9905
Open: Mon–Sat 11–20.00, Sun 12–18.00

Indian vegetarian eat-in and take-away. £1.60 per bowl of curry or rice.

Ambala Foods

Indian sweet shop

324 Soho Road, Handsworth B21 9HA
Tel: 0121-551 1911
Open: every day 10–20.00

also at 552 Coventry Road, Small Heath
Birmingham B10 0UN. Tel: 0121-773 5838
Open: every day 10–20.00

Lots of sweets and savouries for vegetarians, only samosas for vegans.

Peaceful Mind Cafe

Organic vegetarian cafe

46 Poplar Road
Kings Heath, Birmingham B14 7AG
Tel: 0121-443 5422
Open: Mon–Fri 9–17.00, Sat 10–17.00
www.meditateinbirmingham.org

Mainly a coffee and teas place. (Toasted) sandwiches, many vegan. Cakes, some gluten free, one vegan, snacks, spelt bread and Booja Booja chocolates.

Jyoti Vegetarian Restaurant

Vegetarian Indian restaurant

569 Stratford Rd, Sparkhill, Birmingham B11
Tel: 0121-766 7199
Open: Tue–Fri 18–21.15, Fri 12–13.45,
Sat 13.30–21.15, Sun 13.30–20.30

Vegan-friendly all over Indian vegetarian restaurant. Thalis £9.50, 13.25 and £14.75. Set menu for two people £13 each. Mains £6.75 with half of all items on menu clearly marked suitable for vegans. Average £13 a head with a starter, main and dessert including Swedish Glace, mango sorbet. Children welcome, 2 high chairs. Non smoking. Visa, MC. Air conditioned. Bring your own alcohol.

Milan Sweet Centre

Vegetarian Indian take away

191 Stoney Lane, Sparkhill,
Birmingham B12 8BB
Tel: 0121-551 5239
Open: Mon–Sun 9.00–20.00

Some vegan-friendly savouries/ sweets
.

Browns

Omnivorous bar

Earl Street, Coventry CV1 5RU
Tel: 024-7622 1100
www.brownsindependentbar.com
Open: Mon–Thu 9–23.00, Fri–Sat 9–01.00,
Sun 12–18.00, food always available

Omnivorous bar with a lot of veggie food. £5.50 for a meal. At least half of the 15 dishes are veggie and maybe 4 of those vegan. Choice of 5 or 6 veg and 3 kinds of potato. Desserts £2.50. Soya milk available. Bottle of house wine £9.85, glass £2.65. Non smoking section. Visa, MC. No under 18's. Open air roof terrace overlooking the Cathedral. Sometimes weekend DJ's. In the centre next to the Cathedral, art gallery and the university.

Kakooti Restaurant

Omnivorous international restaurant

16 Spon Street, Coventry CV1 3BA
Tel: 02476-221 392
www.kakooti.com
Open: Mon–Sat 18–21.00 (last orders), closed Sun.

16th century listed Grade 2 building. Vegetarian dishes prepared and cooked separately, use a lot of organic and Fair Trade ingredients. 7 Mediterranean starters £2.85–5.50. 8 mains, most of which can be made vegan, £7.85–8.95 such as pasta, or Kakooti: kidney beans with parsley, fenugreek and coriander leaves, lime sauce and rice. The only vegan dessert is fruit salad. Minimum charge £10. House wine £11.95 bottle, £3.15 glass. At least half the wines are vegetarian/vegan and organic. Organic beers, liqueurs and soft drinks. Children over 8 welcome. No smoking. MC, Visa.

Natural Choice

Vegetarian restaurant

Unit 6 The Terrace, West Orchard Shopping Centre, Coventry, West Midlands CV1 1QS
Tel: 024-7623 9580
Open: Mon–Sat 08.30–17.30, Sun 10–16.00

New place with sandwiches, baguettes, wraps, salads, bakes and other take-aways. Juices and smoothies.

The Restaurant at Ryton Organic Gardens

Omnivorous restaurant

Woolsten Lane, Ryton-on-Dunsmore
Coventry CV8 3LG. Tel: 024-7630 7142
www.hdra.org.uk. Open: every day 9–17.00

Starters £3.25–4.50 such as marinated vegetables, mushroom flageolot bean salad, vegan gluten free soup every day. Average of 5 vegetarian mains daily, such as curry, chickpea veg casserole, hummous platter £7.25–£7.95. Desserts include red wine poached pears, summer pudding £3.50 and they have vegan ice-cream and can do you a sundae. Bottle of vegan house wine £11–12, glass £2–3. They are happy to adapt things for vegans. Non smoking inside. Visa, MC. Some outdoor seating. Children welcome, high chairs.

Natural World

Indepdendent health food shop

596 Bearwood Road, Smethwick, West Mids, B66 4BW. www.healthfoodshop.co.uk
Tel: 0121-420 2145
Open: Mon–Sat 9–17.30, closed Sun

Brilliant health food store like the one in central Birmingham.

Walsall

Cat's Tales

Vegetarian restaurant

Unit6, Green Lane, Walsall WS2 8HE
Tel: 01922–611 622
Open: Mon–Sat 11.00–16.00 plus Fri & Sat
18.30–21.30 booking recommended

Closed as we go to press but hoping to
reopen again.
Excellent, high quality home cooking
with friendly service. Nominated for
"Best exclusively vegetarian gourmet
restaurant" in the Vegetarian Society
Awards 2004.

Wolverhampton

City Bar

Omnivorous international bistro

2–3 Kings Street (off Dudley Street)
Wolverhampton WV1 1ST
Tel: 01902–423376
Food open: Mon, Tue Fri, Sat 12–19.00;
Wed–Thu 12–22.30

Menu is very friendly towards vegans
and veggies. Where else can you get a
vegan breakfast at 7.30pm including
Redwoods sausages and vegan bacon?
They stop taking orders at 7pm to close
at 8pm then reopen for the evening
drinking trade at 10pm, though in
future may run on through the evening.
Three course meal anytime or
soups, pates, jacket potatoes, sandwiches and baguettes. 7 or 8 main
courses, two people together for £5.95
all-in, such as roasted Mediterranean
veg on mash with gravy, sausage and
mash, (vegan) ploughman's, (vegan)
lasagne, shepherd's pie, mushroom
stroganof. Vegan pancakes, fruit
desserts, Swedish Glace. Always have
soya milk. Wednesday night is Spanish
flamenco night with a tapas menu,

Spanish main courses and desserts,
both vegan and vegetarian.

Bar Two
(Hatherton Arms)

Omnivorous international bistro

Corner of North Road and Oxley Street,
Wolverhampton WV1 1QL
Tel: 01902–423376
Open: Sat evening, maybe more

New international bistro in the
Hatherton Arms pub, from the same
people as City Bar, opening June 2005.
Starting with Saturday nights and more
if it goes well, with live music.

Rosemary's Health
Food Shop

Health food shop

3 Mander Square, Mander Centre,
Wolverhampton
www.rosemaryshealthfoods.co.uk
Open: Mon–Sat 9–17.00, Sun 10.30–16.30

Although not entirely vegetarian, this is
still the best health food shop in the
West Midlands for the range of vegan
goods available. They have pasties,
sandwiches and cakes for
vegetarians/vegans in store. There is a
15% discount when you buy two
identical products.

Also in Wolverhampton, there is a new
Chinese stall in the Mander Centre
selling nuts, berries soaked in apple
juice, and different flavoured Turkish
delight. Most of it is vegan or veggie.
Excellent value.

Holland & Barrett

Health food shop

98 Church Street, Bilston
Tel: 01902–496 489

1–3 Corporation Square, Birmingham
Tel: 0121–236 7869

6 City Arcade, Coventry
Tel: 02476–222 752

12 Churchill Precinct, Dudley
Tel: 01384–230 610

132 High Street, Erdington, Birmingham
Tel: 0121–382 9897

99a High Street, Harborne, Birmingham
Tel: 0121–427 649

33 Hagley Mall, Cornbow Centre, Halesowen
Tel: 0121–585 0496

33 Alcester Road South,
Kings Heath, Birmingham
Tel: 0121–444 7000

Unit L36 Lower Mall, Merry Hill Centre
Brierley Hill. Tel: 01384–483 608

22 Grosvenor Shopping Centre, Northfield,
Birmingham. Tel: 0121 475 493

2160/2160B Coventry Road,
Sheldon, Birmingham
Tel: 0121–742 0313

Unit 20, 23 One Stop Shopping Centre
Walsall Road, Perry Barr, Birmingham
Tel: 0121–331 1599

54–55 The Pallasades, Central Birmingham
Tel: 0121–633 0104

215 Stratford Road, Shirley, Solihull
Tel: 0121–733 6880

84 High Street, Solihull
Tel: 0121–709 2153

Unit 32 , Ryemarket Shopping Centre
Stourbridge
Tel: 01384–374 112

Sainsbury's Centre, Sutton Coldfield
Tel: 0121–321 2439

34–36 Park Street Arcade, Walsall
Tel: 01922–611 348

43 The Mall, 3 Sandwell Shopping Centre
West Bromwich
Tel: 0121–553 5523

11 – 13 Queens Arcade, Mander Centre
Wolverhampton
Tel: 01902–420937

Birmingham Vegetarians and Vegans
Local social and campaigning group
www.bvvuk.org
Or contact Barbara and Harry
on 0121 353 2442
or Frank on 07770 630121.
5 Esher Road, Kingstanding,
Birmingham B44 9QL.

Worcestershire

Lady Foley's Tea Room

Vegetarian restaurant

Great Malvern Railway Station
Imperial Rd, off Avenue Rd, Malvern
Tel: 01684–893 033
Open: Mon–Sat 9–18.00

On the platform of the railway station. Soup £2 is usually vegan and salads are £1.50. Main courses such as ginger stir-fry veg or red bean chilli with rice and jacket potatoes. Various desserts but none vegan.

St. Annes Well Cafe

Vegan/vegetarian cafe

Victoria Walk, St Annes Road, Malvern
Open: Mon–Sun 10–17.00 Easter–September,
Winter weekends 10–dark

Mostly vegan menu. Cooked meals between midday and 3pm. Mains such as corn on the cob, chilli, aubergine and mango curry, homity pie and spicy burgers £1.90–£6.95. Always some vegan desserts and 4 vegan cakes for 85p–£1.50. Over 100 speciality teas. Always have soya milk available. Friday evenings they have alcohol with food. Most of seating is outdoors. Non smoking. Cash or cheque only.

Chesters

Omnivorous Mexican restaurant

51 New Street, Worcester WR1 2DL
Tel: 01905–611 638
Open: Mon–Tue 18–22.00, Wed–Thu –22.30,
Fri – 23.00. Sat 12–23.00. Sun closed.

Highly recommended by local vegans and veggies. Huge menu with stacks for us and huge mains. Vegan butternut squash risotto £5.25 starter, £10.95 main. Vegan double cheeseburger £6.95. 6 bean chili £9.95. We don't know about desserts, no one ever had room after a main! Licensed.

King Charles II Restaurant

Omnivorous restaurant

King Charles House, 29 New Street, Worcester
Tel: 01905–22 449
Open: Mon–Sat 12.00–14.00, 18.30–21.30,
closed Sun.

Several vegetarian dishes and can adapt for vegans. Mains £9.95 such as pasta and vegetables. No smoking, except in bar upstairs. Children welcome, high chairs. Visa, MC.

GNC

Health food shop

Unit C7, Chapel Walk, Crowngate, Worcester
Tel: 01905 612639

Holland & Barrett

Health food shop

15 High Street, Bromsgrove
Tel: 01527–836 949

Unit 23, Abbey Gates Centre, Evesham
Tel: 01386–40 854

Unit 12 King Charles Square
The Swan Centre, Kidderminster
Tel: 01562–748 822

8 High St, Leominster. Tel: 01568–615 455

Unit 2 New Walk, Kingfisher Centre, Redditch
B97 4HB. Tel: 01527 64062

43–47 High Street, Stourport on Seven
Tel: 01299–822 463

38 High St, Pershore. Tel: 01386–556 495

22–23 Mealcheapen St, Worcester
Tel: 01905–28 153

SCOTLAND

Edinburgh

Scotland Accommodation

Scotland Restaurants

LEWIS

SKYE

HIGHLAND

Inverness

MORAY

ABERDEENSHIRE

ANGUS

PERTH
AND
KINROSS

ARGYLL
AND BUTE

STIRLING

FIFE

4 3 Glasgow 1

2

LOTHIAN

Edinburgh

LANARKSHIRE

ARRAN

AYRSHIRE

SCOTTISH
BORDERS

DUMFRIES AND GALLOWAY

1. GLASGOW CITY
2. EAST RENFREWSHIRE
3. RENFREWSHIRE
4. INVERCLYDE

413

A holiday in Britain is not complete without visiting Scotland. The Highlands are breathtaking, the people are incredibly friendly, and the cities are throbbing with life and culture.

Top of the list of places to visit is Edinburgh, the capital. From the ancient castle, museums and galleries to the many pubs and night clubs, you will never be without something to see or do. Then of course there is the famous Edinburgh Festival every summer. And you will not go hungry in this city. Edinburgh is excellent for vegetarians and vegans. The number of vegetarian restaurants just keeps on growing and it now rivals London as being the best city in Britain for vegetarian eating. Even if you are at an omnivorous restaurant, in Edinburgh they are used to catering for veggies and most know how to knock up a great meat-free meal.

If you want to wake up to a full vegetarian Scottish breakfast, stay at the Greenhouse where you will be in vegan heaven. The friendly proprietors Hugh and Suzanne will be more than willing to help you with tourist information on Edinburgh. They will even give you a free city map with veggie places highlighted.

Don't leave Scotland before you check out Glasgow, the country's largest city. It is lively and cosmopolitan and just as cultural as Edinburgh. Glasgow is particularly known for its architecture due to Charles Mackintosh (1868-1928), the famous Glasgow born architect and designer, who is renowned world wide for his innovative style which helped shape European Art Nouveau. His influence can still be seen around the city. Although not quite the vegetarian paradise that Edinburgh is, Glasgow is catching up fast and is the only city in Europe with three vegetarian and vegan pubs: Mono, Stereo and the 13th Note.

Don't just stay in the city when visiting Scotland. Many people hire a car and go exploring. Around both Edinburgh and Glasgow there is much to see, such as coastal hills, parks, woodlands, historic towns and heritage sites.

If you go further afield into Braveheart country, you will find people more aware of vegetarianism than you might expect. Towns in the Highlands like Fort William and Aviemore are popular ski resorts and although sadly lacking vegetarian restaurants, you can still get decent veggie and vegan food. You can't go wrong in an Italian or Indian restaurant and you will find both in these towns.

All over Scotland there are vegetarian guesthouses in small towns or the remote and beautiful countryside. Imagine waking in the morning to the smell of vegetarian bacon and scrambled tofu, hearing the sound of birds chirping and knowing that all you have to do that day is enjoy yourself. And the Scottish people will do their utmost to ensure that you do.

For general tourist information on Scotland go to www.visitscotland.com

Our Scotland chapter is in three parts. First a giant section on Edinburgh, then accommodation outside of Edinburgh, and finally restaurants outside the capital.

Palace of Holyrood house

Holyrood Park

Regent Garden

London Road

Regent Road

Canongate

Holyrood Road

Clerk Street

Leith Street

Nicholson Street

Broughton Street

South Bri

North Bri

Royal Museum of Scotland

National museum of antiquities, portrait Gallery

Edinburgh Weaverley

Dublin Street

St Andrew Street

George Street

National Gallery

High Street

Place

West Meadow Park

Dundas Street

Gardens

Queen Street

St David Street

Princes Street Gardens

Edinburgh Castle

Johnston Ter

Grassmarket

Lauriston

Henderson Row

Queens

Princes Street

Lothian Road

Approach

Fountainbridge

Queensferry Street

Shandwick Place

Morrison

West

Edinburgh is one of the most attractive and inviting cities in Britain, with stunning limestone buildings overlooked by an imposing castle, and lots of history and culture.

The city centre is full of lively pubs, cafes and shops, and is as good as Brighton and London for vegetarian food. Walking around requires a degree of fitness, as Edinburgh is very hilly, which adds to its atmosphere and rugged good looks. There are several excellent free museums in the city, along with a thriving arts scene. The botanical gardens are also not to be missed.

The annual Edinburgh Fringe Festival draws thousands of people, so if you are planning to visit during August, book your accommodation as far in advance as possible.

Edinburgh

The Greenhouse

A warm welcome awaits you at this friendly veggie guest house. Situated in the heart of Edinburgh, it's only twenty minutes walk to the city centre. There are six rooms, comprised of doubles and twins. One can be converted to a family room. Four have ensuite bathrooms and two have private bathrooms. Stay for £35 per person per night from May–September (inclusive) and £30 the rest of the year. August is £40 per person per night. Single night bookings are not available.

The breakfast menu is extensive and mouth watering. Half of it's vegan and even more can be made vegan by request. Hugh and Suzanne are committed to providing good service and great veggie food. The full Scottish breakfast includes rashers, organic tempeh and home made veggie sausages (choose from mushroom, kidney bean and coriander, chickpea and black olive, walnut and rosemary, or herbed polenta); served with mushrooms, tomatoes, baked beans, hash browns, scrambled tofu and toast. Yum! Vegan kedgeree is on the menu too, or opt for one of the lighter choices like bagels with vegan cream cheese, scrambled tofu with mushrooms on toast, pancakes with maple syrup, Greenhouse tomato bruschetta, or Greenhouse mushrooms on sour dough bread. Soya milk, vegan margarine, vegan muesli and soya yoghurt are available. Organic and GM free ingredients used whenever possible.

No evening meal, but it's hardly necessary in the veg paradise that is Edinburgh! Hugh and Suzanne will give you a map of Edinburgh with veggie places highlighted.

TV's and tea and coffee making facilities in the rooms. Vegans who like their cuppa white don't miss out, as soya milk can be kept in a cooler in your room.

Vegan Christmas packages are available.

Vegetarian guest house

14 Hartington Gardens
Bruntsfield
Edinburgh EH10 4LD
Scotland

Tel: 0131–622 7634

www.greenhouse-edinburgh.com

Email: greenhouse_edin@hotmail.com

Train Station: Waverley, 35 minutes walk or get bus or taxi

Open: all year

Directions: From the M8, go to Newbridge roundabout and take the A8. Then take A702 (Lothian Road). This becomes Earlgrey Street, then Home Street, then Leven Street, then Bruntsfield Place. Turn right down Viewforth, then take your second left into Hartington Gardens.

Parking: available

Vegan bedding. Soaps are home made and vegan.

Children are welcome and those under twelve stay for £20 (based on a shared room with two adults).

Cot available.

No pets

No smoking throughout

Six Marys Place

Omnivorous guest house

6 Marys Place, Raeburn Place, Stockbridge,
Edinburgh EH4 1JH
Tel: 0131–332 8965
www.sixmarysplace.co.uk

Restored Georgian townhouse, a short walk from the Royal Botanical Gardens. 2 singles, 3 doubles, 2 twin ensuites, £35–50 per person. One family room that sleeps 5, with a double bed, double sofa bed, and a single, £100–150 per night. Veggie breakfasts can be adjusted for vegans and special diets. Tea/coffee, internet and TV in room. Also a TV lounge with free internet service. 5% discount for Vegetarian Society members.

No. 1

Vegetarian guest house

1 Gayfield Place, Edinburgh, EH7 4AB
Tel: 0131–557 4752
Train Station: Waverley, 5–10 minutes walk
Open: all year
gayfield–bb@supanet.com

One twin, one single and one double £25 per person, and one double ensuite £30 per person. Flat rate £30 all rooms during festival. Children welcome but no pets. No smoking throughout.

Castle Rock Hostel

Omnivorous hostel

15 Johnston Terrace,
Edinburgh EH1 2PW
Tel: 0131–225 9666
TrainStation: Waverley, ten minutes walk
Open: all year

Located next to the castle, this hostel has 225 beds. There are both single sex and mixed dorms which have 8–16 beds and cost £11 per night. No private rooms. Quads, triples, and twins are £17 per person per night; doubles are £45 per night; and deluxe doubles cost £50 per night. Veggie continental breakfast is £1.90. Free tea and coffee. If you're vegan, you'll need to bring your own soya milk and margarine. There is a newly refurbished kitchen for self catering. 24 hour access. No lockers, but you can leave valuables at reception.

SCOTLAND Edinburgh – accommodation

Edinburgh

Royal Mile Backpackers

Omnivorous hostel

105 High Street, Edinburgh, EH1 1SG
Tel: 0131-557 6120
Train Station: Waverley, ten minutes walk
Open: all year

38 beds costing £12 per night (£13.50 in August) in a dorm of eight to ten people. Single sex dorms. No private rooms. Veggie continental breakfast is £1.90.
Free tea and coffee. If you're vegan, you'll need to bring your own soya milk and margarine. There is a newly refurbished kitchen for self catering. 24 hour access. No lockers, but there's a safe in reception. Smoking areas. No children.

High Street Hostel

Omnivorous hostel

8 Blackfriars Street, Edinburgh, EH1 1NE
Tel: 0131-557 3984
www.scotlandstophostels.com
Train Station: Waverley, five minutes walk
Open: all year

140 beds costing £12 (winter) or £13.50 (summer) per night in a dorm of six to sixteen people. A veggie continental breakfast is £1.90. Free tea and coffee. If you're vegan, you'll beed to bring your own soya milk and margarine. There is a kitchen for self catering. 24 hour access. Single sex dorms. No private rooms. No lockers, but there's a safe in reception. Smoking areas. No children. Laundry service is £2.50. Internet access.

David Bann Restaurant

Situated just off the Royal Mile, a combination of modern décor with candlelight makes this gourmet eatery popular with tourists and locals.

Extensive world menu with snacks and starters from £3-5 and full meals around £10. Examples of food include: walnut, almond and mushroom haggis wellington, roulade, koftas, dosa, mushroom crepes, pan fried smoked tofu. Plenty for vegans. Desserts, £4.50. Many dishes can be made vegan, check website.

Good range of drinks including a gorgeous foamy hot chocolate £1.80 or £2 with soya milk, organic fruit juices £1.80. Licenced for alcohol.

Edinburgh

Vegetarian restaurant

56-58 St Mary's St
(Royal Mile and Cowgate)
Edinburgh EH1 1SX

Tel: 0131-556 5888
Email: info@davidbann.co.uk

www.davidbann.co.uk

Licensed

Open: Daily 11.00 - 01.00.

All credit cards except Diner's

The Baked Potato

Not just your usual spud! Very friendly small vegetarian and vegan take away located just off the Royal Mile, in the heart of Edinburgh, and a favourite of local students.

Good value, generous portions with potatoes starting from £2.40 with fillings including pasta salad, curried rice peppers, mexican, spinach or avocado salad and cous cous. They do a superb vegan coleslaw. Hot fillings such as vegetarian haggis, chilli, vegetable curry or baked beans.

Varied selection of filled rolls, £1.40, and filled pittas from £2.35. Tasty sausage rolls too.

They make their own high quality vegan cakes (carrot, chocolate, cranberry and apple) which start from 55p.

Vegan mayonnaise, margarine and soya milk available. Some gluten-free, wheat-free and raw foods

Lots of fliers for various holistic things and happenings and also leaflets on animal issues.

It can get very busy at lunchtime so expect lively crowds.

Vegetarian take away

56 Cockburn Street
Royal Mile
Edinburgh EH1 1PB

Tel: 0131-225 7572

charlesveggie@aol.com

Train/Tube Train: Waverley Station

Open: Mon-Sun 9.00-21.00 Extended hours during Edinburgh festival (Mon-Sat 23.00).

No smoking

Cash or cheque only

10% discount to members of Animal Aid, PETA, Viva!, Vegetarian and Vegan Society and also to people presenting this book!

Black Bo's

Black Bo's been acclaimed for its vegetarian cordon vert dishes with the chef dedicated to providing imaginative and flavoursome meals.

You won't find a menu like this anywhere else. Somehow the combination of flavours really works. Gluten-free, vegan and special diets catered for or adapted. Modern, fashionable interior.

Almost half the menu is vegan and starters at around £4.50 include chickpea chilli with coriander and avocado, with lemon sorbert and blue bols, smoked tofu and veggies stuffed with garlic and seasoned oil, cashew and carrot roulade with midori sauce, sweet potato and goats cheese steamed pudding with herb oil.

Main courses at around £9.50 include mushrooms with back olive roulade; fried potato balls with fig and rum sauce; aubergine with melon and chilli, asparagus and pasta balls stuffed with pepper, pineapple chutney and mint yoghurt, haggis and garlic cream cheese with green ginger wine and rosemary, Pepper stuffed with sundried tomato and spinach souflee with lemon cream, pecan beanburger on a toasted bagel with red onion and roasted garlc gravy.

Our reviewers visited twice and found the service very variable.

Sorbet appears to be the only vegan dessert. Desserts around £3.50.

All wines have been guaranteed vegetarian by their supplier. House wine £11.95 per bottle, wines from around the World £17.95.

Bar attached open to all.

Vegetarian restaurant

57-61 Blackfriars Street
Edinburgh EH1 1NB

Tel: 0131-557 6136

www.blackbos.co.uk

Open: Mon-Sun dinner 18.00- 22.30, also Fri-Sat lunch 12-14.00

Open lunchtimes throughout the week during the festival.

Henderson's Bistro Bar

Vegetarian cafe-bar

Vegan friendly vegetarian wine bar with cosy atmosphere adjoining the Salad Table (below).

25 Thistle Street
Edinburgh EH2 1DR

Soup £2.95. Patés £2.20. Garlic bread £2.30 or £.50 to share. Wholemeal/Italian style bruschetta with marinated wild mushrooms £3.70 single or £6.75 to share, tomato £3.40/£6.50.

Tel: 0131-225 2605

Train: Waverly Edinburgh

mail@hendersonsofedin-burgh.co.uk

Mains include changing curries such as Thai with rice £6.75; Moroccan stew with aubergine, butternut squash, tofu, apricot and spices served with rice £6.95.

Open:
Mon-Wed 12.00-20.30,
Thu-Sat 12.00-21.30,
Sun 12.00-20.30 Extended hours during festival.

Kaliber and bottled beers and ciders £2.60-3.40. Freshly made blended juices £2-2.80. Coffees £1.50, pot of tea £1.30. House wine (vegan) £2.95 (175ml glass), £3.95 (260ml), £10.95 bottle, plus numerous other wines, many biodynamic, organic or vegan.

Children welcome, high chairs

No Smoking
Visa, MC

Henderson's Salad Table

Vegetarian fast food restaurant

Vegetarian café situated in the centre since 1962, next to the Bistro Bar (above).

94 Hanover Street
Edinburgh EH2 1DR
Tel: 0131-225 2131

Large selection of salads from £1.40. Pastries and savouries from £1.95. Up to 8 different hot dishes which change daily, from £4.25 lunch or £4.95 evening, such as Moroccan stew, roasted butternut squash and aubergine in apricot and cinammon sauce with couscous and flatbread. Sweets such as fresh or dried fruit salad £2.60, or apple or cherry pie £2.50.

mail@hendersonsofedin-burgh.co.uk

Train: Waverly Edinburgh

Open: Mon-Sat 8.00-22.30, Sun 12.00-20.00

They aim to provide at least one hot vegan dish and try to be aware of and cater for special diets. Use seasonal, local and organic produce whenever possible.

No smoking. Visa, MC
Children very welcome, high chairs

Fruit juices, fruit and herb teas 95p-£1.30. House wine £2.75 a glass, £9.50 bottle. Bottled beers from £2.40.

Small health food shop upstairs with take-away food including fruit pies, plus coffee bar. Open Mon-Fri 8am-7pm, Sat -5pm. Closed Sun.

Susie's Wholefood Diner

Vegetarian/vegan café where you can fill up for around a fiver and you'll be spoilt for choice with at least 7 (3 or 4 vegan) hot dishes, including Moroccan stew, sweet and sour tofu stir-fry, vegan cashewnut flan. Salads every day.

Relaxed menu rules allow you to combine several hot and cold dishes together and the portions are generous. Order a small plate for £4.95 or large £5.95 and make up your own feast.

Vegan desserts include banana and date and walnut cake or apricot slices £1.25–2.60.

House wine £8.95 bottle, £2.50 glass. Many more wines and beers and Scottish fruit wines, such as raspberry and bramble.

Vegetarian cafe

51 –53 West Nicolson St
opposite the pear tree
Edinburgh EH8 9DB

Tel: 0131-667 8729

Open: Mon –Sat 12.00–22.00 (Mon 21.00), closed Sun except during festival. Extended hrs during festival.

No smoking

Children welcome, 2 high chairs

No credit cards

SCOTLAND

Edinburgh

Ann Purna

Vegetarian Indian Gujarati restaurant

45 St Patrick's Square, Edinburgh EH8 9ET
Tel: 0131-662 1807
Open: Mon-Fri 12-14.00, 17.30-23.00;
Sat-Sun 17.00-22.00 (not lunch)

Local vegans tells us the food here is very nice, not oily like many Indian places, and they do a good vegan thali even though it's not on the menu. £4.95 for a 3-course lunch, £12-15 evenings. A meal could contain pakoras, bel poori or salad.; vegetable curry or korma or mixed veg curry or dhal; white or brown rice; desserts include fruit salad or strawberry, mango or carrot semolina halva. (They do vegan versions of everything.) House wine £8.25 bottle, £2.10 glass.No smoking throughout. Children most welcome, no high chairs. MC, Visa.

The Engine Shed Cafe

Vegetarian cafe

19 St Leonards Lane, Edinburgh EH8 9SD
Tel: 0131-662 0040
engineshed@aol.com
www.engineshed.org.uk
Open: Mon-Thu 10.30-15.30, Fri 10.30-14.30

Vegetarian café run by charitable organisation Garvald Community Enterprises which works with people with learning difficulties. Vegan options always available and a wheat-free choice in main dishes. Soup £1.40. Mains £3 typically include chillis and casseroles. Salads 90p a portion, £2.50 for a plate of 3 salads, and £3.50 for a substantial plate which you can fill with a helping of all the salads on offer. Hot desserts are occasionally vegan and there is always a fresh fruit salad. Counter service. No smoking. Cash and cheque only.

Forest Cafe

Arts centre and co-op veggie cafe

3 Bristo Place, Edinburgh EH1 1EY
www.theforest.org.uk
Open: almost every day 10.00–24.00

This is the "alternative" place, a veggie cafe run by volunteers. They have events, art shows, internet access, lots of sofas, fairly traded drinks and food, much of it local. Food is cheap but good so you should tip! Mains £3.70–3.90 such as burrito, (Mexican) burger with salad, falafel with salads, daily specials. Salads £2.80 such as rice and bean with salsa, tortillas and guacamole. Design your own sandwich from a long list of ingredients in organic brown bread, bagel or pitta £2, or ciabatta £2.40. Value meals £1.50–2.00 such as burger, falafel, vegan soup, rich muesli. Sweets, cookies, cakes, brownies, flapjacks £1.30. Fair trade organic coffees £1.20–1.60. Pot of tea for one £1.20, two £2, cuppa 90p. Hot chocolate £1.60. Organic soft drinks £1.20. Pint of cool 100% juice £1. BYO 50p beer per can/bottle, wine £1 per bottle. No spirits. No smoking except outside. Talk to them if you'd like to volunteer.

Suruchi

Indian omnivorous restaurant

14A Nicholson St, Edinburgh EH8 9DB
Tel: 0131–556 6583
Fax: 0131–622 7227
Lunch: Mon–Sat 11–14.00, Sun 11–16.00.
Dinner: every day 17–23.00

Around 30% of the food is vegetarian and you can eat for £11–15 per person. House wine £10–11 bottle, £2.50 glass. Children welcome, high chairs. Smoking area if not busy. MC, Visa. 10% discount to Vegan Society members.

Kalpna

Indian vegetarian restaurant

2–3 St Patrick Square, Edinburgh EH8 9EZ
Tel: 0131–667 9890
Lunch: Mon–Sat 12–14.00 (14.30 summer), (not Sun).
Dinner: Mon–Sat 17.30–23.00 (last order 22.30), Sun too during festival.

Gujarati and other dishes from north North and South India, with plenty of choice for vegans. Lunch £6 buffet every day. Dinner mains from £4.95 up to £15 thali. House wine £10.50 bottle, £2.50 glass. Well behaved children welcome, no high chairs. No smoking. Visa, MC (£90 limit). 5% discount for Vegetarian and Vegan Society members.

Filmhouse Cafe–Bar

Omnivorous cafe in cinema

88 Lothian Road, Edinburgh EH3 9BZ
Tel: 0131–229 5932
Open: Mon–Thu & Sun 10.00–23.30,
Fri & Sat 10.00–00.30

Always have vegan options available such as curries, spicy bean chilli, hummous, baked potatoes and a daily special £5–7. Smoking section. MC, Visa. Children welcome till 8pm, 2 high chairs.

The Elephant House

Omnivorous cafe

21 George IV Bridge, Edinburgh EH1 1EN
Tel: 0131–220 5355
Open: 08.00–23.00, Sat 09.00–23.00,
Sun 9.00–23.00

Popular with students, it has some veggie food though little in mains for vegans, but they do have vegan cakes such as carrot cake, chocolate cake and some biscuity things, all around £2.50.

Piemaker

Omnivorous pie shop

38 South Bridge, Edinburgh EH1 1LL
Tel: 0131–556 8566
Open: Mon 9–19.00,
Tue–Thu 09.00–midnight,
Fri & Sat 10.00–02.00am, Sun 11.00–19.00

Several vegetarian pies and about 4 vegan sweet pies including apple, apple and raspberry, maple and pecan nut pie. Average of 5 savoury pies such as Moroccan veg, Mexican veg, Thai mushroom and pepper, vegetarian haggis roll, all clearly marked if vegan, and very good value at £1.39. Not far from Princes Mile and near the studenty area of Southside.

Hanover Health Foods

Health food shop

40 Hanover St, Edinburgh EH2 2DR
Tel: 0131–225 4291
www.hanoverhealth.co.uk
Open: Mon & Tue 9.30–17.30, Wed 10.00–17.30, Thu 9.30–19.00, Fri & Sat 9.30–17.30

Offers personal advice from well trained staff as well as stocking a very wide range of health foods and vitamins.

Helios Fountain

Personal growth bookshop

7 Grassmarket, Edinburgh EH1 2HY
Tel: 0131–229 7884
Fax: 0131–622 7173
www.helios-fountain.co.uk
Open: Mon–Sat 10–18.00, Sun 12–17.00

Former cofee shop which now has become a personal growth bookshop with a variety of crafts, toys, and other eco-friendly kids stuff.

Jordan Wholefoods

Omnivorous world food shop

8 Nicolson Street, Edinburgh EH8 9DJ
Tel: 0131–556 6928
Open: Mon–Fri 9.30–17.30, Sat 10.00–18.00

Jordan Valley make their own range of vegetarian and vegan pates, pies, dips and pastries. The food is mainly Mediterranean, with olives, dolmades, stuffed aubergines and peppers. Take-away sandwiches, pates, pastries, pies, cakes, flapjacks and falafels. Outside catering possible.

Nature's Gate

Vegetarian wholefood shop

83 Clerk St, Newington, Edinburgh EH8 9JG
Tel: 0131–668 2067
Open: Mon–Fri 9.30–19.00, Sat 10–18.00, Sun 12–17.00

Lots of organic stuff, fruit & veg. Pasties and vegan chocolate cake.

Real Foods

Wholefood shop

37 Broughton Street, Edinburgh EH1 3JU
Tel: 0131 557 1911
Open: Mon–Fri 9.00–19.00, Thur til 20.00
Sat 9.00–18.00, Sun 10.00–18.00

8 Brougham Street, Edinburgh EH3 9JH
Tel: 0131 228 1657
Open: Mon–Fri 9–18.00, Sat 9–17.30, Sun 11–17.00

Big shops iwth many products organic. Snacks, breads, vegan wines.

Holland & Barrett

Health food shop

Unit 3 Hanover Building, Rose St, EH2 2NN
Tel: 0131 226 5802

Accommodation

Corry Lodge B & B

Vegetarian B&B set in one and a half acres of garden surrounded by woodlands. The self-contained log cabin overlooks the loch and hills. It comprises of a kitchenette, lounge/dining room, bathroom, one twin room and one double room, both costing £20 per person per night.

Self contained, there is a microwave and fridge, although no cooker. However the vegetarian owner Liz, who cooks with seasonal organic ingredients, will bring cooked breakfast over to you.

For breakfast start with fruit juice, cereal or muesli with (soya) yoghurt and stewed or fresh fruit from the garden. Followed by veggie bacon, veggie sausages, tomatoes, mushrooms, waffles and homemade bread or toast with homemade preserves and tea or coffee. Soya milk and margarine are always available.

A three or four course dinner is offered by arrangement for £10-£15 and could be soup, followed by a curry, nut roast, casserole, hot pot, stuffed vine leaves or a pasta dish. Liz makes her own eggless pasta.

Nearby are nature walks, the beach and sailing. The picturesque port town is a walk away and has a museum, theatre, pubs with live music and numerous restaurants serving vegetarian food.

The cabin has high chairs and a toy box, with swings and a play area in the garden. Be careful not to trip over one of the many hens that run free there!

The cabin has all amenities including an iron and hairdryer. Televisions are in the bedrooms and lounge. A recent guest called it utopia!

Vegetarian bed and breakfast

Garve Road
Lochbroom
Ullapool
Wester Ross IV26 2TB
Scotland

Tel: 01854-612681 / 612777

www.corrylodge-ullapool.co.uk

Email:
lized.corry@btopenworld.com

Train station:
Inverness, 30 miles

Open: all year

Directions:
Corry Lodge is 50miles northwest of Inverness on the A35, two miles from the village of Ullapool

Parking: available

Smoking is allowed on the porch only

10% discount to members of the Vegetarian Society, Vegan Society and people presenting this book

Children and animals welcome.

Cruachan

Vegetarian B&B in Minard, a village on the banks of Loch Fyne. Spend some time just relaxing in this friendly home, in between enjoying some of the many local walks or going on day trips. One single £20, one double £20 per person, one double ensuite £23 per person.

Breakfast is a feast beginning with fruit juice, cereals and fresh fruit, followed by your choice of several dishes, including The Cruachan – veggie sausages, scrambled tofu, tomato, mushrooms, beans and potatoes; The Benedict – tofu in a rich sauce served on a muffin and garnished with herbs; or The Sunshine – French toast with summer fruits. Many items are organic. Soya milk, yoghurt, vegan muesli and margarine, and herbal tea are all available.

Packed lunch is available with prior notice.

Dinner is offered for £13.50 and could be a tofu and roast vegetable plait or Moroccan casserole. Special diets catered for with advance notice. Pinto's vegetarian restaurant is a short drive away and owned by the same people.

Cruachan is close to many places of interest, including Kilmartin Glen with its standing stones, Dunadd Iron Age fortress and the Herb Garden at Lochgair. There's also the restored Highland village of Auchindrain and the Museum of Ancient Culture. At Cruachan, the grounds rise up to the forest and depending on the time of year, deer can be seen coming down the hill to feed.

Tea and coffee making facilities in the rooms.

Argyll

Vegan/vegetarian bed and breakfast

Inverae Farm Road
Minard
Argyll PA32 8YF
Scotland

Tel: 01546–886 378

Email:
iswcruach@talk21.com

Train Station: Glasgow, 20 miles, then bus

Open: all year

Directions: follow the A83 through Inveraray going towards Campbeltown, come into Minard, turn first right up farm track after 40 mph sign. Cruachan is the fourth house on the right.

Parking: available

10% discount to members of the Vegetarian Society and the Vegan Society

No children or pets

No smoking throughout

5% discount to people presenting this book

SCOTLAND Accommodation

Cuildorag House

Veggie bed and breakfast with three rooms amidst some of Britian's most magnificent landscapes. The double and family room are £17.50 per person per night and the double ensuite is £21 per person. Children are half price or free if they're under three years old.

Breakfast is cereal or porridge followed by veggie sausages, potato scones, baked beans, mushrooms and tomatoes. Vegan margarine and soya milk are always available and sometimes soya yoghurt. A three course dinner is offered by arrangement for £12.50. Organic produce is mainly used. There are veggie options at restaurants in nearby Fort William.

Fort William is a popular tourist centre and is close to the ski fields of Ben Nevis (Britian's highest mountain) and Glencoe. Skiing, snowboarding, hiking, climbing and bike riding are top activities in the area and you'll find plenty of shops where you can buy or hire equipment. There are walks for all levels, from strolls along Glen Nevis through the gorge to Steall Meadows, to the strenuous hike up Ben Nevis. Or you could embark on an eighty mile bike ride along the Great Glen Cycle route which links Fort William and Inverness.

The Isles of Skye or Mull make great day trips.

All three rooms have a television and tea and coffee making facilities. There is a video player in the lounge. All rooms have

Vegetarian bed and breakfast

Onich
nr Fort William
Highlands PH3 6SD
Scotland

Tel: 01855-821 529

www.cuildoraghouse.com
enquiries@cuildoraghouse.com

Train Station: Fort William, 10 miles, then a bus

Open: all year, except Christmas

Directions: Take A82 Glasgow Road. It's about 10 miles south of Fort William

Parking: available

There is a cot and high chair for the youngster in the family and the proprietor may even babysit for you

Smoking in the garden only

5% discount on stays of two nights or more to members of the Vegetarian Society, the Vegan Society, Viva! and people presenting this book

Drumskeoch Farm

Delightful detached farmhouse on a hill with outstanding views (see website), set in 11 acres of land with mature and newly planted trees and its own water supply. The nearest neighbours are half a mile away.

There are two double rooms with separate bathroom £25–£28 per person. No supplement for single occupancy. There is organic paint on the walls, organic bed linen and towels.

All the food is organic and vegetarian, with wheat and gluten-free diets catered for. Breakfast is both cooked and buffet: choice of cereals, muesli, fresh fruit (subject to seasonal availability), breads for toast, jams, nut butters, Marmite and pickles. Extras can be ordered: dried fruits, nuts and seeds, veggie sausages, mushrooms, baked beans, grilled tomatoes, hash browns, porridge cooked with water or any milk (including additional fruits, seeds, nuts etc), wholemeal pancakes with various toppings. Fruit compote also available, please order the night before. Also coffee and coffee alternatives, teas, herbal teas and hot chocolate, freshly squeezed fruit juices, fruit smoothies and sometimes fresh green juice.

Evening meals are available by arrangement for £10–£15. Soup, various vegan and veggie starters, goulash, hot pot, main and side salads, pasta, chilli, nut roast etc.

6 miles form the beach, near Galloway Forest providing nature walks and cycle routes. Girvan has a craft centre, boat trips to Aisla Graig Bird Sanctuary, golf course and Aroma's restaurant which has veggie options and is licensed, tel 01465-710071.

Vegan/vegetarian bed and breakfast

Pinwherry, nr Girvan
Ayrshire, KA26 0QB

Tel: 01465-841 172

drumskeoch@wildmail.com
www.drumskeoch.co.uk

Train: Girvan, then 12 mile taxi or Barrhill which has limited service but is only 6miles away and they can collect.

Open: all year

Parking available

Children welcome. Can provide cot and changing area

Guide dogs only

Credit cards not accepted

Directions: 2 miles off A714, 2 miles south of Pinwherry

Smoking outside only

SCOTLAND   Accommodation

East Lochhead

One hundred year old Scottish Farmhouse with views to the south-east over the Barr Loch and Renfrewshire hills. It is set within twenty-five acres of farmland and guests are encouraged to enjoy the two acres of beautiful garden.

There are three rooms; one double, one twin and one family, all with views, ensuite bathrooms, £60–£80 per room per night. There are also six self catering cottages which can accommodate from two to six people, £90–160 per person per week depending on season (see website).

The co-proprietor Janet is an enthusiastic and qualified cook and being almost vegetarian she specialises in veggie food. There is a large breakfast menu, which includes Scottish pancakes with maple syrup. Vegan muesli, veggie sausages, vegan margarine, soya milk and yoghurt are available with prior notice.

They provide evening meals for B&B guests and for those self-catering, if they wish. The vegetables are largely home grown.

Lochwinnoch is twenty-five minutes drive from Glasgow. There is much to do in the area including watersports, golf, walking and cycling. There is a cycle track opposite the house. The Ayrshire coast is only twenty minutes away.

East Lochhead has won many awards including the Scottish Tourist Boards Thistle Award for customer care in 2001, regional final for Vision In Business for the Environment Scotland 2003 and two gold awards for Green Business Tourism.

Tea and coffee making facilities and TV's are in the rooms. There is also a TV lounge.

Omnivorous bed and breakfast

Largs Road
Lochwinnoch
Renfrewshire PA12 4DX
(Glasgow outskirts)
Scotland

Tel and Fax:
01505–842 610

www.eastlochhead.co.uk
admin@eastlochhead.co.uk

Train station:
Lochwinnoch,
then phone for collection

Open: all year

Directions:
From Glasgow take M8, exit junction 28A to Irvine (A737). Road divides at Kilbarchan. Stay on right. At road head roundabout turn right on A760. Travel two miles. Look for East Lochhead on the left.

Parking: plenty of parking

Animals and children are welcome and there are cots and high chairs.

No smoking throughout

5% discount to people presenting this book

Cycles available for hire

Licensed

Accepts credit cards

AA Five Diamonds Award

Rhu Mhor Guest House

Traditional guest house set in an acre of wild tree-shrouded garden with resident roe deer, overlooking Loch Linnhe and the hills of Loch Eil. Owned for the last thirty years by the same veggie kilt-wearing proprietor!

There are seven guest rooms, four of which are ensuite with shower and toilet. Standard double or twin £16-£20 per person per night (£100-126 per person weekly). Double or twin ensuite £20-26 (£126-164). Children 4-12 years sharing with 2 adults £8-13 in family or triple, charged as adults if in their own room. Under 3 no charge. Three adults sharing receive 10% discount. Single occupancy £18-45 (£113-285) according to room and season.

For breakfast there is juice and oatmeal porridge, muesli or cornflakes. You then have the choice of either a continental breakfast or a full cooked breakfast which includes homemade veggie sausages. Soya milk is available. Notify when booking or upon arrival if you are veggie or vegan or have any other dietary needs.

Dinner is not provided, but there are a couple of Indian restaurants in Fort William where you can get a decent curry.

Rhu Mhor is set amidst some of the most beautiful scenery in Scotland and is just around the corner from Ben Nevis, Scotland's highest mountain. It is ideal for a quiet holiday taking in the beautiful scenery while on leisurely walks, or a more active holiday involving long distance walking, ascending to the summits of some of Scotland's highest mountains, rock climbing, canoeing or cycling the quiet back roads and forest paths.

There are washbasins in the rooms and tea and coffee making facilities. TV lounge and separate sitting room.

Omnivorous guest house

Alma Road
Fort William
Inverness-Shire PH33 6BP
Scotland

Tel: 01397-702 213

www.rhumhor.co.uk
rhumhor@btinternet.com

Train station:
Fort William, 10 minutes walk

Open: Easter-October

Children welcome and there is a cot (reserve when booking)

Animals welcome

Separate room for smoking

Directions:
From town centre go north on A82. Turn right into Victoria Road after the hospital, then left into Alma Road.

Parking: available

Visa, MC

SCOTLAND Accommodation

433

Sonnhalde

Victorian villa with an open outlook across the Spey Valley to the Cairngorm mountains. There are seven rooms; two double ensuites and one twin ensuite from £22 per person, two twins from £19 and two family rooms at £19–£22 per person.

Start the day with a hearty breakfast of fruit, muesli or porridge, wholemeal bread with various spreads and buckwheat crepes with tomatoes and mushrooms. Vegan muesli, margarine and veggie sausages are all available, as well as soya milk and soya yoghurt.

Dinner at £13 could be home made soup, then tomato, spinach and pine nut pie with fresh veggies and salad followed by plum and banana crumble. There is a good selection of shops and restaurants in town catering for vegetarians.

Kingussie is an excellent centre for touring the Central Highlands. It's within easy reach of the popular tourist town Aviemore and the Cairngorm ski slopes. The Cairngorm area is a National Park. There are lots of outdoor activities such as hill walking, mountaineering, natural history tours and of course skiing and snowboarding. There is a Folk Museum, Wildlife Park and a Whisky Trail nearby. Inverness is 40 minutes drive away and Loch Ness one hour.

Tea and coffee making and washbasins in the rooms. Televisions in rooms by request. There is a lounge with a TV, the only room which smoking is allowed in.

Omnivorous guest house

East Terrace
Kingussie
Highlands PH21 1JS
Scotland

Tel and Fax:
01540-661 266

Email: sonn.gh@btopen-world.com

Train Station: Kingussie, approx 1/2 mile, then owners can collect.

Open: all year

Children are welcome and they have a cot and a high chair.

Pets by arrangement.

Directions: Directly off A9, take the second exit for Kingussie (travelling north). Turn left into town, then right at traffic lights, then first right. It's the third house on the left.

Parking: available

Three Castle Terrace / Penny Browne

Vegetarian B&B in a bungalow overlooking the sea. Penny Browne, the vegetarian owner is friendly and informative. There are three rooms, one double ensuite at £21 per person, one twin at £19, and one single £19–21.

Wake in the mornings to fresh melon and strawberries with cereal or porridge and a full cooked English vegetarian breakfast. This comprises of veggie grills and burgers, grilled tomatoes and mushrooms as well as wholegrain toast and homemade jams, tea, herbal teas, and fresh coffee. Vegan margarine, soya milk and vegan muesli are always available.

Penny doesn't offer dinner but says there is plenty of veggie and some vegan food available at the restaurants in Ullapool.

From Three Castle Terrace it is five minutes walk to the terminal where you can jump on a ferry to visit nearby islands, such as Summer Isles for bird-watching. It is possible to drive to Handa Bird Island.

There is unlimited hill walking, a golf course, an indoor pool and lots of pubs in and around the town. The subtropical Inverewe Gardens are to the south of Ullapool.

There are no tea and coffee making facilities in the rooms, but you only have to ask and Penny will make you a cup.

Televisions are in the bedrooms and the lounge.

3 Star Award from Scottish Tourist Board.

Vegetarian bed and breakfast

3 Castle Terrace
Ullapool
Wester Ross IV26 2XD
Scotland

Tel: 01854–612 409

Train station:
Inverness, then a bus for 30 miles. Buses run twice daily.

Open:
by arrangement,
usually April–October.

Directions:
Coming from the south arrive at the pier head in Ullapool, turn right, go up hill for about 500 metres to a t-junction and turn left. It's the fourth house on the left.

Parking: available

Animals are accepted by arrangement

Smoking is allowed in the garden only

10% discount to people presenting this book, if staying more than one night.

SCOTLAND Accommodation

435

Woodwick House

Small veggie friendly hotel in the tiny area of Evie. There are two doubles and one twin for £32 per person, two double ensuites and two twin ensuites for £42–£46 per person.

Breakfast begins with cereal or organic muesli, followed by veggie sausages, tomatoes, mushrooms, baked beans and toast. Soya milk, vegan margarine and vegan muesli are available. They can cater for special diets.

The three–course dinner menu, £22–24, is flexible and could start with soup or garlic mushrooms, followed by spicy lentil puffs with spinach and roast veggies and then apple pie or treacle tart.

Evie is a very special, peaceful place which tends to attract those who care for the environment. Orkney has few trees and has always had a lack of wood, so is full of ancient historical sites which have survived because all the buildings were made from stone. The most impressive ancient monuments are all on Mainland like the Village of Skara Brae, the tomb of Maes Howe and the Ring of Brodgar. The best preserved example of a fortified stone tower in Orkney is only one and a half miles down a track from the area of Evie.

Wildlife is abundant and many people come to birdwatch. There are beautiful walks and sandy beaches nearby.

Televisions and washbasins can be found in the rooms. There are also two lounges, one with a TV and one with an open fire.

Omnivorous hotel

Evie
Mainland
Orkney KW17 2PQ
Scotland

Tel: 01856–751 330
Fax:01856–751 383

www.woodwickhouse.co.uk
mail@woodwickhouse.co.uk

Open: all year

Children welcome and they have cots and high chairs

Dogs are welcome for a fee of £7 for the duration of the stay if they come into the house

Smoking is allowed in one of the sitting rooms

Directions: Evie is on the east coast of the largest island, Mainland. Fly to Kirkwall Airport or catch the ferry from Scrabster to Stromness.

Parking: available

Visa, MC

Old Sawmill Cottage

Vegetarian bed and breakfast

Kilkerran, Maybole, Ayrshire KA19 7PZ
Tel: 01655–740 451
Email: kilkerran@breathemail.net
Train station: Maybole, 5 miles
Open: March–October (inclusive)

Cosy traditional cottage with wood burning stoves, set in a woodland garden on the banks of the River Girvan. One double ensuite room £15–20 per person per night. Breakfast is mostly organic. Vegans catered for. Dinner is not offered, but there are restaurants catering for veggies and vegans nearby. There is an abundance of wildlife in the surrounding area and many resident animals, so guests' pets are only accepted under special circumstances. No smoking throughout.

Borders

Wheatears

Vegetarian self catering

Lumsdaine, Coldingham
Borders TD14 5UA
Tel and Fax: 01890–771 375
Email: wheatears2003@yahoo.com
Train: Berwick-upon-Tweed 12 miles,
then taxi, or collection can be arranged

Stone farm cottages built in 1830 on the coast, less than an hour from Edinburgh, with over 2,000 native trees planted in the two acre wildlife garden. Self-catering detached cottage with one double, and a family room with double and single, £230–£400 per week. Vegan owners. Homemade vegan dishes using local, GM free, organic produce. 3-course dinner £17. Pets by arrangement. Children over 10 welcome. If you're interested in buying the place, please contact the owners.

Fife

Covenanter Hotel

Omnivorous hotel

The Square, Falkland, Fife, KY15 7BU
Tel: 01337–857 224
Train: Mark Inch, 4 miles
Open: all year
www.covenanterhotel.com
Email: g.menzies@btinternet.com

Five double ensuite rooms at £25 per person per night, or £39 for single occupancy. A two course meal in their restaurant is £15, or have three courses for £20. Vegans and those with special dietary requirements are catered for with advanced notice. Children welcome. No pets. Smoking in the cocktail bar only. 10% discount on food to people presenting this book.

Inverness–Shire

Glen Mhor Hotel

Omnivorous hotel

9–12 Ness Bank, Inverness,
Inverness–Shire, IV2 4SG
Tel: 01463–234 308
Train: Inverness, ten minutes walk
www.glen–mhor.com
Email: glenmhor@ukonline.co.uk
Open: all year, except New Year

45 ensuite rooms from £29.50 to £44 per person, up to £60 for an executive honeymoon suite. Evening meal is available and open to non residents. Vegans catered for with advanced notice. Children welcome and they have facilities for them. Pets also welcome. Smoking allowed in rooms and some areas. Rooms have satellite TV, ISDN ports, and tea and cofee making facilities.

SCOTLAND Accommodation

Lazy Duck Hostel

Self catering hostel

Badanfhuarain, Nethy Bridge,
Inverness–Shire, PH25 3ED
Train: Aviemore, then £12 taxi ride, or bus
Open: all year
Tel and Fax: 01479–821 642
www.lazyduck.co.uk
Email: veggie@lazy.duck.co.uk

The Lazy Duck is one of Scotland's smallest hostels sleeping only eight people in an open plan sleeping gallery £9.50 per person. Private use by arrangement. Well equipped kitchen, with home baked bread. Advance groceries delivery service. Village shop one mile. Linen provided, but bring own towels. Safe cycle storage. Washing machine and dryer. No smoking.

Sleeperzzz

Self catering hostel

Rogart Station, Sutherland IV28 3XA
Tel: 01408–641 343
Open: all year
www.sleeperzzz.com
kate@sleeperzzz.com

Hostel in a train. Two carriages hold 4 rooms, a showman's wagon has one double bed, and one carriage sleeps 4 with full self-catering facilities, shower and toilet. £10 per person, children under 10 £7.50, 10% discount for rail users and cyclists. Kitchen in the hostel and a Spar shop 100m away which sells organic muesli. Great for hill walking or cycling , and sampling malt whiskies in the inn 100m away which does vegetarian food though not vegan. See website for full details and pictures.

Isle of Barra Hotel

Omnivorous hotel

Tangasdale Beach, Isle of Barra
Western Isles HS9 5XW
Tel: 01871–810 383
www.isleofbarra.com/iob.html
barrahotel@aol.com
Transport: a post bus meets the plane and drops at the hotel, or get a taxi.
Open: Easter–October

Two miles from the ferry and six miles from the airport. Forty rooms; 7 doubles and 33 twins, £42 per person or £60 with dinner. Most have views of the Atlantic. Buffet of fruit juice, fruit, cereals and porridge followed by cooked breakfast. Soya milk and veggie sausages available, though they sometimes need advance notice. Four course meal and coffee is £24.95 to non residents or £18 to residents, always one veggie dish on the menu and vegans can be catered for. Children welcome, they have cots and high chairs. Pets welcome. Smoking allowed in rooms, bar and reception. Some disabled access. 10% discount to people presenting this book.

Ford House

Omnivorous guesthouse

Ford, Lochgilphead, Argyll PA31 8RH
Tel: 0845–456 1208. Mobile 07789 388 146
International: +44–1546–810 273
www.ford–house.com/home.htm

Several rooms and a log cabin, £28 adult, £20 child. Full vegetarian menu available.

Restaurants Scotland

Da Bod Cafe & B&B

Vegetarian and vegan café by day and restaurant in the evening, the only veggie place in Shetland. Open every summer to raise funds for the adjacent wildlife sanctuary in a stunning location. Down on the seafront at Hillswick. The name means the trading post in Norse.

Food is by donation – pay what you can, and all the proceeds go to help upkeep of the sanctuary.

Wholefood and organic as much as possible, they have snacks and light eats during the day such as soup, filled pitta breads, broccoli and cauliflower bake and pizzas (with vegan option).

Evening meals include summer vegetable and cashew nut loaf, mushroom stroganoff and provencal vegetable plait.

For dessert there is a vegan chocolate cake with hot chocolate sauce and apple and strawberry crumble.

The menu changes as they like to experiment. They can always cater for special diets.

They run various children's projects, raising awareness and educating children on animal and environmental issues and hold story-telling and musical evenings.

Bring your own bottle of wine.

Also an internet cafe by donation.

B&B: They now have a room available, with a deluxe king size sofa bed that pulls out and two sofa chairs, ideal for a family. £50 for the room or £30 for two people. You have your own breakfast bar and toaster in the room, or come to the cafe at 11am for a full breakfast. Dogs welcome.

Shetland

Vegetarian cafe and restaurant (plus B&B)

Hillswick Wildlife Sanctuary
Hillswick
Shetland ZE2 9RW

Tel: 01806–503 348

Fax: 01806–503 747

hillswick.wildlife@virgin.net

Open: May–Sept,
Tue–Sun 11.00–late

Non smoking

No credit cards

BYO

Children welcome and they have a playroom for them while you're eating, painted out like an underwater cave.

Directions:
Drive from Lerwick on A971 North as far as you can go until you get to Hillswick then turn left down onto seafront.

Pinto's Restaurant

Vegetarian and vegan restaurant with a fresh modern approach to international dishes and a Scottish flair. Plenty for vegans, with half of all dishes being suitable and clearly marked. Organic where possible.

Visitors have a complete quality dining experience where they will find the wine lists complements the food and the owner can advise on a good choice of wine.

Starters, £2.95–£3.95, such as polenta served with tapenade, or corn chowder, layered Mediterranean gateau, soup, green bean and sun dried tomato spring rolls.

Mains around £9.50, served with salads, potatoes and fresh vegetables, include Morrocan casserole with couscous, Greek pasta casserole, vegetarian haggis with clapshot stacks and whisky sauce, corn pancakes with sweet potato and ginger sauce, mushroom and salsify tartlet, and Southern Indian pasties.

Lunchtime specials around £4.95 – £5.95

Desserts, £3.25–£3.95, such as soya ice cream sundaes, gooseberry tartlet with vanilla sauce, vegan chocolate and pecan torte.

Wine £9.50–£19.50 for a bottle. Beer £2.75. Coffee £1.20

Can cater for gluten and wheat-free diets and they have organic and vegetarian wines.

Linda, the owner, is trained as a wine manager and runs cookery courses for the Vegetarian Society at the restaurant – phone for details.

Vegan/vegetarian restaurant

1 Argyll Street
Lochgilphead
Argyll PA31 8LZ

Tel: 01546–602 547

lswcruach@talk21.com

Open:
Tue–Sat 12.00–15.00, 19.00–22.00 during summer. Reduced hours in winter.

Booking advisable

Non smoking

Visa, MC.

5% discount to people presenting this guidebook

SCOTLAND Argyll

Argyll

The Smiddy

Omnivorous restaurant

Smithy Lane, Lochgilphead, Argyll PA31 8TA
Tel: 01546–603 606
Open: Mon–Sat 10–17.00 (last orders 16.00)

Omnivorous place that caters well for vegetarians. Homemade veggie soups and mains such as vegetarian flans. Daily changing specials such as potato nests with ratatouille, for £6–£7. Non smoking. MC, Visa.

Aberdeen

The Beautiful Mountain

Omnivorous sandwich bar

11 Belmont St, Aberdeen AB10 1JR
Tel: 01224–645353
Open:Mon–Sat 8.30–17.00,Sun 11.30–16.30

Soup and any sandwich you want made, with several vegan. Soya milk available.

The Lemon Tree

Omnivorous cafe–pub

Queen Street, Aberdeen AB24 5AT
Tel: 01224–621610
Food: Thu–Sun 12–16.00 (served till 15.00)

Primarily a live music venue. Local vegans meet here on the first Sat of the month when vegan food is available.

The Foyer

Omnivorous restaurant

82a Crown Street. Tel: 01224–582277
Open: Tue–Sat 10.00–23.30 (last food order 22.00), closed Sun–Mon
www.foyerrestaurant.com

Restaurant with contemporary art in a former church which serves vegetarian and some vegan food. Light lunch

(11am till 6pm) such as soup and bread £3.95, mains £5.50–6.00. Main menu (12–3pm, 5–10pm) starters £3.95–5.00, mains £9.50. Desserts £5. No smoking. Children under 13 welcome until 8pm, high chairs. Wheelchair access.

Soul and Spice

Afro–Caribbean bar/restaurant

15–17 Belmont St. Tel: 01224–645200
Open: Tue–Sat 18–midnight or later (22.00 last orders), closed Sun–Mon
http://soulnspice.freeservers.com/Cafe.htm

Separate vegetarian menu (mostly vegan). 8 starters £3.45, 13 mains £8.95 such as hot and spicy Ethiopian shiro wot with corn, cabbage, chili, sweet potato and plantain in groundnut sauce; 7–vegetable tagine. Rice, couscous, chips £1.50–3.00. licensed. No smoking. Children welcome, high chairs. MC, Visa.

Nature's Larder

Wholefood shop

60 Holburn Street. Tel: 01224–588 120.
Open: Mon–Sat 9–18.00, closed Sun

Grampian Health Foods

Health food shop

5 Crown Street. Tel: 01224–590 886

Dumfries

The Green Tea House

Vegetarian tea rooms

The Old Bank, Chapel Street
Moniaive, Dumfries & Galloway DG3 4EJ
Tel: 077520 99193   www.moniaive.com
Open: Apr–Nov Tue–Sun 11–17.00, Nov–Apr Thu–Sun 11–17.00.

Vegetarian tea room that uses local

organic products, 12 miles south–west of Dumfries. Homemade vegan soups and rolls £2.50. Vegetable pie with salad £5.50. Vegan date and apple slice, chocolate brownies. Fair Trade coffee and tea £1–1.40, served with vegan shortbread. Specialise in people with dietary sensitivities. Theme nights once a month, £20 a head with a choice of four starters, mains and desserts and a complementary drink when you arrive; bring your own wine. No smoking. Pets welcome. Children welcome, high chairs. No credit cards. Large garden. Moniaive has lots of local arts and crafts.

Abbey Cottage Coffee and Crafts

Omnivorous cafe

26 Main Street, New Abbey, Dumfries & Galloway DG2 8BY. Tel: 01387–850 377
Open: Daily 10–17.00 (April–Oct incl.); Sat–Sun only 10–17.00 (March, Nov & Dec)

Omnivorous café with lots for vegetarians. All vegetable based soups, and therefore suitable for vegans and other items can be adapted for vegans. Soups £2.35, homemade bean and hazelnut pate with mango and ginger £2.40. Carrot cake£2.25.

Glasgow

Mono

Vegan restaurant and bar

King's Court, 10 King Street, Glasgow, G1 5RB
Tel: 0141–553 2400
Open: Sun–Thu 12–24.00, Fri–Sat 12–01.00.
Food Sun–Wed 12–21.00, Thu–Sat 12–22.00.

Eat for £3 to £7 in the restaurant which is separate from the bar. Typical mains: pizza, tofu and veg satay with basmati rice, bangers, chips, salads, seitan stir-fry. Leave some room for hazelnut waffles with ice–cream and chocolate sauce £3, ice–cream, cheesecake with various toppings. Wine £9.95, 2.60.

Organic lagers, ciders and bottled beers. They make their own lemonade and ginger beer in their micro–brewery. Some live events. Children welcome, high chairs. Non smoking area in the food section. MC, Visa.

Stereo

Vegan bar

10 Kelvinaugh Street, Glasgow G3 8NU
Tel: 0141–576 5018
Open: Mon–Fri 17–23.45. Sat–Sun 13–23.45

Vegan food, three courses £6.50. Some vegan beers, but not all as they're tied to a brewery. More of a venue for bands on the way up (or down) like Franz Ferdinand. Smoking throughout. No licence for children. MC, Visa.

Balti & Dosa House

Omnivorous Indian Punjabi restaurant

11 Hyndland Street, off Dumbarton Road Glasgow G11 5QE. Tel: 0141–334 0084
Open: Mon–Thu 17.00–23.00, Fri–Sat 17–24.00, Sun 17–23.00

29 veggie dishes prepared separately. £9–10 for dinner. Desserts include vegan gulab jamun. House wine £10 bottl,e £2.90 glass. Children welcome, high chairs. MC, Visa, Amex, Diners.

The Bay Tree

Omnivorous Middle East restaurant

403 Great Western Road, Kelvinbridge Glasgow G4 9HY
Tel: 0141–334 5898
Open: Mon–Sat 9.30–22.00 (last order 21.00), Sun 9.30–21.00

Separate vegetarian and vegan menu with 5 or 6 dishes around £5.95, such as aubergine bakes, falafel. Unlicensed, BYO no corkage. Children welcome, high chair. Separate smoking section. No credit cards.

443

The 13th Note

Vegetarian restaurant and pub.

Vegetarian restaurant

Starters include soup, hummous and pitta and filo wraps for £2-£3. Mains, such as filo wraps, veggie burgers, soba noodles and aubergine cannelloni, £3-£6.

50-60 King Street
Glasgow G1 5QT

Tel: 0141-553 1638
Fax: 0141-552 5797

All desserts, from £3, are vegan including tofu cheesecake.

Open:
Mon-Sun 12.00-24.00,
food served until 22.00

All coffee beans and tea are fair trade. Enjoy a soyaccino, soya latte, soya hot chocolate, or soya mocha for £1.30; and pots of herbal tea for £1.10

Smoking permitted

Visa, MC

10% discount to members of the Vegan Society.

Grassroots Cafe

Vegetarian and vegan organic wholefood restaurant. Most dishes are either vegan or can be made vegan.

Vegetarian restaurant

97 St Georges Rd
Charing Cross
Glasgow G3 6UR

Full breakfast, £5.50. Starters, £2.95-£5.45, include soups, tempura and greek dips. Sandwiches, £5.50, with choice of breads and fillings – eg hummous and avocado.

Tel: 0141-333 0534

www.grassrootsorganic
.com

Salads from £3.50. Mains, £5.75-£7.65, such as burgers, thai green curry, vegetable chilli and a pasta of the week.

Train: Charing Cross
Tube Train:
 St George Cross

Special diets catered for. Soya milkshakes and smoothies.

Open: Every day 10.00-22.00

Child-friendly

Fully licensed. Smoking allowed except in smoke-free area. Visa, MC.

Disabled access

CCA Cafe & Scott St Bar

Omnivorous cafe in arts centre

Centre for Contemporary Arts,
350 Sauchiehall St, Glasgow G2 3JD
Tel: 0141–332 7959. www.cca-glasgow.com
Breakfast: Tue–Sat 9–11.30;
Food: Thu 12.00–21.00, Fri–Sat 12–22.00

Upstairs bar with south facing beer garden, downstairs courtyard cafe. Vegetarian options though not so good for vegans unless asked in advance. Starters £2.95. Mains £5.50. Budget deal all day every day veggie dish for a fiver, e.g. Moroccan veg tagine with couscous and orange salad plus a bottle of beer, glass of wine or pint of soft drink. Children welcome in cafe till 8pm but not bar. Smoking section. Visa, MC.

Fast Food Bar

Omnivorous take-away

66 Woodlands Rd, Charing Cross
Glasgow G3 6HA. Tel: 0141–332 5495
Open: Mon–Wed 8.00–18.00,
Thu–Sat 8.00–03.00

80% veggie fast food take away. Several burgers, 14+ pakoras and pizzas, all have vegan options. No credit cards.

Otago

Omnivorous restaurant

61 Otago Street, Off Great Western Road,
Kelvinbridge, Glasgow G12 8PQ
Tel: 0141–337 2282. www.otagocafe.co.uk
Open: Mon–Sun 10.00–22.00

50% vegetarian. Starters £4–5, mains, £9–12, such as asparagus risotto or Mediterranean roast veg. Desserts from £3.95. Always try to cater special diets including vegans. House wine, £11.95 for a bottle, £2.95 for a glass. Separate smoking section. Visa, MC.

Wagamama

Omnivorous Japanese restaurant

97–103 West George Street, Glasgow G2 1PB
Tel: 0141–229 1468. www.wagamama.com
Open: Mon–Sat 12–23.00 Sun 12.30–22.00

See Manchester entry for menu.

Grassroots

Wholefood supermarket and deli

20 Woodlands Rd
www.grassrootsorganic.com
Tel: 0141–353 3278
Mon–Wed 8–18.00, Thu–Fri –19.00,
Sat 9–18.00, Sun 11–17.00

Not far from their cafe–restaurant (page 444), Glasgow's wholefood super-market is vegan heaven. 70% organic. Fruit and veg, wine and beer, household products, body care. Deli has stacks of ready made dishes you can take home to heat up.

Roots & Fruits

Wholefood shop

351 Byres Rd, West End, Glasgow G12 8AU
Tel: 0141–339 5164
Open: Mon–Sat 07–19.00, Sun 08–19.00

Fresh fruit & veg and flowers. A few take–away pasta dishes in the fridge.

455 Great Western Rd, Glasgow, G12 8HH
Tel: 0141–339 3077
Open: Mon–Fri 8.30–19.00, Sat 8.30–18.30,
Sun 10–18.30

This branch has a hot food counter with veggie lunch £2–3.50, and fresh bread.

Ambala Foods

Indian speciality store

178 Maxwell Road, Pollockshields, G41 1SS
Tel: 0141–929 5620

Inverness-Shire

Cawdor Castle

Omnivorous restaurant

Nairn, Inverness–Shire IV12 5RD
Tel: 01667–404 401
Open: 1st May–13th October, 9.30–17.30

Set within Cawdor castle, as in Shake-speare's Macbeth, one of the Highlands' most romantic castles. Soups (some vegan) £2.85. Baked potato £2.95–4.25. Paninis, toasties, sandwiches £3.55–4.35. Salads £6.95. Little bottles wine £3.50. Lager £2. Children welcome, high chair. Smoking only at outside tables. MC, Visa.
Castle entry including garden: adult £5.80, 9.30–17.30.

Inverness

Pizza Express

Omnivorous restaurant

Unit B Eastgate Centre Inverness IV2 3PP
Tel: 01463–709 700
Open: every day 11.30–22.00

Isle of Skye

An Tuireann Arts Centre and Cafe

Omnivorous cafe

Sruan Road, Potree, Isle of Skye,
Inverness–shire IV51 9EG.
Tel: 01478–613 306
Open: Tue–Sat 10–16.30,not Xmas/New Year

Cafe in an arts centre that caters well for vegetarians and also always have something vegan including daily soups. Mains £5 such as roast veg and couscous salad.   Children welcome, high chairs. Licensed. No smoking except outside seating. Visa, MC.

St Andrews, Fife

Nahm–Jim

Omnivorous Thai restaurant

Crail's Lane, St Andrews, Fife
Tel: 01334–474000. Closed Monday

Tofu and veggie dishes and vegan tempura.

Sutherland

Achins Coffee Shop

Omnivorous cafe

Inverkirkaig, Lochinver, Sutherland IV27 4RS
Tel: 01571–844 262
Open: every day 10.00–17.00 Easter–October

Small coffee shop with some vegetarian options such as nut roast with salad, £4. Non smoking. Visa, MC.

Holland & Barrett

Health food shop

49 Netherkirkgate, Aberdeen
Trinity Centre, 155 Union St, Aberdeen

61 High St, Dumbarton. Tel: 01389–730 754

Unit 31, Kingsgate Shopping Centre
Dunfermline. Tel: 01383–624 915

Unit 20, Wellgate Centre, Dundee

45 High Street, Falkirk. Tel: 01324–633 397

Unit 3, Douglas Bridge, Galashiels

94 Sauchiehall St, Glasgow
9 Queen St, Glasgow G1

34 Eastgate, Inverness. Tel: 01463–234 267

132 High Street, Kircaldy.Tel: 01592–205 349

34 Brandon Parade South, Motherwell

Thistle Centre, Stirling. Tel: 01786–465 350

Unit 13, The Olympia, East Kilbride

WALES

Accommodation

Restaurants

Shops

Isle of Anglesy

Caernarfon

Bangor

Colwyn Bay

CONWY

FLINTSHIRE

Denbigh

WREXHAM

GWYNEDD

Aberystwyth

POWYS

CARDIGANSHIRE

PEMBROKESHIRE

CARMARTHENSHIRE

Carmarthen

Pembroke

Swansea

1

2

3

4

5

6

7

8

9

10

11

Newport

Cardiff

1. North Port Talbot
2. Bridgend
3. Rhondda Cynon Tuff
4. Merthyr Tydffi
5. Caerphilly
6. Blateneau Gwent
7. Torfaen
8. Monmouthshire
9. Vale of Glamorgan
10. Cardiff
11. Newport

Wales

Wales is a different country: The landscape sparkles with extra vitality when you venture west of Offa's Dyke.

History did not begin in 1066 here. Read the ancient stories collected in The Mabinogion and gain the satisfaction of locating the precise scenes. Listen to the language spoken by King Arthur and Myrddin (Merlin). The latter lived on a vegan diet of "roots, grasses, wild fruit and berries, or nuts and acorns." Even the patron saint, Dewi (David), was recorded to have eaten a vegan diet and drank water. And Welsh water is so pure... try "crystal clear Cerist."

The tradition continues, including amongst those labelled "hippies" for seeking refuge in Welsh valleys from English materialism. The self-sufficiency impetus, especially in West Wales where John Seymour lived and wrote his books, is strong and although Seymour killed his own animals, many of his followers chose to be at least vegetarian. Stay in the independent hostel at Brithdir Mawr, near Trefdraeth (that's the Newport in Pembrokeshire) to sample the simple life of a sustainable community.

Industrial erections known as windmills and which attract tempting government grants now threaten to desecrate the solitude of Mid Wales. Yet there need be no conflict of "green interest." The kitchens at the Centre for Alternative Technology, near Machynlleth, are powered by the much more environmentally-friendly and dependable source of renewable energy known as wood. The Vegan Society sponsored the first bio-fuel machine here in the early 1980s to demonstrate how subsidised and environmentally damaging sheep farming could be replaced with the return of the natural climax vegetation of oak woodland, surviving today in pockets such as at Dinas Emrys (National Trust) and Ynyshir (Royal Society for the Protection of Birds). The Foot and Mouth crisis of 2001, when the closure of footpaths devastated the tourist industry, emphasises the need to make this change. Dinas Mawddwy's Meirion Mill (on the site of King Arthur's last battle, at Camlan) now grows willow for renewable energy, while the Greenwood Centre, near Caernarfon, demonstrates the potential of switching from sheep to native broadleaved trees (not to be confused with the alien conifers planted by the Forestry Commission).

Anecdotal evidence suggests that there are more vegans per head of population in Wales than in England. They have their own little magazine, Y Figan Cymreig, while there's no trouble in buying vegan ice creams in little coastal resorts such as Aberaeron. Spot the vegan restaurant as you tour the medieval walls of Conwy. Wales still has its share of flesh-eaters but vegetable samosas can be found in the most surprising of places.

Laurence Main is a director of the Vegan Society and was its Assistant Secretary in the early 1980s. The author of 50 walking guidebooks, he spends much of his life camping and recording dreams on sacred peaks. A Druid, he researches and gives talks on Earth Mysteries (including leys) and King Arthur. His guidebooks include the popular Walk Snowdonia and North Wales, published by Bartholomew (cartography by David Perrott), The Spirit Paths of Wales (Cicerone Press) and A Meirionnydd Coast Walk (Gwasg Carreg Gwaig). Laurence contributes walks in Wales to Country Walking and Trail magazines and writes weekly walks in The Western Mail. Guided walks are sometimes available (telephone Laurence on 01650 531354 or write to him at 9 Mawddwy Cottages, Minllyn, Dinas Mawddwy, Machynlleth, SY20 9LW –GDSH85 9142).

Heartspring, vegan bed & breakfast retreat centre

The Barn

Deep in the beautiful Black Mountains, between Hereford and Abergavenny, amid abundant nature, The Barn is the ideal retreat for walking, resting, reflection and rejuvenation. One double and one twin £20 per person, one double en suite £22.50 per person. Single person £25. Children £10.

The accommodation is heated largely by wood burning stoves and each room has stunning views of the mountains and its own access on to the hill.

Cooked breakfast in the bright conservatory includes tomatoes, mushrooms, beans, sausages and pancakes. Soya milk and vegan musli available.

3 course evening meal available for £12 such as soup with home made bread, shepherd's pie with organic salad and veg, and apple crumble.

The Barn is surrounded by beautiful woodland, historic sites and many local ancient churches and chapels. The 12th century ruins of Llanthony Abbey are 3½miles away. It is close to the Offa's Dyke Path, on the Cambrian Way and just off National Cycling Route 42.

The Black Mountains offer all kinds of outdoor activities and water sports including climbing and abseiling, caving, kayaking, (white water) canoeing and rafting, raft building, mountain bike hire, gorge scrambling/walking and land carting.

The world famous book town of Hay-on-Wye is 8 miles away.

Classes in yoga and painting are available at the Barn at certain times of year.

Tea/coffee making in rooms. No TV. Hairdryer available. Vegan owner.

Vegetarian bed & breakfast

Pen-y-Maes
Capel-y-Ffin
Monmouthshire
NP7 7NP
Wales
(Powys border)

Tel: 01873 890477

www.thebarn-wales.co.uk
alice@thebarn-wales.co.uk

See also
www.hay-on-wye.co.uk

Train station: Abergavenny 14 miles then taxi

Open: all year

Directions:
Half way between Hereford and Abergavenny on the A465, turn off for Hay-on-Wye. Go through Llanthony and Capel-Y-Ffin then turn off left.
(map on website)

Children welcome

No smoking in house

Parking: available

Children welcome

No credit cards

Chapel Guest House

Chapel Guest House lies in the pretty village of St Brides, between Newport and Cardiff. There are seven rooms, all with ensuite bathrooms, single at £30-35, double or twin and one family £26-£27.50 per person per night. Under new ownership from June 2005 but they're keeping the veggie breakfasts going.

Breakfast is fruit and muesli or cereal followed by a full cooked English breakfast. Vegan sausages, soya milk, vegan margarine and vegan muesli are all on offer.

Dinner is not available, but there are two restaurants in the village and there is a veggie cafe in Newport, and a couple of inns opposite which do veggie food.

Chapel House, formerly Rehoboth Baptist Chapel built in 1828, fell into disrepair and in 1982 was converted into the 3 star accommodation it is now. It is only half a mile from the 'special scientific interest' site of the Severn Estuary which can be accessed across footpaths. Tredegar House Stately Home with its boating lake, park and gardens is two miles away. There is a golf course a mile away.

The village is ideally placed for touring South Wales and the Wye valley. It is only four miles from Newport with its premier indoor Go-Kart track and eight miles from Cardiff which has one of the finest Civic Centres in Europe and a great night life.

Children are welcome and those under twelve are half price. Pets are accepted by arrangement.

There are televisions and tea and coffee making facilites in the rooms. TV lounge. There is a ground floor room so disabled access is possible.

Omnivorous guest house

Church Road
St Brides Wentloog
Near Newport
Gwent NP10 8SN
Wales

Tel : 01633-681 018

Fax: 01633-681 431

www.smoothhound.co.uk/hotels/chapel1.html

chapelguesthouse@hotmail.com

Train station:
Newport, 4 miles, then bus or taxi

Open: all year

Directions:
Leave M4 at junction 28. Take A48 towards Newport. At roundabout take third exit, signposted, 'B4239 St Brides'. Follow B4239 for approximately three miles to village centre, turn right into Church Road, then first left into Church House Inn car park. Chapel Guest House is on the left.

Children welcome

No smoking throughout

Parking: available

WALES Accommodation

Graianfryn

Graianfryn is on the northern edge of Snowdonia National Park between the mountains and the sea. One double and one twin at £22 per person per night and one double ensuite at £24 per person.

Breakfast is fruit juice and fresh or dried fruit salad with home made cereals or muesli, followed by veggie sausages, mushrooms, tomatoes, scrambled tofu and potato cakes with home baked organic rolls. Vegan muesli, margarine, soya milk and yoghurt available.

Dinner is £18 and could be tomatoes stuffed with flagelot beans and olives in a tomato and avocado sauce, followed by Jamaican sweet potato casserole with marinated tofu, pineapple rice and salad, and for dessert, strawberry tofu ice cream. Fresh organic produce is used where possible and some of it is from the garden.

Graianfryn is set in magnificent countryside and is an ideal base for walking and exploring North Wales. It is three miles from the foot of Snowdon yet only 20 minutes drive to the nearest sandy beach. Nearby are gentle walks as well as plenty of challenging peaks for the more serious walker or climber. You could take a scenic journey on the Ffestiniog steam railway or visit one of the picturesque villages, castles, stately homes, lakes or botanical gardens.

Children over four are welcome and those under eleven are half price. Children eleven to thirteen years get 25% discount. Picnic lunches can be supplied. Secure cycle storage. There is a lounge with a fireplace, television, books and games. Tea and coffee making facilities in the rooms. Well behaved pets welcome.

Vegetarian guest house

Penisarwaun
Caernarfon
Gwynedd LL55 3NH

Tel: 01286–871 007

www.fastasleep.me.uk
christine@fastasleep.me.uk

Train: Bangor, 7 miles, then a bus or taxi. They can sometimes collect.

Open: all year

Directions:
From the A55 follow signs for Llanberis. Take the Bangor exit. At the round-about at the end of the slip road, turn left then right past the Little Chef. At the next roundabout, turn left along the A547. Pass Beran petrol station on your left, then take the next right to Penisarwaun. Immediately turn right again down a track. Graianfryn is on your left before the farm gates.

From A5 (South and Midlands) turn left at Capel Curig then right over the Llanberis Pass and through the village of Llanberis. After the second lake turn right down the A547 towards Bangor. Ignore the first left turning for Penisar-waun but take the next, then immediately turn right down a track. Graianfryn is on your left before the farm gates.

Parking: available

No smoking throughout

Green Haven

Vegetarian B&B in a modern bungalow close to Pembrokeshire Coast National Park. They have a double and a twin room both costing £19.50 per person per night or £18 for stays of 3 nights or more.

Breakfast is dried fruit salad and cereal, or soya yoghurt with vegan muesli, followed by grilled mushrooms and tomatoes, baked beans and sauteed potatoes with toast and preserves, as well as tea and coffee. Veggie sausages, vegan margarine and soya milk are available.

Dinner is offered for £10 and could be celery soup with garlic bread, followed by tomato and basil gnocci with mixed salad and green beans. For dessert, you may have apple and apricot crumble with soy cream. All the above are home-made, ensuring only vegan ingredients are used. There is also a restaurant, Keeston Kitchen (01437–710 440), which caters for veggies, a five minute walk away. Pelcamb Inn (01437–710 267) and Rising Sun (01437–765 171) are also veggie-friendly and only a short drive away.

A major attraction throughout the year is the famous coastal path, which winds for 186 miles around bays and headlands through the Pembrokeshire Coast National Park. There are beaches within a ten minute drive and surfing is possible.

You can get a ferry to Ireland at Fishguard, half an hour's drive away. There are also plenty of museums, castles, standing stones and other places of interest. Boat trips are also possible to Skomer, Skokholm and Ramsey.

The tiny cathedral city of St. David's is a twenty minute drive. In August 2002 the National Eisteddfod was held near here.

Tea and coffee making facilities are in the rooms and the visitors' lounge has a TV, VCR, CDs, tapes, books, and games. Children are welcome.

Vegetarian bed and breakfast

Nolton Road
Simpson Cross
Haverfordwest
Pembrokeshire SA62 6ES
Wales

Tel : 01437–710 756

Email:
greenhaven710756@
aol.com

Train station:
Haverfordwest, 4 miles, then bus or taxi, or they can collect.

Open: all year

Directions:
From the centrally located market town of Haverford-west take the A487 for about four miles towards St Davids, into the village of Simpson Cross. Green Haven is about fifty yards down Nolton Road.

Parking: plenty available

Disabled access possible

No smoking throughout.

No pets please

WALES Accommodation

455

Gwalia Farm

Gwalia is a small and remote working farm with goats, hens, sheep (whose produce is used for breakfast) and beautiful views of the Snowdonian mountains. There are two rooms: one twin and one family costing £22 per person per night.

They aim to produce as much of their own food as possible. Virtually all their fruit and vegetables are from their own organic garden.

Breakfast could be muesli or porridge followed by veggie sausages, baked beans and home-made whole wheat organic bread with home-made preserves. Vegan margarine and soya milk available.

Dinner is offered for £12 and could be sweet and sour beans with brown rice and home grown freshly picked organic veggies, followed by rhubarb crumble.

As well as the rooms in the house, they also have a self catering caravan, or if you'd rather be out in the elements you can pitch a tent.

If you fancy a swim or a paddle in a canoe, the farm has a lake in the conservation area.

It is an excellent spot for walking and bird watching. The Centre for Alternative Technology is nearby.

There are no televisions, but they do have 'a log fire, spring water and silence.' Children are welcome and they can help feed the chickens.

Machynlleth

Vegetarian bed and breakfast

Cemaes
Machynlleth
Powys SY20 9PZ
Wales

Tel: 01650 511377

www.gwaliafarm.co.uk

Train station:
Machynlleth, 9 miles

Open: all year

Directions:
Take the A489 from Machynlleth, or from Newtown take the A470. Gwalia Farm is on a lane between Cemaes and Commins Coch.

Parking: available

No smoking throughout

High chair available

Pets are welcome

Heartspring

Ecological Victorian country house overlooking stunning coastal conservation area. One single and one twin room at £26–£30 per night and two family rooms at £26–£42 per person. All rooms decorated with chemical free paints, simple country furniture and natural fabrics. Rooms have large south facing windows with stunning views of the sea, village and castle.

Breakfast is an organic buffet with a large selection of fruit and cereals with plant milks and soya yoghurt as well as breads with various jams. Gluten free choices. Vegan margarine and muesli are available. A vegan organic dinner is offered from £8. Special attention is paid to those with allergies.

The house is south facing and due to its elevated position receives long hours of sunshine. It's surrounded by an acre of organic gardens and is only five minutes walk to the beach. Numerous coastal paths to explore and the ruined castle is just up the lane. For the active, there is sailing, canoeing, walking, cycling and swimming.

B&B stays, self catering breaks, group courses and workshops and tailor made individual healing retreats are all possible at Heartspring. There is a therapy room, a wooden meditation sanctuary in the garden and a wood burning stove in the workshop space. Fresh spring water for drinking and bathing. Wide choice of therapies and teaching sessions such as Meditation, Profound Relaxation, Massage, Reiki and more.

Tea and coffe making in rooms. No TV's to spoil the natural environment.

See photo page 451.

Vegan B & B and retreat centre

Hill House
Llansteffan, Carmarthen
Carmarthenshire
SA33 5JG
Wales

Tel: 01267–241 999

www.heartspring.co.uk
info@heartspring.co.uk

Train Station: Carmarthen, 7 miles, then bus taxi or owners can collect.

Open: all year

Directions: Follow the M4 west through South Wales until it becomes the A48. Follow until you reach Carmarthen. Then follow signs for A40 (St Clears). Continue for a 1/4 mile and take the first exit signed Johnstown & Llansteffan. Turn right at the T junction for Llansteffan. Follow this B troad for 6 miles to the village of Llansteffan. Continue to the centre of the village. Go past the Sticks Hotel on your right and after four houses turn right into a narrow driveway (opposite church tower). Heartspring is the big pink house at the top.

Parking: available

Children welcome and there are cots and highchairs

No smoking throughout

Cash or cheque only

The Old Post Office

(Hay-on-Wye)

Vegetarian guest house

Llanigon
Hay-on-Wye
Hereford HR3 5QA
Wales

Tel: 01497-820 008

www.oldpost-office.co.uk

Train station:
Hereford, 20 miles, then
bus to Hay, then taxi

Open: all year

Directions:
From Hay-on-Wye take
B4350 towards Brecon. After
1/2 mile, turn left sign-
posted 'to Llanigon'. Drive
another mile, turn left
before school. It is the big
white house on the right
opposite church.

Parking: available

No smoking throughout

Children welcome
depending which rooms are
available.

Animals welcome.

10% discount to members of
the Vegetarian Society,
Vegan Society, Viva!, PETA,
Animal Aid and people
presenting this book if
staying three nights or more
in the ensuite room or a
week or more in the
standard room. Please
advise her when you book.

Veggie B&B in an outstandingly beautiful area with the Brecon Beacons national park on the doorstep.

There are three rooms in this grade 2 listed house; one twin/double at £20 per person per night and two twin/double ensuites at £30 per person per night.

Breakfast starts with fresh grapefruit and cereals, followed by a choice of main course such as homemade potato cakes, tomatoes, mushrooms, beans, fried bread and fresh locally-baked wholemeal bread with homemade preserves. All washed down with fruit juice, tea and coffee of course. Vegan margarine, soya milk, vegan muesli and soya yoghurt are all available. Ask in advance if you'd like veggie/vegan sausages.

Dinner is not offered but veggie proprietor Linda will point you in the right direction with an eating out guide for Hay, which is only two miles away.

Llanigon is a nice quiet hamlet on the edge of the Black Mountains with not much night life apart from a few pubs. However, there is loads to tire you out during the day so you'll probably just fall into bed in the evenings. Being so close to the Brecon Beacons there are 11 miles of walking and mountain bike trails. The River Wye is not far away where you can go canoeing. Paragliding is also available nearby – the best way to see the amazing scenery and it's not scary – honest!

There are tea and coffee making facilities in the rooms and a TV in the lounge.

Plas Dolmelynllyn

Country hotel in a Welsh Manor house built in 1550. It is situated in Dolmelynllyn, in the southern part of Snowdonia National Park. There are nine rooms all with ensuite bathrooms; one single at £65 per night, four doubles and three twins at £90–£180 per room per night and one family room at £180 per night. Discounts are available out of season and short breaks for dinner, bed and breakfast are available all year.

A number of veggie options are offered for breakfast. The chef, Joanna, provides a six course country house dinner for £29 (a la carte also available). Vegetarian options are always on the menu and most dishes can be adapted to accommodate other diets. Advise them when you book if you are vegan.

The menu changes daily, but expect something like deep fried red onion and corn fritters to begin, then pineapple and lime water ice, devilled field mushrooms on sweet potato mash with chilli dressing for your main course and for dessert, warm coconut crempogs with grilled mango on passion fruit sauce.

They use local and homegrown organic produce whenever possible and are open to non-residents for dinner.

The hotel is set in three acres of terraced gardens with a stream running through it and is surrounded by National Trust owned forests, mountains and meadows. There are many attractions such as gold mines and slate mines, castles and stately homes, superb beaches and little villages nestling in the grand scenery. If you're feeling adventurous why not climb Cader Idris or Snowdon just a short drive away.

Each of the bedrooms has a different decorative theme and all have a television, radio, telephone, hair dryer and tea and coffee making facilities.

Omnivorous hotel

Ganllwyd
Dolgellau
Gwynedd LL40 2HP
Wales

Tel: 01341–440 273

Fax: 01341–440 640

www.dolly-hotel.co.uk
info@dolly-hotel.co.uk

Train station:
Barmouth, 10 miles

Open: February–December
(inclusive)

Directions:
5 miles north of Dolgellau
on the A470

Parking: 20 spaces

Continental breakfast can
be served in rooms if
requested

No smoking throughout

MC, V accepted

10% discount to members of
the Vegetarian Society.
Please notify on booking.

WALES Accommodation

459

Plas Madoc

Vegetarian guest house with splendid views of Llandudno, the sea and the mountains of Snowdonia. There are four bedrooms, all with ensuite bathrooms. One single £32 per night, one double £27–£32 per person, one twin £27 per person.

There is lots on offer at breakfast and all the food is organic when possible. Begin with fruit juice and a selection of cereals with fruit and soya yoghurt. Follow up with veggie sausages, tomatoes with basil, mushrooms, baked beans and potato rosti served with thick crusty toast. Tea, coffee, fruit tea and dandelion coffee are all on offer. They have vegan margarine, muesli and soya milk.

There are miles of breathtakingly beautiful walks in the area and it is a birdwatcher's delight. A 10 minute walk from the house is Great Orme and Ski Llandudno which has a dry slope and 700m toboggan run. Take the longest cable-operated tramway in Britain to the top of Great Orme, or if you have a head for heights take a cable car. The town itself is fronted by a sweeping bay and has much to offer like ten pin bowling, an art gallery, a museum and a theatre. Watersports and bike hire available.

The mountains of Snowdonia are only fifteen minutes drive and the sandy beaches in Anglesey half an hour's drive.

Tea & coffee making facilites and TV's in rooms. The guest lounge is well stocked with books, maps, guides and games.

Llandudno

Vegetarian guest house

60 Church Walks
Llandudno
Conwy LL30 2HL
Wales

Tel: 01492 876514

www.
vegetarianguesthouse.com

plasmadoc@vegetarian
guesthouse.com

Train station:
Llandudno, 1/2 mile

Open:
all year, except Christmas and new year

Directions:
A55 along North Wales coast, then A470 to Llandudno. Go straight through the town, left at Empire Hotel and past tram station. It's the second hotel on the right.

Parking: off road parking available

Well-behaved children welcome

No smoking throughout

Cash or cheque only

10% discount given to members of the Vegetarian Society, Vegan Society and Viva!

Dyfiguest

This comfortable modern bungalow run by vegan owners Carol and Hank, offers panoramic views overlooking the Dyfi valley and Snowdonia National Park. Come here for tranquility and relaxation. One deluxe double ensuite £25–£26 per person or £35 single occupancy. Hot water is solar driven and the room has a large power shower, washbasin, hairdryer and Fair Trade tea and coffee making facilities. Satellite TV in the TV lounge.

Start the day with a choice of four cereals such as vegan muesli, fruit and juice followed by sausages, tomatoes, baked, chilli, or curried beans, garlic mushrooms, hash browns, sausage and lentil surprise, and Spanish barley. There is also organic homemade brown and white toast with marmalade or jams with coffee, tea and herbal teas. Vegan margarine, soya milk and yoghurt are provided. Where possible, all food is organic and sourced locally from the Dyfi Valley. All diets are catered for.

Evening 3-course meal £15 is available on request. There are plenty of pubs, cafes and restaurants in Machynlleth 5 minutes walk away such as Quarry vegan/veggie cafe and health food shop. The veggie cafe at the Centre for Alternative Technology is 2 miles away.

Nearby Cader Idris and Glyndwr Way are ideal for walkers. Traffic-free roads, numerous cycle tracks and routes. Cycle hire in town. Aberdovey and the coast are only 8 miles away, Talylyn Steam Railway 5 miles and Ynyshir Nature Reserve 2 miles.

4 Star Welsh Tourist Board, 4 Red Diamonds AA, Welcome Host Gold Award, Green Dragon Environmental Award. Shortlisted for Best Use of Energy Award for Businesses – Wales Environment Awards 2004.

Machynlleth

Vegan/vegetarian bed and breakfast

20 Fford Mynydd Griffiths
Machynlleth
Powys SY20 8DD
Wales
Tel: 01654–702 562 /
07790–715 256

www.dyfiguest.co.uk
dyfiguest@yahoo.co.uk

Train and bus station: 200 yards Machynlleth.
Free pick-up service to and from railway and bus stations.
For walkers, transfer backpack transport to next destination.

Open: all year

Directions: From Machynlleth town centre take A487 to Dolgellau. Take second right railway station, stay right to top of hill. Bungalow last but one on right. From north, go under railway bridge, take the first left to station, then right to top of hill. Bungalow last but one on right.

Parking: Private secure parking; lock-up garage for bicycles

No children or pets
Cash or cheque only

Easy access, no steps, wide doorways

No smoking throughout

In National Vegetarian Week 2005 10% off donated to Vegetarian Society

Trericket Mill

Vegetarian guest house, bunk house and camp site situated in the Upper Wye Valley. There are three rooms in the house; two doubles and one twin costing £24–£27 per person per night, all with ensuite bathrooms and tea and coffee making facilities.

The bunkhouse sleeps up to eight people from £10 per person per night in two cosy rooms. In the mill, overlooking the garden, there is an ensuite bunkroom for two, a common room with games, books and a TV along with drying facilities.

The terraced orchard provides a few camping pitches for tents and small camper vans with the use of the bunkhouse shower and toilet facilities.

Breakfast can be a continental or a full cooked breakfast, including home-made bean, tomato and basil sausages, mushrooms, tomatoes and baked beans. Breakfast is available for bunkhouse guests and campers by arrangement. Soya milk and yoghurt, vegan margarine and vegan muesli are all available.

Three-course dinner for £15 could be mushroom pate with wholegrain toast, followed by chickpea stew with apricots, wild rice and veggies, completed with apple and raspberry crumble and soya ice cream for dessert.

Trericket Mill is a brilliant base for activities in the Brecon Beacons National Park. The Wye Valley walk passes the door with riverside walks in both directions. A national cycle route is also nearby with opportunities for off road cycling. Wildlife abounds amongst the many delights such as Prince Llewellyn's cave or the fairy glen with its hidden bathing pool.

Builth Wells

Vegetarian guest house & self catering

Erwood
Builth Wells
Powys LD2 3TQ
Wales

Tel: 01982 560312

www.trericket.co.uk
mail@trericket.co.uk

Train station:
Builth Road, 11 miles, then a bus.

Open:
all year, except Christmas

Directions:
Set back from the A470 Brecon to Builth Wells road between the villages of Llyswen and Erwood

Parking: available

Pets are allowed in the bunkhouse only

Smoke free throughout

5% discount to members of the Vegetarian Society, Vegan Society and Viva! on stays of 2 nights or more

Ty'r Ysgol

Veggie guest house in an early Victorian school house situated in a large garden surrounded by field and fells. There are three double ensuite rooms priced from £29–£34 per person per night. Each room is individually designed and all have views over the garden, countryside and hills.

For breakfast begin with fruit juice, fresh fruit and cereal or muesli, followed by tofu sausages, field mushrooms, tomatoes, baked beans and toast. Specials are offered some mornings. Vegan margarine, soya milk, rice milk, vegan muesli, gluten and yeast free breads are available.

Dinner, mostly organic, is offered for £20 and could be carrot and coriander soup to begin, followed by leek and wild mushroom croustade accompanied by salad or vegetables. For dessert, apple, pear and blackberry crumble. If the weather's nice you might like to have your dinner in the garden or the summerhouse. Organic produce is used where possible. Advise when booking if you are vegan or have any food intolerances or allergies.

There are ten beaches all within a twenty minute driving radius of the schoolhouse, including the four mile sandy beach Porth Neigwl (Hell's Mouth) which is popular with surfers. It is possible to get lessons and hire equipment for both surfing and sailing at nearby Abensoch. Wildlife and flora are abundant including seals, dolphins, herons and badgers. Further afield is Snowdonia National Park, Portmeirion Italianate village, the Welsh Highland Railway and many more attractions.

One dog is welcome. Tea and coffee making facilities and TV's in the rooms. Guest lounge. No smoking except in the garden. Parking available.

Vegetarian guest house

Botwnnog
Pwllheli
Gwynedd LL53 8PY
Wales

Tel: 01758-730661

www.tyr-ysgol.co.uk

Email:
maureenlewis@botwnnog.fr
eeserve.co.uk

Train station: Pwllheli, 10 miles, then bus or taxi or collection is possible.

Open: all year

Directions: From the A55 along the north coast road, leave at the second Bangor exit towards and through Caernarfon following the A487. After 5 or 6 miles, there is a roundabout where the A487 goes left towards Portmadog. Take the A499 towards Pwllheli. Continue through Pwllheli to Llanbedrog. After the 30 mph signs, take the next right turn, (B4413) signposted 'Aberdaron, Botwnnog, Sarn and Archery school'. Continue for 6 miles to Botwnnog. After entering the village and passing a large health centre, take the only main road to the right, signposted Llaniestyn. Continue up the hill passing the school and church on your right. Just after the national speed limit signs you will see the entrance of Ty'r Ysgol on the right.

WALES   Accommodation

The West Usk Lighthouse

Beautifully converted lighthouse on the east coast of St. Brides, with the sea a stone's throw from the front door. One of the proprietors is veggie. The lighthouse has one single ensuite from £55 per night, three double ensuites and one family room from £85 per person per night (£10 for children). The single room has a sea view and a four poster bed. One of the double rooms also has a four poster bed, one has a water bed and the other an antique bed.

Begin the day with cereal, followed by a cooked breakfast. Soya milk and veggie sausages available. For added romance, order some champagne with it. If you want to sweep your partner of his or her feet, a Rolls Royce drive to a local highly acclaimed restaurant can be arranged for £30 one way.

Local attractions include the palatial Tredegar House, Castell Coch, the Roman city of Caerleon and the castles of Caldicot Cardiff, Caerphilly and Penhow. There are also dry ski slopes, helicopter rides and go-karting for those who need some action. Both the Usk Valley and the Brecon Beacons are an easy, scenic drive away.

Take in the 360 degree view from the lantern room, or relax in the roof garden, watching the ships go by, whilst basking in the sunset or sunrise. West Usk Lighthouse is the perfect place to come for a romantic secluded break. If you're hoping your partner will propose, you may well get your wish. The host claims that in the last seven years, they've had over thirty marriage proposals among guests.

If you need extra pampering, they have a floatation tank and provide many complimentary therapies including aromatherapy, reflexology, healing, stress relief, hynotherapy, and detox from £40. Tea and coffee making facilities and TV's in rooms.

Omnivorous bed and breakfast

Lighthouse Road
St. Brides
Wentloog
near Newport
Gwent NP10 8SF
(Monmouthshire)

Tel: 01633–810 126

www.westusklighthouse.co.uk
info@westusklighthouse.co.uk

Train Station: Newport Gwent, 5 miles, then taxi or collection can be arranged

Open: all year

Directions: from the M4, at junction 28, take the A48 for Newport, then B4239 St. Brides. Drive for two miles. Turn left at Cattle Bridge into a long winding bumpy road.

Parking: available

Pets accepted by arrangement

Children welcome

Credit cards accepted

No smoking throughout

The Old Post Office

(Rosebush)

Omnivorous small guest house, 24 seat bistro, bar and 15 seat restaurant, open to non-residents, with masses for vegetarians, half of it vegan. One double (or family room with cot available), £20 per person per night. Tea/coffee making, washbasins and TV in rooms. Cooked vegan or veggie breakfast. Pets welcome (not elephants). Laundry and drying facilities.

The restaurant has a Welsh and international menu and a specials board that changes daily. 4 vegan and 7 veggie entrées £2.95-3.95 such as basil and tomato soup, broccoli and walnut vegan pancake. 7 vegan and 7 veggie main courses £6.95-8.00 such as mushroom loaf, Brazil nut pancake, Moroccan stuffed peppers, and apple and onion tart.

Desserts £1.95-3.95 may include vegan sorbets, always a fruit salad, vegan apple pie or treacle tart.

The children's menu comprises a meal, dessert and drink £5.45. Smaller portions of adult veggie/vegan meals are available as are veggie fingers, sausages and burgers.

Beer, two or three real ales each week. House wine from £6.95 bottle, £2.10 for a large glass. Tea or coffee, soya milk and milkshakes. Selection of sugar-free juices.

Smoking in the bar only. No credit cards at time of publication. Children of all ages welcome, they have a toy box in the bistro. Best to book for meals.

Rosebush

Omnivorous guest house and restaurant

Rosebush,
near Maenchlochog
Clynderwen
Pembrokeshire SA66 7QU

Tel: 01437 532205

www.
postofficerestaurant.co.uk

info@postofficerestaurant.co.uk

Restaurant:
Tues-Sun 12-23.00
(Sun eves – bookings only)
Mon closed

Oct-Easter :
Closed Mon all day and
Tuesday afternoons

Directions: from A40 take
B4313 at Narberth.
Rosebush is 8 miles. Head
for Maenclochog.
Not to be confused with
the other Old Post Office in
Powys.

Children of all ages
welcome

Toy box in bistro

Children's menu

Pets welcome

Smoking in bar only

Parking available to the
right of restaurant

Anglesey – accommodation

Bryntirion B&B

Omnivorous B&B

Bryntirion, Lon Ganol, Llandegfan,
Menai Bridge, Anglesey LL59 5YA
Tel: 01248-712 775
Train station: Bangor 3 miles
Open: all year   www.visitwales.com
Email : Mmaggiemccoy@aol.com (Two M's)

Traditional Welsh cotage. All diets
catered for using local produce. Two
twin en suites (probably 3 by end of
2005), one of which is ground floor and
disabled friendly with grab rails etc. One
night £30 per person, 2+ £25. Single
occupancy £35. Evening meal £10 2–
course, £12.50 for 3, packed lunch on
request. Children welcome, high chair.

Gwynedd – accommodation

Tremeifion

Vegetarian hotel

Soar Road, Talsarnau, Gwynedd LL47 6UH
Tel: 01766 770491
www.vegetarian-hotel.com
Train station: Talsarnau, 5 minutes walk
Open: all year, except Dec–Jan (incl.)

Four double rooms £56–£65 per
person per night for bed, breakfast and
evening meal. Children and pets
welcome. No smoking throughout.

Aberystwyth – restaurants

The Tree House

Omnivorous restaurant
and organic shop

14 Baker Street, Aberystwyth SY23 2BJ
Tel: 01970-615791
Restaurant open: Mon–Sat 12–15.00. Will
open evenings for parties and groups.
Shop: Mon–Thu 9–18.00, Fri 18.30,
Sat 17.00, closed Sun

Restaurant upstairs on two floors (stairs

only), shop downstairs. The standard
restaurant menu has 2 veggie mains
including veggieburger £3.50 with
wedges and salad. The specials menu
changes daily and always has soups
which are always veggie and nearly
always vegan, almost all of the 5 to 7
mains are veggie and at least three are
vegan risotto with shitake mushrooms,
stuffed baked aubergine with mixed
salad, spinach dolmades, all £5.75 or
less. Also baked potatoes, salads,
wedges, hummous. Always at least one
vegan cake £2.50. Juices, coffees, soya
milk. No smoking. MC, Visa. House wine
£8.95, glass £2.25. Children welcome,
high chair.
Organic shop stocks fruit and veg,
groceries, take-away food (mostly
veggie) such as soup and rolls, pasties,
little tarts, flapjacks, but not sandwiches, though there's a sandwich bar
next door.
On a Sunday in Aber you could try an
Indian or Chinese restaurant.

Isle of Anglesey

The Harvest Moon Cafe
and Healing Centre

Vegan Cafe

4 Newry Street, Holyhead,
Isle of Anglesey, North Wales LL65 1HP
www.holyhead.com/harvestmoon/
Tel: 01407-763 670
Open: Tue–Sat 10.00–17.00

98% vegan 2% veggie café in a healing
centre which offers various treatments,
runs meditation groups and a lending
library of 1,000 books. Soups £2, with
garlic bread £2.50, homemade veggie
burgers £2.80, chilli and sandwiches.
Baked potatoes £2.50–£3.50 such as
avacodo and mango chutney.
Homemade peanut munchies 60p and
cakes like chocolate cake and lemon
drizzle cake from £1.30. Banana

smoothy £1.20. Swedish glace ice-cream. Selection of fruit teas. Soya milk available. No smoking throughout. Cash and cheque only.

Cardiff

Cafe Naz

Omnivorous Indian restaurant

Unit 8/8c Mermaid Quay, Cardiff Bay
Tel: 029 2049 7333. www.cafenaz.co.uk
Open: Mon–Thu 12–15.00, 18–24.00;
Fri–Sun 12.00–01.00

Classy Indian, south Indian and Bukhara cuisine with many veggie dishes. Starters £2.95–3.95, mains £7–10, thali £11. No vegan desserts. Bottle of house wine £8.95, glass £2.75. Smoking area. Pay and park area in the complex. Reservations essential Fri–Sat. Children welcome, high chairs. Visa, MC.

Crumbs

Vegetarian cafe

33 David Morgan Arcade, Cardiff CF1 2AF
Tel: 02920 395 007
Open: Mon–Fri 10–15.30, Sat 10–16.00

Salads £4, spuds from £1.80–£3.65, hot dishes like curry or pasta £4.75. Desserts include fruit salads, carrot cake £1.40 and muffins. Children's portions, no high chairs. Unlicensed. No smoking except outside in the summer. No credit cards.

The Chapter Arts Centre

Omnivorous cafe

Market Road, Canton, Cardiff
Tel: 029–2031 1050
www.chapter.org
Open: every day 09.00–21.00

Cafe in an arts centre. Always have some vegetarian dishes as a lot of local veggies and vegans eat there, around £5 for a main. Self–serve salad bar £3 large bowl. Flapjacks but none vegan, though as we go to pres they're getting a new chef. There's a bar on site. Teas 50p, coffee £1.20, cappuccino £1.50, they have soya milk. Cafe no smoking (but bar is), and there's a big outdoor patio seated area.

Carmarthen

Waverley Vegetarian Restaurant

Vegan/vegetarian cafe

23 Lammas Street, Carmarthen
Carmarthenshire SA31 3AL
Tel: 01267–236 521
Open: Mon–Sat 9–17.00 (shop), 11.30–14.00 (cafe)

Vegetarian and vegan café. Mains £3.95–£4.50 such as potato cake with salad. Vegan desserts like apple pie and fruit crumble. Herb teas. No smoking throughout. Visa, MC. The health store attached to the cafe has a small amount of wholefoods, including organic veg, cosmetics and supplements.

Llanidloes (Powys)

Great Oak Cafe

Vegetarian cafe

12 Great Oak Street, Llanidloes
Powys SY18 6BU
comptons.powys.org.uk/cafe.html
Tel: 01686–413 211
Open: Mon–Sat 9.00–16.00 , closed Sun

Veggie cafe with many vegan dishes also. Curry, shepherds pie, veggie sausage rolls are all vegan. Specials board changes daily. Mains £5.50. Salads £3. Filled rolls £1.60, jacket potatoes £2.50. Vegan flapjacks and cakes form £1.30. Soya milk and egg–free mayo available. Drinks include soya milkshakes, organic lemonade and vegan coffees such as soyaccino.

WALES Restaurants

Machynlleth (Powys)

Centre for Alternative Technology Restaurant

Vegetarian restaurant

Pantperthog, Machynlleth, Powys SY20 9AZ
Tel: 01654–705950
www.cat.org.uk
Open: Winter 10–16.00, Summer 10–17.00.
Closed Xmas, Boxing Day and two weeks in
January.

Vegetarian wholefood café in the Centre for Alternative Technology. Main course £5–6 such as chilli with rice., vegan clearly marked but not always available. Licensed for alcohol. Non smoking. Credit cards ok. High chair.

The centre itself is open all year apart from above holidays, summer 10.00–18.00, winter 10–16.00. Admission summer adult £8, children (3 years+) £5.50, concessions £7.20, family (2+2) £24, (2+3) £27.50, (+4) £30. Winter adult £5.35, children £3.20, concessions £4.80, families £15.90, £18.95, £22. Three miles north of Machynlleth on the A487. 10% discount if you arrive by bus (every 20–40 minutes on weekdays in the summer), bike, train and show your tickets or put your bike in their shed. Right on Sustrans 8 national bike route.

Quarry Cafe

Vegetarian cafe

13 Heol Maengwyn,
Machynlleth, Powys SY20 8EB
Tel: 01654–702 624
Open: Winter Mon–Sat 9–16.30
(Thu –14.00), closed Sun.
Summer Mon–Sat 9–17.00, Sun 10–16.00.

Vegetarian café and take–away using some organic and fair–traded produce. Part of the Centre for Alternative Technology but this café is in the town not the centre (3 miles away). Soup, hummous, various curries, nut roasts, pasta bakes, salads. Filled rolls £1.50, soups £1.95, £5.95 mains. Desserts including vegan cakes and vegan fruit crumble 95p–£2.50. Teas, coffees, cappucino 60p–£1.20, can be made with soya milk. Prepack soya milk–shakes. Bring your own booze, no corkage charge. High chairs, some children's portions, one step wheelchair access.

Wholefood shop in the same street.

Newport (Gwent)

Hunky Dory Vegetarian Coffee Shop

Vegetarian cafe

17 Charles Sreet ,Newport, Gwent NP20 1JU
Tel: 01633–257 850
Open: Mon–Sat 10–15.30, Sun closed
occasional evening every two weeks

Vegetarian café. Main meals £5.45 such as broccoli bake, pies, pizza, pasta bake. Home made cakes, scones, flapjacks, almost all vegan. Bring your own wine, no corkage. No smoking. Children welcome, no high chairs. Cash and cheque only.

Swansea

Govinda's Vegetarian Restaurant

Vegetarian Indian restaurant

8 Cradock St, Swansea,
West Glamorgan SA1 3EN
Tel: 01792–468 469
Train: Swansea Central
Open: Sun–Thu 12–15.00, Fri–Sat 12–18.00

Vegetarian restaurant 2 minutes from town centre and with three quarters of menu vegan and clearly indicated. Starters, £1.25–£2.25, include soups and salads. Mains, £3.95–£5.45, with burgers and a daily changing Govindas special which includes daal and vegetable dishes. Desserts such as vegan apple pies £1.75 and vegan cheesecake £2.15. Non smoking. No credit cards.

Khushi Khana

Indian vegetarian cafe

36 St Helens Rd, Swansea SA1 4AY
Tel: 01792-411076
Open: Mon–Sat 11-19.00, Sun 11-16.00

Specialise in north Indian food such as dals, biryani, vegetable dishes. Set thali £4.99 to £7.50. Vegan no problem. Desserts include vegan laddoo. Lassis can be made with soya milk. Also a completely vegetarian grocery store open the same hours which sells home made Indian snacks including samosas. MC, Visa. No smoking. Children welcome, high chair. No alcohol.

The Retreat

Vegetarian cafe in wholistic centre

2 Humphrey Street, Swansea SA1 6BG
Tel: 01792-457 880
www.theretreatcentre.org
Open: Tue–Sat 10 till mid evening

Soups with wholemeal bread, corn, rice or oat cakes £2.95. Daily specials such as bangers & mash, chilli and rice, spinach dahl or Moroccan stew, lunch £4.95, dinner £5.95. Vegetable or spicy bean burger with brown rice or wholemeal roll and mixed salad £3.95. Saturday breakfast (served 12-3pm) sausages, hashbrown, mushrooms, beans, tomato & toast £5.95. Desserts from £1.95 include crumbly cakes, brownies, dairy–free ice–cream, hemp flapjacks, Green & Black's Maya Gold, muffins & biscuits. Bring your own wine, small corkage charge.
Swansea Vegans group meet here

monthly for a social evening (contact George Barwick on 01792 518773 for more details).

Cardigan (Ceredigion)

Go Mango Wholefoods

Organic vegetarian wholefood shop

4-6 Black Lion Mews, High St, Cardigan, Cardiganshire (Ceredigion) SA43 1HJ
Tel: 01239-614727
Open: Mon–Sat 9-17.00, Thu – 17.30

Mostly vegan shop, all sandwiches vegan.

Carmarthen

Aardvark Wholefoods

Wholefood shop

2 Mansel Street, Carmarthen, Pembrokeshire
Tel: 01267-232 497
Open: Mon–Wed & Fri–Sat 9-17.00, Thu 9-18.30

Omnivorous wholefood shop with take-away pasties.

Haverfordwest (Pembrokeshire)

Natural Grocer

Wholefood shop

11 Quay Street, Haverfordwest
Pembrokeshire SA61 1BG
Tel: 01437 767499
Open: Mon–Sat 9-17.30 (17.00 Sat)

The fridge contains things like tofu and vegan cheese.

Machynlleth (Powys)

Quarry Shop

Vegetarian health food shop

27 Heol Maengwyn, Machynlleth,
Powys SY20 8EB .Tel: 01654-702 339
Open: Winter Mon-Sat 9-17.00, closed Sun.
Summer Mon-Sat 9-17.30, Sun 10-16.00.
(Thu shuts at 14.00 except in school holidays)

Mainly organic and fair trade, with wholefoods, vitamins, homeopathic remedies, toiletries. 10% discount for Vegetarian and Vegan Society members.

Newport (Gwent)

Beanfreaks Ltd

Wholefood shop

Chartist Towers, Upper Dock Street, Newport
Tel: 01633 666150. Open: Mon-Sat 9-17.30

Wholefood shop. No take-aways.

Porthmadog (Gwynedd)

Vegonia Wholefoods

Vegan wholefood shop

49 High St, Porthmadog, Gwynedd
Tel: 01766-515 195
Open: Mon-Sat 10-17.30

Completely vegan wholefood shop. Sometimes they have pasties and of course vegan ice-cream.

Rhos-on-Sea (Denbighshire)

Natural Choice

Wholefood shop

14 Colwyn Avenue, Rhos-on-Sea,
Denbighshire LL28 4RB (Conwy)
Tel: 01492-549520. Open: Mon-Sat 9-17.00

Cruelty-free toiletries, remedies, supplements and veggie boxes.

Holland & Barrett

Health food shop

4b High Street, Abergavenny NP7 5RY
Tel: 01873-850 429

253 High Street, Bangor LL57 1PD
Tel: 01248-355 934

40 Town Wall, St. David's Centre, Cardiff
CF10 2DQ
Tel: 02920-342 094

Unit 8, Grayfriars, Carmarthen SA31 3BN
Tel: 01267-237 198

Unit 2 Colwyn Centre, Sea View Road,
Colwyn Bay, Denbighshire LL29 8DG
Tel: 01492-534 336

Unit 16, Riverside Key, Haverfordwest
SA61 2EZ
Tel: 01437-762 723

51 Mostyn Street, Llandudno LL30 2NN
Tel: 01492-870 814

73 Monmow Street, Monmouth ND5 3EW
Tel: 01600-772 153

42a Commercial Street, Newport NP20 1LP
Tel: 01633-264 596

58 High Street, Rhyl, Denbighshire
LL18 1TW
Tel: 01745-355 044

10 Union Street, Swansea SA1 3EF
Tel: 01792-644011

27 Hope Street, Wrexham LL11 1BD
Tel: 01978-262 847

IRELAND

This chapter contains a selection of some of the best vegetarian places to stay and eat in Ireland. There are terrific places to eat out in Dublin and wonderful country retreats.

You can pick up additional information at these great Irish websites:

www.vegetarian.ie

www.ireland.travel.ie

www.tourismireland.com

www.visitdublin.com

www.corkkerry.ie

www.irelandnorthwest.ie

www.irelandwest.ie

www.hostels-ireland.com

www.irelandyha.org

Phone +353-830 4555 to get free fold-out leaflets with maps and information about 36 hostels throughout Ireland.

www.ryanair.com (cheap flights)

www.swiftcall.ie (cheap overseas calls)

www.daft.ie (long term accommodation)

www.gcn.ie Gay Community News. Free printed version at Outhouse gay and lesbian community centre, 105 Capel St, Dublin 1, 12-18.00 weekdays. Also at Books Upstairs on Dame St. Gay switchboard Dublin Mon-Fri 8-10pm, Sat 3.30-6pm, 01-872 1055.

As with all internet listings, beware of places that have closed down and always phone first before going.

With grateful thanks to Nana Luke and friends, who compiled the Vegetarian Guide to Ireland, for all their work.
Telephone dialling code for Ireland from the UK is 00 353 then drop the first 0 of the phone number. From overseas +353.

ULSTER

Donegal Bay

Donegal

NORTHERN IRELAND

Balina

Monaghan

Castlebar

ULSTER

Cavan

Dundalk

Westport

CONNAUGHT

Drogheda

Longford

Roscommon

Navan

IRISH SEA

Tuam

Athlone

Galway Bay

Galway

Dublin

Tullamore

Kildane

LEINSTER

Lahinch

Carlow

Arklow

Limerick

Kilkenny

Tipperary

Trabee

Dingle

MUNSTER

Kilarney

Cork

Bantry

Bandon

Cork Harbour

CELTIC SEA

Republic of Ireland

Republic of Ireland

Green Lodge

Vegetarian self catering

Pearson's Bridge, Bantry, Cork
Tel: 027-66146
Open: all year
http://homepage.eircom.net/~greenlodge
Bookings: greenlodge@eircom.net

Self catering apartments for vegans and vegetarians with private cooking facilities, bathroom and own entrance. 8km from Bantry in peaceful wooded surroundings. Ensuite single room 105 euros per week (65e for 3 days), double/twin 130e (80e). Apartment for two with dining room and kitchen 175e per week (110 for 3 days). Family flat from 175-205e for 3-5 people (130-150 for 3 days). Children welcome, babysitting by arrangement, cot available. No pets. Booking deposit 100 euros per week. No credit cards. TV's in all rooms. Wheelchair access. Laundry service. Table tennis and basketball.

Shiplake Mountain Hostel

Youth hostel

Dunmanway, West Cork
Tel: 023-45750
Open: all year except two weeks in winter, phone to check
www.shiplakemountainhostel.com
info@shiplakemountainhostel.com

Youth hostel for 20 people on the side of a mountain, about 5km from Dunmanway. Traditional gypsy caravans for two people (can also take a child) 11.50 euros per person per night in low season, 13.50 in high season. Private room 16.50 all year per person. Dorm for 6-8 people 11 euros. Camping adult 6 euros, child 4 euros. Smoking only in the common room.

Bicycle hire 8.50 euros, maps available. Laundry service. Courtesy pickup from town. Weekly and group discounts.

Chysalis Holistic Ctr

Vegetarian B&B and holistic centre

Donard, Wicklow
Tel: 045-404713
www.chrysalis.ie
peace@chrysalis.ie
Open: all year except Christmas,
office 9.30-17.30

Vegetarian holistic centre in its own grounds. Bed and breakfast, in two lovely cottages. Singles cost 48 euros, for stays of two days and doubles are 75 euros per room per night. Craft shop, sauna, therapies, meditation garden. Non smoking. Call them for a programme of events.

Cussens Cottage Vegan Guest House

Vegan guest house

Ballygrennan, Bulgaden, Kilmallock
Limerick
Tel: 063-98926
cussenscottage.com
info@cussenscottage.com

Set in over 1.5 acres of gardens, Cussens Cottage is believed to be Ireland's only vegan guest house. All rooms are ensuite with their own door opening onto the gardens. Doubles 32 euros (£21.50) per person, call for single rates. Rooms have electric heaters, hairdryers and kettles with teas, coffees and milks. Breakfast is a huge affair which keeps you well fed on vegan food until the four course dinner, 17 euros (£11.50). Much of the food comes from their veganic garden, i.e. organic with no animal manure. They run veganic gardening weekends and other special events. An ideal base for touring the south-west, or stay here and take the train into Dublin. No smoking in public rooms. Not a suitable holiday venue for children.

The Phoenix

Vegetarian guest house & restaurant

4 Shanahill East, Boolteens
Near Castlemaine, Kerry
Tel: 066-9766284
www.thephoenixorganic.com
phoenixtyther@hotmail.com
Open: Easter-Oct, rest of the year bookings only. Restaurant 09.00-midnight Easter-Oct

Organic vegetarian restaurant and farmhouse accommodation resting under Slieve Mish mountains on the Dingle peninsula. Room rates in the main house are 20-27 euros per person. Chalets are 490 euros per week. Always vegan and gluten-free options. The vegan menu could include hummous and olives with popadoms, chargrilled tomatoes and polenta bake with white wine sauce. Lounge with open fire, library, studio for workshops, extensive gardens. Camping (with kitchen available) , group and private facilities. Sandy beach and Kerry airport nearby. Courtesy lifts available to and from Castlemaine. Dublin Express bus stops in Castlemaine. Half an hour drive from Kerry airport. Pets welcome. Children welcome, high chairs and baby bed in family room.

Blazing Salads

Vegetarian take-away

42 Drury Street, Dublin 2
Tel: 01-6719552
blazingsalads@eircom.net
Open: Mon-Sat 9.00-17.30 (later in summer), Sun closed

Vegetarian take-away using mainly organic ingredients, with a regularly changing menu. Soups, self serve salad bar with cost by weight, sandwiches, samosas, tofu and veg spring rolls, apricot slices and fruit and nut bars. They cater for vegan, gluten-free and wheat-free diets and have soya milk, soya cappuccinos, soya milkshakes and Innocent smoothies. Visa, MC, Amex.

Cornucopia

Vegetarian cafe and take-away

19 Wicklow Street, Dublin 2
Tel: 01 6777583
Open: Mon-Sat 08.30-20.00,
Thurs late till 21.00, Sun 12-19.00

Very busy vegetarian counter service café, with a great selection for vegans. There are always two soups, ten salads, five main dishes such as Moroccan lentil stew with rice and salad, cakes and cookies. Freshly baked bread by the slice including vegan soda bread. Breakfast menu served 09.00-12.00. Special diets no problem with all items clearly marked. Organic ingredients are used as much as possible.

Accommodation IRELAND

Cafe Fresh

Vegetarian cafe

Top floor, Powerscourt Townhouse Centre,
South William Street, Dublin 2
Tel: 01-671 9669. www.cafe-fresh.com
Open: Mon-Sat 10-18.00, closed Sun

In a busy shopping mall, this cafe has a couple of vegan dishes daily, which changes with the seasons, such as curry or tagine, and always a casserole, 9.55 euros with two salads to eat in. Vegan, dairy-free, yeast-free, gluten-free, sugar-free or wheat-free clearly marked. No smoking. Children welcome, baby chair. Lift. MC, Visa.

Govinda's

Hare Krishna vegetarian restaurant

4 Auinger Street, Dublin 2
Tel: 01-475 0309
Open: Mon-Sat 12-21.00

Maintaining the reputation of Hare Krishna places around the world for value, cheerfulness and a very full plate of rice, dhal and salad. Also burgers. No eggs used. No smoking. MC, V.

Juice

Vegetarian restaurant

73-83 South Great Georges Street, Dublin 2
Tel: 01-4757856
Open: every day 11.00-23.00

Vegetarian restaurant with a friendly atmosphere which would suit both a romantic dinner for two or a group of friends. It is also possible to sit at the front of the restaurant and just enjoy a fresh juice or a wine. Plenty for vegans, clearly marked. Start with soup, miso broth, yam wedges chilled tofu mayonnaise dip, or a selection of dips. Lots of exotic side dishes. Main courses 14 euros evening, 7 euro daytime, include Asian noodles in Ponzu sauce with tofu or tempeh; vegetable fried rice with tofu, tempeh or seitan; organic aduki Juiceburger and chips. 3 course lunch deal 9.95 euros. Weekday earlybird 5-7pm 14.95 euros. Organic vegan wines. Soya milk, cappuccinos and milkshakes. Homemade desserts and vegan ice-cream. Visa, MC.

Wagamama

Omnivorous Japanese restaurant

Unit 4b, St Stephen's Green Shopping Centre,
South King Street, Dublin 2
Tel: 01-4782152
Open: Mon-Sat 12.00-23.00 (last orders),
Sun till 22.00

Omnivorous Japanese noodle bar. Vegetarian dishes are clearly marked. Some are suitable for vegans. No smoking. Licensed. MC, Visa, Amex, Diners.

Nature's Way

Health food shop

Stephen's Green Shopping Centre,
Grafton Street , Dublin 2
Open: Mon-Sat, (except Thu) 9.00-18.00,
Thu 9.00-20.00, Sun closed.

The Parnell Mall, The Ilac Centre, Dublin 1
Tel: 01-8728391
Open: Mon-Sat 9.00-18.00, Thu till 20.00,
Sun 12-18.00

Unit 121, Blanchardstown Shopping Centre
Dublin 15 (Bus 39). Tel: 01-822 2560
Open: Mon-Tue & Sat 9-18.00,
Wed-Fri 9-21.00, Sun 11-18.00

Blackrock Shopping Centre, Blackrock,
County Dublin, (south of Dublin)
Tel: 01-288 6696
Open: Mon-Wed Sat 9-18.00,
Thu-Fri 9-21.00, Sun 14-18.00

Nouish

Health food shop

Unit 1, GPO Arcade, Henry Street, Dublin 1
Tel: 01-8743290. www.nourishonline.ie
Open: Mon–Sat 9.00–18.00, Thu till 20.00.
Sun closed.

16 Wicklow Street, Dublin 2
Tel: 01–670 3223. www.nourishonline.ie
Open: Mon–Tue 9–18.00, Wed, Fri, Sat 9–18.30, Sun 12–18.30

Nutgrove Shopping Centre,
Rathfarnham, Dublin 14
Tel: 01–493 5289. www.nourishonline.ie
Open: Mon–Tue, Sat 9–18.00, Wed–Fri 9–21.00, Sun 12–18.00

6 Lower Liffey Street, Dublin 1
Tel: 01–873 4098. www.nourishonline.ie
Open: Mon–Sat 9–18.00, Sun 12–18.00

Omni Park Shopping Centre, Santry, Dublin 9
Tel: 01–862 1392. www.nourishonline.ie
Open: Mon–Wed, Sat 9–18.00, Thu–Fri 9–21.00, Sun 12–18.00

Lush

Cruelty-free cosmetics

116 Grafton Street, Dublin, 2
Tel: 01–677 0392
Open: Mon–Sat 10–19,00, Thu till 20.00,
Sun 12–18.00

Holland & Barrett

Health food shop

U67 Donaghmede Shopping Centre, Dublin
Tel: 00353–1867 1174
Open: Mon–Wed 9–18.00, Thu–Fri 9–21.00,
Sat 9–18.00, Sun 13–18.00

U51 Blackrock Shopping Centre, Dublin
Tel: 00353–1288 6696
Open Mon–Wed 9–18.00, Thu–Fri 9–21.00,
Sat 9–18.00, Sun 14–18.00

U236A The Square Shopping Centre
Tallaght, Dublin
Tel: 00353–1459 6268

U121 Blanchardstown NTC, Dublin
Tel: 00353–1822 2560
Mon–Sat 9–18.00, Sun 11–18.00

U115 St Stephens Green Shopping Centre
Dublin
Tel: 00353–1478 0165
Every day 9–18.00, Thu –20.00

U20 Wilton Shopping Centre, Cork
Tel: 00353–214544284
Mon–Wed 9–18.00, Thu–Fri 9–21.00,
Sat 9–18.00, Sun 13.30–17.30

UG5 Merchants Quay Shopping Centre, Cork
Tel: 00353–214275989
Mon–Wed 9–18.00, Thu 9–19.00,
Fri 9–21.00, Sat 9–18.00, Sun 14–18.00

U7 Blackpool Shopping Centre, Cork
Tel: 00353–214212041

U5 Paul Street Shopping Centre, Cork
Tel: 00353–214270729

U14 Market Cross Shopping Centre, Kilkenny
Tel: 00353–5665896

U2 Arthurs Quay Shopping Centre, Limerick
Tel: 00353–61310466

Northern Ireland

Antrim

Ahimsa

Vegetarian bed and breakfast

243 Whitepark Road, Bushmills, Co Antrim
Tel: 028-207 31383
Open all year

Traditional cottage, tastefully modernised. It is warm and cosy inside and vegetables are mostly supplied from the organic garden. Twin room £18 per person with extra sofa bed, double room £16. Accommodates 4, children welcome. Evening dinner with notice £10. It is very close to the Giants Causeway and the surrounding spectacular coastline. An ideal centre for walking, birdwatching, etc. Yoga and reflexology are available on request. No smoking. Tourist Board approved.

Down

Bushymead Bed & Breakfast

Omnivorous bed and breakfast

86 Drumaness Road,
Ballynahinch, Co Down BT24 8LT
Tel: 028-97 561171
Open all year

Non-vegetarian, catering for vegetarian and vegan breakfasts. Large country house built in classical style. All rooms have tea/coffee facilities, TV and central heating. Separate guest lounge. Situated on main A24 Belfast-Newcastle road in the centre of Co Down. Close to all tourist attractions, forest parks, National Trust properties, museums, coast of Down. Nearest railway station – Lisburn. £22.50 pp sharing with reduction for extended stay, £25 single. Breakfast in rooms on request. Nearby Sainsbury's and the owner can get things from health food shops in Newcastle and Lisburn. Buffet breakfast – fruit, cereal, yoghurt (can be soya), cooked food. No evening meal available. Children welcome. Pets welcome provided they are house-trained. Accommodates up to 30, non-smoking, Tourist Board approved. Primrose Bar & Restaurant nearby caters for vegetarians.

Belfast

v2go

Vegetarian cafe and take-away

Food Court Kiosk 4,
Castlecourt Shopping Centre,
Royal Avenue, Belfast BT1
Tel: 02890-325522
www.v2go.co.uk
Open: Mon-Sat 8-18.00, Thu till 21.00,
Sun 12-18.00

The newest opening of v2go, just like the two branches in Manchester. Veggie burger or spicy Mexican beanburger £3. Falafel £4. Hummous and salad pitta £3.75. Mixed salads £3.25. Crunchy potato wedges £1.50. Fries £1.40. Sandwiches £2.25-£2.50. Two types of muffin £1.50 and different flavoured flapjacks £1.
Mineral water £1. Juices from 80p. Fizzy drinks £95p-£1.20.
Children welcome, high chairs. No credit cards. No smoking.

Pizza Express

Omnivorous pizza restaurant

25 Bedford Street, Belfast BT2 7EJ (city centre)
Tel: 028 9032 9050
11.30am to Midnight

Big restaurant that can do vegan pizzas, two minutes walk from the central bus station.

Eatwell Healthfoods

Health food shop

413 Lisburn Road, Belfast BT9
Tel: 028 9066 4362
Train: Adelaide

Excellent range of vegan/vegetarian refrigerated food and deserts; home baked savoury pastries and scones; Beauty Without Cruelty cosmetics; crueltry free toiletries. Vegetarian proprietors – friendly, family run.

Framar Health

Health food shop

391 Ormeau Road, Belfast
Tel: 028–9069 4210
Train: Botanic

595 Lisburn Road, Belfast BT9
Tel: 028–9068 1018
Train: Adelaide

Average range of foods; emphasis on supplements and toiletries.

The Nutmeg

Wholefood shop

Lombard Street, Belfast BT1
Tel: 028–9024 9984
Train: Glengall St

Small city centre wholefood shop, compact and varied range of foods with vegan pastries, cakes and snacks.

IRELAND

INDEXES

Care and feeding of your vegan: he or she will purr with delight at
scrambled tofu, superb buffets, vegan cakes, desserts and soya ice-cream.

Dog friendly

Retreat
centres

Children
welcome

Strictly vegan 2

QUICK
FIND

Scotland

EDINBURGH
Broughton Street, The Greenhouse   418

GLASGOW
Kelvinaugh St, Stereo   443
King St, Mono   443

Wales

CARMARTHENSHIRE
Llansteffan, Heartspring   457

CONWY
Llandudno, Llandudno Vegan   249

GWYNEDD
Holyhead, Harvest Moon Café   466
Porthmadog, Vegonia Wholefoods   470

MONMOUTHSHIRE
Capel-y-Ffin, The Barn   452

POWYS
Machynlleth, Dyfiguest   461

Ireland

LIMERICK
Kilmallock, Cussens Cottage GH   477

For the latest vegan news,
join the Vegan Society and
receive The Vegan
magazine four times a
year. See page 29.

These places told us they welcome the little darlings with high chairs, children's portions or special menus. (Other restaurants may be good too.)

North

QUICK FIND

Strictly vegan

Children
welcome 3

Retreat
centres

Dog friendly

South

West

BRISTOL

GLOUCESTERSHIRE

HEREFORDSHIRE

OXFORDSHIRE

SHROPSHIRE

WARWICKSHIRE

WEST MIDLANDS

WORCESTERSHIRE

Scotland

ARGYLL

AYRSHIRE

BORDERS

DUMFRIES & GALLOWAY

EDINBURGH

FIFE

GLASGOW

HIGHLANDS

INVERNESS-SHIRE

ISLE OF BARRA

Strictly vegan | Children welcome 5 | Retreat centres | Dog friendly

Dog friendly

Retreat
centres

Children
welcome

Strictly vegan

QUICK
FIND

Tranquil revitalising guest houses run by holistic health practitioners or offering extra pampering such as massage, Reiki, yoga or meditation.

North

CUMBRIA
Grasmere, Glenthorne Country House   49

NORTH YORKSHIRE
Bransdale, Lidmoor Farm   49

South

DEVON
Dartmoor, Life Dynamic   277
Throwleigh, Little Burrows   270

SOMERSET
Glastonbury, Ploughshares – The Fisher
King Centre   329
Glastonbury, Shekinashram   328

SURREY
Lingfield, Claridge House   340

West

WEST MIDLANDS
Birmingham, Sibila's / Body & Being   402

Wales

CAMARTHENSHIRE
Llansteffan, Heartspring   457

Ireland

WICKLOW
Donard, Chrysalis Holistic Centre   477

You could also try yoga and Buddhist centres and magazines for other possibilities.

INDEX

Strictly vegan

Children
welcome

Retreat
centres

Dog friendly 1

Well behaved dogs welcome here, or by arrangement.

North

East

South

Accommodation by area

Restaurants by area
A–Z Index
Index of Places

New places at www.vegetarianguides.co.uk/updates

South England

Western England

Accommodation by area

Scotland

Wales

New places at www.vegetarianguides.co.uk/updates

Republic of Ireland

Northern Ireland

Accommodation by area

Restaurants by area

A–Z Index
Index of Places

East England

Restaurants by area

East England

London

South England

Restaurants by area

Western England

Accommodation by area

Restaurants by area

A–Z Index
Index of Places

Accommodation by area
Restaurants by area

A–Z Index

Index of Places

G

H

Holland & Barrett

A–Z Index

Index of Places

Q

R

S

INDEX

Accommodation by area
Restaurants by area
A–Z Index
Index of Places

INDEX

Accommodation by name
Restaurants by name
A–Z Index

Index of Places

INDEX

Accommodation by name
Restaurants by name
A–Z Index

Index of Places

The Veggie Guides Way

Alex Bourke set up Vegetarian Guides to map the world for vegetarians and vegans. His aim was to make it easy to eat cruelty-free anywhere in the world. Since 1991 he's travelled on five continents, working with the coordinators of local and national vegetarian organisations in each country. As well as publishing our own guides, Vegetarian Guides buys in veggie travel guides from other publishers to sell mail order at www.vegetarianguides.co.uk

We don't publish reviews based on one traveller eating once at 1,000 restaurants in 3 months, and there are no vague symbols like ££ or three stars. Instead we include places where local veggies eat out and shop all the time, listing the most popular dishes with real prices, so budget travellers can find the bargains, couples can spot the ones with candles, and business types know where to go to impress.

This guide was compiled by an international team of vegan travellers aided by several researchers and dozens of readers. Suzanne Wright from Southampton previously worked in the library sector and was the lead researcher on this edition. Claire Insley saved whales and forests crewing on Greenpeace's Rainbow Warrior, and has lived and eaten out all over Britain from Devon to Glasgow. Ronny Worsey has worked for campaigning organisations and vegetarian cafes from Kent to Edinbugh and written several vegan cookbooks. Sophie and Stephen Fenwick-Paul are leading vegan activists – look out for their big outreach stall at the WOMAD Festival. Australian Katrina Holland has travelled all over the UK and Ireland and recently backpacked across Asia. Canadian travel writer Sarah Richards has just spent three years in Asia and wrote many of the new chapter introductions.

If you'd like to help research future editions, or you have recommendations, we'd love to hear from you.

Vegetarian Guides Ltd, PO Box 2284, London W1A 5UH, UK
www.vegetarianguides.co.uk
updates@vegetarianguides.co.uk